Social theory as science

International Library of Sociology

Founded by Karl Mannheim

Editor: John Rex, University of Warwick

Arbor Scientiae
Arbor Vitae

Social theory as science

Russell Keat
Department of Philosophy
University of Lancaster

and

John Urry
Department of Sociology
University of Lancaster

Routledge & Kegan Paul
London, Henley and Boston

First published in 1975
by Routledge & Kegan Paul Ltd
39 Store Street
London WC1E 7DD,
Broadway House, Newtown Road
Henley-on-Thames
Oxon, RG9 1EN and
9 Park Street
Boston, Mass. 02108, USA
Reprinted 1976
Set in 10 on 11 point Times New Roman
and printed in Great Britain by
Unwin Brothers Limited
Old Woking, Surrey
© John R. Urry and R. N. Keat 1975

ISBN 0 7100 8125 1 (c)
ISBN 0 7100 8126 X (p)

Contents

Preface

This book is intended to change how we think about and carry out the scientific study of social life. We try to establish an appropriate philosophical and theoretical basis for such a study. Some important books in this area, for instance Alan Ryan's *Philosophy of the Social Sciences*, are primarily philosophical, with relatively limited treatment of substantive social science. Others, such as Robert Friedrichs's *A Sociology of Sociology*, tend to minimize philosophical analysis, and thus reduce discussion to a description of various types of sociological practice. We aim, by contrast, to combine the philosophical evaluation of different conceptions of the nature of social theory with an examination of important sociological theorists and frameworks. In doing so, we try to relate a variety of themes, arguments and controversies that have developed within very different intellectual traditions. The issues we cover are diverse, complex, and difficult, but we have attempted to keep our discussion as clear and simple as is possible. We hope that the book will be relevant to second and third year students taking theoretical, methodological or philosophical courses in the social sciences, and to postgraduates working in these areas. But it is also intended as a general contribution to the problems and issues that we discuss. There are, however, several important topics about which we say little or nothing: the place of mathematics in science; the nature of rules and rule-guided action; functionalism and the logic of functional explanations; and the question of methodological holism versus individualism.

This book has arisen from the many, lengthy discussions we have had together in the last three years while employed at the University of Lancaster. Many of these derived from certain themes in an article by one of us, Russell Keat's 'Positivism, Naturalism and Anti-Naturalism in the Social Sciences'. The discussions also took place in the context of a period of considerable political conflict inside this

University, during which we were both involved, with many other friends, in attempts to combat certain repressive results of the existing power structure. The shared political sympathies engendered by these conflicts have been important to us, and we attach political, as well as intellectual significance to this book. For coherent political thought and activity depend partly on adequate analysis of the social structures within which these take place, an analysis which in turn rests upon a proper conception of the nature of social theory.

The book is, therefore, very much the joint product of personal, intellectual and political cooperation. However, each of us has been principally responsible for individual chapters: Russell Keat for part 1, and chapters 7 and 9 in part 3; John Urry for part 2, and chapter 8 in part 3. A number of stylistic differences remain between these two groups of chapters, which we thought it unnecessary to eliminate. We would not have been able to write this book without the friendship, help and advice of many people. We are grateful to our former teachers; and we hope that those who have taken our courses here will recognize the important contributions they have made to our thinking. We are especially grateful to our friends living in and around Lancaster. In particular, we would like to thank the following for reading and commenting on one or more chapters: Nick Abercrombie, Steve Ackroyd, Ken Baublys, Michael Hammond, Suzette Heald, Mike Howard, John King, David Miller, Linda Nicholson, and Geoff Smith. And we are grateful to the people who have typed the drafts of various chapters: Carole Corless, Carol Fell, Wendy Graham, Margaret Gudgin, Barbara Hayes, Julie Huddleston, Margaret Nolan, Wilga Urry, and Brenda Wright.

Russell Keat would like to thank the academic and assistant staff in the Department of Philosophy at Lancaster for their help, and for enabling him to spend the 1973/4 academic year on leave to write the book.

John Urry is grateful for being an early member of the Department of Sociology at Lancaster, and for the successful demonstration of the possibilities of democratizing university departments.

Introduction

The central debate within the philosophy of the social sciences has concerned the methodological unity of natural and social science. However, the way in which this debate has been conducted is fundamentally misconceived. This is because it has been viewed primarily in terms of the relevance of one particular conception of science, that of positivism, to the study of social phenomena. But we will show that there are a number of different conceptions of science and that it is erroneous to discuss the methodological unity issue simply in terms of one particular characterization of the natural sciences. We will further argue that a neglected position in the philosophy of natural science, theoretical realism, or realism, should be explored as an appropriate framework for the social sciences.

Thus we will attempt to redraw the standard framework of categories and distinctions in terms of which the methodological unity debate is conducted. Normally it is based upon two related dichotomies, naturalism versus anti-naturalism, and positivism versus idealism. Further, these two dichotomies are typically assimilated so that we are presented with exclusive and exhaustive alternatives: naturalism and positivism; *or* anti-naturalism and idealism. Indeed positivism has often been taken as synonymous with naturalism, or at least including naturalism as an essential part of its meaning.

Historically, the reason why these two dichotomies have been assimilated, is because of the dominance of the positivist conception of science in the period during which the methodological unity debate has been conducted. Also positivism, as a distinct position in the philosophy of science, has been part of a more general intellectual and methodological tradition, which has involved naturalism as one of its central elements. The doctrine of naturalism has been mainly supported by those who have adopted a positivist view of science. As a result, it has been difficult to conceive of a naturalist position which is not also positivist. It seems that in the study of social life

1

we have to choose either a positivist (and naturalist) position, or an idealist (and anti-naturalist) position. This is, however, incorrect. We will criticize how positivists have succeeded in dictating the way in which the methodological unity issue has been debated. In discussing three different conceptions of the natural sciences, positivism, realism, and conventionalism, we will attack the normal assimilation of the two dichotomies, and particularly that of the positivist and naturalist positions. We will examine the issues involved in a naturalism based on a non-positivist, realist view of science.

Let us now outline the three parts of this book. In part 1 we analyse and contrast positivist, realist and conventionalist conceptions of the natural sciences. In each case we characterize their basic claims, outline the justifications provided for these, and indicate the main difficulties and criticisms that can be made of them. Our own commitment is to a realist position, modified by certain conclusions which have led others to adopt a non-realist, conventionalist view of science.

In part 2 we use this classification of alternative conceptions of science, and especially the distinction between positivism and realism, to analyse different writers and schools within the social sciences. We consider those who, although adopting a naturalist position, differ in the view of science that they hold. Initially we look at various positivist sociologists and schools of sociology in the nineteenth and twentieth centuries. We then analyse a clear example of realism in the social sciences, namely, Karl Marx and his attempt to found a science of historical materialism. Finally, we consider the concept of structure, which is central to any realist science. We note, however, that there are other forms of structural or structuralist analysis in the social sciences; some of these can be seen as either positivist or as a form of conventionalism.

In the last part, we examine the two central problems in any science of social life: the nature of human action, and the possibly value-distorted, subjective, or ideological character of the social scientific enterprise. We will see that some of the anti-naturalist arguments involved here are analogues of conventionalist claims in the philosophy of the natural sciences. We will consider the plausibility of an anti-naturalist position by reference, not to a positivist, but a realist, naturalist position. First, then, we consider how subjective meanings can be analysed as causes of human action. We will then consider whether there is a distinctive form of interpretative understanding in the social sciences. Second, we examine different conceptions of ideology; we analyse in detail one form of ideological distortion, that of reification; we confront various issues involved in the concept of value-free sociology, especially the relationship between concepts and reality; and we defend a non-relativistic sociology of science and knowledge.

part one

Conceptions of science

In the following three chapters, we will present a critical analysis of three widely differing conceptions of the natural sciences – positivism, realism, and conventionalism. The analysis will be conducted primarily by reference to Anglo-American philosophers of science who have developed and defended these positions in the twentieth century. These positions have important connections with earlier views in the history and philosophy of science, and also with more general philosophical and intellectual movements. But, first, let us provide a brief outline of the three positions.

For the positivist, science is an attempt to gain predictive and explanatory knowledge of the external world. To do this, one must construct theories, which consist of highly general statements, expressing the regular relationships that are found to exist in that world. These general statements, or laws, enable us both to predict and explain the phenomena that we discover by means of systematic observation and experiment. To explain something is to show that it is an instance of these regularities; and we can make predictions only on the same basis. Statements expressing these regularities, if true, are only contingently so; their truth is not a matter of logical necessity, and cannot be known by *a priori* means. Instead, such statements must be objectively tested by means of experiment and observation, which are the only source of sure and certain empirical knowledge. It is not the purpose of science to get 'behind' or 'beyond' the phenomena revealed to us by sensory experience, to give us knowledge of unobservable natures, essences or mechanisms that somehow necessitate these phenomena. For the positivist, there are no necessary connections in nature; there are only regularities, successions of phenomena which can be systematically represented in the universal laws of scientific theory. Any attempt to go beyond this representation plunges science into the unverifiable claims of metaphysics and religion, which are at best unscientific, and at worst meaningless.

The realist shares with the positivist a conception of science as an empirically-based, rational and objective enterprise, the purpose of which is to provide us with true explanatory and predictive knowledge of nature. But for the realist, unlike the positivist, there is an important difference between explanation and prediction. And it is explanation which must be pursued as the primary objective of science. To explain phenomena is not merely to show they are instances of well-established regularities. Instead, we must discover the necessary connections between phenomena, by acquiring knowledge of the underlying structures and mechanisms at work. Often, this will mean postulating the existence of types of unobservable entities and processes that are unfamiliar to us: but it is only by doing this that we get beyond the 'mere appearances' of things, to their natures and essences. Thus, for the realist, a scientific theory is a description of structures and mechanisms which causally generate the observable phenomena, a description which enables us to explain them.

We have noted already that, despite their differences, positivists and realists share a certain general conception of science and its objectives. What is common to those philosophers of science we call 'conventionalists' is their rejection of these shared attitudes. But their reasons for doing so are varied. It may be argued that observations cannot by themselves determine the truth or falsity of theories, and that no useful distinction between theory and observation can be maintained. Or, that there are no universal criteria for choosing rationally between different theoretical frameworks, and that moral, aesthetic, or instrumental values play an essential part in such choices. More radically, the idea of an external reality which exists independently of our theoretical beliefs and concepts may be rejected. Associated with these different claims are different positive conceptions of science. In all of them, there is a sense in which the adoption of theories is a matter of convention. But 'conventionalism', as we use this term, does not denote a homogeneous set of views about science, which can be simply contrasted with positivism and realism. What unites conventionalists is their opposition to the view of science as providing true descriptions and explanations of an external reality, through theories which can be objectively tested and compared by observation and experiment.

So far, these accounts of positivism, realism and conventionalism have been couched, as far as possible, in terms that are not specific to the way in which they have been developed in twentieth-century philosophy of science. For we wish to emphasize that each of these views has a long history in science and philosophy. The realist position, with its emphasis on causal explanations through the discovery of essences, was systematically articulated by Aristotle, developed by various medieval philosophers, and continued through the seventeenth-century scientific revolution and after; for example, in the writings of Locke, who developed an epistemology based on the corpuscularian realism of the science of his time. Positivist philosophy of science was significantly developed in the early eighteenth century, through the work of Hume and Berkeley, with the denial of causal necessity in nature, the defence of a regularity view of causation and explanation, and the rejection of any scientific concepts which went beyond the realm of the observable. Elements of positivism were already present in the writings of medieval philosophers, such as Ockham; and the positivist tradition continued through the nineteenth and twentieth centuries when, until quite recently, its dominance seemed assured. Likewise, several of the ideas involved in conventionalist philosophies of science have a long history, particularly in astronomy. From very early on, there developed the view that all that mattered for an astronomical theory was that it should 'save the appearances', that it should be a computational device which enables us to make correct and useful predictions about the observed movements of the heavenly bodies. Such theories should not be seen as describing any physical reality, or making claims to truth: their value was primarily instrumental. If more than one theory adequately 'saved the appearances' the choice between them should be made on the basis of partly aesthetic criteria, such as mathematical elegance.[1]

These different conceptions of science have also been related to more general philosophical positions and movements. In the twentieth century, these relationships are particularly interesting. Until about twenty years ago, the dominance of positivist philosophy of science was closely associated with the dominance of the logical positivist movement, itself a complex blending of the Humean empiricist tradition with the late nineteenth-century development of mathematical logic. The recent attacks on positivist philosophy of science, which have taken both realist and conventionalist forms, have themselves been linked with some of the philosophical movements that emerged in opposition to logical positivism. Thus, several conventionalist philosophers of science have been influenced by the later writings of Wittgenstein, and realist philosophy of science has partly been developed from the standpoint of 'scientific realism', a position which is opposed both to logical positivism, and also to the movement of analytical philosophy inspired by Wittgenstein, Ryle and Austin.[2]

It should already be clear that our own use of the term 'positivism' is a more restricted one than is usual, particularly in debates about the methodological unity of the natural and social sciences. First, the term is frequently used in such a way that the positions which we distinguish as positivist and realist are conflated under the terms 'positivist', or 'empiricist'. Although positivism and realism have common features, and have both been developed within a broadly empiricist philosophical tradition, the failure to distinguish the two positions is misleading. Indeed, the differences between these positions itself reflects important divergences within the empiricist tradition, several of which are manifested in the differences between Hume and Locke. Second, 'positivism' is sometimes used as if synonymous with 'naturalism', a use which we have already criticized. Third, the term is also applied to a more general intellectual tradition which, although partly constituted by what we have called positivist philosophy of science, also involves other, more sweeping claims. In particular, positivists in this wider sense not only adopt a certain view of the natural sciences, but insist that science, conceived in this way, is the only legitimate form of human knowledge. Other intellectual enquiries must either conform to this model of knowledge, or be dismissed as providing no real knowledge at all. Questions of values, theology and metaphysics are to be rejected in this manner, and the embryonic social sciences must, to deserve the name of 'science', be developed on the lines of the natural sciences.

But positivism purely as a philosophy of science may be maintained without these additional claims. Thus some philosophers have adopted this view of science, without thereby rejecting other forms of knowledge as meaningless or unintelligible. Instead, they may merely wish to distinguish science from, for example, theology, sometimes even to protect theology from the claims of science, rather than using science as a weapon against theology. Similarly, though positivist philosophers of science deny the relevance of values to the conduct of science and the validity of its results, this denial need not be based upon the rejection of value claims *in toto*: they may simply be regarded as having no legitimate part in science.[3]

Our procedure in these three chapters will be as follows. In chapter 1, we examine the positivist view of science, beginning with its analysis of explanation. We then consider its general view of scientific theories, and their relation to observations. An important aspect of this view is its use of a distinction between theoretical and observational terms; this we examine separately. And in the final section, some further characteristics of positivist philosophy of science as a whole are considered, especially those associated with its concept of 'the logic of science'.

Throughout chapter 1, although we emphasize the difficulties and problems that are raised by various positivist doctrines, we do not attempt any systematic criticism of the position. But in chapter 2, we present the realist view of science both as an alternative to positivism, and in terms of its critical diagnosis of the problems facing positivism. Thus in the first three sections, we partly parallel the corresponding sections of chapter 1, by discussing the realist accounts of explanation, theories, and the distinction between theoretical and observational terms. We conclude by pointing to some of the problems for a realist philosophy of science, and drawing out some of the characteristics common to both positivism and realism.

The organization of chapter 3 is rather different from that of the first two chapters. Only in the final section do we consider conventionalism as a general position in the philosophy of science, and even here we emphasize the diversity of positions that may be grouped under this single category. In the earlier sections of the chapter, we confine ourselves to a critical analysis of several writers and arguments which stand in opposition to both positivism and realism.

Finally, the accounts we provide of both positivism and realism are composite constructions, and although there may be philosophers of science who subscribe to every element of one of these, this is not assumed by the procedure we have adopted. Thus, we do not claim that any writer who supports, say, the positivist view of explanation, will necessarily support all the other doctrines we describe as positivist – though support for at least some of them is likely. The various elements of the realist and positivist positions do fit together into coherent, alternative conceptions of science, most fully developed in the twentieth century, but present at many earlier stages in the history of science and philosophy.[4]

1 Positivist philosophy of science

1 The positivist view of explanation

That the explanation of an event consists basically in showing that it is an instance of a well-supported regularity has long been maintained by positivist philosophers of science. By examining the detailed development of this view by twentieth-century positivists, we will also gain insight into the main difference between these more recent writers, and their predecessors. This consists in the considerable reliance of the former upon the techniques and concepts of modern formal logic. These have been used both to express characteristically positivist views of science with a far greater degree of rigour and precision than was previously possible, and to provide a basic framework in which to analyse the nature of scientific theories.[1] There can be little doubt that the attendant rigour and precision have often been highly beneficial to the philosophy of science – though not always to the positivists, since the careful and systematic statement of their views has frequently revealed serious problems and difficulties which may be unresolvable within the positivist framework.

We will examine the positivist view of explanation in the form in which it has been presented and defended by Carl Hempel, since his account is, in several senses, exemplary.[2] Let us begin with the following passage (1965a, p. 246), in which he describes a typical case of scientific explanation, and presents an analysis of it which indicates his general conception of such explanations:

> A mercury thermometer is rapidly immersed in hot water; there occurs a temporary drop of the mercury column, which is then followed by a swift rise. How is this phenomenon to be explained? The increase in temperature affects at first only the glass tube of the thermometer; it expands and thus provides a larger space for the mercury inside, whose surface therefore

drops. As soon as by heat conduction the rise in temperature reaches the mercury, however, the latter expands, and as its coefficient of expansion is considerably larger than that of glass, a rise of the mercury level results. – This account consists of statements of two kinds. Those of the first kind indicate certain conditions which are realized prior to, or at the same time as, the phenomenon to be explained; we shall refer to them briefly as antecedent conditions. In our illustration, the antecedent conditions include, among others, the fact that the thermometer consists of a glass tube which is partly filled with mercury, and that it is immersed into hot water. The statements of the second kind express certain general laws; in our case, these include the laws of the thermic expansion of mercury and of glass, and a statement about the small thermic conductivity of glass. The two sets of statements, if adequately and completely formulated, explain the phenomenon under consideration: they entail the consequence that the mercury will first drop, then rise. Thus, the event under discussion is explained by subsuming it under general laws, i.e. by showing that it occurred in accordance with those laws, in virtue of the realization of certain specified antecedent conditions.

Here, scientific explanation is presented as a form of logical argument. The conclusion of the argument is a statement describing the event which is to be explained – in this case, the behaviour of a mercury thermometer which is immersed in hot water. This statement is termed 'the *explanandum*-statement'. The premises of the argument are of two kinds: statements of general laws, and statements of antecedent conditions. These are termed 'the *explanans*-statements'. Thus, schematically:

$$\text{Explanans} \quad \left\{ \begin{array}{l} L_1, L_2, \ldots L_r \ \text{Laws} \\ C_1, C_2, \ldots C_k \ \text{Antecedent conditions} \end{array} \right\} \text{Premisses}$$

$$\overline{\text{Explanandum} \quad E \hspace{8cm} \text{Conclusion}}$$

So far, we have talked of the 'general conception of explanation' presented by Hempel. But this phrase needs to be made more precise, and qualified in various ways, before we proceed to a further examination of his account. Hempel sees his task as that of providing the necessary and sufficient conditions for something to be properly regarded as a scientific explanation. That is, he wishes to specify certain conditions to which any scientific explanation must conform, and which are such that, if these conditions are satisfied, a legitimate explanation has been given. Such specifications are often termed a 'model' of scientific explanation. Hempel in fact offers more than one model, and these differ in some respects, whilst having several features in common. We can regard these as attempting to provide necessary and sufficient conditions for several, slightly different, types of scientific explanation.

The two most important models, for our purposes, are called 'Deductive–Nomological', and 'Inductive–Statistical'. We shall refer to these as the 'D–N' and 'I–S' models, respectively. It is the former which we described in our initial discussion of Hempel. In the latter, the law-statements of the D–N model are replaced by probabilistic, or statistical, generalizations; and the relationship between premises and conclusion is one of inductive probability, instead of deductive necessity. We begin with the D–N model, considering its use for explaining particular events, though we should note that it may also be used for the explanation of lower-level laws by higher-level laws.[3]

There is no doubt that Hempel's example of the explanation of the mercury column's behaviour, which we quoted above, is a perfectly good example of a scientific explanation. Like many others, it can easily be presented in such a way that it conforms to the requirements of the D–N model. However, it does not follow from this that the model in fact provides an adequate account of scientific explanation. For there are many other examples which cannot be regarded as legitimate cases of scientific explanation despite the fact that they meet this model's requirements. In other words, the model does not provide sufficient conditions for explanation: there is some important element which it fails to capture. And we will suggest, in discussing this objection, that it cannot easily be met by adding further, formal requirements to the model.

The objection can best be analysed by considering a further claim that Hempel makes about the D–N model. This concerns the relationship between explanation and prediction. Hempel argues that the statements of laws and antecedent conditions which are employed as premises in the model, can function either as a basis for explaining the phenomenon described in the conclusion, or as a basis for predicting it. In particular, any argument which, conforming to the D–N model, enables us to predict an event which has not yet occurred, will also enable us to explain that event, after its occurrence.

But this claim is problematic, as Hempel himself now acknowledges. This can be seen from the following passage (1965b, p. 374), where he discusses an apparent counter-example:

One of the early symptoms of measles is the appearance of small whitish spots, known as Koplik spots, on the mucous linings of the cheeks. The statement, L, that the appearance of Koplik spots is always followed by the later manifestations of the measles might therefore be taken to be a law, and it might then

11

be used as a premise in D–N arguments with a second premise of the form 'Patient *i* has Koplik spots at time *t*', and with a conclusion stating that *i* subsequently shows the later manifestations of the measles. An argument of this type is adequate for predictive purposes, but its explanatory adequacy might be questioned. We would not want to say, for example, that *i* had developed high fever and other symptoms of the measles because he had previously had Koplik spots.

Clearly, many cases of a similar kind can easily be found. For example the regular relationship between barometer readings and changes in weather conditions cannot be regarded as providing explanations of the weather, despite their enabling us to make predictions about it. Thus, even if the D–N model adequately represents the necessary conditions for scientific explanation, these conditions are not sufficient.

It might be thought that this objection could be avoided if a suitably restrictive account were given of the law-statements that function as premises in the deductive argument. In other words, if it were possible to distinguish between explanatory and non-explanatory laws, we could then eliminate the latter group as acceptable explanans-statements. Obviously, any direct appeal to the concept of 'explanatory law' is ruled out on the grounds of circularity, since the D–N model is itself intended to provide the analysis of scientific explanation. A more promising approach might lie in restricting the laws to those which express a causal relationship. For, one reason for rejecting the Koplik-spots example as non-explanatory is that we do not believe these spots are the cause of the fever.

However, this approach faces at least two difficulties. First, Hempel, together with many other positivists, does not wish to restrict the concept of scientific explanation to that of causal explanation. Second, the positivist treatment of causal relations is such that a distinction between causal and non-causal laws is very difficult to draw. This is mainly because of their adoption of a Humean, regularity theory of causation. But we will defer discussion of these points until the next chapter.

More will be said about the positivist account of scientific laws in the following section. But let us now examine the I–S model, since its problems cast further light on those of the D–N model. In the I–S model, we explain some particular event by showing that a statement describing it is supported with a high degree of inductive probability by a set of premises, at least one of which is a statement of the statistical probability that an event of one kind will be followed by, or associated with, an event of another kind. Suppose, for example, that we are drawing a marble from an urn that contains 1,000 marbles, one black, and the others white. We draw a white one, and explain this by the high inductive probability of doing so, given that the statistical probability of drawing a white marble from such an urn is 0.999.

The difficulty with such examples, and thus of the model they are based upon, is well expressed by Alan Donagan (1966, p. 133):

> In cases of this sort the obvious thing to say is that there is *no* explanation of any individual outcome. You will be deceived into imagining that there is only if you confound what it was reasonable to expect with what has been explained. Reasonable expectations and explanations differ fundamentally. It is more reasonable to expect at the first attempt to toss heads with a coin than to win roulette on a given number; but the grounds why it is more reasonable do not *explain* why you succeeded in tossing heads and failed to win at roulette. After all, you might have won at roulette and tossed tails. *With respect to explanation,* chance situations where the odds are equal do not differ from those where the odds are fifty to one or a thousand to one.

Where the odds are equal, as in tossing a coin, we do not regard getting heads as explained by the 0·5 probability of doing so. Donagan's point is that although the much higher probability of drawing a white marble enables us to make a fairly certain prediction, it does not thereby constitute an explanation. The difference between explanation and non-explanation cannot consist in differing degrees of probability. We can relate this objection to the one that was made against the D–N model in the following way. In both cases, there is a failure to distinguish between providing the grounds for expecting that an event will occur, and explaining why it does occur. The problem of non-explanatory laws in the D–N model is greatly magnified in the I–S model, where, instead of universal laws, we have only statistical probabilities. To accept the I–S model of explanation requires a prior acceptance of the assimilation of predictive and explanatory knowledge that is involved in the D–N model, and more generally in the positivist view of scientific explanation.

2 The positivist view of theories

For the positivist, scientific theories consist of sets of highly general universal statements, whose truth or falsity can be assessed by means of systematic observation and experiment. The results of these observations and experiments can be known either with total certainty, or at least with a far greater degree of certainty than anything else, including the theories which are evaluated by reference to them. The universal statements of scientific theories are usually termed 'laws', though it is often maintained that there is an important difference between 'theoretical laws' and 'empirical laws', with only the former qualifying as constituents of a theory. This difference itself depends upon a distinction between theoretical (or non-observational) terms and observational (or non-theoretical) terms. We will examine this distinction in the next section. For the moment, we will ignore the difference between theoretical and empirical laws, and concentrate upon the accounts given by positivists of the relations that hold between theories and the results of observations and experiments. (For convenience, we often use the term 'observations' to refer to such results.)

We can begin by noting briefly the various criteria that positivists have offered in their attempts to characterize scientific laws. Though there have been disagreements about these criteria, and their relative importance, there are several which have been widely accepted. First, statements which express laws must have the syntactical form of universal conditionals. In simple cases, they will be of the form: 'for all x, if x has the property P, then it has the property Q.' (Symbolically, $(x)(Px \rightarrow Qx)$, which may be read, roughly, as 'All Ps are Qs'.) Examples of scientific laws which can be cast in this form are: 'all planets move in elliptical orbits', or 'all bodies subject to no external forces maintain constant velocity'. Second, such statements must not be restricted in their application to any finite region of space and time: they must hold true for all times and places. Thus, 'all humans now in this room are mortal' would not qualify as a law, because of the spatial and temporal restrictions in the statement. Third, none of the terms occurring in scientific laws can refer only to particular, individual items. That is, they must not contain what are, logically, 'names'. This category includes both what are grammatically termed 'proper names', such as the names of individual people, places, or things; and also expressions which necessarily refer to one, and only one, item, such as 'the highest mountain in the world'. Finally, scientific laws do not express any form of necessity, whether this is logical necessity, or what is variously called 'empirical', 'natural', or 'causal' necessity. Thus, it is maintained, laws express non-necessary, or contingent, relationships, whose truth or falsity can only be known by empirical means: they cannot be known by *a priori* argument. Nor can they be regarded as expressing some mysterious non-logical necessity, a necessity which somehow inheres in nature itself: for positivists, as we have already noted, deny the existence of natural necessity.[4]

Given this characterization of scientific laws and theories, how can the positivist ideal of science as giving us genuine explanatory and predictive knowledge be realized? We have seen already, in section 1, the way in which scientific laws, for the positivist, perform their double function of explanation and prediction. But neither that account, nor the formal characterization of the laws involved in it, are designed to answer the questions of how we can arrive at true scientific theories, or of how we can evaluate the attempts that are made to formulate such theories. It is here that the relationship between theory and observation becomes vitally important, since, for the positivist, it is only observation that can provide an objective foundation for scientific theorizing.

Though some earlier positivists believed that it is possible, by means of observation, to conclusively verify scientific theories, there is an important feature of scientific laws which, as all modern positivists have emphasized, rules this out. No finite amount of observational evidence (and this is all we ever have) can finally establish the truth of a law which is held to apply to all times and places, and whose instances are therefore potentially infinite in number. This difficulty is, in effect, one version of the 'logical problem of induction', of how one can justifiably argue from past events to future events, from the known to the unknown, and so on. In this century, as before, there have been many attempts to solve (or even dissolve) the problem. But what concerns us here are the positivist responses to the following question: assuming that the logical problem of induction means that no conclusive verification of scientific theories is possible, how should one use empirical evidence to evaluate such theories? We can distinguish two main approaches to this, which we will call the 'confirmationist', and the 'falsificationist'.

The confirmationists argue that one can use empirical evidence to provide a varying degree of positive support for the truth of scientific theories. For example, the larger the number of instances which are in accordance with the predictions that can be deduced from a theory, or the more varied the circumstances in which these instances occur, the more strongly confirmed is that theory. Similarly, rival theories can be compared as to their relative degrees of empirical support. And many confirmationists have tried to formalize these relationships of evidential support for a theory, and to construct a 'logic of confirmation', which is sometimes based upon the calculus of probabilities.

For the falsificationist, however, all these attempts are futile: there is no logic of confirmation, only of falsification. Observations should be used solely to show that putative theories are false. If we deduce from a theory a prediction that turns out to be incorrect, then it follows logically from this that the theory itself is incorrect. Unlike the confirmationist, the falsificationist restricts the concept of valid argument to that of deductive argument, and insists that the only kind of deductive relationship that can be established between theory and observation is that in which the falsity of a theory follows from

15

the falsity of the predictions derived from it. Thus, in evaluating scientific theories by means of observations, we can only use the latter to falsify, and not to confirm, the former.

This falsificationist position is often associated with a more general view of the process of theory formulation and evaluation, the 'hypothetico-deductive method', particularly in the work of Karl Popper. Popper argues that one does not first make observations, arrive at a theory by induction from these, and then seek to confirm the theory by further observations. Instead, the scientist begins by formulating a theory, or hypothesis, and proceeds to test the hypothesis by making potentially falsifying observations. If the theory is falsified, it must be abandoned, and another one formulated to replace it. This formulation of hypotheses is purely a matter of conjecture: there is no 'logic of discovery' by which we can arrive at theories from observations. Indeed, Popper claims that it makes no sense simply to 'observe', without reference to any hypothesis which is being tested. For without such a theory, one does not know what to look for.

Thus the hypothetico-deductive method provides an account both of the way in which the scientist is to arrive at theories, and also of the way these hypotheses are to be evaluated by empirical evidence. But it is important to realize that there is no inconsistency in accepting only one part of this account, whilst rejecting the other. For example, a confirmationist could agree that theory formulation is a matter of conjecture, and not of induction from observations; yet still insist that one should try to accumulate positive support for theories, and that it is possible to measure the degree of confirmation that theories have with respect to this empirical evidence. Similarly, the falsificationist view of theory evaluation could be combined with the claim that one arrives at theories by some process of inductive argument from observations. The hypothetico-deductive method does not have to be either accepted or rejected *in toto*.[5]

But although there are these differences between positivist philosophers of science concerning the relationship between theories and observations, the assumptions that they share are more significant than their disagreements. Two such assumptions will prove especially important in the following two chapters, where we consider the realist and conventionalist positions. First, that the theories which are either confirmed, or falsified, are universal statements about regular, contingent relationships in nature. Second, that the observations used to evaluate such theories provide an objective foundation for science. In particular, the truth or falsity of statements about observations is not dependent upon the truth or falsity of theories; and theoretical disputes can be resolved by reference to agreed observation-statements.

16

3 Theoretical and observational terms

So far, we have discussed the positivist treatment of the relations between theory and observation, in terms of the various responses to the problems posed by the universality and generality of scientific laws. In other words, the distinction between theory and observation has been construed simply as one between universal statements, or laws, and particular statements, that is, statements about observations. However, as we noted at the beginning of section 2, many positivists wish to reserve the title of 'theory' to a special class of such laws, namely 'theoretical laws'. For although science has, as its objective, the explanation and prediction of observable phenomena, many of the terms which actually occur in scientific theories do not, in any obvious way, refer to such phenomena. These terms are usually described as 'theoretical', and the laws containing them, 'theoretical laws'. For reasons which will emerge shortly, this fact about scientific theories has seemed highly problematic to the positivist. Consider the following quotation from Hempel (1958, p. 177):

> Scientific systematization is ultimately aimed at establishing explanatory and predictive order among the bewilderingly complex 'data' of our experience, the phenomena that can be 'directly observed' by us. It is a remarkable fact, therefore, that the greatest advances in scientific systematization have not been accomplished by means of laws referring explicitly to *observables*, i.e. to things and events which are ascertainable by direct observation, but rather by means of laws that speak of various *hypothetical*, or *theoretical*, *entities*, i.e. presumptive objects, events, and attributes which cannot be perceived or otherwise directly observed by us.

Hempel proceeds to give some examples of such hypothetical, or theoretical entities: electric, magnetic and gravitational fields; molecules, atoms, and sub-atomic particles. Other examples which are often classified as 'theoretical' are: genes, viruses, kinetic energy, and electrical resistance.

What is particularly interesting about the quotation from Hempel is the beginning of the second sentence, 'It is a remarkable fact . . .'. For this fact would hardly be described as remarkable by the realist. Indeed, it is just what one would expect, since for the realist, one objective of science is to discover the often unobservable structures and mechanisms which causally generate the observable phenomena. Thus the realist is perfectly prepared to regard terms such as 'electron' or 'molecule' as referring to real entities in the world, in much the same way as non-theoretical terms do – such as 'iron', 'wood', 'red', etc.

17

Why then should the occurrence of theoretical terms in scientific theories be surprising and problematic for the positivist? The answer lies in the consequences that positivists have believed to follow from their general attempts to distinguish science from other intellectual activities, such as metaphysics, theology, or ethics. For the positivist, a statement can only be properly regarded as scientific if it is possible to ascertain its truth or falsity by means of empirical observation. But statements containing theoretical terms, if these terms are construed as making reference to entities which cannot be observed, appear not to meet this criterion of scientificity: thus they must somehow be understood in a different way.

Clearly, much depends here on how stringently this criterion of scientificity is interpreted. In the twentieth century, both positivists and their opponents have paid considerable attention to the problems of formulating such a criterion. Confirmationists and falsificationists have disagreed about whether the criterion should be stated in terms of the possibility of verifying (or confirming), or of falsifying the statements concerned; the concept of 'possibility' involved in the criterion has proved difficult to elucidate; and the degree of directness with which observations are required either to verify or falsify statements has been much disputed. Furthermore, what we have described as a criterion of scientificity has often been regarded as a criterion of meaningfulness. Thus, instead of the contrast being drawn between science and non-science, it has frequently been seen as one between the meaningful and the meaningless.[6]

However, we do not wish to engage with these issues here. It is sufficient to note that positivist philosophers of science have both adopted a criterion of the kind we have mentioned, and regarded it as implying that theoretical statements are genuinely scientific only if they are construed in a way that does not involve ontological commitments to unobservable entities. That is, they have tended to reject the view that theoretical terms make reference to actually existing, yet unobservable, items in the world.

Several different strategies have been adopted by positivists in their attempts to deal with what is often called the 'problem of theoretical terms'. Most of these have involved the construction of an exclusive and exhaustive dichotomy between two 'languages' or sets of terms: theoretical (or non-observational) and observational (or non-theoretical). And a frequent device has been the formulation of 'correspondence rules', through which definitions can be given to theoretical terms by means of statements containing only observational terms.[7] In examining these strategies, we will proceed in the following way. First, we will comment on some characteristics of the theoretical-observational dichotomy. Next, we will outline two of the forms of correspondence rule that have been advocated. Finally, we will note some of the criticisms that have been made of the dichotomy, and of the way it has been used. Other, more fundamental criticisms, will be raised in our discussion of realist and conventionalist views in the next two chapters.

The dichotomy between theoretical and observational terms (and thus between the two 'languages' which contain these terms) has typically been constructed by giving a positive characterization of the observational, and then defining the theoretical as whatever is not observational. An observational term is one which refers to what can be observed, and whose meaning can thus, in many cases, be defined ostensively. Thus statements containing only observational terms satisfy the positivists' criterion of scientificity, since their truth or falsity can be determined by means of observation. The precise content of the dichotomy depends, however, on the way in which 'observation' or 'observable' are defined: here, many different accounts have been given. Sometimes, only the direct perceptual experience of an individual observer is allowed the status of observation. But this definition generates severe problems for the intersubjective agreement amongst different observers which is essential to the positivist ideal of science as objectively controlled by observation. Alternatively, the physical operations involved in measurement and experimental procedures may be invoked as constituting the observable; or the material objects and properties that we commonly encounter and refer to in our everyday life. Another approach, often called the 'pragmatic' theory of observation, is to define as observational all those terms whose correct or incorrect application can be agreed upon by the scientists concerned. Finally, in most of these definitions, considerable significance is attached to the measurability of the observable, to the possibility of quantification: indeed, the difficulties of appealing to direct perceptual experience are partly due to its failure to meet this requirement.[8]

But despite these differences about what is to count as observable, the resulting observation-languages have several common characteristics, which are of central importance to positivist philosophy of science. We can usefully summarize these by saying that the observation language has been regarded by positivists as both *epistemologically and ontologically privileged*. By 'epistemologically privileged' we mean this. First, that the truth or falsity of statements containing only observational terms can be known either with total certainty, or at least with a far greater degree of certainty than those containing non-observational, or theoretical, terms. Second, that observational statements can be verified or falsified without reference to the truth or falsity of theoretical statements, that is, those containing at least some non-observational terms. This second element of epistemological privilege is often termed 'theory-neutrality', and has been attacked

19

by some of the philosophers of science whose views we will examine in chapter 3. By 'ontologically privileged', we mean that terms belonging to the observation-language, and only these terms, can be regarded as making genuine reference to items in the physical world. Only such items can properly be said to exist. Thus it is these items that scientific theories attempt to explain and predict; that provide the basis of our empirical testing of such explanations and predictions; and which, in some sense, our theories are about.

We turn now to the positivist use of correspondence rules. It is by means of such rules that many positivists have attempted to deal with the problem of theoretical terms. Ideally, they have hoped to provide definitions of theoretical terms in the observation language, by linking the former, via correspondence rules, with statements in the latter. By doing this, the epistemologically inferior status of theoretical statements would be remedied, their apparent commitments to unobservable ontologies avoided, and their lack of scientificity made good. Several different types of correspondence rule have been formulated. For various technical reasons, which we will not discuss here, none of them has proved entirely successful. Furthermore, they derive their general rationale from a philosophical theory of meaning, the 'verification theory', which, as we will see in the next chapter, is rejected by the realist. But we will outline two simple types of correspondence rule, in order to give some idea of the procedures that are involved.

Let us consider the theoretical term 'magnetic' (theoretical according to most positivist accounts of what is observable). The first type of correspondence rule, used by advocates of what is called 'operational definition', might be formulated in the following way: 'for any object, x, x is magnetic if and only if, whenever a small piece of iron is placed near it, the piece of iron moves towards it'. More generally, we could say: 'x has the theoretical property Q if and only if, when x is subjected to test conditions C, it manifests the response R'. (Symbolically: $Qx \equiv (Cx \to Rx)$.) Such operational definitions would, if successful, enable the positivist to replace all theoretical terms and statements by observational ones. However, for technical reasons, these definitions also generate highly unwelcome consequences – such as, that any object is magnetic whilst no piece of iron is near it – which soon led to their abandonment by positivists. (Unfortunately, for a long time after this, the ideal of operational definition was pursued enthusiastically by many social scientists.)

In their place, a second type of correspondence rule was proposed, involving what is often called the method of 'partial interpretation', in which the meaning of the theoretical term is only partly specified. A simple example of such a rule for 'magnetic' would be: 'if a piece of iron is placed near x, then x is magnetic if and only if the piece of iron moves towards it'. More generally, we have: 'in test conditions C, x has the theoretical property Q if and only if it manifests the response R'. (Symbolically: $Cx \rightarrow (Qx \equiv Rx)$.) Thus what we get here is a partial specification of the meaning of theoretical terms, that is, the meaning they have in certain test situations. Further specifications can then be given, by correspondence rules which give the meanings of the terms in different situations.

There are several difficulties with this account, which we will not mention here.[9] However, the main point is that the success of this second type of correspondence rule depends partly on whether the list of rules for a particular theoretical term is finite in number. If not, as seems likely, then it will not be possible, even in principle, to eliminate theoretical terms from science, and replace them by observational terms. And if this is impossible, it might be taken to indicate that it is also impossible to avoid the ontological commitments of theoretical terms, and to maintain the ontologically privileged status of the observation-language. Alternatively, it might be taken to provide a rationale for what is called the 'instrumentalist' view of science, in which theoretical statements are regarded not as true or false, but as computational devices for the generation of successful predictions about observables. We will return to this view at the end of chapter 3; whilst in chapter 2, we will consider a realist interpretation of the positivists' correspondence rules. But let us now examine some problems of the theoretical-observational dichotomy itself.

There are many different distinctions that can be drawn between the observable and the unobservable, and also between the theoretical and the non-theoretical. Each of these is of some importance in different contexts, but there is no one distinction that has priority over all the others, and which can be used to perform the several different functions which positivists have assigned to the theoretical-observational dichotomy. Further, it is difficult to state these distinctions as holding between two sets of *terms*, since the status of any one term may change historically, or vary from one situation in which it is applied to another.

Consider, for example, the term 'virus'. If one allows as observable anything that can be detected either by the senses or by instruments, then it is now an observational term (since viruses can be observed by use of an electron microscope), but earlier it was not. A similar historical change of status results from the application of the pragmatic theory of observation, mentioned earlier. Alternatively, if the observable is defined as that which can be detected without the use of instruments, 'virus' remains non-observational. But is it a *theoretical* term? If one distinguishes between terms that are central to a developed scientific theory, and those that are not, then 'virus' is now theoretical, but not earlier on. However, if 'theoretical' is taken to mean 'speculative' or 'purely hypothetical', then viruses, whose existence is now well-confirmed, were once theoretical, but now non-theoretical.

Even at any one time, the status of a particular term with respect to such distinctions is often problematic. Suppose we define as observable that which does not require the use of instruments for its detection. Consider the term 'moon'. Sometimes, as with the Earth's moon, the term is applied as a result of observations with the naked eye: but for most other moons, it is not. Somewhat similarly, one can often detect the presence of an electrical charge without the use of instruments; but to make precise quantitative measurements, instruments are necessary. So are the terms 'moon' and 'electrical charge' to be counted as observational or non-observational?[10]

It seems that the basic error of positivist philosophers of science has been to use a single dichotomy to resolve several different issues. First, there is the problem of finding some epistemological foundation for scientific theories, of distinguishing between the degrees of certainty with which various kinds of statement can be affirmed or denied, and thus of giving some account of the 'objective control' of science. Second, there is the problem of finding some way of assessing the relative merits of competing scientific theories, which themselves often provide different ways of characterizing the results of experiments and observations; of constructing some theory-neutral observation language. Finally, there is the ontological issue, the question of determining in general what sorts of items can properly be said to exist, and to enter into causal relations with each other. In the following two chapters, we will be returning to these problems, and the relations between them.

4 Positivism and 'the logic of science'

So far, we have been examining the specific claims made by positivists about the nature of scientific explanation, the relations between theory and observation, and so on. We will now make some comments about the way in which positivists have conceived of the philosophy of science itself, and of the kinds of results it can establish. 'The logic of science' is a phrase which has often been used to represent this conception of the philosophy of science, and it will be convenient to organize our remarks around its various connotations.

We have noted the reliance of positivists upon the techniques and concepts of formal logic. Thus, explanation is analysed as a form of logical argument; theoretical terms are given definitions through formal correspondence rules; and attempts are made to specify the logical relationships involved in the testing of theories. These features alone justify the use of 'the logic of science' as an appropriate description of the way in which positivists have regarded and carried out their enterprise.[11] But this phrase may also be used to contrast what the positivist sees as the *philosophical* approach to science, with various others, such as the historical, psychological or sociological. Generally, positivists have either been uninterested in these, or, at least, convinced that they have no great relevance to the philosophy of science, which is concerned only with its 'logic'. Thus, the general characterization of the historical development of science, or the psychological processes involved in the theoretical activity of scientists, or the organization of the scientific community and its relations to other aspects of society: all these have been regarded as forms of enquiry quite different from that of the logic of science, and their results as strictly irrelevant to it. This claim of non-relevance may itself be supported by reference to some version of a general distinction between prescription and description. So the positivist conceives of the logic of science as dealing with questions of rational evaluation and justification, in contrast to, say, the sociologist's concern with the empirical description and explanation of scientific activity.

Let us consider two of these contrasts – between the logic of science and, respectively, its psychology and history – in more detail. The first of these is well illustrated in the positivist attitude towards the role of models and analogies in science. An undoubted feature of scientific activity is the way in which many theories are presented by means of analogies with relatively familiar objects and processes. For example, Huygens justified his use of the term 'waves' in his theory of light and sound in the following manner (quoted in Achinstein, 1968, p. 204):

I call them waves from their resemblance to those which are seen to be formed in water when a stone is thrown into it, and which present a successive spreading as circles, though these arise from another cause, and are only on a flat surface.

Such analogies, and the models which are based upon them (in this case, the 'wave model' of light and sound), are typically regarded by positivists as of only psychological interest. They are thus seen as 'heuristic aids': either to the scientist who first formulates the theory, by some act of creative imagination, or to laymen (or other scientists), who find it psychologically helpful in understanding a theory to have it presented in terms of models or analogies. But such features of scientific activity are irrelevant to the logic of science, which is not concerned with these psychological processes.[12]

The contrast between the logic of science and its history is more complex. Most positivists reject the view that, somehow, a correct philosophy of science can be derived from a study of its history; or that philosophical claims about science can be confirmed or refuted by the fact that scientists have, or have not, proceeded in this way historically. However, many positivists have been interested in producing a 'rational reconstruction' of the history of science, in which various episodes are appropriately re-described in terms of the vocabulary and doctrines of the logic of science. Indeed, this may take the form of a very general characterization of the way in which science develops historically. Here we find two main accounts, which bear close affinities with some of the views about the relations between theory and observation discussed in section 2. First, an inductivist account, according to which science can be seen as a process of steady accumulation, in which more and more facts are discovered, with increasing accuracy, and theories become more general and universal in their scope. Second, a hypothetico-deductive account, in which science develops by the successive formulation and rejection of theories, and is thus neither steady nor cumulative in its progress. The history of science is the history of the abandonment of hypotheses which failed to meet the tests of observation and experiment. Nonetheless, there is a sense in which progress is made: although one can never be sure that present theories are correct, they are at least closer to the truth than those which have already been falsified.[13]

Whichever of these two accounts is adopted, positivists tend to characterize the historical development of human knowledge as a process in which various types of pre-scientific explanations of natural phenomena are eventually replaced by properly scientific ones. This view is often supported by reference to a number of 'famous episodes', where the scientific attitude is seen as finally triumphing over theological, animistic or metaphysical explanations. One such example, from eighteenth-century chemistry, is the replacement of the *phlogiston* theory of combustion, by Lavoisier's *oxygen* theory. Positivists view phlogiston as an unscientific concept, which neither belongs to, nor is definable within, the observational language of science. We will now outline these two theories, since the nature of the historical conflict between their proponents raises issues that will be significant in later chapters.

Priestley, a supporter of the phlogiston theory, argued that the combustion of substances such as metals or sulphur was due to the phlogiston present in them being released and absorbed into the air, leaving behind metal calxes, or sulphuric acid. Thus: combustible substance − phlogiston = burnt substance. When calxes or acids were heated, with carbon, they absorbed the phlogiston contained in the carbon, and the original substances were regenerated: burnt substance + phlogiston = combustible substance. Against this, Lavoisier argued that, during combustion, metals or sulphur combined with oxygen from the air. For example: sulphur + oxygen = sulphuric acid. Conversely, burnt substance − oxygen (withdrawn by the carbon) = combustible substance. We should also note that what Lavoisier came to call 'oxygen' had earlier been discovered by Priestley, by heating mercury calx. But Priestley called this gas 'dephlogisticated air', because he believed its properties, such as supporting rapid combustion, were due to its containing less phlogiston than ordinary air, thus being able to absorb more phlogiston during combustion.[14]

Let us now consider another feature of positivism associated with the phrase 'the logic of science'. This is the idea that the philosophy of science involves an analysis of science which is not directly dependent upon the actual and varying specific contents of different scientific theories, but which is conducted at a 'higher' or 'meta-' level. Furthermore, it is often believed that by analysing science in this way, we can discover various abstract, universal and objective criteria to which any actual scientific theory or explanation must conform. Such criteria can also be appealed to as external, rational standards to resolve the disputes between proponents of rival scientific theories or explanations that may occur, and have occurred, in the history of science.

Finally, and closely connected to this last feature, there is an underlying claim that there is only *one* logic of science, to which any intellectual activity aspiring to the title of 'science' must conform. Thus, the so-called 'social sciences' must do this, if they are to deserve their title: and many positivists have argued that, though at present 'immature', they can in fact do so. This claim, which we have earlier referred to as 'naturalism', has been a characteristic feature of positivism, both in this century, and before − so much so that the terms 'positivism' and 'naturalism' have come to be used interchangeably. We have already argued that such a usage is highly misleading. But it is worth adding here, that this belief in the methodological unity of the sciences has itself been only one aspect of a more general commitment to what positivists have termed 'the unity of science'. This latter ideal has involved, in addition to methodological unity, a substantive unity, which is to be achieved by the systematic reduction of all sciences to one basic science, usually physics. Such a reduction (or rather, a series of reductions) can be achieved either by defining the concepts of one science (say, biology) in terms of those of another science (say, chemistry), or by deriving the laws and theories of the former from those of the latter. Thus, ideally, we would have a hierarchy of sciences, beginning with physics, and proceeding through chemistry, biology, psychology and sociology, in which all are 'reduced' to the first.[15]

We will not examine this ideal any further here. Instead, we turn in the next chapter to an analysis of one of the alternative conceptions of the natural sciences – realism.

2 Realist philosophy of science

1 The realist view of explanation

We argued earlier that the main difficulty for the positivist account of
scientific explanation arises from the existence of logical arguments
which, though satisfying the specified conditions, enable us only to
predict, and not to explain, the occurrence of particular events. For
the realist, this difficulty is highly significant, since it indicates a basic
inadequacy of the positivist account. The inadequacy consists in
confusing the provision of grounds for expecting an event to occur,
with giving a causal explanation of why that event occurred. The
premisses which, for the positivist, constitute the explanans may
often be such that they only give us good, or conclusive, reasons for
believing that the explanandum-event either will or did occur. They
do not necessarily tell us *why* that event did or will occur.[1]

For the realist, this problem results from analysing scientific
explanation as consisting of a form of logical argument. Even if it is
a necessary condition of explanation that such arguments can be
constructed, it is not a sufficient one. What is additionally required
is the delineation of the causal processes involved in the generation of
the phenomena we are trying to explain. Instead of establishing, as
in the D–N model, relations of logical necessity between the explanans
and explanandum statements, we should discover the relations of
natural necessity that exist in the physical world. To show that the
truth of the conclusion follows necessarily from that of the premisses
is no substitute for describing the necessary, causal connections
between things in nature.

But this use of the concept of natural, or causal, necessity has long
been rejected by positivists, who have regarded Hume's objections to
it as decisive. Hume accepted that our everyday pre-philosophical
concept of causation involves both the idea of the cause immediately
preceding its effect, and also some idea of a necessary connection

27

between the two. But the crucial question for Hume was what kind of necessity this could be. Not logical necessity, since it is impossible to deduce, from a statement asserting the occurrence of one event, a statement asserting the later occurrence of another event, which we may happen to regard as the effect of the first one. Thus it is not self-contradictory to affirm the truth of the first statement, whilst denying that of the second. Consider, for example, the two events 'striking a match' and 'the match lighting'. Although we may in fact believe that the former is the cause of the latter, whatever necessity we ascribe to the relation between them cannot be logical necessity, since it is not self-contradictory both to affirm that the match was struck, and to deny that it lit. Further, Hume argued that the idea of necessity cannot be derived from observation: there is no non-logical necessity which somehow exists in nature. However closely and systematically we observe any two events that we believe to be cause and effect, we can never discover any necessary link or connection between them. Thus, in the case of one billiard ball's being said to cause another to move, there is nothing to be observed but the one movement immediately followed by the other.

Nonetheless, it is also possible to learn by observation that a movement of the first kind is regularly followed by one of the second kind. And this indicates the nature of Hume's positive account of causal relations. To say that one event is the cause of another is to say that the first is temporally prior to the second, and that whenever an event of the same type as the first occurs, it is always followed by one of the same type as the second.[2]

This Humean view of causation, the 'regularity theory', provides the basis of the positivist analysis of scientific explanation. The statements expressing laws, which constitute one part of the explanans in the D–N model, are essentially statements of Humean regularities. They are not logically necessary statements: as we noted in our outline of the positivist view of scientific laws, they are purely empirical, universal conditional statements. The logical necessity in the D–N model is located in the relation between the explanans (premises) and the explanandum (conclusion). Further, we can now see one reason why the positivist is unlikely to try to avoid the problem of non-explanatory predictions by restricting the law-statements in this model to causal laws. For, on a regularity theory of causation, many of the cases of non-explanatory regularities will qualify as causal relations: it is difficult to distinguish between causal and non-causal laws in a way relevant to this problem.[3]

So the realist objection to the positivist account of explanation rests upon a rejection of the Humean view of causation that provides its fundamental rationale. The realist wishes to substitute an alternative account of explanation based upon a non-Humean view of causal relations. This involves both a criticism of Hume's position, and the construction of a viable alternative. One approach[4] to these can be introduced by considering the comments made by a realist philosopher of science, Rom Harré, on the following passage from the *Enquiries*, where Hume (1902, p. 77) gives an example of the application of his account of causation:

> We say, for instance, that the vibration of this string is the cause of this particular sound. But what do we mean by that affirmation? We ... mean *that this vibration is followed by this sound, and that all similar vibrations have been followed by similar sounds. ...*

Harré comments (1970, pp. 105–6):

> This, Hume contends, must be the correct analysis since we can form no idea of the connection between the vibration and the sound. But the theory and experiments of sonic physics and neuro-physiology give us a very good idea of the connection between the vibration and the sound. We all know nowadays of the train of pressures in the air, the operation of the ear-drum, the cochlea, and so on, and we now know something of the train of electrochemical happenings between the inner ear and that part of the brain identified as the seat of audition. Furthermore, to explain what we mean by 'the vibration causes the sound', rather than something else, typically involves, I contend, reference to the intervening mechanism which links the vibration in the string to the sound we hear. The vibration of the string stimulates a mechanism which then acts in such a way that we are stimulated and hear a sound.

More generally, Harré argues that to view causal relations as consisting only of temporal precedence and regular succession, is to fail to distinguish between the *meaning* of statements asserting such relations, and one kind of *evidence* upon which they may be based. If we discover a regular relationship between two kinds of phenomena, this gives us some reason to believe that they are causally connected: the existence of the regularity is strong, though not conclusive, evidence for a causal connection. But this is not all we mean in claiming that one thing is the cause of another. In addition, we commit ourselves to the presence of some intervening mechanism which links them together, and it is the scientist's task to discover and analyse the nature of such mechanisms. Thus, in the example about the string-vibration and sound, Harré would maintain that the regular relation between these may provide evidence for the existence of a causal relation. But in saying that there is a causal relation, we mean also that there is some intervening mechanism which, in this instance, is described by means of the theories of sonic physics and neuro-physiology.[5]

This claim about the relation between evidence and meaning in the case of causal statements implicitly involves the rejection of a general theory of meaning often supported by positivist philosophers of science. According to this 'verificationist' theory, the meaning of any empirical statement is given by its actual or possible means of verification – that is, by observational evidence, such as Humean regularities. As we will see in section 3, the rejection of this theory is also involved in the realist view of positivist correspondence rules. And in the final section, we will consider some objections to these criticisms of Hume. But let us now look in more detail at the realist alternative to the regularity theory of causation and the positivist view of scientific explanation.

For the realist, adequate causal explanations require the discovery both of regular relations between phenomena, and of some kind of mechanism that links them. So, in explaining any particular phenomenon, we must not only make reference to those events which initiate the process of change: we must also give a description of that process itself. To do this, we need knowledge of the underlying mechanisms and structures that are present, and of the manner in which they generate or produce the phenomenon we are trying to explain. In describing these mechanisms and structures we will often, in effect, be characterizing the 'nature', 'essence', or 'inner constitution' of various types of entity. Suppose we wish to explain an increase in temperature of some particular gas. There are well-established laws relating the temperature, volume and pressure of gases (at least in 'ideal' conditions). Thus we can, with this knowledge, show any particular temperature increase to be an instance of these laws; and we can thereby explain this phenomenon in a manner conforming to the D–N model. But for the realist, a satisfactory causal explanation requires more than this. We need to know the mechanisms at work: and to do so, we must discover the nature or constitution of gases. This is given by the molecular theory of gases, according to which they are composed of a vast number of molecules, which interact in a manner that explains the regular relations represented by the gas laws.

It might, however, be objected by the positivist that this example can easily be accommodated within the framework of the D–N model. The laws relating temperature, volume and pressure can be seen as 'lower level' laws, derivable from, and thus explicable by, the 'higher level' laws of molecular interaction. The latter laws are more general in their scope than the lower level ones, and also contain theoretical terms. But there are several replies to this objection. First, the positivist explanation outlined here is, strictly speaking, of the lower level laws, and not of the particular phenomenon which is the explanandum in our example. For the positivist, this phenomenon is adequately explained by showing it to be an instance of the lower level laws. This the realist denies. Second, the positivist must view the explanatory power of the molecular theory as stemming only from its greater scope and generality, which enable the lower level laws (and, less directly, particular phenomena) to be deduced from it. But the realist regards its explanatory power as due to its description of the nature, or essence, of gas, thereby providing the kind of account of mechanisms and structures necessary for adequate causal explanation. Finally, by their rejection of the ontological commitments of theoretical terms, positivists eliminate this central feature of the molecular theory's explanatory power.

The realist view of explanation can be conveniently summarized in the claim that answers to why-questions (that is, to requests for causal explanations) require answers to how- and what-questions. Thus, if asked *why* something occurs, we must show *how* some event or change brings about a new state of affairs, by describing the way in which the structures and mechanisms that are present respond to the initial change. To do this, it is necessary to discover *what* the entities involved are: to discover their natures or essences. It is sometimes said that science cannot tell us why things happen, but only how; or, that science is concerned only with description, and not with explanation. But the realist rejects the contrasts implicit in such claims. For, to explain why is partly to say how; and causal explanation itself requires descriptions.[6]

We conclude this account of the realist view of explanation by considering one of the positivist developments of Hume's theory of causal relations, due mainly to J. S. Mill. Let us return to an earlier example, striking a match as the cause of its lighting. If Hume's theory is applied to this, the following problem arises. Although we may talk of the former event causing the latter, we would be unwilling to claim that, whenever an event of the first kind occurs, it is always followed by an event of the second kind. For this regularity only holds given the existence of various other conditions, such as the chemical nature of the match-head and striking-surface, the degree of force with which the match is struck, the presence of oxygen in the atmosphere, and so on. Thus the striking of the match is only one of the causes of its lighting, and not the whole or complete cause. The complete cause must be such that, whenever it recurs, an event of the same kind will follow.

For Mill, then, the cause of any event must be a set of conditions or factors which, taken together, are a sufficient condition for it. No one of these conditions is, by itself, sufficient: each may be termed 'a cause', or 'a causal condition', in contrast to the complete cause, which is composed of a conjunction of these conditions. Thus sets of conditions replace Hume's single events. But this difference is of little significance to the realist, as can be seen from the following two objections from a realist standpoint. First, causal relations interpreted as sufficient condition relations are still basically Humean regularities. For no element of necessity is involved in the relation between a sufficient set of conditions and the phenomenon of which they are the cause. Second, the realist finds problematic the manner in which different types of causal conditions are somehow combined or conjoined to constitute the complete cause. The term 'condition' is used by Mill to refer, indifferently, to events, states of affairs, processes, and so on: almost anything can turn up in a list of causal conditions. Indeed, in the example used earlier (admittedly our own, but conforming to the general spirit of Mill's account), two of these items – the chemical composition of the match-head and striking-surface – are of a similar kind to those which would typically occur as the structural component of a realist explanation. But for such items to be simply listed, together with others of very different kinds – the striking of the match, and the presence of oxygen – as jointly forming a sufficient set, is, for the realist, misleading and mysterious. These sets are typically presented as logical conjunctions of discrete conditions, as in '(A & B & C)': but what kind of combination of such disparate items could this possibly represent?[7]

2 The realist view of theories and models

For the realist, the primary purpose of scientific theories is to enable us to give causal explanations of observable phenomena, and of the regular relations that exist between them. Further, such explanations must make reference to the underlying structures and mechanisms which are involved in the causal processes. It is these structures and mechanisms which it is the task of theories to describe. Thus, the central feature of a scientific theory is its description of these items, and of the way in which they operate to generate the various phenomena that we wish to explain.

This brief characterization of the realist position can best be expanded by considering the function of models and analogies in theories. We noted in the previous chapter that many scientific theories are based upon, or involve some reference to, models and analogies that link those theories to other types of phenomena, or other areas of scientific and common-sense knowledge. Stated in this vague and general way, this is a claim that both positivists and realists can agree upon. But, as we will see, they disagree significantly about more precise and specific ways of interpreting it. Let us begin by giving some examples of models and analogies, ignoring for the moment the differences between these two concepts. In the following passage, Peter Achinstein (1968, pp. 203–4) presents some typical scientific analogies, accompanied by illustrative quotations:

1   The analogy between an atom and a solar system, in which the nucleus is likened to a sun and the electrons to planets revolving about it in elliptical orbits:
'The alternative [to a harmonic model of the atom] was to copy the motion of the planets around the sun. The reason planets do not fall into the sun is that they have reached stable orbits in which the centripetal force required to constrain them is exactly the force of gravitation pulling them in . . . Similarly in the atom, a revolving electron if moving fast enough would not fall into the positively charged nucleus.'
2   The analogy drawn by Huygens between waves of light, sound, and water:
'I call them [light and sound] waves from their resemblance to those which are seen to be formed in water when a stone is thrown into it, and which present a successive spreading as circles, though these arise from another cause, and are only on a flat surface.'
3   The analogy between a gas and a container of billiard balls, in which the molecules in the gas are likened to perfectly elastic billiard balls striking the sides of the container as well as each other.

We can use these examples to give some indication of the relationship between analogies and models. In the case of 1, we might talk of the solar model of the atom, based upon an analogy with the solar system; in 2, of the wave model of light and sound, based upon an analogy with the behaviour of water; and in 3, of the molecular model of gases, based upon an analogy with billiard balls in a container. We can also draw distinctions, which are important from the realist standpoint, between a *model*, the *source* of a model, and the *subject* of a model. Roughly, a model is an attempted representation of the nature of that which is the subject of the model; it is analogically related to its source, which is an already understood phenomenon. In other words, models are *of* a subject, and modelled *on* a source. Thus, in 1, the subject of the model is the structure of the atom; the source of the model is the solar system; and the model is a representation of this subject, analogically related to the source. Likewise, with the other examples. Further, we can use these distinctions to draw attention to the diverse ways in which well-known models in science are often named. Sometimes, as with 'The Bohr model of the atom', the name derives simply from the model's author. Or, as with 'the wave model of light', it derives from the basic feature ascribed by the model to its subject. Finally, as with 'the billiard ball model of gases', the name derives from the model's source; though, in this case, we have an alternative name, 'the molecular model', deriving from its subject.

In this account of models, the concepts of analogy and representation are clearly important. In general, to claim that there is an analogy between two items is to claim that there are both similarities and dissimilarities between their various features, and that the similarities enable us to understand one of the items by means of our knowledge of the other. The relevant features may range from the straightforwardly observable, such as size, to the more 'abstract', such as conformity to the same laws. Thus, in the billiard ball model of gas, the features ascribed by that model to the constituents of gas differ from those of billiard balls with respect to colour and size, but are similar with respect to shape and mode of interaction.

The concept of representation is more problematic. It should be noted that the expression 'representational model' is sometimes used to refer to three-dimensional physical objects (or two-dimensional diagrams), such as tinkertoy models of molecules, or engineering models of dams and aeroplanes. Such objects are frequently employed in science, but they involve different senses of the terms 'model' and 'representation' to those so far considered: we will exclude these different senses in what follows.[8] Basically, the realist regards a model as an attempt to *describe* structures and mechanisms which are often unavailable to observation, even with the use of scientific instruments. Thus the relationships between the descriptive terms of a model and the characteristics of its subject are, in principle, the same as those between any such terms and the items to which they refer. However, the description or representation provided by a model typically involves various forms of abstraction and idealization of the actual features of its subject. For example, the billiard ball model abstracts from these features in omitting reference to the attractive and repulsive intermolecular forces. It also presents some of them in an idealized form, in ascribing 'perfect elasticity' to the constituents of gases, a property which is possessed by no actual object in the physical world. Nonetheless, it would be wrong to regard abstraction and idealization as peculiar to models, or to any attempt to describe unobservable entities. They are present at every level of scientific theorizing, as is shown by the use of such concepts as the perfectly frictionless surface, an idealization which need not refer to unobservable entities, nor be part of a model.[9]

Let us now consider the way in which, for the realist, models and analogies function in the processes of theory-formulation and testing. In order to explain observable phenomena, and the regularities that obtain between them, scientists must attempt to discover appropriate structures and mechanisms. Since these will typically be unavailable to observation, we first construct a model of them, often drawing upon an already familiar source. The model is such that, were it to represent correctly these structures and mechanisms, the phenomena would then be causally explained. Having constructed the model, we proceed to test it as a hypothetical description of actually existing entities and their relations. To do so, we work out further consequences of the model (that is, additional to the phenomena we are trying to explain), that can be stated in a manner open to empirical testing. If these tests are successful, this gives good reason to believe in the existence of these structures and mechanisms, the *initial* reason for this belief being that, were they to exist, the original phenomena would be adequately explained. Further, it may prove possible to obtain more direct confirmation of these existential claims, by the development and use of suitable instruments. Finally, the whole process model-building may then be repeated, in order to explain the structures and mechanisms already discovered.[10]

How does this account compare with some of the positivist views of theory-formulation and testing that we outlined in section 2 of the previous chapter? Clearly, the realist must reject the idea that we arrive at theories by an inductive procedure, by moving from particular observations to generalizations about these observed phenomena. Whatever the realist may think about the logical problem of induction, such inductive arguments can never justify the postulation of unobservable entities. The move of generalization, from 'some' to 'all', is not a move from observables to the unobservable structures and mechanisms which explain them.

The hypothetico-deductive method, however, might at first seem closer to the realist view. Models could be regarded as hypotheses, which are tested by deducing their observable consequences. To some extent, the realist can accept this, but with important qualifications. First, whereas the hypothetico-deductivist claims that hypotheses are purely conjectures, which 'come from nowhere', the realist emphasizes the frequency with which some form of analogical argument, from source to model, may be employed. Second, the realist's hypotheses are about underlying structures and mechanisms, whereas the positivist's hypotheses are, at best, theoretical laws, whose theoretical terms are not interpreted as involving ontological commitments. Indeed, many of the hypotheses introduced by realists are of an existential kind. That is, they postulate the existence of entities that have not been observed, and may not be open to any available method of detection. Examples of such existential hypotheses are the postulation of the existence of viruses, of various sub-atomic particles, or of magnetic fields. Thus, to describe the realist view of theories as involving use of the hypothetico-deductive method is misleading if the nature of the hypotheses, and their differences from those advocated by positivists, is not fully recognized.[11]

Let us conclude by contrasting the attitude of positivists and realists to the function of models and analogies in scientific theories. There is an orthodox view of the contrast that should be rejected. According to this, the positivist regards their function as purely heuristic: models and analogies are psychologically helpful in arriving at, and presenting, scientific theories, but their significance is limited to this. Whereas the realist sees them as an essential feature of theories, enabling us intelligibly to represent unobservable structures and mechanisms. But this orthodox account mistakenly assumes that realists and positivists accept the same conception of models and analogies, whilst disagreeing only about their function. Against this, we suggest that their disagreements about what constitutes an adequate scientific theory result in their having different conceptions of the nature of models and analogies. Since the positivist is concerned to arrive at theories which are statements either of empirical or theoretical laws, there is no function at all for models which, conceived from the realist standpoint, are descriptions of actually existing structures and mechanisms. It would be misleading to say that positivists regard such models as serving only a heuristic function, since on their view of theories, there is *no* function for models conceived in this way. The most that the positivist could allow is that we sometimes use an already familiar *source* as a way of suggesting laws that would explain a phenomenon apparently dissimilar to the source, and that we may find it easier to understand a theory if stated in these familiar terms. Indeed, the positivist position tends to deny the relevance of the distinction between models and their sources.

It could also be misleading to say that, for the realist, models and analogies are essential to scientific theories. If theories are seen as attempted descriptions of structures and mechanisms, the distinction between theories and models seems to collapse, since models are characterized in precisely the same way. The distinction can only be maintained by saying that, for the realist, to call something a model is to refer to a relatively early stage in the process of theory-building, in which the use of sources for the construction of the model is of considerable importance, and the status of the model as a correct representation is still highly speculative. However, we will return to some of these issues at the end of the next chapter. Let us now consider the realist view of the distinction between theoretical and observational terms.[12]

3 Realism and theoretical terms

In the previous chapter, we suggested that positivists were mistaken in trying to use the theoretical-observational dichotomy to solve what are, in fact, three distinct problems: the construction of an epistemologically certain foundation for science, the provision of means for comparing and evaluating rival theories, and the delimitation of an acceptable scientific ontology. The relationship between the first two problems will be examined in the following chapter. Here, we will be concerned with the ways in which realists and positivists differ with respect to the relationship between the first and third. And, for the most part, we will ignore the various difficulties of drawing any single distinction between the theoretical and the observational.

We characterized the positivist view of the observation language as ascribing to it both epistemological and ontological privilege. The realist rejects this ascription of ontological privilege. Scientific theories enable us to give causal explanations of observable phenomena by their description of structures and mechanisms that are typically beyond observation (even if we include as observable those items which can be detected by available instruments). Thus, although the realist may accept that the truth or falsity of observational statements is a matter of far greater certainty than that of theoretical statements, any attempt to limit the ontological commitments of a scientific theory to those made in observational statements is strongly rejected. The question of what exists, or can intelligibly be said to exist, must be kept distinct from that of what we can observe, or know with a high degree of certainty.

However, it is not enough for the realist simply to deny the positivist equation of epistemological and ontological privilege. For that equation, as we noted earlier, is itself based upon the positivist's adoption of a general criterion of scientificity, a principle by which scientific and non-scientific statements can be distinguished. It is this principle, according to which a statement is only scientific if it is possible to ascertain its truth or falsity by means of direct observation, which generates the problem of theoretical terms for positivism. It also suggests the manner in which the problem is to be resolved; for example, by the use of correspondence rules which render theoretical statements scientific by providing definitions of theoretical terms in the observation language. The realist must either reject the whole idea of finding a general criterion of scientificity, or else produce an acceptable alternative criterion.

But the latter option, if taken, may not be particularly difficult. For, by making some relatively minor adjustments to the positivist criterion, realists can allow all the ontological commitments they might wish a scientific theory to be able to make. Consider this principle: a statement is scientific only if it is possible to make observations that would count in some way for or against its truth or falsity. Such a criterion of scientificity would enable the realist to accept theoretical statements at their face value, and remove the necessity of translating them into an acceptably 'scientific' observation language.[13]

Since the realist rejects the basis of the problem for which correspondence rules were introduced as one type of solution, it is not surprising that such rules, if used at all, take on a very different function. For the positivist, they are ways of specifying the meanings of theoretical terms by relating these to statements in the observation language. For the realist, they suggest ways of indirectly testing the truth or falsity of theoretical statements; or means by which the presence or absence of the items denoted by theoretical terms can be observationally detected or inferred. Thus, in the case of the operational definition of magnetism (p. 20 above), the results of placing a small piece of iron near an object should be seen as a way of *testing* the claim that the object is magnetic, and not as expressing the *meaning* of the statement 'x is magnetic'. Similarly, with partial interpretations: they should not be seen as partial specifications of the meaning of the theoretical term 'Q', but as stating different ways of empirically detecting the presence or absence of the item to which 'Q' refers.

However, for various technical reasons, the realist cannot accept the logical form of either operational definitions or partial interpretations as adequately representing these relations of empirical testing. Instead, something of the following form is proposed: 'if x is Q, then if test-conditions C are applied, result R will occur'. (Symbolically: $Qx \to (Cx \to Rx)$.) In this form, positive results provide only indirect, and logically non-conclusive, evidence for the truth of 'x is Q'. We postulate that x is Q, and argue that, if this is so, we should get R when we carry out C. If this is what happens, it gives us some reason to believe that x is Q. But there are many reasons why R may happen, of which x's being Q is only one. Indeed, what is often involved in such cases is an argument from effects to causes (that is, from R as the effect of Q in C, to Q): but one can never be sure that there is only one possible cause for any given effect.[14]

Thus the realist regards 'correspondence rules' (if this phrase is still used) as frequently expressing causal relations between theoretical entities and observable phenomena. It is because an entity of some kind exists, or has some property, that when the specified test conditions are carried out, the predicted results occur. This is very different from the positivist view of correspondence rules as specifying the meanings of theoretical terms. Further, this way of stating the difference suggests that here, just as in their criticism of the Humean theory of causation, realists must also reject the verificationist theory of meaning that underlies the positivist conception of correspondence rules. According to this theory (which entails, but is not entailed by, the positivist criterion of scientificity), the meaning of an empirical statement is constituted by its mode of verification. So, for the positivist, in providing correspondence rules that link theoretical terms to test procedures and their observable results, we are giving the meanings of those terms, and thus of statements containing them. But the realist rejects this theory of meaning. Instead, it is maintained that the meanings of theoretical terms can be understood independently of the construction of test procedures which enable us to verify indirectly the presence or absence of the items referred to by these terms.

We will not discuss the general philosophical grounds for rejecting the verificationist theory. But we will conclude this section by considering two of the ways in which realists may give an account of the meanings of theoretical terms. First, it may be possible to give analogical definitions for such terms, by relating their meanings analogically to some already understood terms. Such analogical definitions may often be derived from the source of a model, but not always, as is shown by the following example provided by Achinstein (1968, pp. 117–18):

> When Maxwell introduced the concept of self-diffusion of molecules in a gas he invoked an analogy between molecules and bees in a swarm:
> 'If we wish to form a representation of what is going on among the molecules in calm air, we cannot do better than observe a swarm of bees, when every individual bee is flying furiously, first in one direction and then in another, while the swarm as a whole remains at rest, or sails slowly through the air.'

The second way is suggested by a criticism, made in section 3 of the previous chapter, of the positivist's attempt to state the theoretical-observational dichotomy as existing between two sets of terms. Many terms, such as 'moon' or 'electric charge', are used to characterize both observable and unobservable items. Assuming that the meanings of such terms are relatively unproblematic in their observational uses, the realist can simply maintain that these meanings remain much the same in their non-observational, or theoretical, uses. This is well illustrated in the following quotation from H. A. Lorentz (quoted in Schaffner, 1969, p. 282), discussing the introduction of the concept of the electron:

If we want to understand the way in which electrical and magnetic properties depend on the temperature, the density, the chemical composition, or the crystalline state of substances . . . we shall be obliged to have recourse to some hypothesis about the mechanism that is at the bottom of the phenomena.

It is by this necessity that one has been led to the conception of *electrons*, i.e. of extremely small particles, charged with electricity . . . by whose distribution we endeavour to explain all electric phenomena that are not confined to the free ether. . . .

Here, we are given an initial definition of the term 'electron', not by means of positivist correspondence rules, but by the use of terms that are already understood in observational contexts. There is no reason to believe that these terms, 'small', 'particle', 'charged with electricity', suddenly lose or radically alter their meaning when they are used to characterize a theoretical entity, the electron. Further, Lorentz's comments on the reasons for introducing this concept provide a good example of the realist view of scientific theories and explanation.[15]

4 Some problems for realism

We will now consider various objections that might be made against the realist view of science. Some of these are from a specifically positivist standpoint, but others concern the extent to which realism can provide an adequate account of the major kinds of theoretical activity and achievement that actually take place in science. One such objection, to the realist analysis of explanation, is that it is far too restrictive, since there are many scientific theories and laws that can properly be regarded as providing explanations, but not of the sort advocated by the realist. For example, the laws of free fall, or of pendular motion, certainly have some form of explanatory power, and must surely count as significant achievements in the history of science. When some phenomenon is shown to be an instance of these elegantly stated, economically formulated systematizations, it would be wrong to deny that any explanation has been provided, through an undue restriction of this concept to the kind of causal explanation advocated by the realist. And this objection can be extended to the realist view of theories, as failing to represent an important kind of scientific theory, sometimes called 'reticular' or 'abstractive'. The ideal gas laws, or, indeed, the whole of classical mechanics, are examples of reticular theories, which clearly differ from the causal theories advocated by the realist, such as the molecular theory of gases, or the virus theory of infection. In reticular theories, no attempt is made to discover underlying mechanisms or structures, but only to formulate laws governing the behaviour of a wide range of observable phenomena. Reticular theories typically involve terms, such as 'force', which do not refer to observables: but it would be wrong to interpret them as referring to unobservable causes, unlike terms such as 'virus'. Any descriptively adequate philosophy of science must recognize the significance of both types of theory, and not pay undue attention to either one.[16]

Of course, even if these objections are successful against realism, they do not thereby vindicate the positivist position. For, although positivists might argue that the D–N model, and their account of laws and theories, accurately represent these non-causal explanations and reticular theories, it could likewise be objected that their own account of science is descriptively inadequate with respect to those elements emphasized by the realist.[17] Further, both realists and positivists might defend themselves against this double-edged objection by maintaining that philosophical theories about science cannot be refuted by such claims of descriptive inadequacy. To think that this is possible is to ignore the essentially prescriptive nature of the philosophy of science, which distinguishes it from a purely descriptive approach, such as the historical one.

We will not try to resolve directly this general issue about the relations between the philosophy of science and scientific practice. But some light is thrown on it by the following suggestion that may be made by a realist who tries to tackle the problem of descriptive adequacy. The suggestion is that, although reticular theories are of considerable importance in science, they do not provide a form of explanation acceptable in its own right as an alternative to causal explanation. Instead, such theories must always be replaced eventually by causal theories, which both explain the regular relations represented by the reticular theory, and provide properly causal explanations of the phenomena that can be shown to be instances of those relations. It may also be suggested that a significant theme in the historical development of science is well represented by this account of the philosophical relation between causal and reticular theories: namely, the successive attempts to discover causal theories which explain reticular theories, often motivated by the dissatisfaction felt by scientists about the explanatory power of the latter.[18]

However, the success of this suggestion depends partly on the adequacy of the realist's alternative to the Humean view of causation. Were this to be inadequate, the distinction between the two types of theory would lose much of its force, since if causality is a matter of regularities, the distinctive nature of *causal* theories becomes highly problematic. Further, the positivist might then replace the realist account of the relations between reticular and causal theories by one in terms of the successive D–N explanations of one reticular theory by another. So let us now consider a positivist objection to the realist view of causation. The objection is that the realist has provided no adequate analysis of causal, or natural, necessity; and that what are presented by the realist as descriptions of structures and mechanisms that causally necessitate observable phenomena, are no more than descriptions of Humean regularities of high generality.

A realist reply to this can be stated only briefly. It is true that the concept of natural necessity has not yet been satisfactorily analysed. Indeed, some philosophers argue that it is essentially unanalysable. However, it is increasingly widely accepted that scientific laws cannot themselves be adequately characterized without some reference to this possibly unanalysable concept of necessity.[19] Further, the realist may accept that, in talking about describing structures and mechanisms, no direct analysis is being given of the concept of necessity; and also that such descriptions are, at least partly, of regularities, such as the behaviour of the molecules that constitute gases. But it does not follow from this that the explanatory power of causal theories derives only from the deducibility of one set of regularities from another, as the positivist maintains. Finally, the discovery of one set of structural regularities is not regarded by the realist as ruling out any further explanatory enquiries. Rather, the existence of such regularities must itself be causally explained, by the positing of further structures and mechanisms, and so on.

This last point raises an important question, and one which enables us to state a somewhat attenuated, and perhaps more defensible, version of the positivist view of causation and theories. Are there any ultimate explanations (that is, those for which no further explanations can be given), or is the process of successive causal explanations, and thus of scientific enquiry itself, in principle infinite and unending? The answer to this question depends basically upon that of the finitude of nature, for there can be no ultimate explanations of an objectively infinite nature. But suppose we accept its finitude, and thus the possibility of ultimate explanations and theories. We can then characterize the positivist view as this: such ultimate explanations must be in terms of 'brute regularities', that simply happen to be those that obtain in our physical world.[20]

Let us now consider a rather different objection to realism, that it is *essentialist*. The terms 'essence' and 'essentialism' have been used in a large variety of different ways, and we will only examine two of these here. Popper, a well-known opponent of essentialism in science, characterizes the essentialist as making two claims. First, that it is possible to establish the truth of a scientific theory beyond all reasonable doubt. Second, that the scientist can provide ultimate explanations by discovering the essence or 'reality' that lies behind the 'appearances'. Does the realist position, as we have presented it, entail either of these claims? It would seem not. There is no commitment to the first claim. The realist is concerned primarily with the nature of those theories which the scientist should be trying to construct, and has no inclination to underestimate the degree of difficulty, and uncertainty, involved in such projects. On the question of ultimate explanations, the realist can remain agnostic: as we have already suggested, this turns on the finitude of nature, and there is nothing in the realist position which counts for or against finitude. As for the distinction between reality and appearance, this may often be invoked by the realist, but not in a way that implies belief in either certainty or ultimacy.[21]

The second sense of 'essentialism' is mainly concerned with a theory of definition, and of the function of such definitions in scientific explanation. According to this, definitions are descriptions of the essences, or essential properties, of things, and we can assess various attempts at definition in terms of the truth or falsity of the descriptions given by them. Scientific explanation requires the discovery of such essences, and thus of correct definitions. These views are often ascribed to Aristotle, together with the belief in a world that is objectively divided into 'natural kinds', to which correct definitions must correspond. But, whether or not this ascription is correct, the realist is not committed to this theory of definition, to the view that explanations can be discovered by definitions, or to a belief in natural kinds.[22]

Historically, the term 'essence' is often associated with others, such as 'occult quality' or 'substantial form', which are seen by positivists as denoting mysterious entities that do not belong to genuinely scientific theories. The concept of phlogiston is typically regarded by positivists in this way, as we noted in the last section of the previous chapter. By considering this example, we can examine the claim that the realist position inevitably leads to the postulation of unintelligible entities, and thus retards the development of science. The phlogiston theory is often criticized on the following grounds: that it had no explanatory value; that phlogiston was unobservable; that absurd properties, such as negative weight, had to be ascribed to this entity to explain away the increased weight of metals after combustion; and that only when Lavoisier subjected the theory to the scrutiny of experimental data was chemistry at last established on a scientific basis.

But such criticisms are mistaken. Instead, the postulation of phlogiston was a reasonable attempt to explain, in a unified manner, many apparently disparate phenomena. In its earlier stages, the theory was extremely fruitful. It was recognized that the precise nature of the postulated entity required further specification, and several suggestions were made, such as its identification with 'inflammable air' (hydrogen), or the idea that soot was almost pure phlogiston. The negative weight hypothesis was not essential to the theory of phlogiston, since other explanations of weight increase were proposed, especially in terms of the absorption, during combustion, of matter from the fire and heat. However, Lavoisier's experiments showed this last explanation was highly improbable; and the fact that metallic mercury could be produced by heating mercury calx without the presence of carbon also made the phlogiston theory implausible. Lavoisier's theory enabled most of the same phenomena to be explained without reference to phlogiston: it thus became reasonable to deny its existence. Yet we can find many examples in the history of science (such as the postulation of the 'gene' to explain Mendel's laws of inherited characteristics), where similar postulations were followed by successful identifications of the hypothetical entity (such as the DNA molecule). For the realist, these attempts to explain the regularities of observable phenomena are both necessary and legitimate. The failure of specific hypotheses, which were reasonable at the time they were proposed, should not lead us to eliminate all such hypotheses as, in principle, unscientific. On the contrary, it is only in this way that science can develop so that it deepens our understanding of the physical world.[23]

We conclude this chapter by outlining some of the features common to realism and positivism. Both share a general conception of science as an objective, rational enquiry which aims at true explanatory and predictive knowledge of an external reality. Let us consider the concepts of objectivity and rationality that are involved here. There are two different aspects of the former concept. First, the idea that scientific theories must be objectively assessed by reference to empirical evidence. This evidence is such that all scientists who are competent, honest, and lacking in perceptual deficiencies can agree upon it, though not necessarily with total certainty. Second, there is the idea that there are 'objects', in the broadest sense of the term, which exist independently of our beliefs and theories about them. In other words, there is some commitment to a theory of truth in which there is a clear dichotomy between 'the world', and the various attempts that we may make to describe and explain it correctly. This means a rejection of the view that scientific theories determine that reality, rather than make genuine discoveries about it. Science is descriptive, and not constructive, of the nature of that which exists.

What concept of rationality is regarded by realists and positivists as characterizing science? Both hold that there are general standards of scientificity, of what counts as an adequate explanation, of what it is that we must try to achieve by scientific theories, of the manner in which empirical evidence should be used to assess their truth or falsity, and so on. Whilst disagreeing about what these standards are, both believe that they exist, and can properly be used to evaluate specific cases of scientific practice. They are external and universal standards, independent of particular, substantive theories and explanations, and applicable to all periods in the historical development of science.

It is these shared assumptions of objectivity and rationality which, stated here in a simplified manner, are rejected to varying degrees, and for varying reasons, by the philosophers of science we will consider in the following chapter.

3 Forms of conventionalism

1 Problems of falsification

If empirical evidence is to be regarded as an adequate objective control for the acceptance and rejection of scientific theories, it is essential to specify precisely the logical relations involved in the testing of those theories by observation. We have noted already the impossibility of conclusively verifying scientific theories: the best that can be hoped for is the establishment of degrees of positive confirmation. But it is often maintained, by writers such as Popper, that there is an important asymmetry between verification and falsification. If we deduce predictions from a theory which are then shown by observation to fail, this must entail the falsity of that theory, whether it is a reticular or causal one.[1]

At first sight, this claim seems to be justified as a matter of simple logic. Let 'T' stand for a scientific theory, and 'O' for a statement of the observable results of some test-procedure. If we can deduce O from T, and show that O is false, it follows logically that T is also false. If, however, O is shown to be true, it does not follow that T is true: thus the impossibility of conclusive verification. But several problems arise when this simplified logical model of falsification is applied to the actual process of testing a scientific theory. The degree of certainty with which we can assert the falsity of T depends upon the corresponding degree of certainty of the falsity of O. Logically, all that can be shown is that if O is false, then so is T: any uncertainty about the former is necessarily reflected in the latter. Further, what is in fact deducible from a theory is not a statement describing the observable results of a test-procedure, but a hypothetical, or conditional statement, asserting that if the relevant procedure is carried out, such results will occur. Failure to get the predicted results does not, therefore, directly falsify the theory, since it is always possible that the test-procedures have not been carried out satisfactorily.

However, we will ignore these two difficulties in what follows, and concentrate on a more fundamental problem. This arises from the fact that, in order to derive testable consequences from a theory, it is usually necessary to make assumptions additional to those involved in the theory itself. For example, if an optical microscope is employed in making observations to test a theory, we have to assume the theoretical principles upon which the construction and use of the microscope are based. The general problem raised by such examples was clearly articulated by Pierre Duhem (1954, p. 187):

> The physicist can never subject an isolated hypothesis to
> experimental test, but only a whole group of hypotheses; when
> the experiment is in disagreement with his predictions, what he
> learns is that at least one of the hypotheses constituting the
> group is unacceptable and ought to be modified; but the
> experiment does not indicate which one ought to be changed.

If we represent the additional assumptions, sometimes called 'auxiliary hypotheses', by 'A_{1-n}', then the problem can be described in this way: if O can be deduced only from T together with A_{1-n}, then the falsity of O does not entail the falsity of T, but the falsity of either T or one of the assumptions A_{1-n}. We know that at least one of these must be false, but not which one. In particular, the falsity of O is logically compatible with the truth of T. (Symbolically: $[(T \& A_{1-n} \to O) \& -O] \to -(T \& A_{1-n})$. This contrasts with the simplified logical model of falsification, where we have: $[(T \to O) \& -O] \to -T$.)

A simple illustration of this problem is provided by Hempel.[2] The Hungarian physician Semmelweiss, investigating the high rates of women's mortality in childbirth, put forward the theory that these were due to blood poisoning, caused by infectious matter carried on the hands of doctors who examined the women after performing dissections in the autopsy room. From this hypothesis, he argued that the mortality rates should decrease if the doctors washed their hands in a solution of chlorinated lime, so destroying the infectious matter. Appropriate experiments were carried out, and the rates decreased as predicted, thus confirming the theory, though not, of course, conclusively verifying it. Suppose, however, that the predicted decrease had not occurred: would this have falsified the theory? Not conclusively, for it might have been an additional assumption, that chlorinated lime solution destroys infectious matter, that was false, and not the theory itself.

W. V. Quine has raised a more radical objection to the possibility of conclusively falsifying scientific theories, in the course of a general critique of the orthodox empiricist distinction between analytic and synthetic statements. He says (1961, p. 43 – our insertion):

Any statement can be held true come what may, if we make drastic enough adjustments elsewhere in the system. Even a statement very close to the periphery [i.e. one apparently directly testable by sensory experience] can be held true in the face of recalcitrant experience by pleading hallucination or by amending certain statements of the kind called logical laws. Conversely, by the same token, no statement is immune to revision.

If we apply these remarks specifically to the empirical testing of scientific theories, it would seem that Quine's claim is that it is always possible to rescue a theory from apparently falsifying evidence, by making some further assumption that maintains the consistency of the theory with this evidence. In other words, if we derive O from T, together with assumptions A_{1-n}, and find that O is false, we can always make some further assumption, A_o, which is such that the falsity of O is consistent with the truth of T and A_o. (Note that A_o may sometimes be the denial of one of A_{1-n}.)

It is unclear quite how this claim could be shown to be true. We will confine ourselves to making three points about it. First, the scope of the 'adjustments' that might have to be made to preserve a theory is extremely large: thus Quine explicitly mentions changes in logical laws, and the plea of hallucination. Second, and related to this, the claim involves the idea that it is our whole system of knowledge that is being put to the test at any one time. This is a considerable extension of Duhem's objection to the possibility of testing single, isolated hypotheses. Third, we must distinguish the view that it is always *possible* to make the necessary adjustments, or additional assumptions, from the view that it is always *reasonable* to do so. Thus, even if no apparently falsifying evidence can constitute a logically conclusive falsification of a scientific theory, it does not follow that it is always, or normally, more reasonable to make the necessary adjustments than to abandon the theory.[3]

This suggests that the problem of theory-falsification should be seen primarily as that of finding criteria for the reasonable abandonment of scientific theories, not for their logically conclusive disproof. Looking at the problem in this way, the simplest solution would be to adopt the following rule: always abandon a theory when it is apparently contradicted by observation, even though it is logically possible to save the theory by adding further assumptions. However, this rule (sometimes called 'naive methodological falsificationism', and ascribed to Popper in his earlier writings) has some obvious disadvantages. In particular, it can be shown that had scientists consistently followed it, many major scientific achievements would never have occurred, since theories which eventually turned out to be highly sucessful would have been abandoned too soon.[4]

Partly in response to this difficulty, Imre Lakatos has proposed an alternative doctrine, which he calls 'sophisticated methodological falsificationism'. He suggests that we cannot rationally decide to abandon any one theory, T, unless there exists some alternative theory, T', which is in certain important respects preferable to T. The decision to abandon T rests not only upon its relation to the empirical evidence, but also upon its relation to alternative theories. The problem, then, is to define what makes T' preferable to T. Lakatos's solution to this is given in the following passage (1970, p. 116):

> The sophisticated falsificationist regards a scientific theory T as falsified if and only if another theory T' has been proposed with the following characteristics: (1) T' has excess empirical content over T: that is, it predicts *novel* facts, that is, facts improbable in the light of, or even forbidden by, T; (2) T' explains the previous success of T, that is, all the unrefuted content of T is contained (within the limits of observational error) in the content of T'; and (3) some of the excess content of T' is corroborated.

Simplifying this slightly: it is reasonable to abandon T if and only if there is an alternative theory T' which explains everything that T explains, and generates predictions not derivable from T, some of which have been confirmed by empirical testing.

Several objections can be made to this rule. It will sometimes be too stringent, since an alternative theory may be preferable, despite its not, at least initially, explaining everything that its predecessor explained. And some theories may become so hopelessly at odds with experimental results that it is reasonable to abandon them, even if there are no viable alternatives. Further, there is no analysis of the stage at which it becomes rational to develop alternative theories to the one in trouble. One possibility here, suggested by Paul Feyerabend, is that scientists should adopt a 'principle of proliferation'. According to this, a wide range of competing theories should always be formulated, and scientists should never be concerned solely with the development and testing of any one theory. Indeed Feyerabend argues that, in many cases, it is only by means of this proliferation that counter-evidence to the dominant theory can emerge, or be recognized as such.[5]

However, the most fundamental objection concerns a necessary assumption of both Lakatos's and any similarly 'comparative' account of theory abandonment. The assumption is that it is possible to describe the observational consequences of two or more theories in such a way that we can intelligibly talk of one theory explaining or predicting more than another. In other words, it must be assumed

49

that we can make observation statements 'in the same language' for each theory. If this is not possible, it makes no sense to talk of comparing their predictive and explanatory powers, since there would be no common, theory-neutral language in which these comparisons could be stated. But it has been argued by several philosophers of science that such a language does not, and cannot, exist.

2 The problem of theory-neutrality

Recent attacks on the theory-neutrality of observation, and thus, implicitly or explicitly, on the possibility of an objective, observationally controlled science, have taken two main forms. First, it is claimed that sensory perception is somehow influenced by theoretical beliefs and expectations. Second, that the meanings of observational terms are in some way dependent upon those of theoretical terms or of the various statements that constitute a scientific theory. Both raise difficult issues in epistemology and the philosophy of language. We will concentrate here on the relation between theories and perception, and on the account of this given by Norwood Hanson.[6]

Hanson's account is based upon an analysis of the concept of seeing, or visual perception. He is concerned to rebut the orthodox distinction between visual *data* and their *interpretation*. By using this distinction, many philosophers have claimed that the proponents of rival theories can be said to agree on what they see, or observe, whilst disagreeing about the theoretical interpretation of such data. Further, agreed observations can be used to resolve disagreements over interpretation: competing theories can be assessed by reference to uninterpreted data. Against this, Hanson argues that, in the sense of seeing relevant to scientific enquiry, the proponents of different theories do not agree on what they see. They see different things just because of their different theoretical beliefs. Each scientific theory provides its own way of describing what we see. It is not that they give different ways of interpreting the data which are what we all, whatever our theories, in fact see. Rather, our theories determine what we see, and there are no separable components of data and interpretation.[7]

The issues involved here are examined by Hanson with reference to a number of examples. The one he discusses most frequently is introduced as follows (1958, p. 5):

> Let us consider Johannes Kepler: imagine him on a hill watching the dawn. With him is Tycho Brahe. Kepler regarded the sun as fixed: it was the earth that moved. But Tycho followed Ptolemy and Aristotle in this much at least: the earth was fixed and all other celestial bodies moved around it. *Do Kepler and Tycho see the same thing in the east at dawn?*

Hanson argues that, although there are ways of answering this question in the affirmative, these do not provide us with the sense of 'seeing' that is primarily involved in scientific observation: in this sense, Kepler sees a static sun, and Brahe a mobile one.

He rejects the view that the similarity of the retinal stimulation received by the two astronomers could justify the claim that they saw the same thing. For it is mistaken to claim that these physical stimulations are *seen* by their recipients. He also rejects any recourse to the idea of pure visual experience, and thus to the claim that both Kepler and Brahe had the same such experience, namely of 'a brilliant yellow-white disc centred between green and blue colour-patches' (1958, p. 8). Hanson argues that no general distinction can be drawn between uninterpreted visual experiences, and the different interpretations that may be made of them. To show this, he considers a series of examples from Gestalt psychology, such as the Necker cube, Köhler's goblet-and-faces figuration, and the antelope-bird. He describes these as 'shift-of-aspect phenomena'. In these cases, we cannot talk intelligibly of some uninterpreted visual experience: in seeing the figures first as one thing, and then as another, we cannot be described as giving different interpretations to the same visual data. The interpretation is, as it were, *constitutive* of the seeing, and not a separable component. Or, rather, the concept of interpretation has no place here, and so neither does the distinction between interpretation and data.

Hanson regards these shift-of-aspect phenomena as providing relevant analogies for what is involved in the relation between different scientific theories and what their proponents can be said to see. Thus (1958, p. 17):

> You see a bird, I see an antelope; the physicist sees an X-ray tube, the child a complicated lamp-bulb; the microscopist sees coelenterate mesoglea, his new student sees only a gooey, formless stuff. Tycho and Simplicius see a mobile sun, Kepler and Galileo see a static sun.

Further, Hanson argues that the concept of seeing appropriate to scientific observation, is such that what it is that scientists see is essentially related to their knowledge and beliefs. To the extent that these beliefs differ, what they can be said to see also differs[8] (1958, pp. 23–4 – our italics):

> Tycho sees the sun beginning its journey from horizon to horizon. He sees that from some celestial vantage point the sun (carrying with it the moon and the planets) could be watched circling our fixed earth. Watching the sun at dawn through Tychonic spectacles would be to see it in something like this way.

51

... But Kepler will see the horizon dipping, or turning away, from our local fixed star. The shift from sunrise to horizon-turn is analogous to the shift-of-aspect phenomena already considered; *it is occasioned by differences between what Tycho and Kepler think they know.*

We can begin to assess Hanson's account of seeing by showing its implications for the use of observation in testing and comparing scientific theories. If what we see or observe is determined by our beliefs or knowledge, then we cannot, without circularity, test the truth or falsity of those beliefs by means of observation. This radical consequence of Hanson's position can be brought out in the following way. If what we observe depends upon our beliefs, and these beliefs are expressed in our theories, then the truth of our claims about what we observe must depend upon the truth of those theories. This means that if our observation-statements are true, our theories must also be true. But if this is so, we cannot falsify our theories by means of true observation-statements, since if the latter are true, the former cannot be false. Furthermore, we cannot judge between two competing theories on the basis of what is observed since, in the crucial cases, the proponents of these theories will not be able to agree on the truth or falsity of the relevant observation-statements. If their differences of belief result in differences of observation, they cannot settle their theoretical differences by reference to agreed observations.

Such conclusions seem counter-intuitive: is it possible to avoid them, without completely rejecting some of Hanson's insights into the concept of scientific observation? At least two of his claims can certainly be accepted. First, that when asked to describe what they see or observe, the proponents of rival theories will typically give different answers, which reflect their theoretical differences. Second, that it is not possible to provide descriptions of what we observe that are totally free of any conceptual and theoretical implications and assumptions. However, it does not follow from these claims that there is no way of correctly describing observations which is independent of the specific theory, or theories, that are being tested and assessed. If we believe some theory to be true, we will tend to describe our observations in terms of it. But this does not mean that, when the truth of this theory is in dispute, we cannot describe those observations in a manner that does not presuppose its truth. Similarly, though rival theorists will often disagree in their accounts of what they observe, they may be able to find agreed descriptions by reference to which the relative merits of their theories can be compared. Such descriptions will not be totally 'theory-free', but free of the particular theoretical beliefs at issue.

Let us consider how the position just outlined might be applied to

Hanson's example about Kepler and Brahe. Although, when asked what they see at dawn, they may give different answers – such as 'horizon-turn' and 'sunrise', or 'static sun' and 'mobile sun' – there are several other answers they could agree upon. One of these would be in terms of the 'visual experience' of 'a brilliant yellow-white disc centred between green and blue colour patches'. Another might be 'a brilliant heavenly body', a suggestion which Hanson makes at one point. Notice that this latter answer might itself be disputed by scientists whose theoretical disagreements were not those of Kepler and Brahe, but instead concerned some other issue, such as whether it was legitimate to apply the term 'heavenly' to the sun. In this (perhaps unlikely) case, Hanson's 'yellow-white disc . . .' description might nonetheless be agreed upon.

It must not be thought that this 'visual experience' description is an example of some uniquely privileged observational language, to be used in all cases of theoretical disagreement, and providing an epistemologically incorrigible foundation for science.[9] Hanson's arguments about shift-of-aspect phenomena, together with other philosophical arguments, and results from the psychological study of perception, make any such view untenable. These results are summarized by C. A. Hooker (1973, p. 65):

> A perceptual judgment then may be a function of our past experiences, our current emotional state, our current beliefs, our current foci of interests and so on, as well as the actual patterns of stimulation of our sensory receptors.

But, as Hooker goes on to argue, there is little evidence that the kinds of theoretical beliefs normally involved in scientific disputes figure significantly amongst the determinants of perceptual judgments. In other words, although the ideal of science as based upon some pure, uninterpreted realm of perceptual experience is untenable, the opposite view, that theoretical disagreements typically result in perceptual differences, is equally so.

Hanson, as we have noted, presents his own account in terms of an analysis of the sense of 'seeing' that is 'relevant for science'. We can now see an important ambiguity in this phrase. The sense that he regards as relevant is that involved in the way that scientists typically talk about what they see or observe. But we may also be interested in the sense that is relevant to the problems of theory testing and comparison, and there is no good reason to believe that an account of seeing that is relevant to the former concern is equally relevant to the latter. Further, although Hanson may be right in regarding shift-of-aspect phenomena as vitiating any general distinction between data and interpretation, the analogy he suggests between such phenomena, and what occurs in cases of theoretical disagreement, is too tenuous to establish his conclusions. For Hanson, scientific observations are, as it were, 'shift-of-theory phenomena'. But whereas, in examples such as the antelope-bird figure, it seems that we necessarily see them either one way or the other, this is not so in the kinds of observational situations relevant to the assessment of scientific theories.

Let us conclude by suggesting one of the implications of the position we have been developing in opposition to Hanson's. Much of the language used to describe what we see – the results of experiments, and so on – is theory-laden, in that it assumes the truth of various scientific theories and beliefs. Thus it will often seem that alternative theories to those presently accepted are contradicted by established facts. The ways in which we describe observations will be such that they appear to constitute fairly conclusive counter-evidence to theories that are opposed to those assumed by these observational descriptions. It follows that, in the formulation and defence of alternative theories, an important element will be the detection and challenging of the theoretical assumptions made in the existent observational language. Otherwise, many such alternatives will be prematurely dismissed, through a failure to see that the evidence against them is 'loaded' by theories that may themselves be defective.

It is partly for these reasons that Feyerabend, as we noted in the previous section, defends the principle of proliferation, and argues that without this principle, much evidence that is inconsistent with existing theories may never be revealed as so. Not only does the incorporation of such theories in the observational language distort the apparent relations between observations and alternative theories; it may also conceal what is counter-evidence to accepted theories.[10] For Feyerabend, the proliferation principle forms part of what he calls 'an anarchistic theory of knowledge', which involves a denial of the possibility of formulating rational standards for the assessment of scientific theories. We will examine this in the next section. But we begin by considering an account of science in some respects similar to Feyerabend's, that of Thomas Kuhn.

3 Paradigms and anarchy: problems of rationality

In *The Structure of Scientific Revolutions* (Kuhn, 1970a), Kuhn's central concern is to characterize the way in which science historically develops. He regards this characterization as having important consequences for the philosophy of science. His conclusions challenge not only several features of the conception of science as a rational and objective enquiry, but also the view that philosophical theories cannot be undermined by recourse to historical, sociological and psychological studies.

For Kuhn, the development of each branch of science alternates between two recurrent stages: normal, and revolutionary science. In the former stage, scientific activity is governed by a 'paradigm'. Paradigms are initially defined by Kuhn as 'universally recognized scientific achievements that ... provide model problems and solutions to a community of practitioners' (1970a, p. viii). In normal science, the scientist's work is devoted to the articulation and wider application of the accepted paradigm, which is not itself questioned or criticized. Scientific problems are regarded as *puzzles*, as problems which are known to have a solution within the framework of assumptions implicitly or explicitly embodied in the paradigm. If a puzzle is not solved, the fault lies in the scientist, and not in the paradigm.

By contrast, in the relatively brief periods of revolutionary science, the scientist is confronted by increasingly perplexing *anomalies*, which call into question the paradigm itself. Scientific revolution occurs when a new paradigm emerges, and becomes accepted by the scientific community. But the acceptance of the new paradigm does not take place solely as a result of a process of critical argument and assessment between the proponents of the competing paradigms. For individual scientists, the change of allegiance from one paradigm to another is often a 'conversion experience', akin to gestalt-switches or changes of religious faith. And for the scientific profession as a whole, Kuhn quotes with approval Max Planck's famous dictum: 'A new scientific truth does not triumph by convincing its opponents and making them see the light, but rather because its opponents eventually die, and a new generation grows up that is familiar with it' (1970a, p. 150). Such changes require sociological and psychological categories for their explanation: not a rational reconstruction in terms of the standard conceptions of philosophers of science, according to which theories are accepted and rejected by reference to observations, subject to the agreed universally applicable standards of scientific rationality.

Some philosophers of science might accept these claims as historically correct, but deny their philosophical relevance. However, such a response not only rests upon too restrictive a view of the relation between philosophical and historical studies, but also ignores the distinctively philosophical basis of many elements in Kuhn's account. For example, one reason which Kuhn has for rejecting 'the methodological stereotype of falsification by direct comparison with nature' (1970a, p. 77) is his rejection of the theory-neutrality of observation. This rejection is partly based on the same grounds that we discussed in the previous section, and leads him frequently to make assertions of the following kind (1970a, p. 117 – our italics):

During the seventeenth century, when their research was guided by one or another effluvium theory, electricians repeatedly *saw* chaff particles rebound from, or fall off, the electrified bodies that had attracted them. At least that is what seventeenth-century observers *said they saw*, and we have no more reason to doubt their reports of perception than our own. Placed before the same apparatus, a modern observer would *see* electrostatic repulsion (rather than mechanical or gravitational rebounding). . . .

We have already criticized the use of this concept of seeing; and we can also note that many of the examples that Kuhn cites against the 'methodological stereotype of falsification' could be accommodated within the sophisticated methodological falsification of Lakatos, discussed in section 1.[11] But there is another reason for Kuhn's rejection of the possibility of rationally assessing competing paradigms, which raises different issues. He argues that the relevant standards of assessment are typically *internal* to each paradigm, and vary from one to another. To understand this argument, we must examine further his conception of paradigms. Kuhn's initial definition rapidly broadens into the idea of a set of shared assumptions, often implicit, that govern the activity of a scientific community. In later writings, he distinguishes two concepts of a paradigm, termed 'exemplars' and 'disciplinary matrices' (1970a, pp. 181–90), and it is the latter we will consider here. This consists of a 'strong network of commitments, theoretical, instrumental, and methodological' (1970a, p. 42). An example is the corpuscularian paradigm in seventeenth-century science. This included what Kuhn calls the 'methodological' principle that ultimate explanations must be given by means of the laws governing the interactions between corpuscles, the imperceptible particles of matter of which all objects in the physical world were thought to be composed. Principles of this kind, says Kuhn, provide criteria for the selection, evaluation, and criticism of the problems and solutions arising within any one scientific community.

What happens, then, at times of paradigm-conflict and change? Paradigms (1970a, p. 103) are

the source of the methods, problem-field, and standards of solution accepted by any mature scientific community at any given time. As a result, the reception of a new paradigm often necessitates a redefinition of the corresponding science . . .
And as the problems change, so, often, does the standard that distinguishes a real scientific solution from a mere metaphysical speculation, word game, or mathematical play. The normal-scientific tradition that emerges from a scientific revolution is not only incompatible but often actually incommensurable with that which has gone before.

56

In other words, such changes will often involve 'changes in the standards governing permissible problems, concepts and explanations' (1970a, p. 106). Thus scientific revolutions are partly constituted by changes in the standards governing legitimate explanations, and even in those that define what it is to be scientific, as opposed to, say, metaphysical. So it is not surprising that disputes between proponents of rival paradigms cannot be settled in a rational and objective manner. For, not only are there no mutually agreed, theory-neutral observational facts, but there are also no agreed standards of assessment to apply to them. In both these respects, competing paradigms are 'incommensurable'.[12]

Let us now examine this claim that standards are relative to paradigms. First, Kuhn fails to show that such standards differ from one paradigm to another. This failure is partly due to an ambiguity in expressions such as 'methodological principles' or 'standards governing permissible explanations'. The ambiguity can be illustrated in Kuhn's example of the corpuscularian paradigm. In one sense, it is true that corpuscularians were committed to the 'methodological principle' of explaining all phenomena by reference to interactions between corpuscles. But in another sense, this would not count as a methodological principle at all, since it clearly involves substantive, scientific claims about what kinds of entities exist, what relations obtain between them, and so on. In this latter sense, the D–N model of explanation would be an example of a methodological principle, which lays down standards for permissible explanations, but in a manner independent of substantive issues such as the existence and nature of corpuscles.

Thus, whilst paradigms, and scientific communities, have different methodological principles in the first sense, they may often not differ with respect to principles or standards in the second sense. Both corpuscularians and their opponents might agree on what, in general, constitutes an adequate scientific explanation, and be prepared to argue out their substantive disagreements by reference to such criteria. And to a considerable extent, this was true in the seventeenth-century. For example, the disputes between proponents of wave and corpuscular theories of light did not always involve disagreements about general criteria for scientific explanation. Conversely, although there were many methodological arguments between seventeenth century scientists, these were often conducted *within* what Kuhn would, on other criteria, regard as a single paradigm.[13] Finally, even if Kuhn were correct in his claims about the historical relationships between paradigms and standards, it would not follow that differences between such standards are rationally unresolvable. For at least some of these differences are open to philosophical argument, of the kind we have already engaged in, in our assessment of realist and positivist views about explanation, theories, and scientificity.

We turn now to another writer who has attacked the image of science as a rational and objective enterprise, Feyerabend. For him, this image is both mythical and undesirable. It is mythical, because it misrepresents the historical realities of scientific development, and because it is, in any case, impossible to justify any methodological rules and standards for science: 'There is only *one* principle that can be defended under all circumstances, and in *all* stages of human development. It is the principle: *anything goes*' (1970, p. 26). And the image is an undesirable one, since it directs scientists to pursue an ideal that is in total conflict with the 'humanitarian attitude'. The ideal of rationality is, says Feyerabend, 'unworthy of a free man'; and he quotes with approval J. S. Mill's endorsement of 'that culti-vation of individuality which [alone] produces, or can produce well developed human beings' (1970, pp. 20–1).

Like Kuhn, Feyerabend denies the existence of a theory-neutral observational language, and of universal methodological rules and standards. But he also denies, both as reality and ideal, Kuhn's picture of normal science. We noted earlier Feyerabend's defence of a 'principle of proliferation', clearly opposed to Kuhn's puzzle-solving normality.[14] Here, we will consider the nature and rationale of his views about rules and standards in scientific practice. Feyerabend argues that there are no rules whose breach cannot be shown to be justified. Indeed, it is often best to act in a way directly contrary to that required by any rule (1970, p. 22):

> there are circumstances when it is advisable to introduce, elaborate and defend ad hoc hypotheses, or hypotheses which contradict well-established and generally accepted experimental results, or hypotheses whose content is smaller than the content of the existing and empirically adequate alternatives, or self-inconsistent hypotheses, and so on.
>
> There are even circumstances – and they occur rather frequently – when *argument* loses its forward-looking aspect and becomes a hindrance to progress.

Further, in the absence of universal rules and standards, we must rely upon 'esthetic judgments, judgments of taste, and our own subjective wishes' (1970, p. 90). We can, if we wish, *choose* to conduct science in an apparently rational, objective, and 'professional' manner. But such a choice should be resisted by all who value human freedom and individuality (1970, p. 21):

> Without universally enforced standards of truth and rationality we can no longer speak of universal error. We can only speak of

what does, or does not, seem appropriate when viewed from a particular and restricted point of view, different views, temperaments, attitudes giving rise to different judgments and different methods of approach. Such an *anarchistic epistemology* ... is not only a better means for improving knowledge, of understanding history. It is also more appropriate for a free man to use than are its rigorous and 'scientific' alternatives.

Thus one significant and distinctive feature of Feyerabend's position, as compared with most Anglo-American philosophers of science, is his insistence upon the essential function of 'human values' in science. First, there is his claim that the choice between one conception of science and another is partly an *ethical* choice, and not one that can be decided by reference to the kinds of limited, 'professionally' philosophical criteria that are normally invoked. Second, in Feyerabend's preferred image of science, there is an important part to be played by the individual values, wishes and tastes of the scientist: science must be a fully *human* activity, not one which engages only the cerebral and academic elements of human beings. In suggesting the first of these connections between science and values, Feyerabend is perhaps closest in his concerns to Popper, who persistently emphasizes the links between the critical, rational nature of scientific activity, and the political values of an 'open', liberal-democratic society. But, whereas Popper often argues from the 'correct' view of scientific method to the 'correct' social values, Feyerabend's argument proceeds in the opposite direction. And, in any case, he dismisses both Popperian method and Popperian values as 'ratiomania'.[15]

We will make two critical comments on Feyerabend's position. First, his use of phrases such as 'methodological rule' or 'standards of rationality' is insufficiently discriminating. Most of his arguments against the existence of universal rules and standards are addressed specifically to the practical problems of how scientists should proceed in the actual construction, testing, and rejection of theories. He concludes that, at best, we can only formulate a number of 'rules of thumb', and there will always be circumstances in which it is right to ignore these. But it is possible to accept this, whilst denying that this entails the rejection of rational standards concerning the general nature of scientific theories, explanations, the relations between theories and observations, and so on. We may, for example, know what it is that would constitute an adequate explanation of some phenomenon, without this giving us any practical guides that will guarantee success in discovering one, or tell us when to abandon or continue any particular approach to the problem. But a defence of the rationality and objectivity of science does not require the formulation of such guides.[16]

Second, it is difficult to see how Feyerabend can both dismiss the existence of universal standards, and continue to talk, as he does, of scientific 'progress'. For example, he defends his anarchistic epistemology on the grounds that '[this] liberal practice . . . is not just a *fact* of the history of science . . . [and] not merely a manifestation of human inconstancy and ignorance . . . [but] reasonable *and absolutely necessary* for the growth of knowledge' (1970, p. 22). But it is also necessary to adopt standards and criteria for what it is that constitutes such scientific knowledge, if one is to defend or reject various means towards its growth and progress.

4 Conventionalism and instrumentalism

So far, we have avoided ascribing the term 'conventionalist' to any of the writers discussed in this chapter. The definitions that can, and have been given to this term are highly varied. A fairly standard one is given by Kolakowski (1972, pp. 158–9):

> The fundamental idea of conventionalism may be stated as follows: certain scientific propositions, erroneously taken for descriptions of the world based on the recording and generalization of experiments, are in fact artificial creations, and we regard them as true not because we are compelled to do so for empirical reasons, but because they are convenient, useful, or even because they have aesthetic appeal. Conventionalists agree with empiricists on the origin of knowledge, but reject empiricism as a norm that allows us to justify all accepted judgements by appealing to experience, conceived of as a sufficient criterion of their truth. Or, to put the same point somewhat more accurately, the data of experience always leave scope for more than one explanatory hypothesis, and which one is to be chosen cannot be determined by experience.

There are several different strands in this definition, each of which may be developed in a number of directions. We will now elaborate on some of these, thereby providing a characterization of conventionalism as a group of three, loosely yet significantly related elements.[17]

(1) There is the idea that many scientific statements are not to be seen as true or false descriptions of some external, independently existing 'reality', but rather as creations or constructions of the scientist. This may develop into the more radical claim that, in some sense, the physical world of the scientist is created or constructed by scientific theories, and not described by them. In other words, theories are determinative of what is real, and when they change in a fundamental way, we are not faced with a different conception of the same world, but a different world. (2) There is the claim that the

kinds of considerations that are relevant in accepting or rejecting a scientific theory are somehow 'subjective', in that they are essentially related to the scientist's practical interests, aesthetic or moral values, and so on. The source of this subjectivity may be seen as the individual scientist, or the scientific community. In either case, there is a denial of the existence or adequacy of rational, universally valid criteria and standards for the evaluation of scientific activity. (3) There is the view that the truth or falsity of theories is 'under-determined' by empirical data. Observation cannot provide an objective control for science: the idea that agreed facts can enable us to choose between theories is denied.

Taken together, these three elements of conventionalism constitute a rejection of those common assumptions of objectivity and rationality that we ascribed to realists and positivists at the end of chapter 2. Let us now consider how the arguments we have examined in this chapter are related to them. The Duhemian and Quinean objections to the simple logical model of falsification would give support to, respectively, weaker and stronger forms of (3). Both indicate the difficulties in formulating the kinds of criteria whose existence is denied in (2), though much depends on whether the concept of rationality is restricted to that of logical proof. The attacks on a theory-neutral observational language would support an extreme form of (3) and render inoperative any universal standards which presuppose the existence of theory-free observations. In addition, they could form the basis, together with other philosophical assumptions about the relations between the real and the perceptible, for an ontologically radical version of (1); not only observations, but the world, are theory-dependent. A move of this kind is indicated in these comments by Kuhn (1970a, p. 118):

> Lavoisier, we said, saw oxygen where Priestley had seen
> dephlogisticated air and where others had seen nothing at all. . . .
> At the very least, as a result of discovering oxygen, Lavoisier
> saw nature differently. And in the absence of some recourse
> to that hypothetical fixed nature that he 'saw differently', the
> principle of economy will urge us to say that after discovering
> oxygen Lavoisier worked in a different world.

And Kuhn, like Feyerabend, has argued directly in favour of (2). But whereas Feyerabend lays stress on the individual scientist's tastes, attitudes and values, Kuhn is concerned primarily with the shared standards of the scientific community, and their paradigm-relativity.[18]

However, the relationships sketched out here are only hypothetical: the actual degree to which these three elements are supported by the arguments we have considered depends upon the validity of those arguments. We have criticized all of them to some extent, and if these criticisms are correct, either the degree of support is weakened, or less radical versions of conventionalism are established. However, our piecemeal discussion of these arguments has perhaps concealed an important feature of science whose recognition underlies many of the specific claims made by the writers concerned. This is the way in which, during its historical development, there have been recurrent and radical changes in both the theoretical and observational vocabularies of science. It is no accident that most conventionalist-inclined contemporary philosophers have also made contributions to the history of science. In doing so, they have demonstrated the inadequacy of positivist views of its historical development, whether of an inductivist or hypothetico-deductivist nature.[19] But what we will now suggest is that this general feature of science can more readily be accommodated within a realist, than a positivist, conception of the scientific enterprise.

If theories consist either of empirical laws, or of theoretical laws whose non-observational terms can be suitably defined in the doubly-privileged observational language, it is difficult to see why the development of science should be accompanied by major changes in the way that scientists talk about what they observe, and by clearly marked discontinuities in their theoretical conceptions of the physical world. For the realist, these facts are less surprising. The replacement of one theory by another often means the introduction of new onto-logical classes, and the rejection, as non-existent, of the entities described by the previous theory. An example of this is contained in the last passage from Kuhn that we quoted above: the discovery of oxygen, and the denial of the existence of phlogiston.[20] But whereas, for Kuhn, Priestley and Lavoisier are to be seen as 'working in different worlds', the realist maintains that they worked in the same world, whilst their theories made conflicting claims about the nature and existence of some of its constituents.

Let us explore this example in more detail (see the last sections of chapters 2 and 3). Priestley discovered a previously unknown gas by heating mercury calx. He noted some of its properties, especially that it supported rapid combustion, and was respirable. He called the gas 'dephlogisticated air', thereby indicating his explanation of these properties in terms of the phlogiston theory of combustion. Lavoisier, who produced the same gas, having been informed about it by Priestley, rejected this description of it, since he rejected the phlogiston theory. He first called it 'eminently respirable air', and later, 'oxygen'. The latter name derived from Greek terms, and meant 'begetting acid'. This description reflected Lavoisier's belief that oxygen, when combined with, for instance, sulphur, produced sulphuric acid upon combustion. We have here a clear example of how theoretical beliefs are assumed in the descriptive vocabulary of science. But, as we argued in section 2 of this chapter, when theories conflict, there is normally a way of describing phenomena that is neutral as between the competing theories. Thus, in this case, both Priestley and Lavoisier could agree on some of the gas's properties, whilst disagreeing about their theoretical explanation. There is no reason to regard the two theories, and their 'observational vocabularies', as incommensurable; and only in the most metaphorical sense of 'seeing' is it true that Priestley and Lavoisier 'saw differently', as Kuhn claims. Further, there is no justification for the view that these two scientists 'lived in different worlds'. Lavoisier denied the existence of an entity, phlogiston, that Priestley believed in. But they lived in the same world, and even shared many beliefs about one of its constituents, that 'eminently respirable air' whose properties they explained differently.

We conclude this chapter by considering one other position in the philosophy of science, *instrumentalism*, and its relations with those we have already discussed. We can distinguish two main senses that have been given to this term. First, 'instrumentalism' may refer to a view about the general purpose of scientific enquiry, that it should aim to give us predictive and manipulative power over our physical environment. Thus the justification of scientific activity lies in its practical results, in improving our ability to make useful predictions and changes. Second, the term may denote a view about the logical status of scientific theories, that they are computational devices which generate testable predictions. Theories are instruments, and, as such, only their utility can be assessed, and not their truth or falsity. They do not provide any knowledge of the physical world over and above the predictions that can be derived from them.

Clearly, these two views are closely related. In particular, the first may be seen as providing a strong reason for adopting the second. But either one may be accepted independently of the other, and in what follows we shall be concerned only with the second. Often, a contrast is drawn between instrumentalism and 'realism', as two mutually exclusive and exhaustive views about the nature of science. Here, 'realism' is used in a very broad sense, to denote the view that scientific theories are to be assessed for their truth or falsity, and not merely for their instrumental power: theories are genuine statements, not computational devices. This general contrast has some significance, but it also conceals important similarities and differences. We have already noted the important differences between realism and positivism, which are both termed 'realist' in the instrumentalism-realism dichotomy. But there are also similarities between positivism and instrumentalism.

Consider, for example, the positivist account of scientific explanation. If, as we have argued, this account tends to assimilate predictive and explanatory knowledge, it may become difficult to distinguish the positivist view of scientific theories as providing true explanations, and the instrumentalist view of theories as devices for the generation of predictions. Of course, the positivist regards the laws in a D–N explanation as either true or false, whilst the instrumentalist considers them only as performing a function in the deductive argument. But it is easy to conflate these two attitudes, or to slide from one to the other. In practice, they tend to generate the same kind of scientific activity, which is distinctly different from that required by the realist position. A similar point can be made about the status of theoretical terms, and the positivists' attempts to reduce these to statements in the observational language. Suppose that these attempts were successful. For the positivist, this would mean that theoretical statements are properly scientific, and can meaningfully be ascribed a truth-value. The instrumentalist, however, could argue that this showed how theories are merely convenient devices, and theoretical terms simply shorthand statements about observables. Alternatively, if these attempts fail, the instrumentalist may continue to accept the use of non-replaceable theoretical terms, on the grounds of their utility in generating testable predictions. Though positivists may be worried by whether theoretical statements are properly scientific, instrumentalists are not concerned by this, since their criterion of scientificity is a purely pragmatic one.

Thus, in this case, the difficulties of the positivist programme for theoretical terms may provide a rationale for the adoption of an instrumentalist view of theories. But whichever of these positions about theoretical terms is adopted, both positivists and instrumentalists have in common their rejection of the realist view, according to which theoretical terms are to be interpreted as referring to actually existent, even if unobservable, items. It is this disagreement which seems to us fundamental.

We can see this further by considering an argument sometimes used to support instrumentalism against realism. It concerns the function of models. The instrumentalist may point out that many models have been used by scientists without regarding them as having the ontological implications typically ascribed to them by the realist. Thus, in the twentieth century, both wave and particle models of light have been employed simultaneously, but they are not viewed, as they were earlier, as competing representations of the nature or constitution of light. Neither model can account for all the relevant phenomena, but each can be used to make successful predictions about different, and restricted ranges of those phenomena. There is no claim that light is composed either of waves or particles: the use of such models has a purely pragmatic, instrumental justification.

But this kind of example does not refute the realist position.

Realists can maintain that the existence of such situations in science normally indicates that no adequate theory has yet been developed. In the absence of an adequate theory, which would embody a model that is not regarded in this pragmatic manner, the realist can accept the use of these stop-gap devices. But this must be seen as an essentially unsatisfactory state of affairs, not one which demonstrates the truth of the instrumentalist position. And the realist may add that, here as elsewhere, the adoption of a realist standpoint injects a strongly dynamic element into scientific practice.[21]

Finally, how should we locate instrumentalism within our classification of positivist, realist, and conventionalist philosophies of science? We can see it best as, in principle, a form of conventionalism, which in practice has several affinities with positivism. It is conventionalist in its denial of the truth or falsity of scientific theories, and its emphasis upon practical interests as a criterion for their acceptance or rejection. But it often comes close to positivism in the kinds of scientific activity that its adoption tends to generate. It is, we suggest, for these reasons that historically, instrumentalist and positivist positions have been so closely intertwined in particular writers.[22]

part two

**Conceptions of science
in social theory**

In part 1 we have identified and analysed several different conceptions of the natural sciences. It follows that the advocacy of a naturalist or an anti-naturalist position requires the specification of the particular conception of the natural sciences which has been adopted. Most of the writers that we will consider in part 2 have explicitly taken a naturalist position. We will thus use our classification of alternative methodologies, and especially the distinction between positivism and realism, to identify the different conceptions of science on which various naturalist claims are based. In particular, we will show that being a naturalist does not commit one to a positivist conception of science. We should note that in our identification of the methodological bases of different social theories we will not be concerned with providing criticisms of their substantive content. Also we will not make any methodological criticisms since these follow from the arguments developed in part 1. We will discuss some important problems for a naturalist science of social life in part 3.

In chapter 4 we analyse certain positivist writers, schools, and tendencies. We begin with the Comtean positivists, and conclude with twentieth century American social science and its positivisation of the concepts of role and class. The writers and schools discussed in this chapter are both historically important and represent diverse sociological positions within the positivist framework. Just as the dominant tradition in the philosophy of science has been positivistic, so too is the predominant orientation in the historical development of social science. Thus there is relatively little social science based on a realist conception of science. In chapter 5, in our analysis of realism we consider the methodological bases of the political economy of Karl Marx. He is one of the main writers who clearly and systematically embodies such an approach. One result of taking Marx to be a realist is that we do not have to choose between viewing him as either humanistic and philosophical, or positivist and scientific.[1] We argue that Marx's method is scientific, but non-positivist.

A central concept in our interpretation of Marx is that of structure. In chapter 6, we analyse certain aspects of this concept and various types of structural analysis. We show that one can fruitfully distinguish between positivist, realist, and instrumentalist concepts of structure. In particular we discuss the 'structuralist' analyses of Chomsky and Lévi-Strauss, noting the degree and manner of their realist approach to structure. We also consider features of Louis Althusser's interpretation of Marx, and conclude the chapter by noting some of the criticisms made of the concept of structure and of the nature of structural analysis.

The transference of conceptions of science from the natural to the social sciences is not simple and direct. This is partly for general reasons. First, we have presented the three methodologies in terms of positions that are not necessarily identified with any given writer. As a result even philosophers of the natural sciences will not fit unequivocally into any single position; and a given writer may embody different conceptions of science in different works, or in different parts of the same work. Further, some writers may adhere to one position in their methodological writings yet carry out substantive analyses governed by a different conception of science. Also, as we noted, some positions do in fact tend to merge into each other at the margins; for example, positivism and instrumentalism. Occasionally we do find a natural or social scientist, who explicitly adopts and adheres to a single distinctive conception of science. However, this is unusual and normally scientific methodology can only be identified more indirectly.[2] Turning specifically to the social sciences, the relating of methodological positions to given writers will be more problematic than in the case of natural science. We can illustrate this by considering the positivist attempt to base theories on the observable, that is, on the sensory or the perceptible. But positivists in social science have rarely adhered to such a fully-fledged behaviourist programme. First, their work is normally based upon the *sui generis* character of the social, or of society, although on a strict positivist programme, references to the social level of reality ought to be ruled out on grounds of non-observability. Second, few positivists in sociology have been able to avoid referring in some way or other to the subjective states of individuals, that is, again to essentially unobservable structures and processes.

Finally, we do not provide any historical explanation of the changes in the conceptions of science held by different social theorists. However, it is interesting to note that these different conceptions themselves influence how we conceive of this historical development. This can be seen in two respects. First, for some positivists, sociology is a cumulative science, whose development only lags behind because of its later beginnings and intrinsically more complex subject-matter. By contrast, someone who applied the Kuhnian model to the history of sociology, would see that history as the replacement of one outdated and incommensurate paradigm with another, with no clear unilineal development or progress. Second, the different methodological positions will influence how we characterize the social sciences. For the positivist, there is a tendency to identify each science as different, holding that within each there are sets of given and potentially discoverable general laws. A realist may be more likely to emphasize the artificial character of these disciplinary distinctions, and to argue that we must analyse the causal interrelations between the different orders of reality. Consider also the origins of sociology. For positivists, it is usual to say that sociology began at the beginning of the nineteenth century, with Henri de Saint-Simon and Auguste Comte. Realists, by contrast, might argue that the subject of sociology, conceived of more broadly than in the positivist formulation, lies in the eighteenth-century Scottish Enlightenment and especially in the work of Adam Ferguson and John Millar. These latter writers provided alternative explanations, based upon the distribution of property as the crucial structural mechanism, of certain phenomena analysed positivistically; the nature of industrial society, the effects of the modern division of labour, and the consequences of hierarchy and social conflict. Nineteenth-century sociology, or social science, it has been suggested by Alan Swingewood, was poised between two paradigm-competitors, the positivism of Saint-Simon, Comte, Mill, Spencer, and Durkheim; and the realism of Millar, Ferguson, Marx and some later Marxists.[3]

4 Sociology and positivism

1 Comtean positivism

Saint-Simon, Comte, and the Positivist Movement in general advocated the development of a new positive outlook, or Positive Philosophy, founded upon the certainties of science.[1] The old traditions and values no longer moved people, society was in a state of chaos and anarchy, and the eighteenth century Enlightenment had not stemmed but had contributed to the decline. What therefore was needed was a new basis of intellectual, moral and social life. This would be provided by the methods, findings and instrumental utility of science; sociology would be the crowning pinnacle in this new order. The problems of the emergent industrial society (of competition, social conflict, ideas of free enterprise) were seen as scientifically calculable. Social and political beliefs could be matched to the scientifically possible. The discovery of the laws of social physics would ensure that people accept the inevitable and would only change that which could be changed. Order and progress were seen as reconcilable, the working class in particular would believe in the social ethic of science and industry, and the realm of the social or Society would be omnipotent. Let us consider Comte's argument in detail, beginning with his view of science.

He sees the natural sciences positivistically; and his naturalist characterization of sociology is also positivist. His arguments here rest on two central and quite distinctive theses. First, there is historically a progression from theological, to metaphysical, to positive modes of thought and related types of social organization. Second, there is a hierarchy of the sciences with mathematics at the bottom and sociology at the top, and each of them passes in turn through the three stages, theological, metaphysical and positive. Let us describe what these stages consist of and specifically how the positive stage is distinguished from the other two. We will then discuss Comte's views about the character of the new science of social physics, or sociology, and briefly consider whether his sociological practice departs from his positivist assumptions.

The theological stage for Comte is one in which people explain events and phenomena in the world in terms of supernatural forces, such as particular gods or spirits; in the metaphysical stage, all phenomena are explained in terms of abstract forces or personified entities; and in the positive stage, explanation is given by the establishment of regular law-like connections between empirically observable phenomena. In the first two stages there is a search for hidden, underlying, deeper forces which are taken to account for the phenomena in question. In the last stage there is no attempt to discover such theological or metaphysical forces. Positive science is concerned only with observable phenomena and consists of the establishment of law-like relations between them through the careful accumulation of factual knowledge. This occurs by means of observation, experimentation, comparison, and prediction. In his 'dynamic' sociology Comte argues that there is a particular type of society corresponding to each of the three stages: military/aggressive, military/defensive, industrial/pacific; each results from the prevalent mode of intellectual thought. Thus there is, corresponding to the movement of thought, a similar development of social organization.

Positive Philosophy is based on the belief that we cannot have knowledge of anything but observable phenomena and of the relations between them. Science cannot inform us of the essence, or the underlying structure of such phenomena. The relationships between observables, either of coexistence or of succession, are seen by Comte as constant or regular sequences. Phenomena are thus regularly linked with each other in sets of invariable and universal laws. Our knowledge of such laws is always tentative, provisional and corrigible. We may note however that Comte does not specify how one distinguishes between empirical regularities (night following day) and the scientific law which would explain such regularities (rotation of the earth) (see Mill, 1965).

Let us amplify some of these points. Comte argues that we can demarcate scientific from non-scientific statements, not in terms of their certainty or infallibility, but rather in terms of their testability. Thus scientific statements are those that make general claims about nature or society which are open to empirical control. This means that statements are only properly scientific if they have predictive consequences that can be tested. Comte emphasizes that such predictions do not have to be about the future. Past, present, and future events can all be used to test predictions, for prediction is merely the leap from the 'known' to the 'unknown'. Further Comte suggests that there is a symmetry between prediction and explanation.

He says that every law-like connection 'discovered between any two phenomena enables us both to explain them and foresee them, each by means of the other' (Comte, 1844, p. 20). He also claims that: 'any proposition which is not strictly reducible to the simple enunciation of the fact – either particular or general – can have no real or intelligible meaning for us' (Comte, 1844, pp. 12–13). Thus meaningful statements are those which can be checked, tested and possibly refuted. It is this which clearly distinguishes the positivist approach from theology or metaphysics. But, although the only meaningful statements are those which can be factually tested, science is not merely the discovery of single isolated facts but their systematic and generalized organization into sets of laws. Two further points: first, although he argues that the scientific method is that of induction he does not think that how scientific theories are actually arrived at is particularly important – rather 'their scientific value depends entirely on their conformity . . . with the phenomena' (Comte, 1844, p. 13). Second, Comte argues that we only know that there are universal and invariable laws because when we test certain laws they turn out to be invariable. We cannot prove such invariability, only assert that the testing of laws shows us that some are invariable.

What role do scientific theories play in Comte's positivist philosophy of science? He argues that we construct hypotheses and test them against our observations, although he does not articulate what counts as an *adequate* confirmation or verification. Scientific theories consist only of linking together the facts relating to the observed phenomena in the constantly conjoined sequences of coexistence and succession. We can only attribute reality to observable phenomena. Where reference is made in scientific theories to unobservable entities and processes these are at best only useful fictions. They may help us to see how phenomena are linked together; but the crucial issue always is whether we can observe the law-like relations between observables. Atomic theory, for example, must not be treated as an actual discovery. Comte thus combines an instrumentalist attitude to scientific theories with his generally positivist methodological position; we discussed this possibility in chapter 3, section 4.

He also holds to a more general instrumentalist or pragmatist view of science, which in some ways runs counter to his positivism. Here he claims that the main basis of positive knowledge is its practical applicability. He sees science as an instrument of control over our physical and social conditions. And the factual knowledge that science provides us with will fairly directly imply changes in our beliefs, values and principles of social organization. Thus one criterion of true, or positive, knowledge for Comte is that it is of *practical* use to people in their day-to-day lives. So he rejects as metaphysical large sectors of science, such as the theory of probability, investigations into the structure of matter, or the theory of evolution, since these are realms of enquiry lacking practical exploitation.

Comte thinks that any kind of knowledge reaches the positive stage, the more it is general, simple and independent of other sciences. Since social physics, or sociology, is for Comte the most complicated, individual and dependent of the sciences, it will be the last to reach that stage. Comte's hierarchy has many bizarre and interesting features. It is bizarre because of its omissions; in the realm of social science he excludes both psychology (to J. S. Mill's great annoyance) and political economy (because of its abstract nature and isolation of the economic aspect of life). It is interesting because of his claim that the different types of science correspond to the study of different phenomenal levels each with its own autonomous character. In particular, he argues that there is a social level of phenomena with its distinctive features and laws. And, although sociology is dependent upon the other sciences, both for empirical data and development of their methodologies, sociology is not reducible to these other sciences. Comte therefore opposes any theoretical reduction of the social to some other level. Especially, he rejects all those theories which suggest that the only real human phenomena are individual people and that society is merely the consequence of some form of contract entered into by each of the people living in that society.[2] Comte explicitly and clearly regards society as the basic reality. It is social life which is natural, given and real. What sort of method does Comte advocate for its study?

He says that in the simpler inorganic sciences the individual elements are much better known to us than the whole which they constitute; in this case we must proceed from the simple to the compound. However, the reverse method is appropriate in the study of man (biology) and society (sociology); here we must view each element in the light of the whole. This in turn suggests to Comte the need for two different but complementary approaches: either, we study the laws of coexistence of the various elements at an instant of time (social statics), or we study the laws of succession by which each social state is seen as the product of the preceding state (social dynamics). In the latter case, we employ what Comte calls the historical method. This consists of the comparison between successive states of human development, or of Humanity, so as to reveal the laws of the inevitable transition from one to another. Sociology also uses to varying degrees the methods of the other sciences, which are ordered hierarchically: observation (as in astronomy), experimentation (as in physics and chemistry), and comparison (as in biology), of which the historical method is a subcategory.

Let us consider finally another implication of Comte's advocacy of studying the whole prior to the analysis of each element or part.

Sometimes Comte suggests that this is a matter of convenience, since the whole society is better known and more *accessible* to us; othertimes, it is because of the existence of a social level or society which constitutes a reality *sui generis*. In either case, sociological explanations involve using concepts such as the 'social' or 'society' to refer to the causes of particular events or phenomena. Thus the growth of social conflict between workers and managers is explained by the fact that modern society is passing through a 'critical' stage before the re-establishment of the new 'organic' stage, which will be positivistic. However, it is unclear whether we can 'observe' society, since all that can be observed are various features, elements and consequences. There are two points to note. First, Comte fails to specify just what he means by the observable, and hence by the unobservable and the scientifically illegitimate. Second, when Comte argues that it is society which produces invariable and constant sequences, he uses society as a concept referring to the unobservable. The 'social' or 'society' thus refer to real entities which for Comte cause other phenomena to exist or persist. Consequently, Comte employs here a mode of explanation which in terms of his positivistic philosophy of science should be rejected as metaphysical.

2 Mill and Spencer

Both Mill and Spencer were in different ways influenced by the Comtean Positivist Movement, and both wrote books analysing the Comtean system (Mill, 1965; Spencer, 1968). Although Mill made important criticisms of the system, these were mainly motivated by his belief that Comte had not lived up sufficiently to his positivist principles. Mill did not himself produce any sociological analysis because he thought such an enterprise premature. However, he is of importance in that he wrote explicitly about the proper character and methodology of social science, and there is good reason to believe that his claims have had a considerable influence of a broadly positivist sort.[3]

For Mill, the nature of things in themselves or the hidden causes of phenomena, are inaccessible to the human mind. Nothing can be the object of knowledge except our experience and what can be inferred from our experience. Such sense-experience yields sets of particular facts about individual events. Further, Mill is concerned to develop rules governing the logics of induction and deduction. The former involves rules of inductive inference, Mill's Methods, by which we can infer from these individual facts to the general propositions governing all natural phenomena. The rules of deductive inference are then used to explain particular cases by deducing them from the laws and the antecedent conditions: although there is some controversy as to whether Mill always distinguishes between the laws and the conditions. Mill also argues that we can deduce lower level laws from higher laws, and practical policies from general principles. Scientific progress is seen by Mill, as in much modern positivism, as the reduction in the number of laws involved, together with an increase in the number of phenomena which the laws will account for.

The logics of induction and deduction are taken to be universally applicable. Indeed Mill believes that all phenomena belong to a single natural world, and that the same kinds of scientific procedures are appropriate throughout. More particularly, in relation to the study of man in society, Mill argues that the new social science should be modelled upon Newtonian mechanics; this is interesting for three reasons. First, it is linked to his desire that science, and particularly social science, should enable us to predict events so that they can be more effectively controlled. Second, Newtonian mechanics can be seen as conforming well to the positivist ideal of explanation and as exemplifying a non-necessitarian view of causation. Third, Mill holds to an atomistic view of the universe which can be seen specifically in his methodological individualist interpretation of the social sciences. He argues that the laws governing the behaviour of people in social interaction can be inferred from the laws which govern the behaviour of individuals apart from society. Since the basic elements or atoms in society are individual people, it will be the laws of psychology from which all the laws and regularities relating to social life must ultimately be deduced. This is also because the law-like relations between social phenomena cannot be observed in any simple sense, nor can they in general be arrived at through experimentation. Thus for both ontological and epistemological reasons the laws of psychology are the only secure basis for social science. Thus Mill advocates a kind of theoretical reductionism which we do not find in Comte. It is consequently surprising that Mill thinks that the one sociological law which has been well established is Comte's law of the three stages of intellectual and social development.

Spencer, on the other hand, has no such enthusiasm for Comte's law of the three stages of development.[4] Although we can approximately identify Comte and Spencer as both holding a positivist view of science, Spencer himself denies that he is a Comtean positivist or that the Postivist Movement had any important influence upon him. Let us list some obvious points at which Spencer's position differs from Comte's: Spencer undertakes empirical comparative research which involves systematic documentation and team-work collection and classification of data; he believes that sociology is not the Queen of the Sciences – scientific unity is provided by his own Synthetic Philosophy; and he holds both that sociology should minimize bias in its study, and that it should not be the basis for governmental interference. Spencer claims that Comte attaches too much importance to men's ideas, as opposed to the organization of society; he disagrees with Comte's views that the species are immutable, will not evolve, and that evolution is not a master-principle of explanation; and he finds inadequate Comte's hierarchy of the sciences and the law of the three stages of development.

We can begin to understand the significant affinities between their respective conceptions of science by considering the last point above. Spencer criticizes Comte's hierarchy for being serial, maintaining rather that the sciences have developed in coordination. Spencer sees the observations and laws within different disciplines as influencing each other, rather than one science being the condition for the development of the next. The historical progress of any science depends upon the frequency and obviousness with which the relations between the relevant phenomena are experienced by the senses. Such relations will thus be more perceived and identified, the greater their apparent and actual frequency, the greater their conspicuousness, the more they involve direct personal welfare, the more concrete they are, and the more simple they are (the last one is all that Comte focuses upon). Spencer's classification of the sciences is as follows. He distinguishes between those sciences which consider the forms in which we come to know phenomena (logic and mathematics), and those sciences which study the phenomena either in their individual elements (mechanics, physics, chemistry, etc.) or in their totalities (astronomy, biology, psychology, sociology, etc.).

Spencer also distinguishes between commonsense and scientific knowledge, although he does point out the important similarities between them. Commonsense knowledge, where it takes a fairly systematic form, can understand and explicate only those combinations of phenomena that are directly apprehended by our senses. We can merely predict those phenomena which are in constant, direct and simple causal relations with each other. Scientific knowledge is likewise based on our sense-impressions; but it arises where the relations between phenomena are not of a direct and unproblematic kind. Scientific thought is found where inference and reasoning have to be applied to give a plausible account of how phenomena are linked together in law-like relationships. In other words, scientific thought involves what we now call scientific theories. Like Comte, Spencer is not willing to introduce terms referring to non-observable entities into his strongly positivistic science. The sole function of scientific inference and reasoning is to enable us to establish lawful relations between phenomena, these relations not being immediately apparent to our senses. Once established these laws form the bedrock of science; the whole natural universe is governed by laws relating to all physical and social phenomena.

There are two further distinctive features of scientific thought. First, the indirectness of the relations between phenomena means that prediction is here far more problematic than in the case of common-sense knowledge. Second, Spencer argues that proper scientific knowledge only results when we are able to measure the phenomena and their relationships. For Spencer it is the reduction of phenomena to relations of magnitude that gives to any branch of knowledge its scientific character. We see here an important aspect of modern positivism, that is, the further specification of the privileged category of the observable to refer to that which is measurable. Comte makes no claim that the observable is that which is measurable.

Comte also, it will be remembered, uses science to attack religion and metaphysics. Spencer, by contrast, noting the apparent universality of religious beliefs and practices, believes that religion must perform some useful function for human life. Consequently, he characterizes science in a way that does not invalidate religious experiences. We have seen that for Spencer, as a positivist, science consists in the establishment of law-like relations between observable phenomena. But Spencer also believes in an Unknowable, a set of religious and metaphysical forces or noumena which can only be felt, not known, and which are ultimately incomprehensible. Religion, which Spencer takes to be the belief in this absolute being or realm of the Unknowable, is quite consistent with science provided neither try to transgress their respective boundaries. Religion therefore has nothing to do with knowledge of the world but only in how we transcend it to this Unknowable realm.

There is however a further aspect to Spencer's analysis of the Unknowable which is more directly methodological. Spencer is deeply interested in the way in which we can acquire knowledge of the phenomenal world. He denies that we discover the relations between phenomena by the imposition of forms and categories upon what we experience and observe. Rather the external world imposes limitations and restrictions upon our senses; these limitations consist of the actual lawful relations between the observable phenomena. However, Spencer sees these relations as manifestations of the Unknowable. The Unknowable then is responsible for producing the natural law-like regularities throughout the universe. This means that there is much that we cannot know; that there are sets of unanswerable questions. Spencer says that we can never identify the ultimate origins or essential nature of any phenomenon.

Let us now consider two central features of his sociology, the organic analogy and the process of evolution, and see how they reflect his positivist methodology. Spencer insists that there is no perfect, direct and specific analogy between the social body and the human organism; and indeed he considers this one of the errors made by both Plato and Hobbes. He considers merely that there are some analogical similarities in the growth of animal and social organisms. They both start as small aggregates and increase in mass, both develop a more complex structure as they grow: in both the functionally differentiated parts become increasingly interdependent, and the life of each organism is independent of any of the individual elements that makes it up. One major difference between the two is that in an animal organism only a particular part is endowed with feeling and consciousness; while in society all individuals are endowed with consciousness.

This last point raises an apparent inconsistency in Spencer's use of the analogy. On the one hand, Spencer takes society to bear analogical similarities with an animal body. In particular, he takes the functional interdependence within the living organism as the source for his model of society in which there is an integration of the functionally differentiated elements. On the other hand, Spencer is an individualist, both in the sense that he believes that the free spontaneous development of each individual is the most important political and social goal, and that social life is explicable in terms of the feelings, sentiments and beliefs of the individual members of a given society. Spencer reconciles the functional organization of the whole with the primacy of the individual by arguing that we should conceive of the elements within society (corresponding to the parts of the body) as individual people. Thus within 'industrial society', as opposed to 'militant society', Spencer sees a multitude of private individuals entering into freely arranged and mutually profitable contracts, the consequence of which is to realize social and political harmony; a harmony or functional integration of the differentiated elements is produced spontaneously. It is noteworthy that the source of Spencer's model of society is an organism and not a mechanism; while the latter may support planned change and artificial construction, the former suggests self-generated growth and the non-necessity of externally imposed development.

The reason why Spencer's use of models is positivist is as follows. We have to locate his employment of the organismic source of the model of society within his general positivist desire to identify and establish the law-like regularities of social life existent between empirically observable phenomena. Thus we see that the source is not chosen by Spencer because it will provide us with the means of describing underlying mechanisms and processes productive of observable regularities. Rather we use the organismic source to produce a model of society which comprises a set of law-like relations between observables. Spencer says that this: 'alleged parallelism' between living organisms and society is: 'a scaffolding to help in building up a coherent body of sociological inductions' (Spencer,

1893, p. 581). Once we remove the scaffolding the general law-like relations will stand by themselves to be judged against our empirical observations.

Spencer's analysis of evolution is similarly positivistic. He believes that he has generated a new philosophy, not like those in the past which have been metaphysical, but one centred upon scientific fact and established inductive procedures. His belief is that there is a single process, that of evolution, which can be discerned in all realms of the universe, animate and inanimate. Evolution refers to the process of increasing differentiation (specialization of functions) combined with increasing integration (mutual interdependence of the structurally differentiated parts).

Spencer is thus interested in showing how social phenomena are instantiations of these general laws of evolution. He is not interested in articulating the specific causal mechanisms responsible for particular species-changes. Evolution, for Spencer, is a universal feature of life which furthermore can be induced from our observations. Evolutionary theory is one based upon the observation, the classification and the ordering of facts in the universe relating to different species. Indeed, while in the study of evolution in nature we can only observe the ontogenetic process of differentiation and integration (fertilized egg into an adult individual), in the study of social evolution we actually have records of and personal experiences of phylogenetic development (from one social species to another). In the latter case then we are even more able to ground our theory upon our observation of the process of evolution.

We should note in conclusion that we shall discuss aspects of the British anthropological analysis of social structure in chapter 6; an analysis historically indebted to Spencer.

3 Durkheimian positivism

We have so far discussed three nineteenth-century positivists. We are now going to discuss one of the most important social theorists writing at the end of that century and at the beginning of this. As an introduction to Émile Durkheim we should note two sets of points.

First, it is significant that neither Durkheim nor his positivist predecessors hold to an extreme positivist position, which would be, in the study of human beings, both methodologically individualist and behaviourist. The reason for the first point lies, either, in the tendency to theoretical reductionism in the positivist tradition, so that the social is reduced to the psychological, and then to the biological, and so on; or, because of the fact that the social is less obviously observable than the individual and social laws are less clearly universal. This means however that there is a certain tension between the positivism of Comte or Durkheim and their belief in the irreducibility of the social. It would be wrong to characterize the sociological work of such writers as *simply* positivistic. The reason why a fully positivist social science would be behaviouristic is that this would avoid all reference to the internal mental characteristics of individuals, their states of consciousness, moral beliefs and values, and their motives and reasons for acting. The fully positivist programme would give behavioural definitions of all such mental states. Thus again there is a certain tension involved here for all these writers, between their positivist methodology and the partial adoption of non-behaviourist explanations.

Second, Durkheim was part of a general intellectual movement which occurred at the turn of the century in which many of the general assumptions shared by the writers we have already discussed were questioned and rejected.[5] One aspect of this general anti-positivism was a belief that positivist social science, although not entirely behaviourist, had paid insufficient and inadequate attention to the individual's subjective mental states. The writers concerned, who included Bergson, Croce, Dilthey, Durkheim, Freud, Gramsci, Jung, Lukács, Pareto, Sorel and Weber, were also generally less optimistic about the beneficial consequences of science and of the possibility of a completed social science in the near future. They also criticized the attempt to construct systems of general laws from which particular events could be deduced and explained. There was a greater concern for the nature and particularity of historical development. Even so, the professional sociologists amongst this group departed much less from nineteenth-century positivism than did many of the other writers listed above. Durkheim and Pareto were naturalists and the model of science which they both had in mind was a modified positivist one. Weber was more obviously anti-positivist and anti-naturalist. One final point to note here is that we are also interested in how these various writers have been *interpreted* by later generations of social scientists. In the final section of this chapter we shall briefly discuss how Durkheim has been read by those who claim to be his followers.

Durkheim's methodological views would appear easy to summarize.[6] After all he wrote *The Rules of Sociological Method*, and a reading of this together with *The Division of Labour in Society* and the positivistically famous *Suicide* apparently confirm his location within the positivist camp. This is however too simple, since there are in Durkheim elements of both positivist and realist conceptions of science. We shall suggest in fact that the former is the predominant orientation and that the realist elements are more perspicuously viewed as essentialist. One important reason why Durkheim's methodological views may be at some variance particularly with his substantive analyses is as follows. For Durkheim, and for the other positivists, there is the strongest desire to reject the suggestion that mysterious metaphysical or theological forces are responsible for producing the contours of the empirically observable world. However, in the positivist rejection of such forces there is also the rejection of the sorts of entities that the realist seeks to identify and describe, that is, causal structures and mechanisms. Yet, when positivists seek to put into operation their methodology they often find themselves employing realist arguments or positing realist-type entities, albeit in an unsystematic and confused way.

Durkheim himself describes his position as that of a 'scientific rationalist'; he wishes to extend to the study of human behaviour the methods and procedures of natural science. Conceiving of science as the careful and clear establishment of law-like relations of cause and effect Durkheim argues that sociology should be similarly concerned with the identification and establishment of such relations within the field of social behaviour. Durkheim also believes that the time will come when the science of society will be far enough advanced for theory to govern practice, for it to provide rules of action for the future. The time however has not yet arrived because of the inadequacy of existing sociological work. Such work, according to Durkheim, has been far too bound to overall philosophies of history, too concerned with system-building, and too uninterested in developing, through careful study, bodies of well-established and verified findings about social phenomena. He thinks that the establishment of such findings will help to integrate the already existent social sciences into a synthesizing science of society.

Durkheim, although wishing to dispense with philosophical doctrines such as what he calls Comte's 'positivist metaphysics', believes that Comte has laid the foundation for such a science. He has discovered and elucidated its object, he has a keen sense of the interdependent character of the social, and he correctly identifies the overall method for its study. But he has failed to produce any actual sociological analysis or to examine anything but general types of society, or Humanity. Spencer, Durkheim thinks, has made an important contribution to sociology because of the particularly fruitful organic analogy; this compensates for both his untenable methodological individualism and his bizarre attempt to verify the grand law of evolution. Durkheim, then, considers neither Comte nor Spencer sufficiently positivist in their scientific practice.

Durkheim sees his task as giving to sociology 'a method and a body', a realm of phenomena to be studied scientifically by the sociologist. That realm consists of social facts, those morphological, demographic and ecological features, legal rules and institutionalized norms, established beliefs and practices, and uninstitutionalized social currents, which constitute the organization of society into which any member is born and continues to act. What, for Durkheim, distinguishes a social fact from any other kind of fact?

There are three distinguishing features of a social fact. First, they are external to us. It is a feature of social life that there are sets of external expectations and obligations, beliefs and practices, outside our individual consciousness. Thus the first feature of social facts is that they are not part of us but are external. However, it is unclear whether Durkheim considers that social facts are external to all individuals or merely to each one as we consider them in turn. Sometimes in his analysis of the 'collective conscience' he argues for the former. Elsewhere he maintains that he has no intention of reifying society as something external to all constituent individuals, since there is nothing in society but individuals or individual consciences and that he is only interested in the social properties which result from the organization of these individuals. It would seem that Durkheim's argument is problematic because of his overdifferentiation between the 'individual' and 'society'. In rejecting certain individualist claims Durkheim adopts instead an overstrong belief in the primacy of the social.[7]

The other two distinguishing features are seen by Durkheim as empirical criteria. They are means by which we can identify the presence and nature of social facts. The first of these is that a social fact is one which is general in society, irrespective of individual manifestations. For example, in *Suicide*, Durkheim points out that there is great regularity in the rates of suicide in a given population over time. Individuals with different dispositions cancel each other out and we thus arrive at the general independent social phenomenon. In *Suicide* we are able to infer such a phenomenon, or social fact, from the regularities in the revealed statistics. The final feature of social facts is the coercive power which they impose upon each individual independent of the person's will. The external social pressure constrains or forces people to behave in specified ways. Such pressure may take a variety of forms ranging from direct physical coercion, to where the individual unselfconsciously internalizes an external social force. Thus one difficulty with this constraint criterion is that, while the most observable kind of constraint is prohibition enforced by the law and its agents, that which is most effective is where moral or normative beliefs are taken into or internalized by the individual. Durkheim later admits the difficulties involved in this criterion; especially how it refers to such a variety of types of social pressure. We can note a further point here. This is that, although Durkheim is concerned to provide external, observable criteria, he in fact finds that the most salient factors are internal psychological states. Such mental states are misleadingly characterized as 'coercive'.

This is moreover a general feature of Durkheim's work; namely, that he wishes to eliminate all references to mental, psychological states, as in his definition of suicide, but is unable to do so. Again we see one of those tensions involved for the positivist which we mentioned at the beginning of this section.

To show how Durkheim actually uses this concept of a social fact, we will present the structure of the argument found in his three best known substantive works, *Division of Labour*, *Suicide*, and *Elementary Forms*. Each work is tripartite. First, there is a definition given of the subject in question, of the division of labour, of suicide, and of religion. Second, he considers various explanations of this phenomenon which have previously been suggested, many of which are individualistic or psychological. By the use of both argument and empirical data, he shows the inadequacy of these explanations; for example, of Spencer's thesis that the division of labour results from the pursuit of increased happiness, that suicide rates are explicable in terms of insanity, and that religion can be seen as the outgrowth of natural or cosmic forces. Finally, in each case he puts forward his own sociological explanation in which the social fact in question, the growth and division of labour, the comparative rates of suicide, totemic beliefs and practices, are explained in terms of other social facts. In the *Division of Labour* the growth in population volume, population density and then in 'moral density' produces a growth in social differentiation, the division of labour, and the emergence of organic solidarity. In *Suicide* the comparative rates of suicide are determined by different suicidogenic currents which are themselves the result of religious and political values in that society. While in *Elementary Forms* Durkheim argues both that religion serves certain functional needs that bind people together and that what people worship is really society itself.[8]

Let us consider in more detail the first and third stages of this general structure of argument.[9] Durkheim claims that since the properties of social phenomena cannot be determined in advance of actual empirical study, the social analyst must not rely upon the definitions of phenomena provided by laymen. He is consequently very self-conscious about the correct procedures to be followed in defining and classifying phenomena. Durkheim says that we should define a phenomenon in terms of readily visible external characteristics. We thus use observable criteria to distinguish the members of a class of phenomena from non-members. For Durkheim, the social scientist is a passive receiver of sense-impressions. He believes that the 'articulations of reality' will yield themselves to the scientist in a direct and unproblematic way. Durkheim further holds that the phenomena falling into the class distinguished by this definition will all embody the essence of the phenomenon in question. Thus, although the definitions themselves are not seen as descriptions of essences, in fact all phenomena meeting the criteria given in the definition will embody the phenomenon's essence. Let us now try to see why this is the case by considering Durkheim's closely related approach to explanation.

Durkheim argues that the cause of one social fact must be another preceding social fact. Thus, of all the instances of the phenomenon classed together by our particular definition, there will be some other single social fact or cause which has produced them. If by chance there appear to be different causes of the same phenomenon this is because there are in fact different phenomena in question. Thus, since there are different causes of suicide, different suicidogenic impulses, there must be different types of suicide: egoistic, altruistic, anomic, fatalistic, defined in terms of different causes. The same effect, according to Durkheim cannot be produced by different causes. The same effect must always be produced by the same cause.[10]

Let us summarize his argument here. We define a phenomenon in terms of certain external characteristics which class together the instances of the phenomenon in question. All such instances are seen as produced by a single cause. It is this single cause which gives us the essence of the phenomenon. We can consider as an example of his definitional and explanatory method his theory of religion (stated in non-functionalist terms). Durkheim commences by defining religion in terms of the distinction between the sacred and the profane. He is then led to deny any fundamental differences between totemism and religions of salvation, and finally he proposes that all religion is caused by society and consists of its worship. Thus, although his definition is merely intended to class together these individual instances of a phenomenon with common external characteristics, by linking a single cause with all such instances he in fact identifies the essence of religion. The cause of religion gives us the essence of religion.

Thus far we can see that Durkheim is part-positivist and part-essentialist. There are various reasons why we do not think his approach is realist. First, Durkheim aims to discover through Millian causes the essence of phenomena; while realists seek to discover essences or structures so that they may then causally explain the observable. Second, the realist does not identify such essences, or underlying structures, by Durkheim's curious method of definition; namely, classing together all phenomena that happen to share certain common external characteristics. Third, while Durkheim links together a single cause and a single effect, the realist argues that any such effect results from the complex interrelations between mechanisms, structures and background conditions.

A final point to note here is Durkheim's strong tendency to give operational definitions of his central theoretical terms. Let us approach this point by considering Durkheim's injunction to see social facts as things. Both terms, 'facts' and 'things' are problematic. Basically however the injunction involves considering social facts as having characteristics independent of the subjective inclinations and desires of both the observer and the actor. These characteristics can only be discovered by empirical observation and investigation and not through *a priori* reasoning or intuition, and not by relying upon the concepts and ideas which people hold about their own social activities. It is an injunction to concentrate upon those phenomena in social life which can be observed, or can be built up from our observations and empirical investigations. Durkheim says that all that is subject to observation has the character of a thing, and that such observations are the fundamental base for any scientific enterprise.

His position here is clearly positivist. A difficulty arises however when we consider that in both the *Division of Labour* and *Suicide* he employs terms which refer to unobservable entities. Thus, in the former work, Durkheim is faced by the fact that solidarity 'is a completely moral phenomenon which, taken by itself, does not lend itself to exact observation nor indeed to measurement' (Durkheim, 1933, p. 64). Thus he argues that it is necessary to: 'substitute for this internal fact which escapes us an external index which symbolizes it and study the former in the light of the latter' (Durkheim, 1933, p. 64). The external facts which he takes as the indices of the internal facts are the sets of legal rules in a society. This is because after some time the moral rules in a society become codified into laws. Thus by looking at the externally observable laws we can ascertain the character of the underlying moral rules, and hence the differing types of solidarity. Durkheim says that there are two types of legal codes, repressive and restitutive: the former is the index of mechanical solidarity, the latter of organic solidarity. There are two related problems that arise here. First, since law only reflects a part of social life and the normative expectations present within a society may be inconsistent with the legal code, the empirical adequacy of the index is highly questionable. But second, the relationship between the index and the theoretical term, for example, between repressive law and mechanical solidarity, is unclear and unresolved. Is the former the means by which we confirm the existence and causal efficacy of the given theoretical entity? Or is it the means by which, positivistically, we reduce such entities to empirically meaningful and testable statements in the observation-language?

Our view is basically that Durkheim's position is ambiguous between different conceptions of science. However, as we suggested at the beginning, we are concerned, not only with what a writer says, but with how he is generally interpreted. Let us now consider the positivist interpretation of Durkheim in American social science.

4 American positivism

Suicide in particular has been seen as the model of a positivistic scientific sociology. Although there is an acknowledgment of certain technical deficiencies, it has been taken both as the starting point for the scientific study of suicide, and as the exemplar of how other social phenomena should be analysed. The positivist interpretation of *Suicide* is firmly embodied in Merton's famous essay: 'The Bearing of Sociological Theory on Empirical Research', written in 1948. He says that we can restate certain of Durkheim's theoretic assumptions as follows (1957, p. 97):

1. Social cohesion provides psychic support to group members subjected to acute stresses and anxieties.
2. Suicide rates are functions of *unrelieved* anxieties and stresses to which persons are subjected.
3. Catholics have greater social cohesion than Protestants.
4. Therefore, lower suicide rates should be anticipated among Catholics than among Protestants.

Also we can see how positivistic interpretations can be given of a wider range of suicidal phenomena.[11] The basic law of Durkheim's theory is: 'Suicide varies inversely with the degree of integration of the social groups of which the individual forms a part' (Durkheim, 1952, p. 209). From this it is possible to derive three lower level laws, that suicide varies inversely with the degree of integration of religious society, domestic society and political society. Finally, from these lower level laws we can deduce, given the statement of antecedent conditions, empirically testable hypotheses. The formal symmetry of explanation and prediction also is clearly evident. Let us see these two points in one of Durkheim's best known examples set out in accordance with one of Hempel's models of explanation:[12]

	L_1	Suicide rates vary inversely with the degree of integration of domestic society.
Explanans	C_1	There are two groups, one of married, one of unmarried people.
	C_2	Married people are more integrated.
Explanandum	E	There is a lower suicide rate among the married group compared with the unmarried group.

Thus, we can predict that in certain groups there will be a lower rate of suicide; alternatively, given that we have discovered a lower rate in one group rather than in another, we can explain it by showing how it follows from the general law and the antecedent conditions.[13]

In this consideration of the positivist interpretation of Durkheim, let us now analyse the concept of social integration, which plays a central role in his theory of suicide. It is linked to the various types of suicide, egoistic, anomic and altruisitic, and is itself caused by certain external social factors or forces. Its meaning is, however, left unexplicated in Durkheim; all he provides is the following character-ization of a lack of social integration (1952, p. 209):

> But society cannot disintegrate without the individual
> simultaneously detaching himself from social life, without his
> own goals becoming preponderant over the community ... The
> more weakened the groups to which he belongs, the less he
> depends on them, the more he consequently depends on himself
> and recognizes no other rules of conduct than what are founded
> on his private interests.

This has normally been interpreted as follows: a lack of social integration is an increase in the degree to which people follow their own interests, wants and desires, and do not follow those of the social groups of which they are members. However, this still remains a somewhat unclear notion which is hardly amenable to direct observation as the positivist would desire. Thus in the positivist interpretation of *Suicide* it is argued that we are able to measure the degree of social integration by a number of factors which are im-plicit, but not spelled out, in Durkheim's ambiguous account: the number of individuals interacted with in a given time, the frequency of such interaction, the number of different types of relations, and the degrees of intimacy of such interaction (see Douglas, 1967, p. 39). For the positivist social integration is given by these measures.

We have now set out a few features of the positivist reworking of Durkheim's *Suicide*. Let us now consider some more general features of the interpretation of *Suicide* which are present in other positivist writings. First, in modern theories of suicide, and in the study of much else, it is often argued that patterns of suicidal or other behaviour are explicable in terms of status incongruence or role conflict (see Douglas, 1967, part 2 for summaries). In other words, there is a search for various general laws of social life from which it is possible to derive empirically testable consequences. What is problematic about such claims is the inadequate analysis of the ways in which these general external causes are actually experienced and interpreted, and cause patterns of observable behaviour. There is a failure to detail the mechanisms at the level of meaning which actually cause people to behave in certain ways. We shall discuss the issues of meanings and causes in chapter 7.

A second characteristic of a positivist approach is to operationalize theoretical terms so that the meaning of statements containing them becomes their method of verification. This stems from the positivist suspicion of theoretical entities and the belief that science involves only the establishment of law-like relations between observable phenomena. A clear example of this in a field related to that of suicide is the operationalization of the concept of alienation, most famously by Melvin Seeman (Seeman, 1959). He tries to show that we can identify five different aspects or dimensions of the alienation concept, and that each of them can be given a meaning corresponding to its method of verification. For example, powerlessness is defined by Seeman as: 'the expectancy or probability held by the individual that his own behaviour cannot determine the occurrence of the outcomes, or reinforcements that he seeks' (Seeman, 1959, p. 784).

Third, the positivist student of suicide adopts a rather uncritical attitude to the statistics which provide the epistemologically and ontologically privileged basis for the articulation of general laws (see Douglas, 1967, part 3). The sociologist of suicide presumes that Durkheim's social facts are given by the officially collected statistical rates of suicide based on coroners' interpretations of the cause of each individual death. So whatever definitional anxieties Durkheim and his followers may have, they use in fact an operational definition of suicide which is that employed by coroners and officials in each society. Furthermore, this is misleading since the evidence that is taken by coroners as indicating a suicidal death is arbitrary and highly variable both within and between societies.[14] The problem is that one can only observe dead bodies, and it is then a matter of inter-subjectively managed interpretation as to whether or not any such body is defined as a death by suicide. Thus, in part, suicide rates are matters of construction depending upon the expectancies, meanings and understandings of the officials concerned. This point clearly has a more general relevance: criminal statistics depend upon police vigilance, their use of resources, how much the public report, and so on.[15] However, the significance of the socially constructed nature of such statistics varies. Suicides are such that it is necessary to re-construct the probable intentions of the agent prior to his death. To do so clearly requires coroners and officials to use all sorts of background knowledge and interpretative procedures to make sense of the agent's intentions; thus the officially produced statistical rates of suicide are essentially social constructions. However, it does not follow that anything like the same problem is faced with official statistics relating to income, wealth, housing, births and non-suicidal deaths. Even so two more points should be made. First, the

89

positivist social scientist largely wishes to measure not these sort of phenomena but rather specified aspects of the individual's mental state, such as values, attitudes and beliefs; and this clearly involves highly controversial problems of operationalization. Second, the really important criticism of the positivist analysis of social statistics of any sort is that there is a presumed rigid dichotomy between the theoretical and the observable. We have seen in chapter 3 that this cannot be maintained. All statistics are the product of a specific system of concepts and related set of technical instruments of measurement. They are all theory-dependent (see Hindess, 1973).

From the 1930s to the 1960s American social science has been largely positivist. Its predominant concerns have been the establishment of general laws of social life from which empirically testable consequences can be derived; operationalizing concepts such that they refer to the observable and especially to the measurable; and the statistical manipulation of naively collected and organized empirical data. Facts are sharply distinguished from both values and theories; facts, particularly statistical facts, are neutral between different theories.[16] We do not intend to give a full account of all aspects of American positivism. We are merely going to consider the following. First how, historically, American sociology coped with the holist elements in Durkheim's social theory. Second, we will consider one of the most important interpreters of Durkheim, namely Talcott Parsons and certain features of his general methodological position. Third, we will briefly analyse two of the central concepts of American social science, role and class, and show how they were interpreted and used in a positivist fashion. We will thus refer to various types of sociological work, small-scale empirical studies, middle range theorizing, and Parsonian grand theory. We believe that such work shares certain common positivist assumptions; and that the writers who produced it are concerned to establish in the future a unified system of general sociological laws. They see themselves as and are part of the same positivist enterprise.[17]

For the first quarter of this century, Durkheim's influence within American sociology was negligible. This stemmed from the clear incompatibility between his belief in the *sui generis* character of the social and the underlying individualistic nature of American social science. Especially in the 1920s Durkheim's concepts, such as the 'conscience collective', appeared metaphysical and empirically unintelligible. It was in the 1930s that Durkheim came to be favourably received. Thus translations appeared of the *Division of Labour* and the *Rules*, Durkheim was the subject of a number of doctoral theses including Alpert's (Alpert, 1961), he was discussed in various historical accounts of the development of sociology (Becker and Barnes, 1938), and most importantly, Merton and Parsons used

Durkheimian theses as the foundation for their own significant and influential writings (see Merton, 1957; and Parsons, 1968). It appears that he was accepted because of his advocacy and use of positivist methods and procedures of inquiry. As American social scientists came to demand careful description, the comparative analysis of patterns of concrete social behaviour, and inductive empirical study, they saw Durkheim as involved, brilliantly in *Suicide*, in the same sort of sociological enterprise. Alpert's thesis is thought to have been influential, because he argued that Durkheim did not adhere to such a strong interpretation of the social as had often been claimed, and that Durkheim's aim was to build up, inductively, general laws of social life through the accumulation of statistical findings and well corroborated observations (Alpert, 1961, pp. 82–3).

Let us turn to Talcott Parsons. Our reason for doing so is twofold. First, Parsons's interpretation of Durkheim's work was very significant in the 1930s in encouraging an interest in the Durkheimian position. Second, if our general claim about the positivist character of much American social science between the 1930s and 60s is correct, then we would have to demonstrate that the most abstract and grand theorist of the epoch betrays many elements of a positivist position. Parsons is concerned to establish sets of universal laws of social life which will explain any particular empirical facts. In particular, he says that theory proper 'is confined to the formulation and logical relations of propositions containing empirical facts in direct relation to the observations of the facts and thus empirical verification of the propositions' (Parsons, 1968, p. 49). From such a theory it should be possible to deduce empirical facts which will be present in various sets of circumstances. Parsons distinguishes between the theoretical system and the empirical system. The former for Parsons does not refer to anything which actually exists; it merely defines various properties of empirical variables and states the general relations holding between their values. The theoretical system is not itself a characterization of anything real. Each theoretical term has to be interpreted, that is, given empirical meaning, for it to be applicable.

That Parsons's position is positivist can also be seen from the writings of George A. Lundberg, a well-known positivist philosopher of the natural and social sciences. In 1939 Lundberg argued that the methods of natural science are directly applicable to the study of human behaviour. In particular, the supposed subtleties, complexities, and dynamic character of social phenomena in fact necessitate, and do not preclude, the use of symbolic logic, mathematization and quantification. Without methods of measurement, it is impossible to characterize adequately the enormous variety and gradations of social life. Lundberg says (1964, pp. 81–2):

> We need . . . to develop quantitative units and forms of
> expression so that we may utilize in the description of societal
> phenomena the tremendously powerful technics of mathematics.
> . . . By regarding all qualitative gradations as *degrees* or *amounts*
> of that quality, already existing numerical units and
> manipulating devices can be utilized in accurate and objective
> description of qualities and relationships.

By 1950 Timasheff (1950, p. 26) concluded that:

> The school dominating present-day sociology at least in
> America is the neopositivist one. It is best represented in
> G. Lundberg's *Foundations of Sociology* (1939), [and] in its
> companion volume which is S. C. Dodd's *Dimensions of Society*
> (1942) . . .

By 1964, when Lundberg brought out a revised edition of his
Foundations of Sociology, he considered that the battle for the
positivist method had been more or less won. He says that in the
previous twenty-five years very significant advances have been made
in both the methods of quantitative research (Guttman, Lazarsfeld,
and Stouffer), and in more comprehensive positivist theorizing (Levy,
Merton, and Parsons). Lundberg talked of the now 'enthusiastic
appreciation' of quantitative methods and sociological scaling
techniques. In particular he suggested that there is convergence
between the two apparently quite different theoretical schools, that of
S. C. Dodd and of Talcott Parsons 'in the direction of the theory and
methods of natural science' (Lundberg, 1964, p. 162).

We can also see positivist aspects of Parsons in *Working Papers
in the Theory of Action* (Parsons, Bales, Shils, 1953). Parsons argues
that the meaning of certain of his theoretical concepts, in particular
the so-called pattern variables, is given by the categories of the
interaction process discovered experimentally by Bales. One is thus
able to provide operational definitions of Parsons's concepts.
Lundberg concludes that the problems of quantitative techniques
and operational definitions are not features of some forms of
scientific thought, whilst absent in others. Rather they are the devices
of any form of scientific work; and Parsons and his collaborators
realized this by 1953. Further, the famous chapter written by Parsons
and Bales in the *Working Papers* is entitled: 'The Dimensions of
Action-Space', and they conclude it with the following (1953,
pp. 102–3):

> it would seem likely that there is a very important analogy
> between the scheme we have developed in this paper and the
> classical mechanics. If this supposition stands up to critical

testing of a variety of sorts, it is evident that it should turn out to have far-reaching implications in that it should open up possibilities of quantitative as well as qualitative systematization which are far beyond those which the sciences of action have yet attained.

It will be remembered that the system of classical mechanics provides a good example for positivists of what form scientific explanation should ideally take. Interestingly, then, we find Parsons arguing that there are four generalized laws of equilibrium, that the first three of these are identical with those of Newtonian mechanics, and that the fourth is of the same type. Lundberg points out how significant it is that such natural scientific or positivist theses are produced by the most sophisticated theorist of the epoch.

Finally, let us consider two of the central concepts that are used in this positivist tradition; role, and class or stratification.[18] The former concept, normally defined as the sets of rights, obligations and expectations of attitudes and behaviour which are attached to the incumbent of a given social position, has been criticized in two different ways. First, since role theory is often part of a functionalist analysis of the properties of a social system (as in Parsons), it suffers from certain of the well-known defects of particular types of functionalism.[19] Second, it is often taken to suggest a model of the relationship between social groupings and people in which people's actions are explained in an implausibly one way and deterministic mode. A person's role is taken as given, fixed and determinate. People are viewed as slotting into such a role and acting in conformity with it. In opposition to this it is argued that no such action is ever purely conforming, that a role is never fully defined with completely articulated and congruent obligations and expectations, and that role behaviour always involves reworking and redefinition of those very expectations.

Furthermore, role analysis normally involves a deductive- or inductive-statistical model of scientific explanation (see Hollis, in Bradbury, Heading, and Hollis, 1972). There is a concern to develop sets of probabilistic laws, which given the appropriate antecedent conditions, enable us to predict patterns of attitudes or of behaviour. Thus, to take a simple example: the following low level law might be held by a role analyst: 'All occupants of the role of school teacher tend to display more authoritarian attitudes both to school children and to other people.' Let us consider two groups of people, otherwise identical in terms of a number of demographic and social criteria; one group consists of school teachers, the others are not teachers. We may predict that the first group will contain more individuals displaying authoritarian attitudes; or if we find such attitudes more prevalent among members of the first group we may explain this in terms of the law stated above; that law itself being part of a system deduced from higher level laws.

Role analysis is obviously more complex than this. Let us note, first, that the concept of role was developed in American positivist social science from the writings of G. H. Mead and others in the earlier part of this century (see Mead, 1934). For Mead the individual is able to exert purposive control and organization of his/her conduct; in particular, there is a dialectical relationship between the I, that which gives the sense of freedom, initiative and self-conscious action, and the me, that organization of the generalized attitudes held by others and internalized by the individual. Thus it is not simply that people respond to external stimuli, such as expectations about role behaviour. Rather, for Mead, action is seen as constructed. However, the positivisation of the role concept obliterates this interest. For the positivist the concern is to establish regular relations between external stimuli and patterns of behaviour. There is no interest in how such behaviour is produced, as to how people deliberately and self-consciously interpret external pressures, such as role-expectations. There is no analysis of the meaning-structures at the level of each actor which produce the behavioural responses. Second, in role analysis each person is seen as the sum of the roles that they play. Or more accurately, given certain biological and psychological properties, expressed in terms of particular general laws, each individual is seen as the combination of the particular roles that he or she plays. That person is the instantiation of the set of laws intersecting at his or her particular point. Thus, we can see how the sets of reasons, wants, purposes, desires, and intentions that people have and are causes of their behaviour, are ignored in the analysis of social roles and the positivist search for the empirical regularities of social life.[20]

In conclusion, let us consider the notion of class. We have described this as one of the key concepts of American positivism. But this is misleading, since although the *term* 'class' is employed by many American writers there is a certain unhappiness or tension involved in its use. As we shall see in the next chapter, 'class' is part of the European tradition of social theory, particularly in the writings of Marx and Weber (see Giddens, 1973). This term has been imported into American social science and cast in a positivist framework. The changes involved here should be clearer after our discussion of Marx. For the present, we can say this. The term 'class' is used by Marx in a realist manner. It refers to social entities which are not directly observable, yet which are historically present, and the members of which are potentially aware of their common interests and consciousness. The existence of classes is not to be identified with the existence of inequalities of income, wealth, status, or educational opportunity. For Marx, and generally for realists, class structures are taken to cause such social inequalities. The meaning of the term, 'class', is not given by these inequalities. Rather it is the structure of class relationships which determines the patterns of inequality. The positivization of class involves treating these more or less observable inequalities as providing us with the meaning of 'class'.

For the positivist, the study of class, or more accurately, of stratification, is seen as that of the aggregate of individuals who are differentiated from each other in terms of various kinds of demographic, social and psychological criteria. The focus is on the individual and analysis is made of the various dimensions along which the individual is located, such as the types of inequality mentioned above. The individual is seen at the centre of these various stratificational dimensions; and he or she will exhibit attitudes and behaviour predictable from the operation of the general laws discernible within these dimensions.[21]

5 Marx and realism

1 Introduction to Marx's method

In our interpretation of Marx as a realist we must avoid giving an interpretation of realism so specific to the natural sciences that no social analysis could possibly resemble it; and giving a Marxist reinterpretation of realism such that nobody could be a realist without being a Marxist. In the following we will only consider Marx's later writings, so we will not be involved in the debates as to whether these writings are inconsistent with his earlier works, particularly the *1844 Manuscripts* and the *German Ideology*.[1] Marx's main intention in *Capital*, as well as in the *Grundrisse* and indirectly in *Theories of Surplus Value*, is to reach a successful characterization of the internal structure of the capitalist mode of production (CMP). More generally he intends to produce descriptions of the structures of various modes: primitive communist, ancient, Asiatic, feudal, capitalist, and so on. He takes the more apparent and observable features of social life to be explicable in terms of these underlying structures. They can be comprehended by the discovery of the causal mechanisms central to each structure; these mechanisms are characterized in terms of the relations between a small number of theoretical entities. Marx's advocacy here of analysing the nature of these mechanisms implies a non-Humean view of causal relationships. Likewise he rejects the ideal of positivist science, the search for general laws and its connected model of explanation.[2] He does however believe in the possibility of an objective science of social formations. He is both a naturalist and a realist.

However, to describe Marx as a realist is to suggest general similarities between his position and that of the realist approach to natural scientific explanation. In chapter 2 we gave as two examples of realist explanation, the change in temperature of a gas and the ignition of a match. In the latter case, the realist explains the particular event by providing a description of the mechanism so that we have precipitant-mechanism-effect. In the former, the molecular theory provides a description of the structure of different gases that enables us to explain the particular phenomenon. Marx is similarly concerned with the description of structures, but we might note some differences of approach. First, Marx's structuralism is one in which there is unity of the elements which comprise each structure. This unity is brought about by a single causal mechanism which is specific to that structure and is its defining characteristic. Second, Marx's explanations are rarely similar to the match-ignition example. For him, the causes and effects of social phenomena are aspects, or applications, of the structural relationships between the elements. Finally, Marx's theoretical purpose is to produce descriptions of the structures of different modes of production. However, no such mode is ever found in a pure form. Different modes are always co-present within any actual society, although if the capitalist mode is dominant we will characterize that society as capitalist: for example, nineteenth-century Britain. It thus follows that social analysis consists of at least two stages: first, the elucidation of the internal structure of each mode of production, a theoretical activity involving the positing of models of the relevant causal structures and mechanisms; second, the analysis of the ways in which different modes of production are co-present within a given society and the social and political consequences that follow. We will be mainly concerned in this chapter with describing Marx's method as related to the first of these stages; in the next chapter we will consider some problems of the second stage.

Let us commence this analysis of Marx by considering four of the methodological objections that he makes to the political economy of the late eighteenth and early nineteenth centuries. He distinguishes between the earlier 'scientific' classical economists, such as Adam Smith or David Ricardo, and the later 'vulgar' apologists for capitalism, such as James Mill or Samuel Bailey. All four objections are applied to the latter group; while only the third is in general relevant to the former.[3]

The first objection stems from the overall materialist view which Marx takes of the role of labour in history. Labour, he argues, creates a human world through the production of material objects. Such production, or objectification of oneself, is the means by which men create themselves as human and can be distinguished from animals. By acting on the external world they both change it and change themselves. They develop their human powers through this process of labour; and this is an inherently social process. Men cannot be conceived of apart from society. Their existence is dependent upon their relations with other people; for labour or production is itself inherently social. In particular, the process of material production is one of continuous creation, satisfaction and regeneration of men's needs through labour. Furthermore, this is a process in which there are definite stages. Distinctive types of society exist in which different sets of human needs are satisfied through particular ways of organizing men's labour. But these needs, and people's abilities and wants, are themselves historically produced. They depend not on people's essential attributes, but upon the specific modes of organization of human labour found within particular societies. Thus Marx objects to all studies of human behaviour which assume an isolated individual (for example, the Robinson Crusoe of some classical economics), or individuals whose needs, abilities, or wants, are regarded as independent of the social organization within which they live and work. He objects to those economic theories in which society is taken to be merely an agglomeration of individuals with given eternal natures, who come together not in production, but only in the market-place to buy and sell goods, services and labour-services. So Marx rejects various types of individualist or psychologistic explanations, and any theory which posits a given and unchanging human nature consisting of a fixed set of human needs. However, as we have seen, this does not mean that Marx has no conception of human nature. The point is that the way in which labour, or productive activity, expresses itself is historically variable. Thus Marx says that one must always study people within specific historical structures which are themselves founded upon different modes of organization of productive activity. For example, he criticizes the utilitarian theory of Jeremy Bentham for taking 'the modern shopkeeper, especially the English shopkeeper, as the normal man' (Marx, 1965, p. 609n); for Marx, what is useful to 'this queer normal man, and to his world' (Marx, 1965, p. 609n) is not necessarily useful to other classes in Britain, or to people in other societies founded upon different systems of production.

Second, Marx argues that the specific social relations of material production govern the way in which *things* enter into the process of production. Thus in capitalism the thing, the spinning jenny, is only capital because of the particular function which it performs in the CMP, the capitalist mode of production. And it only performs this function because the central social relation within the society is that between capitalists and wage-labourers. It is the relations between the central *social* constituents that determine the functions that *things* perform within that mode. Further, Marx argues that certain properties of things, such as their productivity, derive from the structures of social relationships: how they are used by specific social groups in relationship to other social groups within a given structure. It is therefore erroneous to see such properties as *naturally* produced. The productivity of the spinning jenny belongs to it only and in so far as it has a social function, that is, is embedded within specific social

relations of production, whether capitalist or otherwise. Two implications follow. First, capital, which is such an important element
within Marx's theory, is not to be seen as a thing; it is rather one
element in a definite social relationship of production corresponding to a particular historical formation and is only manifested
in things, such as the spinning jenny. Second, it is important to
realize that for Marx all social phenomena are inherently relational.
Thus, for example, the category of wage-labour cannot be defined
or understood without reference to that of capital. Further, wage-
labour, capital, and Marx's other concepts all refer to sets of relationships.[4]

Marx's third methodological objection is that it is incorrect to
argue that there are natural economic laws which are applicable to all
societies. There are no general laws of economic life which are
independent of given historical structures. He is particularly critical
of the attempts to develop such laws based on the workings of one
society, capitalism. One consequence of such attempts is the presumption that capitalism is eternal, since the properties of capitalist
society are taken to be the properties of all societies. Marx thus
criticizes the Ricardian analysis of distribution in terms of the two
natural laws of diminishing returns and the Malthusian population
principle. Laws should be seen as specific to particular modes of
production, such as the laws of the feudal mode or the capitalist
mode. We may note two related points. First, Marx's preference for
the analysis of the different structures of society further indicates his
anti-positivist and realist methodological position.[5] Second, Marx
believes that the postulation of natural laws of economic life is an
example of 'commodity fetishism'. Marx's analysis of fetishism, a
concept which includes the erroneous interpretation of certain
properties of things as natural rather than social, is presented in
Capital in the context of a more general methodological distinction
between appearance and reality.

Thus fourth, Marx argues that 'vulgar economics' analyses only
the superficial, phenomenal or apparent features of social and
economic life, and fails to penetrate to their deeper underlying
substratum, essence or reality.[6] Marx supports his view that the
distinction between appearance and reality is important by an
argument about science in general, and by arguments specific to
political economy. First, he says that there would be no need for
scientific theories unless the outward appearance of things and their
inner essence did not coincide. Thus while the air that we breathe
appears undifferentiated, the scientific analysis of how it is *in reality*
shows that it is mainly comprised of nitrogen and oxygen in proportions four to one. No science could proceed if it did not attempt to
explain appearances in terms of the reality, and if it did not show how

the appearances are themselves misleading. But this interpretation of the appearance/reality distinction is fairly general and imprecise. It fails to provide Marx with criteria specific to *his* approach to political economy, and does not even clearly exclude 'vulgar economics'.

What about his specific arguments about political economy? Marx believes that it is a particular feature of capitalism, namely, commodity fetishism, which causes the appearances of things and their reality to diverge. He thinks that some of the most serious difficulties in political economy arise within capitalism since its subject-matter is the production of commodities. Commodities are objects which are produced which have both a use-value (usefulness to their consumer) and an exchange-value.[7] In systems of production where commodity-production prevails, objects are produced for their exchange-value. These exchange-values attach themselves to the objects in question. People view the exchange-value of a given commodity, not as the consequence of men's labour, but as a naturally given fixed property of the commodity. Commodities in general, including machinery, are taken merely to be things, to have thing-like properties, and to stand in thing-like relations with each other. Commodity fetishism for Marx means seeing the results of social relationships, or those relationships themselves, as natural inanimate things. Social relations and socially endowed qualities and properties are seen as natural phenomena. How does this relate to the distinction between appearance and reality?

Commodity fetishism means that reality, that is, the social relations of production, does not appear as it is. There is a gap between the appearances of capitalism and its essence or reality. It appears that social life is governed by general lawful relations between things; for example, that capital is a thing and earns its profit because of its natural productivity. However, according to Marx, any social science which merely analyses this fetishistic level of appearances is false and distorting. Rather we must analyse reality, the organization of capital and labour based on the production and appropriation of surplus value. It is this reality which differs from the appearances of capitalism and which produces the false and distorting forms in which capitalist society appears to its members. It is not that people simply misperceive the nature of capitalism. Rather it is that reality presents itself in an inverted form. However, the visual metaphor of 'appearance-reality' is problematic and we will not use it in this present chapter.

2 Historical materialism

We have mentioned the materialist basis of Marx's theory. To help understand his historical materialism let us consider briefly the well-known passage in the Preface to *A Contribution to the Critique of Political Economy* where he presents a simplified account (Marx and Engels, 1962a, pp. 361-5). Marx argues that in order to produce, men enter into definite connections and relations with each other. It is only within such relations that their action in working on nature, that is production, takes place. Each set of the relations of production corresponds to a definite stage in the development of the material forces of production. Such forces of production consist of land, labour power, raw materials, plant, machinery, tools, technical and scientific knowledge, and the technical organization of production. Further, what is important is the organization of these forces within a particular mode of production. The social relations of production consist of the relatively enduring connections between people, and people and things, which result from the functions to be fulfilled in the process of production and in the control of the forces of production. Such relations of production include relations of serfdom, mastery and lordship; relations of ownership, hiring, and the leasing of men or things; relations of working with or supervision of other men; and relations of working on materials with implements (see Cohen, 1970). Marx argues that a specific set of such relations constitutes the economic base of each type of society, 'the real foundation', from which arises a legal, political and ideological superstructure.[8] Further, if the economic base changes so too does the superstructure. The principal source of change from one type of society to another is the contradiction between the forces and the social relations of production. Beyond a point the latter act as a restriction or limitation upon the further development of the former. Exacerbation of this contradiction results in conflict between the social classes found within the relations of production, and may result in social revolution. However, no social order disappears until all its productive forces have been fully developed. Any new society is always generated within the womb of the old. Specifically the society, or 'social formation' of capitalism is the last antagonistic system of production. With the ending of capitalism, prehistory is brought to an end and a non-antagonistic true communist society can be established.

This passage in the Preface has been much discussed and criticized, partly because of its simplification or even contradiction of Marx's arguments elsewhere. Let us now consider his views about the relationships within the economic base and its determination of the superstructure. Later, in section 6, we shall discuss his analysis of contradictions.

First, Engels in particular claims that not every aspect of the superstructure is determined by the economic base.[9] He emphasizes the partial autonomy of the superstructure, in that each element within

101

it has a degree of independence from, and influence upon, the workings of the base. Thus Engels discusses how legal codes are not a simple expression of class domination; how magical and spiritual theories have a partially independent source; how State power reacts back upon the character of economic development; and how ideology, although developing for economic reasons, may react upon the very forces that produced it. Engels says that we can see the 'dialectical' interaction of cause and effect, between base and the elements in the superstructure. Such ever-present interaction is, however, always unequal, since the 'economic movement' is 'by far the strongest, most primeval, most decisive' (Marx and Engels, 1962b, p. 496). However, this is a very imprecise formulation; let us look rather at Marx's own discussion of the CMP, the capitalist mode of production, beginning with the Introduction to the *Grundrisse* (Marx, 1973).

In the CMP the capitalist relations of production determine the place and broad influence of all the other elements or parts of that society. It is capital which is 'the all-dominating economic power of bourgeois society' (Marx, 1973, p. 107). Thus, the place and function of agriculture can only be understood in terms of its domination by capital within the structure of the capitalist mode. We must locate all elements by the relationship which they bear to one another within the developed mode of capitalist production. So, although one might expect that we should study such a society by tracing the historical development of the various elements, in fact we must start the other way round. For example, the techniques and methods of organization of agriculture should be studied at the end of the analysis and not at the beginning.

More generally, Marx considers how the same social phenomenon, such as a particular type of agriculture or of merchant-capital, may be present in different modes of production. We must always establish the connections of such a phenomenon with the particular elements comprising the structure of each of the different forms of society within which it is present. Thus, we must consider how merchant-capital operates in the capitalist as opposed to the feudal mode: what connections it has with other elements, what functions it serves, and so on. We can only comprehend it adequately by analysing it in relation to all the other elements of capitalism and especially to the general domination of capital.

Marx makes two claims about the structure of any type of society. First, in the completed capitalist mode, as in any other organic system, each element or part is both causally interrelated with every other element and is also a condition of functioning of those elements. Second, the social relations of production dominate all the other elements in the mode; thus, in capitalism it is the social relations of capital and labour which are dominant. Marx attempts to reconcile reciprocal interaction and functional interdependence on the one hand, and the dominance of the economic on the other, through the claim that it is the economic base which determines the character of the reciprocal interrelations. It is the base which determines the 'specific gravity' of each of the elements and of their relationships with each other. It is the base whose condition 'assigns rank and influence' to the other elements within a particular society (Marx, 1973, p. 107). But it is problematic whether this is consistent with the claim of functional interdependence; for example, with the claim that the base functionally requires a particular superstructure and the superstructure requires a given base. We can partly see how Marx tries to solve this problem of the possible divergence between the symmetrical character of the functional relationships and the asymmetrical character of the base's dominant relationship with the superstructure, by presenting his analysis of the economic base.

So far we have talked of the economic base as being composed of the relations of production. We can gain a fuller understanding of this by seeing what Marx says about production in the *Grundrisse*. He criticizes two accounts given of the relations between production, distribution, exchange, and circulation, and then provides his own.[10] First, there is the 'most shallow' account provided by some economists in which the four elements, each subject to its own general laws, are seen as conceptually distinct from each other, and involved in a simple, sequential chain of interactions. Second, there is the Hegelian approach which, through a criticism of the lack of organic unity posited between the elements in the shallow account, maintains the conceptual identity of production, distribution, exchange, and circulation. Marx criticizes both of these interpretations. His account emphasizes the organic connections of the different elements, the functional dependence of certain elements on others, and the predominance of production.

For Marx production and distribution are 'the reverse sides' of each other. Thus wages, which are an aspect of distribution, are implied by the existence of wage-labour, which is an aspect of production. Likewise wages imply the existence of wage-labour. So we have the mutual functional (and conceptual) interdependence of wages and wage-labour. But furthermore, according to Marx, production dominates distribution. Thus we see Marx trying to reconcile two claims: that production and distribution are functionally dependent upon each other; and that production predominates over distribution.

Marx attempts to deal with this difficulty partly by developing a more complex concept of production. He does not think that every aspect of distribution is determined by production, since there are aspects of distribution (as well as of exchange and circulation), which are properly regarded as what he calls 'factors of production', and are thus part of production. Thus the distribution of people among the means of production is part of production and also determines the distribution of products between people, which is part of distribution. Thus distribution, exchange and circulation can be divided into those elements which are 'factors of production' and those which are not. Further, Marx argues that while production, distribution, exchange and circulation 'all form the members of a totality, distinctions within a unity' (Marx, 1973, p. 99), they are not identical as on the Hegelian account. Marx posits two different levels at which interaction takes place between these different elements.

Firstly, within production in the wider sense there is a narrowly defined 'mutual interaction' between production and the 'factors of production' of distribution, exchange and circulation. Second, production in this wider sense predominates over the other aspects of distribution, exchange and circulation, although there is some degree of unequal interaction. Furthermore, although not said in this passage, it is production in this wider sense, which is itself a set of mutually interdependent elements, which determines the 'specific gravity' of the remaining elements in each society. We must now consider production in more detail beginning with the analysis of commodities.

Commodity production occurs where the producers of goods not only produce for themselves but also for sale on the market. In the buying and selling of such goods relatively uniform quantitative relationships are established between each type of good. Marx terms these relationships, 'exchange-values'. Where there is a developed system of exchange these are normally expressed in money terms. Commodities are goods whose utility or use-value is distinct from their exchange-value. Furthermore, according to Marx, the exchange of these commodities expresses the social character of production. Such exchanges are, in a way, exchanges of the activity of the different producers engaged in the production of each commodity. Thus the relation between commodities, the exchange-relation between things (which can be taken as the price of commodities) is essentially a relation between people, the producers of the different commodities. Moreover, if we consider all of these different exchanged commodities the only characteristic which they share is that they are all the product of human labour, albeit of different amounts.

This common labour component of all commodities is the basis of Marx's theory of value. The value of a commodity is given by the amount of labour embodied in it as measured in standard social units.[11] It is distinguished from use-value, because while the latter refers to the relation between a person and a thing (that is, how useful the thing is for a person), value is an expression of the relations between people, between the producers of the different commodities. It is also distinguished from the exchange-value of a commodity. The 'exchange-value' sometimes refers to market prices, othertimes to long run equilibrium prices. The value of a commodity determines these long run prices, or 'prices of production'. However, exactly how values and prices are related depends upon the particular form of commodity production. Let us now present Marx's characterization of the different forms of such production. In so doing we will move from simple commodity production to Marx's partially completed and complex theory of the CMP. At each stage restrictive assumptions are discarded, although all four stages represent idealizations.

In simple commodity production, independent producers own their own means of production and there is no hiring of labour by one group or class. Values equal and determine prices. In the second stage not everyone owns means of production. Owners therefore employ non-owners, and receive profit from the employment of their capital. This arises because the workers or non-owners produce more value than they are paid for. Such surplus-value is the source of capitalists' profits, these being proportional to the quantities of labour employed in each enterprise. Values still determine and equal prices. In the third stage, free competition is introduced between the different branches of production. Values no longer equal prices but depart from them systematically. Marx says that only in the aggregate are values equivalent to prices. In the different branches of production there is variation in the organic composition of capital, that is, in the ratio of constant to variable capital. Values are higher, lower, or the same as prices such that the rate of profit (ratio of surplus-value to constant and variable capital) is equalized throughout the economy. In the fourth stage Marx introduces landed property and mercantile and money-lending capital as further elements, although these were historically present during the earlier stages. Surplus-value is not here completely absorbed by profit, but also furnishes the source of rent and interest. Values still diverge from prices in the way described in the third stage.[12]

In this simplified account we can see how Marx explains the more obvious and easily identifiable features of capitalism. Prices, profit, rent and interest are explained in terms of the central structural mechanism of the capitalist mode. Profits, rent and interest are derived from the rate of surplus-value, prices from values and variations in the organic composition of capital. For Marx any explanation of these features of capitalism which fails to articulate the process by which value is produced and partially appropriated by capital is false, and constitutes part of the ideological superstructure of that society.

Let us now consider aspects of this argument in more detail in the following three sections: the nature of surplus-value and the development of classes; the analysis of those mechanisms found in non-capitalist modes of production analogous to the appropriation of surplus-value within capitalism; the use of models, abstractions and idealizations.

3 Surplus-value and the development of classes

For Marx the mode of production which existed in western Europe prior to capitalism was that of feudalism. Here the lord receives his income by directly appropriating part of the product or value of the product produced by the serf (or by compulsory labour-services). There is nothing concealed about the process. Because of political force and legalized custom it is clear that the lord will alienate part of what the serf produces. In capitalism, however, the fact of appropriation is concealed. There is freedom of choice for both employers and employees, for producers and consumers. There is competition between individuals to buy and sell labour and to buy and sell commodities. No single individual controls the price of labour or of commodities. Each individual worker is able to work for whom he wishes. The relationship of labour and capital seems to be an example of a free and equal exchange relationship. It appears to be economically insignificant and analysable like any other relationship. There seems to be no special need for the political economy of capitalism. Moreover, the rewards that accrue to labour and capital are analysable in similar ways. Both are factors of production and both are paid for their specific contribution to production. Profits are the reward for the contribution of capital, just as wages are the reward to labour.

Marx however argues that the capital : labour relationship is different from other economic relationships, and that the payments to capital and labour are not analogous. Profit is a residual which results from the specific features of the CMP.[13] Marx says (1973, pp. 283–4) that

> because the worker receives the equivalent in the form of
> money, the form of general wealth, he is in this exchange an
> equal *vis-à-vis* the capitalist, like every other part in exchange;
> at least, so he *seems*. In fact this equality is already disturbed
> because the worker's relation to the capitalist as a use value . . .
> is a presupposition of this seemingly simple exchange.

He is of use-value to the capitalist because the capitalist buys his *labour-power*, his capacity to labour over a given period of time. The capitalist pays to the worker the value of his labour-power, that is, no more than the amount of wages necessary to sustain him and his family in food, clothing, housing and so on. What in fact induces the capitalist to buy each worker's labour-power is that such power produces an amount of value greater than the value of his labour-power. This difference constitutes surplus-value and is the source of the capitalist's profits. Surplus-value thus arises in the process of production as a consequence of the existence of labour-time for which the worker is unpaid. The ratio of such unpaid, or surplus, labour time to necessary labour time (that period in which the value created by the worker is equivalent to the value of commodities he must receive for himself and his family to live) is the rate of exploitation.

What is it about the capitalist mode which generates the contrast between the apparently free exchange of equivalents and the actual exploitation of labour by capital? In the CMP the worker is not only free to sell his labour-power but *has* to sell it in order to live. This is because he does not own any of the means of production. He is forced to sell his labour-power to that class of people who have monopolized the ownership of such means. Free choice is limited to choosing for which of the owners of capital one will work. Thus the exchange relations within capitalism are dominated by production in the wider sense which we outlined earlier.

Furthermore, we may note the self-sustaining nature of the process described by Marx. The worker is forced to sell labour-power; that power is used to create value, including surplus-value; this surplus-value is partly embodied in capital owned by the capitalist; the worker is further forced to sell labour-power, and so on. Marx thus points out that capitalist production not only produces commodities, value and surplus-value, but it also *reproduces* the social relations between capitalist and wage-labourers which are the very basis of production. In general all modes of production sustain themselves by continually reproducing the social relations of production pre-supposed by their functioning. One significant consequence of this is that classes are themselves functions of the process of production. Class relationships are for Marx generated within and by the fundamental structure of the capitalist mode.[14]

Labour and capital, the two central elements within the CMP, are defined functionally in terms of the dependence of labour on capital. The relationship between labour and capital is structured exploitatively through the capitalist appropriation of surplus-value created by labour. The nature of wage-labour is determined by this mode of appropriation. The central relations of production are the relations of exploitation. Each mode of production is associated with the domination of a different class; in capitalism, there is dominance of capital and hence of the capitalist class. Capitalism is constituted by this antagonistic unity of opposites, of capital and labour.

We should note that at this level of analysis Marx is only concerned with specific structurally defined patterns of action from the members of the two classes, from the bearers of the capital and labour functions. Marx says that the characters who appear on the economic stage are but personifications of the economic relations existing between them. Any bearers of the capitalist function are taken to pursue certain ends, namely, to expand value, to subordinate enjoyment, and to accumulate. Each capitalist is forced to keep extending his capital, because of competition with other capitalists, because of technical change, and so on; one consequence is that this conflicts with the structurally imparted interests of the other class, that of wage-labourers. The relationship between the two classes is thus founded upon both dependence and conflict.

For Marx this capitalist : wage-labourer relationship is a specific example of his general characterization of modes of production as comprised of dichotomistically related classes, such as patrician and plebeian in Ancient society, or lord and vassal in feudalism. Yet, although we understand theoretically a mode by its central class relationship, there are always present in a society numbers of other social groupings in varying relations with each other (see, for example, Marx, 1960). But for Marx these other social groupings are explicable in terms of the basic structure of productive relationships within the society; they depend upon the specific modes of production and their interrelationship. We may classify these various social groupings as follows. First, there are *transitional* classes: either new classes which emerge out of an existent and soon to be obsolete mode, such as capitalist within feudalism; or, leftovers from the previous historically dominant mode, such as the feudal classes within industrial capitalism. Second, there are *sectors* of the major classes, such as managers within the capitalist class, or more problematically, the lumpenproletariat within the working class. Third, there are *intermediate* classes identifiable within all societies, such as the petit bourgeoisie or the 'new middle class' within capitalism. Finally, there are *quasi-classes* such as slaves in the Ancient mode or the peasantry in mediaeval Europe. Although they are generated by the structure of productive relationships, both lie outside the dominant dichotomous relationship.

Also, for Marx, the peasantry only constitutes a class-in-itself and not a class-for-itself (see Marx, 1963, pp. 123–5). This is because the organization of peasant production is such that the members of this class are unable to become conscious of their common interests, or to develop patterns of organized, class-conscious action. A class for Marx only properly exists when it assumes a directly *political* character. Social classes, then, are not merely elements of the economic base; class relationships are importantly determined by the superstructure. Any adequate analysis of classes must refer not only to their place and function within the relations of production but to the complex configuration of related constituents of any given mode of production, including the ideological superstructure, the state machinery, patterns of political action, and so on. They are then the overall effect within the field of social relations of the structure of the mode of production (see Poulantzas, 1973, pp. 57–98).

4 Pre-capitalist modes

We have already discussed some of the general properties of modes of production, such as the sorts of causal and functional relations that are found within them. But we have so far concentrated on Marx's analysis of the capitalist mode. This of course reflects his own primary interest. Let us now consider whether, when he studies other forms of society, he also provides realist-type descriptions of structures and structural mechanisms.

Marx is interested in the various forms of society that lie, historically and analytically, between primitive communal society, on the one hand, and capitalism, on the other. Marx identifies a number of such forms, Asiatic, Ancient, Germanic, and Feudal. He has however often been criticized for adhering to a philosophy of history in which certain historical laws, universally and inevitably, determine the movement from one form to another, specifically from feudalism to capitalism and then to communism.[15] But this interpretation is questionable. Rather Marx analyses structurally these different modes. In a couple of cases he outlines their central structural mechanism (the enforced extraction of surplus product in feudalism), mentions features that led to their historical emergence from some previous mode, and specifies their internal contradictions that may generate disintegration and transition. His main concern is to analyse these different modes, so that we can explain features of any particular society in terms of the interrelationships between them. Such relationships may be, either, of one mode as dominant, as in the case of capitalism in late nineteenth-century Britain, or of a period of transition with no dominant mode, as in seventeenth-century Britain (see Balibar, 1970, pp. 273–308). Let us now mention the main pre-capitalist forms which Marx analyses.[16]

First, there is the *Asiatic* mode founded upon tribal or community property. The organization of both agriculture and manufacture is self-sustaining within each local community. Where there is central organization a proportion of the surplus product is used to support the expenditure of the larger community on war, irrigation or communication. There are no cities founded upon production but they may develop because of external trade. In the *Ancient* mode the fundamental social relation of production is that of chattel-slavery. This is linked to the growth of cities and of communal city property, including that of slaves. In the *Germanic* mode neither the village community nor the city constitutes the basic unit. Rather each separate household contains an entire economy. The existence of each household is guaranteed by the loose links between it and the other homesteads. Finally, there is the *Feudal* mode. Let us quote Marx's description of this (1962, p. 772), so illustrating the identification of a mechanism and structure which is analogous to that within capitalism:

> The specific economic form, in which unpaid surplus-labour is pumped out of direct producers, determines the relationship of rulers and ruled, as it grows directly out of production itself and in turn, reacts upon it as a determining element . . . It is always the direct relationship of the owners of the conditions of production to the direct producers . . . which reveals the innermost secret, the hidden basis of the entire social structure, and with it the political form of the relation of sovereignty and dependence . . . the labour of the direct producer . . . is still separated in space and time from his labour for the landlord, and the latter appears directly in the brutal form of enforced labour for a third person.

Within capitalism the production of value and surplus-value occur simultaneously. In the feudal mode, however, necessary-labour and surplus-labour are distinct processes. Surplus-labour cannot be extracted without the particular combination of economic and political power. It is this power which forces the direct producer to labour for his landlord as well as to labour for himself.

Marx's discussion of these modes of production is generally sketchy and incomplete. In the Ancient mode he outlines the importance of internal contradictions which bring about the disintegration of that form of society. In the case of the feudal mode he describes the emergence of the new structure of productive relationships centred in the towns which emerges from within the womb of the old society. But much of the time he is only interested in these modes to the degree to which they elucidate aspects of the capitalist mode. Thus he is concerned with why, in western Europe, capitalists and wage-labourers could emerge only from within the feudal mode and not from within other modes.

Finally, let us consider the distinction between 'dominance' and 'determination'. In the CMP, the social relations of production are dominant, although we have noted the mutual but one-sided interactions between the elements comprising the mode. However, if we consider other modes of production, the situation is different. Marx says (1965, p. 81n.):

> my view . . . that the economic structure, is the real basis on which the juridical and political superstructure is raised, and to which definite forms of thought correspond . . . all this is very true for our own times, in which material interests preponderate, but not for the middle ages, in which Catholicism, nor for Athens and Rome, where politics, reigned supreme . . . This much, however, is clear, that the middle ages could not live on Catholicism, nor the ancient world on politics. On the contrary, it is the mode in which they gained a livelihood that explains why here politics, and there Catholicism, played the chief part.

Thus, in these other modes the relations of production are not *dominant*; but such relations *determine* the way in which some other structural element, such as religion or politics, dominates. For example, it is held that Marx believes that kinship relations are dominant in primitive communal society because of the particular character of the primitive economic base.[17]

5 Abstraction and idealization

It is said that Marx's analysis of capitalism, how he constructs his model and theory of the capitalist mode through the four stages of commodity production (outlined in section 2), employs the *logical-historical* method (see Meek, 1973, Introduction and Appendix). By this is meant that Marx's method of constructing progressively more complex models of reality, or 'logical stages', approximately mirrors the manner in which capitalist-dominated societies have developed historically from pre-capitalist formations. However, the 'logical' and the 'historical' do not perfectly mirror each other for two reasons. First, actual historical development is always highly complex, full of events and incidents irrelevant to the general development of a society.[18] Second, and more important, Marx's 'corrected history' requires the abstraction and idealization of relationships which were historically more complex. Only after these relationships have been elucidated can other features, like merchant-capital, be introduced into the model.[19]

For Marx this logical analysis is the means by which he both arrives at and presents his theory of the central mechanism and general structural description of the capitalist mode. Furthermore, because it is 'historical' as well as 'logical', there is a specific basis for the models of the different stages. This is provided by the actual historical development in western Europe, and particularly by the transition from feudalism to capitalism. That history suggests the main lines of development and the central relationships. He uses it to construct the models of the different stages. We may also note that Marx thinks that the goal of the model is to enable us to establish a structural analysis of different forms of society. Models are thus used by Marx to provide descriptions of structures.

Throughout his political economy Marx makes many simplifying assumptions. For example, when analysing the origin of profit through the specific properties of the commodity of labour, he assumes that value equals price in all branches of production. By making such assumptions, 'the phenomena may be observed in their purity, and our observations not interfered with by disturbing circumstances that have nothing to do with the process in question' (Marx, 1965, p. 166n.). Furthermore, Marx's account of the central relationship discussed in his political economy, namely that between capital and labour, involves both abstraction and idealization. This can be seen in two ways. First, within that mode of production all social relations apart from this one are initially assumed away. The capital-labour relationship is then what is extracted from the mass of social relations, some of which are introduced back into the analysis at a later stage. Second, Marx concentrates upon that aspect of the relationship between labour and capital which is for him central. There are other aspects of the relationship which he might have analysed. As it is, he simplifies and idealizes the relation between capital and labour to one of exploitation.

It is sometimes said that Marx constructs an ideal type of capitalism with which actual societies can be compared; and that in so doing he follows Max Weber (see Weber, 1949, pp. 90–112). For Weber reality is infinite and can be divided up in an infinity of different ways. Weber argues that the social scientist should self-consciously construct ideal types, one-sided exaggerations of reality that form conceptually coherent wholes, and which provide points of comparison with, and suggest fruitful hypotheses about, the real world. There are two reasons why Marx's approach differs from this. First, Weber argues that one constructs that ideal type which is most useful or appropriate for one's particular scientific purposes at the moment. Marx however believes that there is a central structural mechanism within capitalism and that it is necessary to organize one's concepts so as to grasp *its* essential features successfully. The omission of some aspects of capitalism and the purification of others is forced on one by the need to produce the correct description of the relations between capital and labour. Secondly, Marx does not believe, as Weber appears to, that we construct our models and develop our theories simply by the process of abstraction from, and idealization of, the concrete social relations found within actual societies. For, since certain modes of production, especially capital-

112

ism, are so structured that they present themselves to their members in such a way that their underlying and central mechanisms are obscured, any process of concept formation which is based on the way society presents itself will be inadequate, misleading and ideological. To use the visual metaphor, abstractions and idealizations based on appearances cannot hope to represent or capture reality. Further, we have noted that Marx's theoretical object in *Capital* and in most of his later writing is the capitalist mode of production in general. Any attempt to develop such a theory by abstracting from a given society is misleading since within such a society there are always co-present more than one mode of production.[20] It is often said that in building models of society, that is, systematizing social reality, it is necessary to abstract from, and idealize, social life. Now although Marx's models are represented in an abstracted and idealized way, it is not the case that his model is generated by abstracting and idealizing actual capitalist societies. For the realist, and for Marx, the fact of abstraction and idealization is not what is crucial to the production of models of different structures.

Finally, in our consideration of Marx's method of abstraction in his political economy, let us analyse his apparently most systematic discussion (see Marx, 1973, pp. 100f.). He says that when we consider a given society, we are tempted to begin by considering its population, the way in which it is distributed into classes, its distribution within towns and country, the occupational structure, its imports and exports, and so on. But the concept of population is inadequate unless we know of what classes that population is constituted. We then need to be able to identify each of the elements constituting the classes, wage-labour, capital, and so on. Likewise these elements demand analysis of exchange, division of labour, prices, value, and money. Thus although we commence from the concrete we are forced to proceed from there to less and less complex abstractions until we arrive at the simplest determinations. This method of political economy, that which proceeds from the concrete to 'abstract general principles' (that is, partial and one-sided), is criticized by Marx for failing to make the return journey. For Marx the correct method is as follows. First, any scientific analysis must begin with a certain preliminary observation and conceptualization. But second, the scientific method proper is to use the abstract general principles to reconstitute the concrete as a highly complex combination of many determinations, 'a unity of the diverse' (Marx, 1973, p. 101). We analyse how the objects of analysis are determined by the complex combinations of relations between the various abstractly realized notions. Thus, a given social group is not seen abstractly but as determined by the 'rich totality of many determinations and relations' (Marx, 1973, p. 100).

This analysis is for a number of reasons problematic.[21] The difficulties appear to result from his attempt to state his methodological position in terms of the single contrast between abstract and concrete; just as earlier we mentioned how it is problematic to characterize his methodology merely in terms of the appearance–reality distinction. Our description of his method has been more complex. It has centred on his clear intention to produce descriptions of structures of modes of production. But it is exactly this consideration that is missing in the description of his method in the passage we have just discussed. In the final section of this chapter we shall examine some further aspects of Marx's analysis of modes of production in general.

6 Function and contradiction in modes of production

Marx sees any mode of production as multi-faceted, complex and holistic.[22] Each mode is a specific and determinate combination of distinct and interdependent structures and processes. Such elements are functionally related to each other. Thus, within the capitalist mode, the economic base is functionally dependent upon the superstructure, and the superstructure is functionally dependent on the base. Further, any mode is unified through the specific structure that is dominant within it. In capitalism the economic base determines the causal rank and influence of each constituent structural element. It is the social relations of production between labour and capital which give to the capitalist mode its irreducible unity, although they in turn cannot exist without certain superstructural elements. But whilst there are functional alternatives to superstructural elements, such as aspects of particular legal systems, there are no such alternatives to the relations of production between labour and capital, since it is they which are definitive of capitalism.

Despite these claims of functional interdependence, Marx does not attempt to explain the origins or the persistence of some element in terms of its being functionally required by some other element or by the structure as a whole. That is, Marx does not employ functionalist explanation.[23] However, his analysis of modes of production does depend on the establishment of functional interrelationships between its elements. Thus he claims that there are certain functional needs that must be satisfied for a particular mode to exist. For example, within capitalism there is the functional need for 'bourgeois ideology'. This does not mean however that we should explain the existence of such ideology merely by demonstrating that it is in the interests of the dominant class, or that it can be shown to serve functions for the structure as a whole. This sort of functionalist explanation is inadequate for Marx. A satisfactory explanation would require the analysis of the co-presence of various modes of production, their changing historical relationships, the specific social formations that result, and so on. Further, unlike orthodox functionalist analysis, the functional interdependencies which Marx identifies are only to be understood within the context of the relations of domination that have characterized all forms of society, apart from primitive communism, up to the present. Such social relations are always based for Marx on the contradiction between the dominant and the dominated class. At the centre of his analysis is the concept of contradiction. Any structure is in some way a unification of opposites. Thus a mode of production is founded upon contradiction between its two constituent elements. Let us consider this by analysing two of the functional needs of the CMP.

The first need is for agents who perform the capitalist function; buying labour-power, directing the use of such power in capitalist enterprises, converting money into capital, and so on. The second need is for agents who perform the labour function; selling labour-power and producing exchange-value for the capitalist. These are functional needs that have to be realized for capitalism to exist and for the system to be reproduced. But they are at the same time incompatible with each other. They form a contradiction which is at the very basis of the mode of production. This is because the structured interests of the agents are incompatible with each other. Each capitalist is forced to compete with other capitalists and the organization of production is such that he must continuously seek to expand his profits through accumulation. But the expansion of his profits is at the direct expense of those who provide labour-power. In the short-run (and given a constant level of exploitation), anything which increases the proportion of exchange-value which goes to the capitalist must reduce that which wage-labourers receive. In the longer run the situation is more complex. The interests of capitalists and wage-labourers remain structurally antagonistic though both profits and wages may rise. But there is still conflict between the shares received by the two classes. As Marx says (1933, p. 39):

> If, therefore, the income of the worker increases with the rapid growth of capital, there is at the same time a widening of the social chasm that divides the worker from the capitalist, an increase in the power of capital over labour, a greater dependence of labour on capital.

Thus, for Marx, those elements which reproduce the capital-labour relationship, the basis of the capitalist mode, simultaneously produce a structural contradiction that threatens its continued existence. Labour and capital are separate from each other, antagonistic, but unified within the structure. Marx's analysis of contradictions and

115

his concept of the dialectic are controversial and we will only examine certain aspects here.[24]

For Marx each contradictory relationship is reconcilable given particular material circumstances. The contradiction between labour and capital can be overcome provided the structure, of which they are the basic elements, namely the CMP, is itself superseded. But such transformations depend upon specific historical mediations. In particular, they are only made possible by the fact that all modes of production are founded upon a number of contradictions – although in each mode one is primary, the others secondary. In capitalism the primary contradiction is between the forces of production and the relations of production. Marx claims that a single contradiction will not by itself generate a new higher unity. Rather this can only result from specific sets of contradictions working through their interdependent effect upon the structure of which they are part. Also, it is not that there are specific elements which somehow happen to contradict each other. For Marx each pair of contradictory elements is generated by a single structural cause. Such elements cannot be reconciled within the given structure. For example, the process of production of surplus value reproduces the contradiction of labour and capital. Similarly, the growth in the size and inter-dependence of capitalist industrial enterprises, that is, the development of the forces of production, has the effect of raising the total amounts of surplus and profit received by the capitalist which are necessary for further development, and also of increasing the degree of organization of wage-labourers within and between different workplaces and hence of heightening class conflict.

This completes our account of Marx. We have argued that his methodology is analogous to that of the realist in the natural sciences. However, from the standpoint of this interpretation there are certain central problems in his analysis. For the realist the aspects of his work which have to be developed are summarized in the question: how do we apply his models and theories of different modes of production to actual societies?

A first problem lies in how we can identify the degree to which any mode of production dominates a given society. We need criteria to detect the empirical presence of the given theoretical entities to be found in Marx's analysis. We also need to know how to examine the relationship between two or more modes present in a society. Further, we have to be able to assess how many and what sorts of social events can be explained in terms of the structures of these modes. Such a structural analysis may only explain the general character of historical development and not the particular events or their details. We saw in chapter 3 that the explanation of particular events in the natural sciences involves more than a structural analysis.

But if this is so in the case of Marx, we have to identify what other types of consideration are involved and their relationship to the analysis of the structures of the different modes of production. In Marx, also, there are great difficulties in the explanation of transition from the dominance of one mode to the dominance of another. Any account depends upon the analysis of contradictions. But it is unclear whether they determine what happens, or merely set limits. There is a need for a theory of the conjunction of contradictions. Just as the realist in the natural sciences criticizes the view that causal explanation is provided by a list of conditions or factors, so here also we need not merely a list of contradictions but a theory specifying the consequences of specific patterns of their accumulation and exacerbation. The degree to which Marx is able to explain particular forms of class-consciousness, class-action and especially revolutionary action, is problematic. We also need to elaborate a theory of class and revolutionary consciousness.

These are the sorts of issues and problems involved in a realist-interpretation of Marx. This interpretation must be evaluated alongside many others, including the humanistic and the positivistic. In the latter, Marx is not seen as involved in the descriptions of structures and of their interrelationships, but in a different sort of intellectual undertaking. As a consequence, quite different problems and deficiencies are identified in his analysis. For the positivist the goal of science is the discovery of sets of general laws to explain particular events, by showing them to be instances of these laws. Marx is thus evaluated for his success in formulating empirically supported social and historical laws. He is criticized because of the way in which his ethical beliefs and political values apparently enter into and distort the methods and findings of his economic and social analysis; and because of the untestable nature of many of the laws that he posits, such as the general pronouncements about man and nature and the dialectics of labour. Other items in his analysis are regarded as testable but refuted by empirical evidence; for example, the prediction of working class revolution in advanced capitalist society. Also, the positivist criticizes Marx for using concepts that make little or no reference to measurable or observable phenomena. The concept of value has often been dismissed as metaphysical. However, Marx is credited with the discovery of some correct empirical laws, such as the increasing concentration of ownership within capitalism. For the positivist, Marx's work must be purged of its metaphysical elements, and can then be exploited as a useful source of empirically testable propositions.[25]

Lukács writes (1971, p. 1):

Let us assume . . . that recent research had disproved once and

117

for all every one of Marx's individual theses . . . Orthodox
Marxism . . . does not imply the uncritical acceptance of the
results of Marx's investigations. It is not the 'belief' in this or
that thesis, nor the exegesis of a 'sacred' book. On the contrary,
orthodoxy refers exclusively to *method*. It is the scientific
conviction that dialectical materialism is the road to truth and
that its methods can be developed, expanded and deepened only
along the lines laid down by its founders.

To the extent that this quotation is a rebuttal of the positivist interpretation of Marx we support it. And in this chapter we have
attempted to describe what we take to be the nature of Marx's
method.

6 Structure and structuralism

1 Structural approaches

In our discussion of Marx's political economy we often referred to the 'structure' of the capitalist mode of production, and to the underlying structure and structural mechanisms of different modes. Indeed, Marx's realist method is clearly displayed in his structural analysis of different modes of production present in various social formations. A realist social science will typically involve a structural analysis. However, the use of the term 'structure' or 'social structure' does not mean that the writer in question adopts a realist position in the social sciences. There are many different structural and structuralist methods and theories: for example, Chomskyan linguistics, structural-functionalism in anthropology, Marxist structuralism, Lévi-Straussian and French structuralism, and so on. It has been argued however, that there is a single structuralist method appropriate to all fields of at least human study,[1] from anthropology to literature, from politics to linguistics. But this view has been questioned by others who argue that there are only specific structural theories found within the context of different disciplines, such as linguistics or anthropology; there is no single structuralist method to analyse and evaluate.[2]

In this chapter we will argue that although there are certain common features of most types of structuralist analysis, there are significant differences between them. But we can best locate these differences by making use of the categories developed in part 1. We will analyse positivist, realist, and instrumentalist conceptions of structure. Thus our identification of the distinctive nature of each form of structuralism will be based not upon the disciplinary context but upon the differing conceptions of science they presuppose.

Let us begin by outlining some common features of most forms of structural analysis. First, there is commitment to the view that the

119

relations between the constituent element of a structure are more important than the individual elements; and indeed that the elements themselves are comprised of sets of relations. Marx, as we saw, argues that the class-position of wage-labourers cannot be defined or analysed except in terms of its relationship with the capitalist class. In anthropology it is claimed that a kinship system must be understood by analysing the set of relationships between terms (brother, sister, mother, etc.), each of which is defined and analysed through its relations to some or all of the other terms. Or, it has been said that the cultural significance of one type of jacket cannot be identified without understanding its relationship both to other jackets and to the other constituents of a person's clothing.

Some further aspects of the notion of structure can be seen from these examples. There is the implication of regular, systematic and orderly relations between the elements which comprise the structure. Thus the structure of the capitalist mode, or of kinship, or of the clothing system, consists of given, patterned and relatively enduring relationships. These form a structure or system; and some of its properties cannot be understood without considering the total set of relationships or the totality. Thus, taking an architectural example, we can only identify the features of the Palladian style from the overall structure discernible within such buildings and not from any single element (classical columns) or related pair of elements (columns and pediment). This raises a further point. When we refer to the structure of a building we are not referring to an observable property such as height or size.[3] A structure is not something that can be directly perceived by our senses. The concept of structure involves abstraction from the observable properties of any such building.

From this outline of common features, it is not difficult to see where serious differences of method and approach will arise: the nature of the relational properties, the sorts of elements relationally analysed, the explanation of the structure's orderly character, the nature of the totality, the forces which produce or maintain wholeness, the relationship between one structure and another, and, most importantly, the relationship between the 'structure' and physical or social reality. Let us consider this last problem by noting two sorts of interpretation that might be given of the relationship between a building and its structure.

On the first, the structure of a building may be taken to consist of the way in which building materials are assembled and combined together to produce an object created for particular purposes and serving certain functions. In our representation of such a structure we may use arrows, for example, to symbolize the pressures exerted by one element upon other elements. If our model of that structure is correct then each arrow will represent a set of given physical facts. We picture these physical facts by means of the arrow. However, they are nonetheless physical realities which comprise the structure of the building. That structure is not immediately visible to us but it is nevertheless present. We have a model of that structure pictorially symbolized by the arrow; the structure is the concealed but physically real relations between certain elements comprising that building.

On the second interpretation, it is argued that because we cannot directly perceive a structure, we have to consider the concept of structure as essentially a fictional construction. A structure is a mental construct formulated to provide a simple and economical device, to predict observable features of the phenomenon in question. The structure is not intended to conform to the object, such as the building; but is merely instrumental in enabling predictions about the object, such as its stress behaviour, to be made. The significant issue in this instrumentalist interpretation is whether the relationships postulated in the structure are predictively fruitful.

Let us consider the implications of this discussion for the analysis of social structure. On the one hand, we can identify the positivist and realist conceptions of structure; on the other, the instrumentalist.[4] For the latter, as we have said, the content of any structural analysis is given by its predictive fruitfulness. There are different kinds of instrumentalist study: first, limited empirical studies where there is prediction of correlation coefficients between a small number of specific variables (for example, income, education, racial attitudes); and second, systems analyses in which a system is defined mathematically in terms of a number of equations, and predictions are mathematically deduced about major properties of the system as a whole. These constitute the part-positivist and part-instrumentalist type of study referred to and discussed briefly in the final section of chapter 4.

We will now consider analyses in which 'structure' is taken to reside in some sense in the object itself. Here we will distinguish positivist and realist conceptions. For the positivist to talk about the social structure is to talk of the laws and regularities found to obtain between observable phenomena. For the realist a structure consists of the system of relationships which underlie and account for the sets of observable social relations and patterns of social consciousness. We will now fill out these two conceptions by first considering a clear case of the former, the positivist analysis of social structure in British social anthropology.[5]

Radcliffe-Brown, for example, argues that it is the task of the scientist to identify and record the law-like regularities of the natural and social world and ultimately to produce a system of universal laws of the universe. Such regularities can be observed through our senses. Reality consists of more or less observable phenomena which are related to each other. Any particular observation can be explained by being shown to be an instance of a general law. Scientific concepts are empirical since they refer to these observable phenomena. Thus, for Radcliffe-Brown and for British social anthropology in general, the concept of social structure is seen positivistically. It refers to the totality of empirically given social relationships within each tribal society. Social structure is given in the observation of each society. Structural analysis refers to the detailed description of the observed patterns of social relations, particularly dyadic, and of the social institutions that are discovered. This detailed observation of social life, from which in a fairly unproblematic way we can identify the structure of a society, is achieved by the research method of fieldwork. The constituent social institutions are seen as essentially systems of norms which can be inferred by the anthropologist in the field. The totality of a society is seen as functionally organized so that each institution is 'functional' for the system as a whole. The organization of society is thus taken to have a functional unity or wholeness.

Let us consider some implications of this general methodological position by briefly discussing one of its more sophisticated theoretical applications. Nadel's position in *The Theory of Social Structure* is based on the concept of role and on the properties of role systems (see Nadel, 1957). Social structure is that ordered arrangement of the social relationships which occur between people as a consequence of their playing of roles relative to one another. The role system provides the matrix of the social structure, and most of the book consists of analysis of the properties of roles and role systems. In considering an individual role we can analyse the temporal nature of its enactment, the context within which it is enacted, whether its underlying properties are ascribed or achieved, and whether there is a 'halo' effect (for example, the teacher didactic outside as well as inside school). In considering a role system we can analyse the degrees of role summation, the number of roles linked together within a single person; of role coherence, the interrelatedness of roles within a system; and of role dependence or independence, the enactment of roles *vis-à-vis* specific other roles or the society in general. Nadel also argues that the ordered arrangement of groups and sub-groups is only a special case of the general relatedness of role relationships. All such relationships can be analysed in terms of two criteria: the degree of command over another's actions, where the role involves specific relationships with actors in other roles; and the degree of command over existing benefits and resources, where an actor plays a role *via-à-vis* a general public.

Nadel maintains that we have to develop a strictly positional picture of society, in which we bracket off the aims, needs, ideas and emotions involved in human behaviour. The identification of social structure is thus realized by abstracting from the qualitative relationships between people. This positional picture is, however, still grounded in concrete reality although partially abstracted from it. For Nadel structural analysis is not explanatory and consists of no more than a means of description. This denial of the explanatory function of his conception of social structure may seem odd, since we have so far suggested that Nadel's general methodological position is positivistic. But it follows because Nadel is assuming a non-positivist account of explanation; and on this view of explanation his structural analysis is descriptive and not explanatory.[6] This can be seen from the following (1957, pp. 150–1) where he contrasts his view of social structure with that of Lévi-Strauss, for whom

> structure is an explanatory construct meant to provide the key to the observed facts of social existence, the principles or formulae accounting for its character, and hence the logic behind social reality. I consider social structure . . . to be still the social reality itself, or an aspect of it, not the logic behind it, and I consider structural analysis to be no more than a descriptive method.

We can also note that Nadel claims that social structure should not be seen as a 'model', in the sense given to that term by Lévi-Strauss. He says that Lévi-Strauss regards models, and thus social structures, as logical constructions in the mind of the anthropologist, that have 'nothing to do with empirical reality' (see Nadel, 1957, pp. 149–50). Nadel suggests that to view social structure in this way is arbitrary and unhelpful, since it is then impossible to talk intelligibly of investigating or studying a society's structure: one does not investigate, in this sense, structures that exist only in the mind of the investigator. Thus Nadel rejects what we earlier called the 'instrumentalist' view of structures, and instead adopts a positivist one. But we have already suggested that there may be conceptions of social structure that are neither instrumentalist nor positivist, but realist. Indeed we will argue that Nadel is wrong in identifying Lévi-Strauss's position as straightforwardly instrumentalist since it is partially realist.

2 'Structuralism'

Let us now consider Lévi-Strauss and the 'structuralist' movement. Besides Lévi-Strauss's own work in anthropology, some of the other writers associated with this contemporary intellectual movement are: Lacan in psychoanalysis, Chomsky in linguistics, Foucault in the history of science, the Bourbaki school in mathematics, and Godelier in historical materialism.[7] We will commence our consideration of 'structuralism', and particularly our analysis of its realist elements, by noting its main features, bearing in mind that not all 'structuralists' adhere to all of them.

First, 'structuralists' argue that phenomena should not be broken down into their individual elements and studied atomistically. Rather each system must be studied as an organized set of inter-related elements. When we acquire knowledge of a set of signs, such as that of traffic lights, this is not the result of identifying the significance of each individual sign. Rather, we learn the system within which each sign finds its place and from which its significance derives. Red only means stop because green means go and vice versa. When we see red we see red-and-not-green. Each element is therefore only intelligible because of its relations with the other constituent elements.

Second, 'structuralists' seek to identify the structure which lies behind the directly observable and knowable social reality. Thus, if we consider language, it is clear that we are able to speak and to be understood although we are unaware of most of the grammatical rules of the language that we are speaking. Common to most 'structuralists' is some version of Saussure's distinction between *la langue* and *la parole* (see Saussure, 1960). The former is that structure of regularities which, within each natural language, underlies the utterances of native speakers; the latter refers to actual linguistic behaviour.

Third, most post-Saussurean linguists argue that behind both surface phenomena (which Chomsky calls linguistic-performance), and its structure (linguistic-competence), there is an innate genetically transmitted structuring mechanism within the mind. It is held that there are certain universal mental characteristics, which constitute the logic or code by which the human mind operates. 'Structuralism' is thus the analysis of the ways in which both surface and deep structural phenomena are expressions of the structural properties of the mind.

The fourth aspect of 'structuralism' follows another argument of Saussure's, namely, his advocacy of semiology, or the general science of signs. Here it is presumed that the methods and distinctions developed in the analysis of language can be applied to non-linguistic social activities which are nonetheless code-like in form. Just as the rules of English enable sequences of sound to have meaning, so certain rules of social life enable one to write a poem, score a goal, or prepare a meal. Semiology emphasizes the way in which meanings of events or objects in the social world are conventional or socially structured rather than natural. To give a brief example of the sort of distinction made, we can consider Barthes's analysis of the cultural system of food (see Barthes, 1967). He distinguishes between alimentary language, which consists of rules of exclusion and association, rituals of use, and the analysis of relevant oppositional terms (such as savoury/sweet); and alimentary speech, which consists of all the individual and family variations of preparation of, and association between, different items of food.

The fifth aspect of 'structuralism' is indicated by the oppositional relationship between savoury and sweet in Barthes's discussion of the food system. At the structural level it is held that various cultural systems can be analysed by means of binary oppositions – terms which are taken by specific social groups as mutually complementary. The warrant for this form of analysis lies in the work of the Prague School of linguists and their analysis of the phoneme.[8] They argued that any phonemic system could be economically and satisfactorily described in terms of a single and small set of a dozen or so binary oppositions (such as grave/acute). This was seen in a realist and not in an instrumentalist way; such oppositions reflecting something inherent in the nature of the mental processes of both encoder and decoder. Lévi-Strauss in particular presumes such binary oppositions to be the central categorizing process in the mind. He takes such oppositions to order both mind and nature.

Sixth, 'structuralists' usually make use of some version of Saussure's distinction between synchrony and diachrony. Prior to Saussure, linguists mainly analysed historical changes in individual linguistic items. When a language as a whole was analysed it was common for texts from quite different periods to be used as examples of such a language. Saussure, however, emphasized that one had to study the structure of each synchronically present language-system. Because different language-systems underlie the texts of the different periods, it is illegitimate to treat such texts as examples of a single language-system.

Finally, 'structuralists' try to identify isomorphic structures within different aspects of social life. They argue, either that such isomorphism is universal, or that the 'structuralist' method is one in which one tries to discover which structures are isomorphic. Lévi-Strauss thinks that 'structuralist' anthropology should become a science of relationships like economics or linguistics. Each would analyse a different form of communication (anthropology, of women(!); economics, of goods and services; and linguistics, of messages). As a result the 'structuralist' identifies systematic regularities between the rules of kinship, the rules of economic life, and linguistic rules, even claiming that they are all variants of a single set. Furthermore 'structuralists' analyse possible rules by which the structure of one type of communication is transformed into another. Thus, for example, Marx is said to have applied a rule of transformation to the capitalist economic base so as to produce the capitalist superstructure. Generally 'structuralists' are anti-causal and anti-historical in their methodological pronouncements. They argue that they are not interested in the cause of the structure of a group of myths; merely how that structure is the logical transformation from some other structure.

However, the claims that 'structuralists' are anti-causal and anti-historical are problematic. First, it seems that the kind of causal analysis that they oppose is a positivist one in which regular relations are established between logically independent events and phenomena. There is a failure to consider how causal explanation may take the realist form which we have been discussing. Thus, in our interpretation of Marx's argument, we saw him as identifying a complex causal relationship, of a realist rather than a positivist sort, between the capitalist base and particular superstructural forms. Second, the claim that 'structuralists' are not involved in historical analysis can be shown to be problematic if we consider Lévi-Strauss's analysis of the Oedipus myth. He argues that this myth is a logical technique to reconcile the belief in man's autochthony with the knowledge that he is in fact born of a man and a woman. The myth provides a socially structured solution to this central ontological problem. However, it has been argued that Lévi-Strauss's 'structuralist' explanation provides in fact an historical explanation involving assessable causal claims concerning the relation between problems of ontology and the content of a group of myths.

We will now examine the writings of two 'structuralists' in more detail. In so doing we must consider what sorts of relationships are being posited between the structure of the mind and social life, between the structural properties of different elements, between the surface and deep structure, and between structure and history. We will consider whether and in what ways Chomsky and Lévi-Strauss employ a realist methodology.

We can approach Chomsky's theory by the contrasts that he draws between it and two other approaches to linguistics.[9] First, Chomsky distinguishes his position from that of Saussure. This is because Saussure takes the object of linguistics to be the word, and argues that their combination into sentences is mainly a matter of individually free creation outside the sphere of linguistics proper. Apart from a few general patterns, syntax is a trivial matter relegated to *la parole* and is not part of *la langue*. Further, Saussure holds that the only proper methods of linguistics are segmentation and classification, essentially the construction of a taxonomy of linguistic items. Chomsky, however, argues that it is the syntactic structure of sentences which should be the object of linguistic theory; and that the Saussurean classification of the surface structure fails to identify the deep structure and the transformational operations by which the deep structure generates the surface structure.

Second, Chomsky distinguishes his position from that of

'empiricists' and 'behaviourists'. Besides B. F. Skinner's radical behaviourist theory in *Verbal Behaviour* Chomsky dissociates himself from the Bloomfieldian tradition, in which he was originally trained (see Skinner, 1957; Chomsky, 1959; and Bloomfield, 1935). Chomsky argues that these empiricist approaches to language and especially to its learning are inadequate for two reasons. First, for Bloomfield the only admissible scientific data are those which are directly observable or physically measurable. The empirically observable data are restricted to those utterances attested by their hearers as grammatical, that is, the utterances which can be observed among the native speakers of a language. However, for Chomsky, this approach to linguistic theory fails to eliminate all those actually ungrammatical sentences which have nevertheless been attested as grammatical. And it fails to include many grammatically correct sentences of a language which have not been uttered. According to Chomsky, the grammar *generates* all the sentences of the language and does not distinguish between those that have been attested as grammatical and those that have not. Second, Chomsky objects to the empiricist approach, because it cannot explain the young child's acquisition of a language. Chomsky notes that such learning seems to be unrelated to the degrees of intelligence and reinforcement, and to be inexplicable in terms of the 'behaviourist' concepts of sense-perception, retention, and association. Chomsky emphasizes that by the age of five or six children are able to produce and understand an indefinitely large number of utterances they have not previously encountered. The empiricist cannot account for this *creative* aspect of language use. There are an infinite number of sentences in our native language that we can understand immediately although we have not previously heard or uttered them.

Let us state more positively certain of Chomsky's central concepts and arguments. He says that none of the theories and models that have been developed to describe simple and immediately given linguistic phenomena can account for the crucial underlying system of linguistic *competence*. This term refers to the fluent native speaker's largely tacit knowledge of the grammaticality of his language. Linguistic *performance*, by contrast, is the actual use of language in concrete situations.[10] It is competence which enables speakers in a language to generate the grammatical sentences of the language. Such grammatical sentences exhibit a surface structure; and Chomsky argues that such surface structures are generated from deep structures by means of formally specifiable operations of 'grammatical transformation'. In this way all and only the infinite number of grammatical sentences of the language in question can be generated.

An important aspect of this argument is that at the level of the deep structure different languages show remarkable similarity. They make use of the same formal operations in the construction of grammatical sentences. Thus, for Chomsky, there are universal principles of language; and the only coherent explanation of this is that human beings are genetically endowed with a highly specific 'language faculty' which determines the universal features of transformational grammar. Thus Chomsky argues that children are not born with a tendency to learn one language or another. Rather they are born with a general language faculty combined with a predisposition to use it in analysing the utterances that they hear. It is the innate knowledge of the universal linguistic principles which explains how it is that a child learns a language. Chomsky's position then is one in which the structure of language and pattern of language learning is determined by the structure of the human mind, the mentalistic embodiment of linguistic principles that causally produce the deep and surface structures of language.

Thus Chomsky's position should be seen as realist, in contrast with both positivism and instrumentalism. We saw his objections to positivism, or what he calls 'empiricism', earlier. Against instrumentalism, he rejects the view that it is sufficient for a theory to discover merely the formal rules and principles that logically generate the grammatical sentences of a language. Instead, we must locate these rules in the human mind, and causally explain linguistic performance by the psychological structures and processes involved.

However, we should note that Chomsky himself describes his position as 'rationalist' (see Chomsky, 1967). It might be thought that this is incompatible with our view of him as a realist; for, historically, both realism and positivism have developed within a generally empiricist standpoint that was opposed to rationalism. But this incompatibility disappears if we separate different elements in the rationalist tradition. Rationalists and empiricists disagreed on at least two issues. First, about how it is that humans come to acquire various types of knowledge. Rationalists argued that it was necessary to assume the presence of innate ideas and principles in the human mind: sensory experience, and the association of ideas, could not by themselves explain these processes of acquisition. Second, about the logical status of the knowledge that we acquire of the external world. Rationalists were inclined to advocate, in opposition to empiricists, an axiomatic science of nature, whose first principles could be known to be true *a priori*, without recourse to observation and experiment.

Chomsky's rationalism, we suggest, is related to the first of these elements, rather than the second. He is rationalist in his emphasis upon the need for positing complex, and often innate, mental structures in humans to explain their acquisition of language. He does not support the ideal of a science of language whose axioms can be discovered *a priori*. Further, we can now see why Chomsky's rationalism requires the adoption of a realist view of science. He has to investigate the nature of unobservable, theoretical entities that causally determine human behaviour. Chomsky rejects any attempt to eliminate such mentalistic, theoretical terms, which regards them as not genuinely referring to existent items, but as translatable into a privileged observational language. In other words, he rejects positivism, and substitutes neither instrumentalism nor *a priori* rationalism, but realism.[11]

Lévi-Strauss applies aspects of the study of language to other social but non-linguistic systems.[12] This advocacy of a non-linguistic semiology is rejected by Chomsky because of his belief in the special and irreducible character of language. Lévi-Strauss, however, while not wishing to reduce other forms of communication to language, believes that we can derive from its study an established logical model which renders intelligible the structure of other forms of communication. In particular, as we mentioned, he believes that the work of the Prague School provides us with a well-confirmed set of logical principles which constitute the structural properties of the human mind. Lévi-Strauss is led to this view because he believes that the basic unit of anthropology, that of kinship, directly corresponds to the basic unit of linguistics, the phoneme. Furthermore, just as the phoneme is reduced to its structural elements and then related in terms of opposition, correlation, permutation and so on, so in the study of kinship we analyse the similar relationships between the kinship terms, brother, sister, father and mother.

Many writers have questioned whether there is such an analogy between the phoneme and kinship. However, what is crucial is Lévi-Strauss's consequent conviction as to the general significance of binary oppositions. Although many linguists, including Chomsky, query their importance in linguistics and even in phonetics, Lévi-Strauss's structural anthropology is founded upon such oppositions. Initially we can characterize his method as one in which we search out within each cultural system all the relevant and related binary oppositions. For example, in considering the cultural system of English cuisine two pertinent oppositions are endogenous/exogenous (national versus exotic ingredients) and central/peripheral (staple food versus accompaniments). Thus in English cooking the main dishes, prepared from endogenous ingredients, are sharply distinguished from their accompaniments, prepared from exotic ingredients. If we wanted to analyse other types of cuisine, we would have to introduce further oppositions, such as sweet/sour to Chinese cooking.

Further, Lévi-Strauss is interested in the way in which the structural properties of different systems are logical transformations of each other. Let us return to the system of traffic lights mentioned in section 1. The ordering mechanism in the brain is such that we feel that green is opposite to red in the way in which black is opposite to white. As a result we find it appropriate to use red and green signals as if they were (+) and (−). And, probably because of the association of the former with blood, red is normally taken to signify danger or stop, green to signify go. Now suppose we wish to devise a further signal meaning 'about to stop' or 'about to go'. Invariably, the colour that will be chosen is that of yellow or amber, the colour midway between red and green on the spectrum. Thus, the system of traffic signals is a transformation of the colour system, that is, of the brain's reading of the colour spectrum.

Let us consider some further aspects of Lévi-Strauss's method by returning to the food system. Animals simply eat food; human beings, on the contrary, eat what is defined as edible by the social group of which they are members. What is eaten, how it is prepared, how the items are related systemically (different sorts of entrée, for example) and syntagmatically (sequence of dishes during a meal), are all social products. Within different societies there is great variation in the sorts of goods regarded as edible. However, in the organization of the underlying types of food and of their respective statuses, we find considerable global similarity. We can see this by noting how cooking is a significant mediator between nature and culture. We may, says Lévi-Strauss, think of cooked food as fresh raw food which has been transformed culturally; rotten food is that which has been transformed naturally. Thus we have a culinary triangle as in Figure 1:

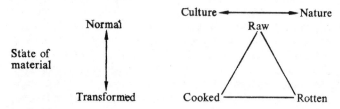

FIGURE 1

There are thus two central oppositions, culture/nature and transformed/normal. Lévi-Strauss then introduces a secondary set of distinctions concerning roasting, boiling and smoking food. These yield further culinary triangles. We need only note here that roasting, and especially roast meat, is universally given the highest status, while boiled food, for example, is given lower status and is generally thought most suitable for children. Thus, for Lévi-Strauss, just as in the social use of red-amber-green for the traffic signal, we find in the use of food categories similar cultural universals of social life. It is these universals which render intelligible the specific cultural practices of particular social groups.[13]

Lévi-Strauss is well aware that the human mind is not itself open to observation, and so any claims that we make about it must be inferred from other observations and theories. In particular, he believes that the knowledge of linguistic principles provides the basis for the understanding of our mental processes. In most social activities, there are various conscious models held by the agents concerned which are not intended as systematic explanations of the phenomenon, but are merely intended to perpetuate them. However, in the case of language there are no conscious models, there is no conscious grammar. It is the only type of social behaviour governed by rules and structures which are unknown to the agent. There are no conscious models which obscure our identification of the unconscious models. We can therefore use these identifiable unconcious models of language to make intelligible the conscious and unconscious structures of other forms of social life. These structures are for Lévi-Strauss expressions of *the* structure, that is, the logic by which the human mind operates. The anthropologist will discover nothing new about this structure, only about the interrelated ways in which it is expressed, in the various relationships between the conscious and unconscious models. 'Structuralism' is a method for sorting out these relationships.

Let us consider three final aspects of Lévi-Strauss's structuralism. First, he argues that no society can be grasped as a whole. Rather it consists of diverse 'orders' of relationships between people and objects; such objects may exhibit isomorphic structures. Lévi-Strauss is not concerned with the systematic causal interpenetration of these different orders; only in showing the possible logical transformations from one to another. Further, within any particular order, such as that of kinship, food, myth or religion, the 'structuralist' method is to decode, to identify the underlying sense, but not to demonstrate the causal interrelationships within that order. Second, we noted above that there is controversy as to whether binary oppositions do actually exist as categorizing devices in the mind. However, it is interesting to note that even if we discovered that they did not exist this would only matter on a realist and not on an instrumentalist reading of Lévi-Strauss. Unlike Chomsky's realist position, Lévi-Strauss's claims are more ambivalent. As a consequence it is unclear how damaging is the criticism that binary oppositions do not really exist within the mind. Third, Lévi-Strauss adopts a strong dichotomy between theory and observation. He says that the first stage of scientific enquiry consists of the observation and careful description of all the relevant facts without any theoretical preconceptions as to the greater importance of some rather than others. It is only after we have assembled this data that we attempt to identify structures.

131

Lévi-Strauss thus argues that the point of structuralist analysis is to be able to decode within each particular order the mass of theory-free ethnographic data. He aims to identify or render intelligible that data but not to explain it causally. In particular he does not show how the categories of the mind cause the conscious and unconscious structures and the mass of ethnographic data. Unlike Chomsky, Lévi-Strauss's 'structuralism' is concerned only with the identification of the meaning or sense lying behind the observable world of appearances. Unlike a realist Lévi-Strauss is not concerned to explain what causes the world, only to show the meaningful patterns into which each order of the world is cast.

Lévi-Strauss therefore is concerned with the meaningfulness of the products of human behaviour. Especially, he elucidates how different cultural items gain their meaning from their relationship with other items constituting a given semiological system. In chapter 7 we shall return to the relationship between such interpretative understanding of the meaning of any cultural item and the kind of realist social science we have been discussing.

3 'Structuralism' and Marxism

In this section we are going to explore further the realist conception of structure by considering aspects of Louis Althusser's reading of Marx. We will contrast our structural and realist interpretation of Marx with that of Althusser, this containing certain non-realist elements. Although Althusser rejects the label, it is clear that there are 'structuralist' aspects of his work, and that he has been influenced by certain 'structuralists'. Further, while we shall criticize aspects of his interpretation of Marx, in our own account in chapter 5 we made use of several features of his analysis, that is, of modes of production, of structure-in-dominance, of the distinction between determination and dominance, and so on.[14]

Like us it is one of his central concerns to establish the exact nature of Marxist science. Central to Althusser's approach is his notion of a problematic, the system of basic related concepts which fit together to form the conceptual framework of a particular science. Such a system has as its focus a particular object which is constituted in thought. Any such problematic is given as much by the questions that it neglects as by the questions that it poses. Any individual term only acquires meaning when it is located within such a problematic; and the same term embedded in a different problematic will have a different meaning. Clearly there are similarities between this notion and that of a Kuhnian paradigm which we discussed in chapter 3. Also, similar to Kuhn's notion of a scientific revolution, Althusser analyses the 'epistemological break' in a discipline, when ideological work becomes scientific for the first time. In chemistry the epistemo-logical break occurred when dephlogisticated air theories were replaced by oxygen-based theories.[15] Marxist science is only properly established in the later writings which employ the distinction between labour and labour-power, the concept of surplus-value, and so on. There is a break between them and both classical political economy and Marx's own early writings derived from Hegel and Feuerbach.

There are, however, three interesting differences between the Althusserian and Kuhnian accounts. First, it is unclear whether Althusser is right in considering that the two examples above, of chemistry and of Marxism, are analogous. It is wrong to suggest that pre-oxygen chemistry is essentially pre-scientific or ideological. Kuhn would say rather that the change in theory represents a change in the paradigm, that is, a move within the science and scientific community of chemistry. Further, once a science has been established Althusser appears to believe that breaks do not occur, unlike Kuhn who maintains a theory of continuing and intermittent scientific revolution. Second, Althusser's account of science is concerned principally with the conceptual level and with conceptual changes. Thus it is the conceptual innovation of oxygen in chemistry, or surplus-value in Marxism, which produces and guarantees scientifi-city. For Kuhn, by contrast, scientific change is not only conceptual but also involves problems of empirical testing, types of instrumenta-tion and so on. Further, while Althusser fails to analyse what it is that produces such conceptual changes, Kuhn argues that scientific change results from anomalies which confront scientists conducting puzzle-solving research within a paradigm. Finally, for Kuhn, a paradigm is firmly located within a particular scientific community, the members of which are, often implicitly, agreed upon the central assumptions, methodological rules, concepts, appropriate instru-ments, and exemplars of research. A problematic, however, for Althusser, is not remotely like this. It is clear that there is no single Marxist science, no single Marxist model of scientific research, no fully agreed-upon presuppositions or rules. Moreover, while Kuhn wishes to provide a sociological grounding for each scientific community, Althusser is concerned to separate theoretical activity from specific social practices. We can see this in his characterization of four types of production.

He says that each of the four types, economic, political, ideological, and scientific, is autonomous and structurally homologous. In each there is the transformation of a given raw material into a determinate product by means of human labour. Corresponding to each type is a specific form of practice. The validity of scientific practice, as opposed to ideological practice, derives from its independence from the values, perspectives and interests of any social group or social class. Scientific practice is conducted theoretically, the only interests at work being interests internal to knowledge.

To understand Althusser's position here let us consider his objections to what he calls 'empiricism', a term he uses to refer to a wide variety of epistemological positions. Empiricism has three features. First, it takes the starting point for theoretical practice to be the given, observable, concrete object. Second, knowledge consists in extracting the essence of this real object by abstraction. Third, models are taken to represent the essence, that has been abstracted from the inessential features of the concrete. Althusser argues, against this empiricist position, that there is a complete dichotomy between the object of knowledge and the real object. The idea of a circle, which is the object of knowledge, must not be confused with the circle, which is the real object. Presuming that Althusser is saying more than that scientific knowledge necessarily consists of concepts and propositions and not of the concrete objects themselves, we can best understand his view by returning to the Marxist distinction between appearance and reality or essence. Althusser argues that this distinction is not, as Marx claims, a distinction at the level of the real or the concrete. It refers rather to the difference between the real object and the thought object. The real object (actual capitalist societies) is the appearance, the thought-object the reality or essence. For Althusser the object of knowledge is internal to thought and is distinct from the appearance which is the real object. Marx's analysis of capitalism is then not a theory at the level of real objects – it is theoretical, that is, concerned with the production of knowledge of the thought-object.

Althusser's general position raises several problems. First, so as to avoid the dangers of relativism, Althusser argues that *scientific* practice, is separate and detached from economic, political, and especially ideological practices. In terms of the normal Marxist scheme, scientific practice for Althusser lies outside both base and superstructure, and is, in some sense, independent. He seems to maintain this because of his belief that if the nature of a scientific theory can be causally explained by social determinants, then its truth or falsity cannot be assessed. We will criticize this position in chapter 9, section 2. Furthermore, Althusser's position fails to provide us with a way to distinguish between different social sciences. Althusser's characterization of a scientific problematic is couched very generally and fails to distinguish Marxist science from other possible social sciences. Indeed to show what is the specific character of Marxism which makes *it* scientific, Althusser has to cite aspects of its substantive content. On strictly methodological grounds it would seem that he cannot object to a wide variety of social scientific theories, provided they are not empiricist in the sense just described. Nor does he indicate how to resolve differences between these various social sciences, for example, between psychoanalysis and Marxism. Finally, Althusser's characterization of empiricism fails to distinguish between what we have termed positivist and realist approaches. The realist would, for example, accept Althusser's criticism of what he sees as the empiricist view of models, because, as we saw in chapter 5, it conflates the concept of essence with that of abstraction (and idealization). For the realist the essence is the unobservable structure and mechanism responsible for producing the concrete features of social reality. The model of that essence will probably be presented in an abstracted and idealized form. However, for the realist, one does not identify this essence by a process of abstraction and idealization of the concrete. Rather abstraction and idealization are involved in the relationship between the elements of the model and the essence that it represents.

Let us now turn in more detail to Althusser's analysis of the relationship between the thought-object and the real-object. He says that, although there is a rigid dichotomy between the two, political economy ultimately studies a raw material provided by 'real concrete history', and that it is real-objects which are the 'absolute reference point' for the process of knowledge production. It appears here that Althusser considers that whatever will enable us to account for, and specifically to predict, the development of real-objects, is thereby scientific. In other words, the thought-objects, since they do not themselves refer to anything real, may be judged in terms of how useful or instrumental they are in comprehending features of the real. Thus, what we take to be Marx's realism, in which his concepts refer to real but obscured mechanisms of a mode of production, is not found in Althusser's apparently more instrumentalist essays in *Reading Capital* (1970). Interestingly, however, in *Lenin and Philosophy* his interpretation of Marx is more realist: 'What makes abstraction scientific is precisely the fact that it designates a concrete reality which certainly exists but which is impossible to "touch with one's hands", or "see with one's eyes" ' (Althusser, 1971, p. 75). His formulation here suggests a simple relationship between real-objects and thought-objects. In *Reading Capital* he suggests an analogy, as we have noted, between Marx's analysis of the CMP and Lavoisier's 'discovery' of oxygen. It is relatively unproblematic in the latter to suggest that the thought-object, the concept of oxygen, directly corresponds with the real-object, oxygen. However, it is incorrect to argue a similar correspondence in the case of *Capital*. For Marx, the thought-object, the CMP, never corresponds exactly with the real-object, an actual capitalist society, because of the presence of more than one mode within any such society.

Let us finally consider some implications of Althusser's argument that history is made by social classes, and that it is the class struggle

135

which is the motor of history. People are only part of this process because of their membership of distinct social classes. Any given society has to be analysed in terms of the different classes present, the relations between these classes and constitutive fractions (such as financial capitalists), and the different forms of class ideology. Whether or not a revolutionary conjuncture materializes depends, for Althusser, on the operation of the law of uneven development, on the presence of primary and secondary contradictions, and on the possible ruptural unity of such contradictions (see Althusser, 1969).

What is significant for our purposes is the relationship between this view, that the class struggle is the motor of history, and Althusser's interpretation of the CMP. He says (1970, p. 180):

> The structure of the relations of production determine the *places* and *functions* occupied and adopted by the agents of production, who are never anything more than the occupants of these places, insofar as they are 'supports' (Träger) of these functions. The true 'subjects' (in the sense of constitutive subjects of the process) are therefore not these occupants or functionaries, are not, despite all appearances, the 'obviousness' of the 'given' if naive anthropology, 'concrete individuals' – 'real men' – but the definition and distribution of these places and functions. The true 'subjects' are these definers and distributors: the relations of production (and political and ideological social relations).

For Althusser the relations of production constitute the subject of the historical process. The 'agents of production' are nothing more than 'supports' or 'bearers' of the functions of the system of production. There are a limited and given number of places in this system, these places being continually reproduced by its operation as a whole. There are specific laws within the CMP which operate to reproduce these places and their relationships. The objective requirements of the structure's continual reproduction become each bearer's subjective aim. Thus human beings, although active in the process of production, are not themselves the subjects of that process. But nor are they simply its object. As a result of performing the necessary functions, the objective needs imposed on the individuals become their subjective aims.

Althusser is not claiming here that every aspect of each person is determined by what part that person plays in the system of production. Rather, to the extent to which agents are bearers of some functions within that system they have to perform certain tasks, and it is these which become incorporated into the agent as subjectively necessary. However, there are aspects of each person's social life which are unrelated to his or her place in the process of production, and others only partly related.

So far Althusser's account is consistent with our interpretation of Marx in the previous chapter. However, the last line of the passage quoted above is problematic. Althusser says that the 'subjects' of the process are the social relations of political and ideological production, as well as of material production. However, it is unclear what it means to say that people are 'supports' or 'bearers' of ideological practice. There are, of course, parts to play within the state and within the ideological superstructure, but it is questionable whether these are defined and distributed by political and ideological social relations of production. Althusser may well wish to accord degrees of independence to non-material relations. But, it does not follow from this that there is equivalence in these different social relations. This unargued and clearly uncertain (because it is bracketed) generalization from the analysis of material production to the analysis of other practices, is a consequence of the 'structuralist' influence in Althusser. Instead of seeing Marx as involved in the study of the causal impact of the social relations of material production, Althusser wishes to identify isomorphic structures of social relations of material, political, and ideological production.[16]

We will return to these issues at the end of chapter 8 when we have considered the analysis of meanings and of reification. We will now prepare the way for our examination there by briefly considering some of the criticisms made of both positivist and realist analyses of structure. These criticisms depend upon varieties of anti-naturalist argument.

4 Criticisms of structural analysis

First, it is claimed that in much structural analysis there is a failure to consider the subjective meanings that actors place upon their experiences within given structures. There is no adequate analysis of such meanings, of how they are shared, of their systemic inter-relationships, and of how actors do not simply and directly respond to objective structural factors. Between the structure of a given social formation and typical patterns of individual action lie sets of shared meanings by which actors identify, interpret, evaluate and indicate to themselves and others, the significance of objects and events present in their social world.

It might seem that this criticism would not apply to Lévi-Strauss and to some other 'structuralists', since they are interested in the decoding of structures of meanings (as well as of social organization). However, analysis of the structural level of meaning omits consideration of how the actors themselves interpret and respond to such structures. We will discuss the subjective states of individuals, and their relationship to causal explanation in the next chapter. A specific instance where a structural analysis has been held to be inadequate, is Marx's explanation of revolutionary transformation from one type of social formation to another. It is unclear how the contradictory character of the structure of the CMP actually generates the necessary forms of political consciousness and political action. Marx, it is claimed, either fails to provide or merely provides an inadequate, explanation of working class consciousness, of what sort of interpretation the 'bearers' of the wage-labourer function place upon their experiences within the structure of capitalist society.[17]

In a second, and sometimes connected, criticism of structural analysis, it is argued that just as we analyse how human action is caused by social structures, so also we must consider how these structures are themselves produced by human activity. This requires a dialectical emphasis in which analysis is made of how social and meaning-structures result from constitutive human activity. Structures are not simply present out there, but are seen as socially constructed, and it is just as much the task of sociology to analyse the nature of this construction as it is to consider how such structures cause various patterns of human action. This criticism of structural theories has been developed from Marx's analysis of labour, of how human beings produce historically structured material and social worlds. Much 'structuralist' writing likewise emphasizes how the structures of meanings are socially constructed and are not simply given in nature. In chapter 8 we will consider various issues in the analysis of reification, that is, of the ideological distortion by which social phenomena are seen not as constructions of human activity, but as material things having natural rather than social properties.[18]

Let us now turn to a third more radical criticism. We will consider aspects of the ethnomethodological school and its apparently in principle critique of the practices of orthodox sociology.[19] Ethnomethodology, although it incorporates the previous two criticisms, is not intended as any type of 'repair' for structural analysis. It is concerned not with the structure of a given social phenomenon but with the method members use to interpret, or make sense of, such a phenomenon. It thus submits the concept of structure to the same type of analysis that is given to any other device used by 'lay' or 'professional' sociologists to account for features of their world. What, briefly, is the warrant for this ethnomethodological concern?

Ethnomethodology rests on the contention that all forms of social interaction, including the most commonplace, have a systematic and organized character. This organization does not stem directly from the nature of the interaction but from how it is made 'accountable'. How members address themselves to an action, describe it, summarize it, present it, or explain it, are the means by which practical actions are organized. Crucial here is the reflexivity of this phenomenon. That is to say, by making it accountable, such interaction is systematized and organized. But ethnomethodologists do not claim that there is interaction on one hand, and accounting practices on the other. Rather interaction itself, how people produce and manage everyday activities, depends upon the accounting practices by which such activities are organized. Garfinkel says that 'the activities whereby members produce and manage settings of organized everyday affairs are members' procedures for making those settings "accountable" ' (Garfinkel, 1967, p. 1).

The aim then is to discover members' methods (or formal structures) of commonplace, everyday actions from within actual settings, as accomplishments of members within these settings. And since everyone is engaged in practical sociological reasoning, the ethnomethodologist is interested in both lay members and professional sociologists. In analysing the latter, the ethnomethodologist will be concerned with, among other things, how sociologists use the notion of structure or social structure as a device to account for, or make rational, methodic, and objective sense of, features of the everyday world. Ethnomethodologists in general abstain from enquiring into whether the structure of a particular social phenomenon is actually of the form suggested by the professional sociologists. Rather they analyse how the accounting practice of structure is an ongoing practical achievement of sociologists within particular settings, so as to make sense of these settings. Garfinkel and Sacks, for example (1970, p. 345), say of the formal structures:

> Ethnomethodological studies of formal structures are directed to the study of such phenomena, seeking to describe members' accounts of formal structures wherever and by whomever they are done, while abstaining from all judgments of their adequacy, value, importance, necessity, practicality, success, or consequentiality. We refer to this procedural policy as 'ethnomethodological indifference'.

However, this principle of indifference is problematic. Ethnomethodologists must, after all, be concerned with whether their analyses of the formal structures of practical actions are correct, with whether there are typical openings or closures in conversations, or with whether a particular member is actually opening or closing a conversation. Further, although ethnomethodologists are not concerned with whether a given social phenomenon to which members refer, really does have a particular structure, they are systematically involved in the analysis of the organized structure of *everyday*

139

activities. Ethnomethodologists concern themselves with the identification of how such activities exhibit the properties of uniformity, reproducibility, repetitiveness, standardization, typicality and so on. Furthermore, these properties are seen as independent of the specific members who produce and recognize such structures. Ethnomethodologists thus are irreducibly involved in trying to provide a correct account of the organized or structural features of everyday activities, and especially of the general properties of conversations. As a consequence it is difficult to know whether ethnomethodology does constitute an in principle criticism of much orthodox structural analysis. Our suggestion is that ethnomethodology provides a further set of repairs, especially in taking the everyday world and members' methods for treating this world, as a topic in its own right and not as a resource in providing orthodox sociology with its data.

part three

Meaning and ideology

In part 2 we examined a number of major social theorists who have regarded their work as attempts to gain a genuinely scientific understanding of social phenomena. We showed how, despite their sharing this naturalist standpoint, the content and method of their enquiries displayed differing views of what it is to be scientific. We were able to identify these differences by using the distinctions drawn in part 1, between realist, positivist and conventionalist conceptions of the natural sciences. In the following part we will examine what we see as the central problems in the defence of a realist naturalism in the social sciences.

The arguments of those who reject naturalism have been diverse. It is claimed, for example, that each person, or each social phenomenon, is unique, and that therefore no general laws relating to them can be discovered; that it is impossible, for various reasons, to conduct controlled experiments on human subjects; and that no accurate predictions can be made about phenomena dependent upon human activity. The apparent force of these claims, if correct, often presupposes a positivist view of the natural sciences: the discovery of high-level generalizations, the use of experiments to directly confirm or falsify theories, and a predictivist account of explanation. Though important issues are occasionally raised by these claims, we will not discuss them here.[1]

The two most significant problems, for us, concern the nature of human action, and the possibility of objective theories of social reality. Each involves a number of partly separable elements. The former, human action, requires answers to two main questions. First, is the type of explanation appropriate for human actions causal or non-causal? Second, is there a distinctive kind of knowledge involved in the understanding of beliefs, values, intentions, and so on: a form of knowledge that has no parallel in the natural

142

sciences?[2] We try to answer these questions in chapter 7. In response
to the first, we defend the view that a typical mode of explaining
actions, in terms of the agent's reasons, should be analysed as
causal; and we reject the way in which positivist social scientists
systematically devalue the importance of such explanations. In
answering the second, we distinguish various senses of 'understanding', or *verstehen*; and argue that one of these, 'interpretive
understanding', is peculiar to knowledge of social reality. But we
further maintain that an adequate philosophical account of the
natural sciences must also include this concept of understanding.
Thus no straightforward advocacy of anti-naturalism can be justified
by reference to the nature of human action.

Our discussion of the second main problem, objectivity, is
organized in a more complex way. We begin chapter 8 by noting how
a contrast is frequently drawn between 'objective' and 'ideological'
social science. We argue that there are two distinct concepts of
ideology. Both involve the idea of *distortion*, but the specific kinds of
distortion differ considerably. In one, the Marxist concept, *reification*
is regarded as a central defect of ideological beliefs. The rest of
chapter 8 is concerned with an analysis of this notion of reification,
especially its articulation and development in the writings of Lukács,
and Berger and Pullberg; in the last section, we consider, and reject,
the view that a realist social theory must involve reification. In the
second concept of ideology, it is the intrusion of *values* that is seen as
the primary source of distortion. Thus ideological social science is
contrasted with 'value-free' social science. In the first section of
chapter 9, we distinguish different elements in the ideal of value-
freedom, and show, by examining a number of objections to this
ideal, that these elements are partly independent of each other. We
argue that the most important question, whether the truth or falsity
of social theories depends upon the acceptance or rejection of
particular values, requires for its solution an examination of the
relations between the knower and the known, the 'subject' and
'object' of knowledge. The nature of these relations is one of the
main concerns of 'critical theorists', and in the final section, we
examine some of their claims, especially in the work of Habermas.

Closely connected with the subject-object problem, is that of the
relations between concepts and reality. We discuss this in the context
of the well-known dispute in anthropology, how to interpret Zande
witchcraft. One contender in this dispute, Winch, supports the view
that criteria of reality, and of rationality, are specific to different
forms of social life. We note the similarities between his position,
and Kuhn's claims about scientific revolutions. Both apparently
adopt a form of relativism, in maintaining that there are no universal
standards of truth and reason that can be used to evaluate every

system of beliefs. Further, relativism is often thought to follow from any general commitment to the causal determination of beliefs, a commitment implicit in Marx's concept of ideology. We reject this argument about determinism and relativism, and defend the legitimacy of the sociological explanation of beliefs, including scientific ones.

It should be clear that there are important analogies between several of these arguments against objectivity in the social sciences, and those used by the conventionalist writers we discussed in chapter 3: the denial of universal standards of rationality; the emphasis upon the part played by values in choosing between theories; the rejection of the idea of a real world existing independently of beliefs and theories 'about it', and so on. In other words, many anti-naturalist arguments rest upon the assumption of a non-conventionalist view of the natural sciences. We have already noted the possibility of adopting a non-positivist, realist naturalism. We can now see a further possibility, conventionalist naturalism.

But in our discussion of conventionalist writers we argued that most of their claims should either be rejected, or modified in a way that does not involve the abandonment of a realist position. In particular, we developed an account of the relations between theoretical beliefs, and the description of observations, which allows the objective assessment of competing theories, without commitment to the positivists' observational language (see chapter 3, section 2). We make use of this account in part 3, especially in our defence of the causal explanation of human actions (chapter 7, section 2), and in giving a realist analysis of Marx's distinction between 'essence' and 'appearance' (chapter 8, section 1).

A central figure in many of the disputes about the methodological unity of the natural and social sciences is Max Weber. This is particularly so with respect to the two main problems we examine in part 3: the explanation and understanding of human action, and the objectivity of social science. On both of these problems, Weber tried to develop a position that mediated between the more extreme forms of naturalism and anti-naturalism.[3] It is partly for this reason that his writings have been interpreted in many different ways, and that his claims have been attacked and defended on a variety of different grounds. An understanding of his complex views is an essential starting-point for most of the discussion which follows. Thus we begin both chapters 7 and 9 with an account of the relevant features of his methodology.

7 The explanation and understanding of social action

1 Weber and interpretive sociology

Max Weber (1947, p. 88) defines sociology as

> a science which attempts the interpretive understanding of
> social action in order thereby to arrive at a causal explanation
> of its course and effects. . . . Action is social in so far as, by
> virtue of the subjective meaning attached to it by the acting
> individual (or individuals), it takes account of the behaviour
> of others, and is thereby oriented in its course.

In this definition, Weber indicates his belief in the need to integrate
two apparently competing conceptions of the social sciences: the
naturalist insistence upon causal explanation, and the anti-naturalist
demand for the interpretive understanding of subjective meanings.
Weber wishes to establish a sociology that combines both of these
elements, and much of his writing, substantive and methodological,
is directed towards this aim. We will begin by considering how he
tries to do this, and go on, in later sections, to examine a number of
issues that are raised by his attempt.[1]

What does Weber mean by 'interpretive understanding'? One
important component in his complex account of this is a distinction
between 'observational', or 'direct' understanding (*aktuelles
Verstehen*), and 'explanatory' or 'motivational' understanding
(*erklärendes Verstehen*). The nature of this distinction is problematic,
but Weber's examples of the two give some idea of it. He says that
when someone states or writes down the proposition '$2 \times 2 = 4$', we
have direct understanding of its meaning. Similarly, we directly
understand someone's outbreak of anger, manifested in various
bodily expressions; the action of a woodcutter chopping wood; or a
person's aiming a gun at an animal. But explanatory understanding
involves knowledge of the 'motives' because of which these directly

145

understood actions are performed. Weber defines a 'motive' as 'a complex of subjective meaning which seems to the actor himself or to the observer an adequate ground for the conduct in question' (1947, p. 98). Possible motives in the examples above would be: balancing a ledger; jealousy; getting a supply of fuel; and obeying a command.

Weber makes it clear that, in ascribing these motives to the agents, we should be seen as attempting to give causal explanations of their actions. Thus he says that when we have explanatory understanding of someone writing or stating '2 × 2 = 4', 'we understand what makes him do this at precisely this moment and in the circumstances' (1947, p. 95). Motivational explanations must be empirically tested in the same way as any other types of causal hypothesis. For, he argues, there are often motivational hypotheses that seem quite plausible, but which may nonetheless turn out to be incorrect. He notes several reasons why this may happen. First, the apparent conscious motives may conceal, from both the agent and the observer, the 'real driving force' of the action. Second, the agent may be subject to different, and conflicting motives, so that it is difficult to ascertain their relative strength or importance. Third, the agent and observer may perceive the agent's situation differently, so that what seems a plausible motive to the observer may be based on a mistaken identification of how that situation appears to the agent. Weber accepts, however, that fully satisfactory empirical testing of motivational hypotheses is rarely possible. Controlled experiments are typically not available. The most that can normally be done is to use comparative methods, trying to find cases that differ from the one we are examining only in the absence of the particular motive or factor that has been postulated as a cause. But often, we have to resort to the highly uncertain procedure of the 'imaginary experiment'. In this we try to work out what would have happened in the absence of the hypothetical cause, on the basis of generalizations for whose truth or falsity we may have little evidence.[2]

To the extent that these empirical tests are satisfied, a motivational explanatory hypothesis is 'causally adequate'. But Weber insists that it must also be 'adequate on the level of meaning'. What precisely is meant by this requirement is unclear. In general terms, Weber claims that the components of a motivational explanation must, according to our habitual modes of thought and feeling, constitute a 'typical' complex of meaning. More specifically, he maintains that the requirement is most fully met when we can show that the motivational pattern is a 'rational' one. Weber considers two central cases of rational action. First, where someone is correctly carrying out a logical or mathematical argument, and where we can thus see that the conclusion follows deductively from the premisses. Second, where a person's action involves the choice of the most effective means for the attainment of some particular end or objective. In both cases, we can be said to have 'rational understanding', and this is one way in which the criterion of adequacy on the level of meaning can be met. Alternatively, we may have varying degrees of 'empathic understanding'. Here Weber refers to the similarities that may exist between the emotions ascribed to agents and those which observers have themselves experienced.

Let us examine in more detail these concepts of rational and empathic understanding, and their relation to the previous distinction between direct and explanatory understanding. Consider first a situation where someone performs a particular action, and where we can show that, given a set of assumptions about a desired objective and the different likelihoods of various courses of action leading to its realization, this action is the most efficient means to that objective. We can regard the relationship between these assumptions and the action in a purely formal or logical manner, and assess the action as a rational one. For Weber, 'rational understanding' refers to the grasp that we have of these formal relationships when we recognize their rationality or validity. Indeed, he sometimes claims that rational understanding is more '*certain*' than any other kind, and it seems likely that he is pointing to the different, *a priori* status, of our knowledge of logical relationships, in contrast to our empirical knowledge.

However, Weber does not regard rational understanding as necessarily linked to explanatory understanding. In the situation outlined above, we would only have explanatory understanding if we knew that it was *because* the agent had that objective, and regarded the action as the best means of achieving it, that the action was performed. To know this would involve the empirical testing, for its causal adequacy, of the motivational hypothesis concerned. If such tests were successful, we would have both explanatory and rational understanding of the action. But Weber insists that this kind of case is quite rare. More frequently, explanatory understanding will involve the ascription of various non-rational, affective motives to the agent. In these cases, we may have varying degrees of empathic understanding, depending upon the extent to which we have ourselves experienced the kinds of affective states that are ascribed in the motivational hypothesis. Further, partly because of the possible similarities between the experiences of the social scientist and the agent, it may sometimes be helpful, in arriving at motivational hypotheses, to use the psychological device of imagining oneself in the agent's situation. But Weber emphasizes that this is not always necessary or helpful, and that, anyway, the hypotheses formulated in this way must then be empirically tested. Finally, he notes that we can often only achieve an 'intellectual' grasp of the agent's motives, including the ends or objectives of rational actions. Empathic understanding is necessarily limited by the experiential biographies of social scientists, and their cultural and historical distance from the agent.[3]

We will leave consideration of the relationship between direct and explanatory understanding until the next section. Let us now examine the way in which the methodological position we have outlined operates in Weber's well-known account of various elements involved in the historical genesis of Western European capitalism. For Weber, capitalism is characterized not only by the relations between its constitutive social classes, but also by the systematic embodiment of the principles of rational organization in its form of economic activity. The emergence of capitalism in sixteenth- and seventeenth-century Europe required, in addition to various 'material' conditions, the adoption of a specific set of values and attitudes, the 'spirit of capitalism' (S. of C.). The S. of C. involved the idea of a worldly calling or duty to engage in economic acquisition as an end in itself, rather than as a means to hedonistic satisfactions; the justification of virtues such as honesty, industry, punctuality and frugality by reference to their usefulness in promoting economic acquisition; and the insistence upon a systematic use of one's time in pursuit of this end. Weber contrasts the values and attitudes of the S. of C. with those of 'traditionalism'. He illustrates the contrast by comparing the ways in which traditional, and non-traditional workers respond to an increase in piece-rates. The former may often decrease the amount of work they do, since their aim is to earn the wage they earned before, and thus to continue living in their accustomed manner. The latter respond by increasing their output, earning more, and thus potentially changing their pattern of life.

Weber argues that the S. of C. was not a later *product* of capitalism, but a necessary pre-condition of its initial development. The S. of C. requires independent explanation, and, for Weber, some indication of the nature of such an explanation is provided by nineteenth-century occupational statistics. These show a marked tendency for Protestants, rather than Catholics, to be business leaders and owners of capital, and to study scientific-technical subjects in higher education.

The first stage in Weber's account of the genesis of the S. of C., and thus of capitalism itself, involves the demonstration of a 'congruence at the level of meaning' between the S. of C. and the ethical doctrines of ascetic forms of Protestantism, especially Calvinism; together with a lack of meaning-congruence between the S. of C. and the ethics of Catholicism. Catholics regarded monastic life as the apex of a hierarchy of activities; and their organic, traditionalist

148

conception of society involved a strongly non-individualist ideal of social relations. Lutherans, while rejecting the privileged status of monastic life, maintained a similarly traditionalist view of society, and insisted that salvation was achieved by faith, not works. In contrast to both Catholicism and Lutheranism, the ethics of Calvinism demanded methodical, systematic, this-worldly activity. This Protestant Ethic (P.E.) took a highly individualistic form, and also involved the rejection of hedonistic pleasures. Such an ethic, though not explicitly requiring that worldly activity should be economic, specified a form of life whose nature was very similar to that demanded by the values and attitudes of the S. of C. Traditionalism is rejected; work is to be rationally ordered; and capital must be accumulated, not dissipated in hedonistic consumption.

Thus, for Weber, there is a meaning-congruence between the P.E. and the S. of C., and he argues that the adoption of the former led to its application in economic activity as the S. of C. But Weber is also concerned to explain how it was that the P.E. was itself generated from the specifically *theological* doctrines of Calvinism. For, unlike the relation between the P.E. and the S. of C., there is no obvious congruence between Calvinist theology and the P.E. Three elements in this theology are particularly important. First, the belief in the predestination of all human souls to eternal salvation or damnation. God, who has determined this predestination, is incomprehensible to humans, and not even priests can aid them to salvation. Second, the belief that God has created the world, and placed men in it so that they may increase His glory by labouring to establish His Kingdom upon Earth. Third, the belief that nature and the flesh mean sin and death, unless men escape from this by divine grace.

Weber argues that the implications of the first element were too terrible for the human psyche to tolerate. An acute sense of isolation and inner loneliness were generated, and led to the adoption of an ethic that was logically incompatible with the doctrines of predestination and God's incomprehensibility to men. The form taken by this ethic was determined by the other two elements in Calvinist theology. Thus Weber constructs a complex motivational explanation of the P.E., by reference to the psychological tensions resulting from theological doctrines. For Calvinists, the question of whether or not their souls were predestined to salvation was of the utmost significance. Yet there was no way of knowing their fate, nor could anything they did in this world bring about their salvation. Faced with this situation, they inevitably came to adopt attitudes inconsistent with their theological beliefs. They could not resist the temptation of trying to discover external signs of salvation, and then of practising the self-deception of trying to lead the kind of life that would provide such signs. What kind of life would be appropriate? A passive, mystical, other-worldly existence was ruled out by the second element of their theology, the duty to labour on Earth for God's glory. The third element prohibited any indulgence in the pleasures of the flesh. Instead, the appropriate kind of life was seen to be the systematic, individualistic, worldly activity of the P.E.

Thus, having already shown the meaning-congruence between the P.E. and the S. of C., and the latter's necessity for the initial development of capitalism, Weber is able to claim that Calvinism was one of the determinants of the successful emergence of that economic system. And in other writings on non-Christian religions, he finds further support for this claim. In particular, Weber argues that the ethics of Indian or Chinese religions could not perform the same function as the P.E. did for capitalism in Europe, though they were not such as to prevent capitalism's taking root when introduced from outside.

We will conclude this discussion of Weber by noting some of the connections between his historical claims about Western capitalism, and his methodological position outlined earlier. First, we can see his account of the relationship between Calvinist theology and the P.E. as an attempted motivational explanation which, even if correct, would not provide us with rational understanding, since the relationship is not a logically valid one. Whether or not it provides empathic understanding depends upon the similarity of our own experiences with those of Calvinists. Second, it is possible that Weber may have arrived at his motivational hypothesis partly through imaginative re-enactment of the Calvinist's plight: but for the validation of the hypothesis, Weber tries to find evidence, from various writings, of the changes in beliefs and attitudes suggested by it. Third, his studies of Indian and Chinese religion can, to some extent, be considered as applications of the comparative method for testing causal hypotheses. But, as Weber was aware, neither India nor China corresponded exactly to Europe with respect to other factors, such as the special characteristics of the Western city, that were also relevant to the emergence of capitalism in Europe.[4] Finally, what is the significance of the meaning-congruence between the P.E. and the S. of C.? We will suggest later, in the last section, that Weber's analysis of this indicates an important sense of 'understanding' that is not adequately represented in his methodological writings. For the moment, however, we should note that he regards the connection between the two sets of values and attitudes as existing not only at the level of meaning, but also at that of causality. It was the adoption of the P.E. that led to the adoption of the S. of C., and thus contributed causally to the emergence of European capitalism.

Weber's methodological position, and the substantive studies based upon it, depend crucially on his view that motivational explanations are a type of causal explanation. In the following two sections, we will examine two different, and opposing, rejections of this view. On the one hand, it is argued that Weber was correct in seeing motivational explanations as central to our understanding of human action, but wrong in identifying these as a form of causal explanation. What is needed, instead, is an approach to the study of humans in society that departs radically from the causal and pre-dictive objectives of the natural sciences. On the other hand, it is argued that Weber was right in his insistence upon causal explanation in the social sciences, but mistaken in thinking that the kinds of items typically referred to in motivational explanations – such as intentions, purposes, emotions, values and beliefs – can meet the requirements for empirically testable scientific explanations. We will argue that both these positions are erroneous. But in the final section, we will give some support to the view that there is a form of under-standing that is distinctive of our knowledge of human action and social reality.

2 Reasons, causes and action

The motivational explanations whose importance Weber maintained are not, of course, the invention or special technique of the social scientist. Whatever refinements the social scientist may add, their general characteristics are located in the ways in which human beings explain and justify their actions in the course of everyday life. Thus we will here be mainly concerned with the logical status of these explanations in such everyday contexts. Weber, in his definition of 'motive', refers to the idea of an agent regarding something as an 'adequate ground' for the action in question. This indicates a signifi-cant element in many everyday explanations: the giving of *reasons*, or *grounds*, for what someone does. For example, 'my reason for walk-ing to work is that I think walking improves blood-circulation', or 'my reason for giving her a present was to express my gratitude'. The general form of these explanations is: 'my reason for doing Y was R'; and even where actual explanations do not use the 'reason for' locution, they can often be restated in this form without signifi-cant changes in meaning.

What is it about such explanations that might lead us to regard them as non-causal?[5] One important feature is that we often respond to them, not by arguing that this was not really why the agents acted as they did, but instead by *evaluating* the reasons and actions con-cerned. Thus we may consider the agent's reasons good or bad, sufficient or insufficient, coherent or confused, and so on. And the actions may be evaluated as appropriate or inappropriate, rational or irrational, correct or incorrect. For example, it might be objected that walking is an ineffective means of improving blood-circulation, or that giving presents is an inappropriate way of expressing gratitude. Clearly, arguments of this kind are different from those involved in the assessment of causal explanations, and cannot intelligibly arise in the study of natural phenomena. Admittedly, we sometimes use an apparently similar verbal form in explaining such phenomena, as in 'the *reason for* the plank's breaking was that a 100-pound weight was dropped on it'. But it would be wrong to say that this was the plank's reason for breaking. Planks have no reason for breaking, despite there being reasons *why* they break.

Thus reason-explanations of human action have a distinctive quality. They are open to 'evaluative assessment'. (Here the concept of evaluation is a broad one, not restricted to *moral* evaluation.) But the question remains of whether they also have the characteristics of causal explanations. A clear indication that they do is given by considering a different type of response that might typically be made to the explanations in our two examples. It might be claimed that the woman walking to work never did anything else to improve her health, and that her 'real reason' was to save money. Or someone might note that the man never gave presents to anyone else, and that it was in his interests that the woman he gave the present to should have a favourable attitude towards him. Such responses presuppose that the reasons proffered by the agent are being assessed as potential causal explanations. They rely upon the kinds of claims that are relevant to the testing of causal hypotheses. Further, the acceptance or rejection of the proffered reasons, in this causal assessment, is independent of the conclusions arrived at in the evaluative assessment. For example, we might accept the man's explanation of why he gave the present, despite rejecting this kind of action as an appropriate or proper way of expressing gratitude.

Here we can see an important similarity to one feature of Weber's account of the relation between Calvinism and the P.E. Weber did not regard Calvinist theology as providing logically adequate reasons for adopting the P.E.: the connection between the two, although not rational, was nonetheless causal.[6] Further, we can use this general difference between causal and evaluative assessment of reason-explanations to distinguish two ways in which the citing of *rules* may be relevant to accounts of human actions. To show that an action conforms to some rule, norm, or convention may serve either an evaluative or an explanatory function. But the conditions that must be met in the two cases are different. An action may conform to a rule, in that it is of a kind specified as required or allowed in that rule. To show such conformity may therefore justify the action, though we may also wish to assess evaluatively the rule itself. But conformity to a rule is not an adequate proof that the person's action is causally explicable by reference to that rule. For this, we would need to show that the agent was *following* the rule. Indeed, it may sometimes happen that, although the agent is 'following a rule', the action does not conform to it, since various 'mistakes' may be made by the agent in applying it.[7]

Let us now examine in more detail the way in which an agent's reasons can function as possible causes of action. We will adopt a slightly modified version of the general account of reason-explanations given by Donald Davidson. In giving reasons for their actions, agents are referring, explicitly or implicitly, to sets of beliefs and desires which they regard both as causally explaining, and as providing grounds for, those actions. The term 'desire' is used here in a very wide sense, to indicate the presence of any kind of favourable attitude towards something. It thus includes '... wantings, urges, promptings, and a great variety of moral views, aesthetic principles, economic prejudices, social conventions, and public and private goals and values ...' (Davidson, 1963, pp. 221–2). Sometimes, the explanatory context may require the agent to make explicit reference to both beliefs and desires, but more often it is necessary to refer only to one of these. Thus, in our two examples, the reason cited is in one case a belief, that walking improves blood-circulation, and in the other a desire, to express gratitude. In the first, there is an implicit desire, to aid health, and in the second an implicit belief, that giving a present is an appropriate expression of gratitude.

This general account of reason-explanations provides a framework within which we can locate many of the concepts typically used in everyday explanations of human actions: purposes and intentions, rules and motives. When agents state their purposes or intentions, they can be seen as specifying the objects of their desires. For example, we might say that the woman walked to work with the intention, or purpose, of aiding her health. When agents refer to rules in explaining their actions, these rules often provide the basis for either their beliefs or desires. For example, the man's desire to express his gratitude might reflect his acceptance of a moral norm or rule requiring such expressions; and his belief that present-giving is an appropriate means of expression might be based upon a social convention or rule to this effect. With motives, the situation is more complex. Terms such as 'jealousy', 'greed', or 'revenge' should not be interpreted as referring directly to specific desires or beliefs. They seem rather to refer to typical clusters of emotions, objectives and beliefs, that are commonly related to a variety of different kinds of actions and circumstances. The more we know about the nature of these actions and circumstances, the more informative is the citing of a particular motive, since it indicates the sorts of beliefs and desires that were causally relevant in this particular context. Thus, as Davidson notes,

153

to say that an agent poisoned someone through jealousy is to suggest, amongst other things, that '. . . the poisoner believes his action will harm his rival, remove the cause of his agony, or redress an injustice, and these are the sorts of things a jealous man will want to do' (Davidson, 1963, pp. 225–6).[8]

However, we must now consider some objections to the general account of reason-explanation we have adopted, which are designed to show that it cannot be regarded as a type of causal explanation. Though differing in some respects, these objections all involve the claim that there is some kind of *conceptual* or *logical* connection between actions, and desires and beliefs. And it is argued that the nature of this connection is such that a necessary condition for any relation to be a causal one cannot be satisfied: for causal relations must be contingent, not logically necessary. One of these objections can be introduced by considering the following example. Suppose someone is asked why she made a right-turn signal while driving, and she answers 'because I wanted to signal that I was turning right'. Here there is a close conceptual connection between the description of the action, 'making a right-turn signal', and that of the desire, 'wanting to signal turning right'. The object of the desire, 'signalling turning right' is given roughly the same description as the action. But, it is argued, if this is so, the desire cannot be a cause of the action, since the relation between them is logical, not contingent.[9]

Two replies can be made to this objection. First, the conceptual connection between the descriptions of the action and the object of the desire does not entail that the occurrence of the action can be logically deduced from the presence of the desire. Yet only if this were deducible would the relation between desire and action be a logical, and thus non-causal, one. That the deduction cannot be made can be seen by noting that, although the woman wanted to make this signal, there are many reasons why she might have failed to do so. Second, the example itself is somewhat peculiar. Given the initial question, more typical answers would be, 'because I wanted to turn right' (not *signal* right, as in the original answer), or, 'because I wanted to take the quickest route to Lancaster'. In these answers, the close conceptual connection between the action and the object of desire is absent. Normally, to describe the action as 'signalling right', as is done in the initial question, is to assume that the person *wanted* to signal right. The question is directed at discovering *why* the agent wanted to signal, and the two alternative answers presented above would provide this information, unlike the original answer. However, there are circumstances in which the assumption made in the initial question may prove to be incorrect. For example, the driver might have been stabbed in the side, her hand hitting the indicator-stick unintentionally. In this case, no straightforward answer could be given to the question 'why did you signal a right-turn?', since the action-description involved here would itself have to be rejected for any reply to be made. For example: 'I wasn't signalling right – I was stabbed.'

We will now present a critical response to these replies, which involves a more serious challenge to the view that beliefs and desires can constitute causes of human actions. Consider the explanation of signalling right in terms of wanting to turn right. It is argued that, although the occurrence of the action cannot be logically derived from the presence of this desire alone, the action's occurrence *can* be derived if we include two further assumptions. First, that the woman believed signalling right to be a required preliminary to turning right; and second, that there were no other conditions present that would prevent the desired action being performed. More generally: if an agent A desires X, and believes Y to be the appropriate means towards X, then, in the absence of preventing conditions, it *follows logically* that A will do Y. But if this is so, beliefs and desires cannot be causes of actions, for there is a logically necessary connection between the presence of these beliefs and desires and, in the absence of preventing conditions, the occurrence of the appropriate action.

The apparent force of this objection can be seen from the way in which we typically regard the failure by agents to perform the actions appropriate to their professed beliefs and desires, as demonstrating that they do not 'really' believe or desire what they claim to. If someone professes to want X, and to believe that Y is the best means of getting X, but then fails to do Y, despite not being prevented from doing so, we will naturally come to doubt these professions. Thus: 'if you really believe Y is the best way of achieving X, but you don't do it, you *cannot really want* to achieve X.' According to the objection we are now considering, what is presupposed by a remark of this kind is that, if the person really does want X, it follows necessarily that Y will be done. In other words, the '*cannot*' in this remark is a matter of *logical* impossibility, and its use reflects the fact that the connection between beliefs, desires and actions is a logical one.

The issues raised by this objection are complex, and we confine ourselves to two criticisms. First, the fact that we use failure to act to cast doubt upon an agent's professions of beliefs and desires can perhaps be accounted for without assuming the existence of a logical connection as is claimed in this objection. Instead, it may be that this use of action-failure is explained by our belief that, if the agents genuinely believe and desire what they profess to, this will typically cause them to act in the appropriate manner. We can give some support to this alternative account by considering an example involving the causal explanation of natural phenomena. Suppose we believe that striking matches causes them to light. If, on some particular occasion, a match fails to light after being struck, we will be inclined to suspect, amongst other things, that the match is itself defective. We are justified in suspecting this by our general confidence in the causal relation concerned. Here, it seems, there is an analogy with our being led to suspect the agent's professions, when the kind of action that we believe to be caused by the professed beliefs and desires fails to occur. In neither of these analogous cases need we assume that logical, rather than causal, relations obtain.

However, the extent of this suggested analogy is problematic. If the match fails to light, we must, in principle, be prepared to abandon our general causal belief, if no suitable defects can be discovered; although, as we noted in section 1 of chapter 3, it is difficult to state at precisely which point we should abandon such beliefs. But the question is: are we, even in principle, prepared to abandon our beliefs about the relation between desires, beliefs, and human actions? What is perhaps involved here is a deeply-rooted conception of what constitutes a rational agent. A person who persistently fails, in the absence of preventing conditions, to act in the manner appropriate to his or her beliefs and desires may come to be regarded as fundamentally irrational. In other words, it is part of our concept of rational agents that their beliefs and desires typically cause them to act in the appropriate manner. Systematic failure to act in this manner will lead us to withdraw the application of this concept of rationality to them. But this does not mean that, where the concept *is* applicable, the relations between beliefs, desires and actions is non-causal.

Our second criticism concerns the nature of the clause asserting 'the absence of preventing conditions', which is an essential part of the characterization of the logical connection said to exist in the objection we are considering. If no advance specification is given of what are to count as preventing conditions, then the claim that actions follow necessarily from desires and beliefs, in the absence of such conditions, is in danger of becoming vacuous. For any apparent counter-example can be easily 'explained away' by citing some previously unspecified preventing conditions. If, on the other hand, an attempt is made to state these conditions in advance, the claim that there is a logically necessary relation becomes implausible. For, given any finite number of specified preventing conditions, it always seems possible to conceive of cases where an agent fails to act appropriately, but where, despite the absence of preventions, there is no need to doubt the agent's professions of belief and desire.[10]

Underlying many of the arguments against regarding reason-explanations as causal is a recognition of the close connections between the ways human actions are described, and the reasons for which they are performed. We conclude this section by showing that these connections are perfectly compatible with a causal analysis of reason-explanations. We can see this by noting how our descriptions of natural phenomena are typically *causal* descriptions. In some cases, these descriptions involve assuming the truth of a positive claim about the causes of the phenomenon. In others, what is assumed is only the falsity of various possible causes of the phenomenon, with no positive specification of the actual causes. Thus, to describe a particular noise as thunder is to make implicit reference to its cause, and to rule out alternative explanations, such as the firing of a gun; to describe a hole in the ground as a crater is at least to deny that it was brought about by human digging. Similarly, when Priestley described what we now call 'oxygen' as 'dephlogisticated air', he was adopting a particular theoretical explanation of the properties of this gas, in terms of the absence of phlogiston. To reject the explanation, as a consequence of denying the existence of this entity, is necessarily to reject the description 'dephlogisticated air'.

We have already suggested, in our discussion of the right-turn signal, that this description of the action would be rejected if the 'signal' were caused by a stab in the side. We can now provide a clear rationale for this. The initial description has to be rejected, since it assumes the falsity of several possible explanations of the phenomenon, one of which is now discovered to be true. Likewise with another of our examples, the man who 'gives a present' to express his gratitude. To describe the action in this way is to rule out various causal explanations of his handing over an object to the other person. This item of behaviour might have been caused by a desire to bribe, or to get rid of an unwanted article, or to show how much the object weighed; or by the belief that the recipient would regard it as an insult. If any of these were the reason for which the action was performed, the description 'giving a present' would be mistaken.

If these remarks are correct, we should be sceptical of attempts by anti-naturalists to distinguish radically the ways in which we conceptualize natural and social phenomena. Peter Winch, in defending such a distinction, compares the concept of thunder with that of an act of obedience. Whilst acknowledging the kind of point we have made about thunder, he insists (1958, p. 125) that:

> An event's character as an act of obedience, is intrinsic to it in a way which is not true of an event's character as a clap of thunder; and this is in general true of human acts as opposed to natural events. . . . An act of obedience contains, as an essential element, a recognition of what went before as an order. But it would of course be senseless to suppose that a clap of thunder contained any recognition of what went before as an electrical storm; it is our recognition of the sound, rather than the sound itself, which contains that recognition of what went before.

We can agree with Winch about the senselessness of ascribing 'recognition' to the clap of thunder. But there is an important similarity between the two cases which Winch ignores. To describe an event as an act of obedience is to assume that it was brought about by the agent's recognition of 'what went before' as a command. In other words, just as with 'thunder', the description can be seen as a causal one, since the agent's recognition is a causal reason for the action.

Winch, though, opposes the interpretation of reason-explanations as causal. If he were right about this, and we were wrong, then there would indeed be an important difference between the concepts of thunder and obedience. But what must be emphasized is that the conceptual connection between action-descriptions and reason-descriptions does not by itself constitute an objection to the causal interpretation of reason-explanations. The connection is perfectly compatible with that interpretation, and can be illuminatingly accounted for by it, provided that we also have an adequate analysis of the general relations between descriptions and causal explanations.

Further, on the basis of that analysis, we can now see a deficiency in Weber's distinction between direct and explanatory understanding. He contrasts, for example, our direct understanding of the fact that someone is angry, or is aiming a gun at an animal, with our explanatory understanding that the anger is caused by jealousy, or that the gun is aimed because of a command to do so. It is tempting to see this distinction as holding between the description and explanation of actions; the former being arrived at immediately, by direct observation, and the latter by a process of explanatory hypotheses and empirical testing. But this would be incorrect, as can be seen by noting that we might often be mistaken about these 'descriptions', and that our mistakes would typically be *explanatory* ones. Thus, what seems to be an expression of anger might instead be that of some other emotion; and the person described as 'aiming a gun at an animal' might instead be checking the sights of the gun, whilst it happened that an animal was in line with the gun-barrel. In both cases, the mistaken description would be due to mistaken explanatory assumptions, just as we earlier suggested about the description 'giving a present'. If this is so, then Weber's category of 'direct understanding' is not separable from that of 'explanatory understanding'; though, as we have now argued, he is correct in regarding the latter as involving causal explanations of human actions.[11]

Finally, let us consider some implications of the position we have defended for the significance of a distinction frequently used by anti-naturalist writers, between 'action' and 'behaviour'. They often maintain that a 'scientific' treatment of humans in society would require the causal explanation of (observable) *behaviour*, whereas

158

what is needed instead is the non-causal explanation of human *action*. And it is claimed both that the same item of behaviour can be seen as the performance of several different actions, and that the same action can be manifested in different items of behaviour. But this anti-naturalist view rests upon a misconception of what is involved in a 'scientific' approach, upon the acceptance of a positivistic conception of the natural sciences. More specifically, it assumes that scientific descriptions of the world must be given in terms of some pure, theory-neutral observational language, and that this would mean, in the social sciences, purely behavioural descriptions. In chapter 3, we accepted some elements of the conventionalist arguments against the existence of such a language, and we have used these in our comments about description and explanation in this section. Further, we should note that it is possible to challenge the explanatory assumptions embodied in action-descriptions, without resorting to a 'purely behavioural' description of the action in question, just as we argued in the analogous cases in the natural sciences. So, for us, it is legitimate to describe human actions in terms that do not belong to a privileged observational language, whilst accepting that these descriptions are themselves open to theoretical, explanatory criticisms.[12]

[handwritten margin note: WEBER SUBJECT- MATTER OF SOCIO- LS DISTINCT.]

3 Positivism, realism, and the agent's viewpoint

We argued in the last section that anti-naturalists are wrong to deny the causal nature of reason-explanations, and suggested that their position is partly due to their positivist conception of natural science. We will now argue that the tendency of many naturalist social scientists to reject, or devalue, the importance of reason-explanations is also due to positivistic assumptions about science, and that a realist view of science enables us to avoid this mistaken tendency. The main features of positivism relevant here are the commitment to an ontologically and epistemologically privileged observational language, and the related treatment of theoretical terms.

We can begin to see the consequences of a positivistic naturalism for social theory by noting some of its manifestations in psychological theory, where the adoption of positivism has led to a variety of methodological positions that can loosely be termed 'behaviourist'. What is common to these is a rejection of the explanatory value of terms referring to 'subjective states', such as purposes, intentions, feelings, emotions, values, beliefs, and so on. Such states are regarded by behaviourists with considerable suspicion, primarily because of their apparently unobservable character. Sometimes, this has resulted in trying to eliminate from psychological theories terms that belong to the vocabulary of subjective states. But more often, attempts have been made to deal with these terms by the techniques developed by positivist philosophers of science in their treatment of theoretical terms in the natural sciences. As we noted in section 3 of chapter 1, one important technique is the use of correspondence rules, to provide definitions of theoretical terms in the observational language.

One type of correspondence rule is that involved in 'operational definitions'. As an example of such a definition, let us consider the well-known attempt by E. C. Tolman to define 'the rat expects food at location L' (quoted in C. Taylor, 1964, p. 79):

> When we assert that a rat expects food at location L, what we assert is that *if* (1) he is deprived of food, (2) he has been trained on path P, (3) he is now put on path P, (4) path P is now blocked, and (5) there are other paths which lead away from path P, one of which points directly to location L, *then* he will run down the path which points directly to location L.
>
> When we assert that he does *not* expect food at location L, what we assert is that, under the same conditions, he will *not* run down the path which points directly to location L.

This is an attempt to translate a statement using a term apparently denoting the unobservable state of 'expectation', into a set of statements in the privileged observational, behavioural language. As Charles Taylor has argued, this translation, and any like it, are open to serious objections. Suppose, for example, that a cat were placed on the path leading to L: we would not then regard the rat's failure to run down this path as indicating its lack of expectation of food at L. Conversely, if this path were a different colour from the others, we would not regard the rat running down it as necessarily indicating the presence of this expectation. Although these particular difficulties could be avoided by adding further conditions to the definition, there will always be an indefinite number of additional circumstances in which the definition does not hold. Furthermore, such definitions are subject to the problems deriving from the logical form of hypothetical statements: for example, the rat must be said to be expecting food at L whenever it is *not* placed in the specified test-conditions.

A somewhat different manoeuvre favoured by some positivist psychologists is to define the general concept of purposive action in terms of statements about behaviour, and then to define particular purposes by specifying the content of different patterns of behaviour. Often, this manoeuvre is based upon analogies from cybernetics. For example, it is sometimes claimed that purposive action is that which tends to result in some definite state of affairs, despite the presence of events or circumstances that might otherwise be expected to prevent this state from being realized. This claim, if correct, would then enable psychologists to use the concept of purpose, without any reference to the beliefs and desires of the human agent.[13]

For the realist, the necessity and legitimacy of these various forms of behaviourism is undermined by the general deficiencies of the positivist view of theories and theoretical terms upon which they are based. As we saw in section 3 of chapter 2, the realist rejects the positivist's attempt to remove the ontological commitments of theoretical terms by defining them in the observational language. An item's unobservability is not regarded as ruling out its existential status, and observations are seen as providing evidence for the nature or presence of such items, not the meanings of the terms referring to them. For the realist, then, there can be no presumption that the theoretical terms of psychological theories do not refer to existent items, including subjective states, that stand in causal relations to observable behaviour.

Thus, in psychology, the differences between realist and positivist naturalism can be clearly articulated and illustrated, and we can see how realist arguments can be used to defend the legitimate place of subjective states in the causal explanation of human action.[14] In sociology, however, the situation is more complex. Occasionally, a strong form of behaviourism is advocated. Thus, Lundberg, whose positivist conception of science we noted in section 4 of chapter 4, makes the following claims (1964, p. 17):

> Today, however, [c. 1939], a considerable number of students of societal phenomena are still firmly convinced that the phenomena with which they have to deal cannot be adequately described or explained without, for example, a category called 'mind', which carries with it a whole vocabulary of subsidiary terms (thought, experience, feeling, judgement, choice, will, value, emotion etc. etc.) . . . These are the phlogiston of the social sciences. Argument or demonstration that the behaviour represented by these words is accorded full recognition within the present framework of the 'physical' sciences are to some apparently as futile as were the arguments against phlogiston to Priestley . . . I have no doubt that a considerable part of the present content of the social sciences will turn out to be pure phlogiston. That fact will be discovered as soon as someone attempts operational definitions of the vocabulary which at present confounds these sciences.

Quite apart from the positivistic behaviourism of this passage, it is interesting to see how Lundberg uses one of the standard items in positivist folklore, the 'non-scientificity' of the concept of phlogiston, in rejecting the place of subjective states in a scientific theory of society. As we argued in section 4 of chapter 2, there is no good reason to regard the concept in this way. The change from Priestley's theory of combustion to Lavoisier's did not involve the replacement of non-science by science, but the denial of the existence of an entity which had been mistakenly, but not unscientifically, held to exist.

However, such outright rejections of the legitimacy of explaining social phenomena by reference to subjective states are rare amongst positivist sociologists. More often, both their methodological claims and their actual practice have displayed a considerable degree of ambiguity or inconsistency on this issue. The consequence has been a strong tendency to ignore or undervalue the significance of such states, and a failure to analyse adequately the theoretically mysterious realm of the subjective. We noted earlier several examples of this: in the explanation of revolutions (chapter 6, section 4), in the positiv-ization of the concept of role (chapter 4, section 4), and in Durkheim's *Suicide* (chapter 4, section 3). Let us now examine this last example, since it raises a number of important points.

Durkheim (1952, p. 44) defines suicide as follows:

> the term *suicide is applied to all cases of death resulting directly or indirectly from a positive or negative act of the victim himself, which he knows will produce this result.* An attempt is an act thus defined but falling short of actual death.

In arguing for this definition, Durkheim considers whether reference should be made to the agent's *intending* his death, as distinct from *knowing* that this will happen. He rejects this, partly on the grounds that intentions are not easily observable. This reason is closely related to Durkheim's emphasis upon the 'externality' of social facts, one aspect of which is that they should be detectable by perception. Yet Durkheim's own definition of suicide does not entirely eliminate the unperceivable, since it makes use of the concept of knowledge: this necessarily involves the concept of belief, and a belief is, in principle, no more external and perceivable than is a purpose or intention. It may sometimes, of course, be easier to discover what people believe than what they intend. But if this is Durkheim's reason for including knowledge and excluding intention, his definition is inconsistent with the strict requirements of his methodological principal of externality. Indeed, as we noted in our earlier discussion of Durkheim, there is also a considerable tension between different elements in his methodological position. For example, he adopts a criterion of 'coercive power' for social facts, which involves, in some cases, reference to internalized social pressures: and these can hardly be described as perceivable.

Durkheim is opposed not only to definitions, but also to explana-tions, which make reference to the subjective states of individual agents. We can see some of his reasons for this by examining his response to the view that the relative constancy of suicide-rates could be explained by supposing that 'various incidents of private life . . . regularly recur annually in the same proportions'. On this view, all we need assume is that humans, faced with such incidents as unhappy marriages, bankruptcies, disappointed ambitions, or poverty, 'reason generally in the same way', and thus respond to them by committing suicide (Durkheim, 1952, p. 305). But Durkheim rejects this view (1952, p. 306 – our italics):

> we know that these individual events, though preceding suicides with fair regularity, are not their *real causes*. To repeat, no unhappiness in life necessarily causes a man to kill himself unless he is otherwise so inclined. The regularity of possible recurrence of these various circumstances thus *cannot explain* the regularity of suicide. Whatever influence is ascribed to them, moreover, such a solution *would at best change the problem, without solving it*. For it remains to be understood why these desperate situations are identically repeated annually, pursuant to a law peculiar to each country. How does it happen that a given, supposedly stable society always has the same number of disunited families, of economic catastrophes etc?

Thus, for Durkheim, the main defect of this view is that it is seriously incomplete: it fails to account for the regularity of the incidents that are postulated as the causes of suicide. We can endorse this criticism, while noting that there is a tendency on Durkheim's part to deny *all* explanatory power to such incidents, on the grounds that they too must be explained. But this is mistaken, since it would mean that only an ultimate explanation – that is, one for which there is no further explanation – can have *any* explanatory value.

However, there are other important criticisms of the account of suicide rejected by Durkheim which, though sometimes implicit in his work, are never fully developed. Many people find themselves in 'desperate situations', but only some of them commit suicide. Any adequate analysis of suicide must explain why, for some individuals, a particular set of circumstances or incidents are perceived as requiring or justifying the response of suicide. To do this, we would need to examine the subjective states of the people involved, their beliefs, values, purposes, emotions, and so on. In other words, we would have to analyse those circumstances 'from the agent's viewpoint', since it is the way they are interpreted that partly determines the agent's action. Furthermore, we can expect to find characteristic differences between the ways in which the members of different societies or social groups interpret these circumstances. What is regarded as a situation sufficiently desperate to make suicide appear an appropriate response, may differ from one such group to another.

It is important to discover these differences, and also to explain them. Thus it is not only the occurrence of desperate situations that requires analysis, but also the ways in which people experience them, and the differences between these experiences.

We suggest that Durkheim's failure to explore the kinds of issues raised by these comments is due partly to his positivism, and partly to his attempts to defend the autonomy of sociology from individualist, psychologistic approaches. We agree with him that such approaches are inadequate and incomplete. But we reject his tendency to deny any value to the analysis of subjective states. By doing so, he excludes an important range of sociological questions, such as why what is regarded as a sufficient reason for suicide in one social group is not so regarded in another. We can only pose such questions when we have first understood social phenomena from the agent's viewpoint.[15]

Durkheim's general opposition to a sociology that is sympathetic to the concepts and explanations used by agents, is clearly indicated in the following passage (1897: quoted by Winch, 1958, p. 23):

> I consider extremely fruitful this idea that social life should be explained, not by the notions of those who participate in it, but by more profound causes which are unperceived by consciousness, and I think also that these causes are to be sought mainly in the manner according to which the associated individuals are grouped. Only in this way, it seems, can history become a science, and sociology itself exist.

In marked contrast to this view, several anti-naturalist writers have argued that the central aim of sociology should be the reconstruction of the ways in which agents themselves explain their actions; and that the theoretical concepts used by sociologists must not depart radically from those of the agents. For example, Alfred Schutz claims that 'the actor and he alone knows what he does, why he does it, and when and where his action starts and ends' (Schutz, 1954, p. 243). And, discussing the sociologist's use of abstract models of typical agents and actions, he insists (1954, p. 247) that:

> each term in such a scientific model of human action must be constructed in such a way that a human act performed within the real world by an individual actor as indicated by the typical construct would be understandable to the actor himself as well as to his fellow-men in terms of common-sense interpretations of everyday life.

Winch, whose position is similar to Schutz's, says (1958, p. 89):

> liquidity preference is a technical concept of economics: it is not generally used by business men in the conduct of their affairs but by the economist who wishes to *explain* the nature and

consequences of certain kinds of business behaviour. But it is logically tied to concepts which do enter into business activity, for its use by the economist presupposes his understanding of what it is to conduct a business, which in turn involves an understanding of such business concepts as money, profit, cost, risk etc. It is only the relation between his account and these concepts which makes it an account of economic activity as opposed, say, to a piece of theology.

Let us now consider the nature and rationale of these attempts to limit the theoretical concepts of the social scientist. We can note that the proposed connection between agent's and sociologist's concepts is not necessarily a very close one. Thus, Schutz's criterion, that the sociologist's concepts should be 'understandable' to agents in terms of their everyday interpretations of the social world, could in practice allow a wide range of technical or theoretical concepts. The actual extent of this would depend upon people's ability to grasp the meaning of such concepts in relation to those of their everyday life. Indeed, we must remember how concepts, at one time belonging exclusively to the vocabulary of the professional social scientist, come to be widely used in everyday discourse – though often not in precisely the same senses. Similarly, Winch's requirement that the social scientist's concepts be 'logically tied to' the agent's, need not be very restrictive, depending on how we interpret this phrase. Consider Marx's concept of surplus-value: unless 'logically tied to' is taken to mean 'completely definable in terms of', it is not obvious that this concept is incompatible with Winch's requirement.

Why, anyway, should Winch and Schutz be concerned to place restrictions on the theoretical concepts of social science? Their position derives, we believe, from an important feature of those explanations in which we ascribed subjective states to the agents. It is often held that, in making such ascriptions, the agent's professions must be regarded as having some special authority or priority. One plausible interpretation of this claim is that there is something objectionable or improper in characterizing people's subjective states in terms of concepts that are unavailable or unintelligible to them. If we ascribe beliefs or intentions to someone, we must recognize that these are, in some way, constituted by the person's concepts: what one believes or intends is essentially related to the conceptual framework within which one operates. Thus, for example, it would be absurd to explain the actions of a medieval surgeon as intended to prevent the spreading of 'virus infections' since this concept was unavailable at that time. Similarly, it would be erroneous to ascribe to medieval merchants, beliefs specified by means of concepts that are peculiar to those engaged in monopoly capitalist enterprises.

It is difficult to state precisely the conceptual limits of the ascriptions that can intelligibly be made in such cases. However, we will not pursue this problem here. For what must be emphasized is that any general proposal to limit theoretical concepts to those 'available to the agent', can only be justified by restricting social science to the type of explanation in which a limitation of this kind has some reasonable basis. This type of explanation is *reason*-explanation. As we argued in the previous section, such explanations typically refer to the beliefs and desires of the agent; and, as we have now suggested, there are good grounds for some form of restriction on the concepts used to describe such items. Thus, if one limits sociological theories to a reconstruction of the agent's reasons for action, it makes sense to restrict the sociologist's concepts in this way. But, although we accept the importance, and causal status, of such explanations, we see no reason to limit sociology to this level of analysis, as our earlier comments on Durkheim have indicated. In other words, advocacy of conceptual restrictions depends on advocacy of explanatory restrictions, and the latter is unacceptable. Conceptual restrictions of the kind we have been discussing must themselves be restricted to a particular level of explanatory analysis.[16]

We conclude this section by considering the relevance of our argument for a common interpretation of Marx's concepts of ideology and false consciousness. It is often thought that Marx's use of these concepts involves him in a systematic devaluation of the explanations given by agents for their own actions. It is held that, for Marx, such explanations typically display false consciousness, in that they do not provide the 'real causes' of human action, which instead are to be located in, for example, class interests. The following passage from Engels (Marx and Engels, 1962b, p. 497) could be interpreted in this way:

> Ideology is a process accomplished by the so-called thinker consciously, it is true, but with a false consciousness. The real motive forces impelling him remain unknown to him; otherwise it simply would not be an ideological process. Hence he imagines false or seeming motive forces.

In other words, to say that an agent's explanation is ideological is to claim that it is a 'rationalization', that it conceals the real reasons for the action, and gives reasons that appear to justify it, but in fact do not.

But this is a mistaken interpretation of Marx's concept of ideology, and of its implications for agent's reason-explanations. For Marx, the primary reference of this concept is to systems of belief. To describe them as ideological is both to criticize them on the grounds of distortion, and to suggest a relationship between them and the interests and structural features of a particular class. We will explore these ideas in the following chapters. For the moment, though, we should note that it in no way follows from the fact that agents' beliefs are ideological, that they do not form part of the causal explanation of their actions. We may be interested in evaluating these beliefs, and also in explaining why they are so widely accepted amongst the members of a particular social class or society. But to do this does not involve any systematic rejection, as mere rationalizations, of the agent's professed reasons, which include their beliefs. We can, of course, challenge the agent's reasons in this way: for reason-explanations are open to causal assessment. But in judging an agent's beliefs to be ideological, we are not making this kind of challenge. Rather, we are evaluating those beliefs negatively, and indicating the way in which their acceptance by the agent should itself be explained. Both these types of analysis are legitimate and significant, but they do not entail a total rejection of the agent's viewpoint.[17]

4 Meaning and understanding

So far in this chapter, we have been primarily concerned with analysing the nature of reason-explanations, and their relation to other levels of explanation in sociological theory. We have claimed, against both anti-naturalists and positivist naturalists, that subjective states can properly be regarded as causes of human action. And we have argued that explanations of this kind are not made redundant or irrelevant by the sociologist's legitimate emphasis upon further modes or levels of causal explanation. In this section, we will examine a different, though related, set of issues, which are centred around the general claim that, unlike the natural sciences, the social sciences are typically involved in the process of *understanding meanings*. Thus we will consider whether or not there is a form of understanding or *verstehen*, that is peculiar to our knowledge of social reality.

Let us begin by noting that there is an important sense of 'understanding' in which we can be said to understand anything for which we know the causal explanation. In this sense, understanding is an aim of both the social and natural sciences. We can call this 'explanatory understanding', and it includes, as one type, the understanding that we gain from explaining human actions by reference to the agents' subjective states. Whether or not additional forms of understanding are also involved in such explanations is a separate question. Often, these additional forms are characterized by saying that they have 'meanings' as their objects. But we must recognize that there are several senses of this term in which the understanding of meanings is not significantly different from explanatory understanding. We will now consider briefly two such senses.

First, there is the sense in which 'meaning' can be used more or less interchangeably with the concepts of purpose and intention. Most of the examples we used in discussing the nature of reason-explanations, in section 2, could be re-formulated by using this sense of 'meaning'. Thus, in place of 'why did you give the present?', and 'my reason was to express gratitude', we could have 'what did you mean by giving the present?', and 'I meant (or intended) to express my gratitude'. When we ask what people meant by doing something, we are often asking for their reasons, intentions or purposes. If, as we have argued, it is correct to analyse these reasons as possible causes, then understanding the meaning of an action is, in this sense, a case of explanatory understanding. Second, there is the sense of 'meaning' involved in examples such as these: 'his getting drunk means that he'll be in an unsympathetic mood tonight', or 'the drop in the barometer means bad weather'. Here, the meaning-relations are based upon knowledge of empirical regularities, and to understand the meaning is to be able to make predictions on this basis. We can regard this form of understanding as a general category of which explanatory understanding is a special type, where the empirical relations are causal. Clearly, there is nothing peculiar to the social sciences about these senses of 'meaning' and 'understanding'.[18]

We turn now to the way in which positivist philosophers of the social sciences have treated the claim that there is a form of understanding distinctive of our knowledge of social reality. Perhaps the most dismissive response to this claim is Otto Neurath's: 'Empathy, understanding, and the like may help the researcher, but it enters into the system of statements of science as little as does a good cup of coffee, which helped the researcher to do his work' (quoted in Apel, 1972, p. 15).

Less exuberantly, Hempel (1942, pp. 239–40) discusses

the method of empathic understanding: The historian, we are told, imagines himself in the place of the persons involved in the events which he wants to explain; he tries to realize as completely as possible the circumstances under which they acted and the motives which influenced their actions; and by this imaginary self-identification with his heroes, he arrives at an understanding and thus at an adequate explanation of the events with which he is concerned.

This method of empathy . . . is essentially a heuristic device; its function is to suggest psychological hypotheses which might serve as explanatory principles . . . but it does not guarantee the soundness of the historical explanation to which it leads.

For positivists, 'understanding' is merely a psychological device by which we postulate the nature of other people's subjective states. The use of this device in no way establishes the validity of its results, and therefore it does not belong to 'the logic of science'. To think otherwise would be to claim a special, intuitive form of non-empirical knowledge, and this the positivist rejects. There is thus no form of understanding that is both peculiar to social science and relevant to its epistemological character.[19]

We will examine the most important grounds for rejecting this positivist view of understanding further on. But first we will introduce a sense of 'understanding' that is certainly peculiar to social science, whatever the epistemological implications it may be thought to have. This can best be seen as an extension of Weber's concept of empathic understanding, and we will call it 'experiential understanding'. For Weber, we have empathic understanding when we know what other people's emotions are, and have also experienced similar emotions ourselves. The same is true for experiential understanding, except that all subjective states, not merely affective ones, are included. It is clear that we often have, in varying degrees, experiential understanding of others, and that this cannot exist in our knowledge of natural phenomena, since subjective states are not amongst their characteristics. Thus, we can give some positive answer to the rhetorical question put by Ernest Nagel: 'Do we really understand more fully and with greater warranted certainty why an insult tends to produce anger, than why a rainbow is produced when the sun's rays strike raindrops at a certain angle?' (Nagel, 1961, p. 483). For, without claiming any greater *certainty*, we can reasonably say that a 'fuller' understanding is possible, in that people may often have experiential understanding of the subjective processes involved in angry responses to insults.

Further, we suggest that humans also have the capacity to extend the range of their own experiences as a result, for example, of the perceptive and sensitive presentation to them of other people's experiences. It is this which often occurs in reading novels, poetry and drama. We can, then, distinguish a sense of 'understanding' that is closely related to experiential understanding, and can be called 'vicarious experiential understanding'. In this, we not only know other people's subjective states, but are somehow able to understand them in the sort of way that we would if we had previously had similar experiences ourselves. We gain a kind of experiential understanding, but not subject to its limitations to earlier experience. It is arguable that the capacity for vicarious experiential understanding is an important one for social scientists to possess, in that it may be associated with a general sensitivity and perceptiveness of considerable value in arriving at explanatory understanding of human actions. We are not, however, claiming that these capacities are directly relevant to the justification or substantiation of causal explanations. Instead, as we will now argue, the view that there is a form of understanding which is epistemologically distinctive of social science should be defended in a very different way, with no reference to the concepts of experiential or explanatory understanding.

We noted, in section 1, that one important element in Weber's account of the emergence of capitalism in Western Europe was his attempt to establish 'meaning-congruence' between the values and attitudes endorsed by the Protestant Ethic and the Spirit of Capitalism. As a provisional statement of the position we will defend, we can say that, involved in this attempt, is a form of understanding that has no direct analogue in our knowledge of the physical world: we will call it 'interpretive understanding'. We begin by considering the way in which Weber arrives at his characterization of the S. of C. He first examines a number of passages from the writings of Benjamin Franklin, including these (quoted in Weber, 1930, pp. 48–50):

> Remember, that *time* is money. He that can earn ten shillings a day by his labour, and goes abroad, or sits idle, for one half of that day, though he spends but sixpence during his diversion or idleness, ought not to reckon *that* the only expence; he has really spent, or rather thrown away, five shillings besides . . .
> The most trifling actions that affect a man's credit are to be regarded. The sound of your hammer at five or six in the morning, or eight at night, heard by a creditor, makes him easy six months longer; but if he sees you at a billiard-table, or hears your voice at a tavern, when you should be at work, he sends for his money the next day; demands it, before he can receive it, in a lump . . .
> Beware of thinking all your own that you possess, and of living accordingly. It is a mistake that many people who have credit fall into. To prevent this, keep an exact account for some time both of your expenses and your income. If you take the pains at first to mention particulars, it will have this good effect: you will discover how wonderfully small, trifling expenses mount up to large sums, and will discern what might have been, and may for the future be saved, without occasioning any great inconvenience.

Weber proceeds to interpret these and other remarks in a particular way. He ascribes to Franklin the views that 'honesty is useful, because it assures credit; so are punctuality, industry, frugality, and that is the reason they are virtues'; that the *summum bonum* consists in 'the earning of more and more money, combined with the strict avoidance of all spontaneous enjoyment of life'; and that everyone has a duty, or calling, to pursue this end (Weber, 1930, pp. 51–4). Weber claims

that these views are both typical of, and peculiar to modern capitalism, and goes on to argue that they are 'congruent' with the P.E. We
are not concerned with these last two parts of his argument. Rather,
we want to examine what exactly is involved in Weber's *interpretation*
of Franklin's writings, and thus the general nature of interpretive
understanding.

The first point to note is that this interpretation depends upon
Weber's ability to understand the words and sentences in the
passages we quoted. Thus, although the interpretation clearly involves
more than this, it presupposes the understanding of linguistic meaning. Though this may seem a trivial point, we will argue that it is in
fact significant. For the understanding of language cannot be assimilated to any of the forms of understanding that we have so far
discussed, and it involves a concept of meaning that is similarly
distinctive. We can see this by considering, and rejecting, the possibility that what is involved is explanatory understanding, where the
causal explanation is in term of the reasons for which the agent
performs the action of writing or uttering linguistic items. In particular, we should reject the view that the meaning of an utterance is
given by the intention with which the speaker makes this utterance.
If this 'intentionalist' view were correct, we could analyse the understanding of linguistic meaning as a case of explanatory understanding,
with the speaker's intention as the cause of the action.

Consider, for example, the statement 'the ice over there is thin!',
shouted at someone walking across a frozen lake. An 'intentionalist'
might claim that to understand its meaning is basically to know the
intention with which the utterance was made: here, this would
probably be to warn the person against walking on a particular area
of ice. But this account of meaning is, at best, seriously incomplete.
For it ignores the fact that, in order that someone can use the statement to carry out the intention of warning the person, the statement
must already have a meaning. It is only by virtue of this pre-existing
meaning, which is independent of the speaker's intentions or purposes,
that the speaker can 'mean' to warn someone by uttering the statement. It follows that the understanding of language cannot be
analysed as the explanatory understanding of actions caused by the
agent's intentions.[20]

If the understanding of linguistic meaning differs from explanatory,
or experiential understanding, this has important consequences for
an analysis of our knowledge of social reality. First, linguistic
utterances are a species of social action, and we must therefore be
able to account for our knowledge of their meanings. Second, the
connection between language and social action is much closer than
this first point suggests. For, as we argued in the previous two
sections, many social actions which are not themselves linguistic

utterances are nonetheless essentially related to language, in that they are characterized by their agents in terms of the conceptual framework within which they operate. Actions are typically described by reference to their agents' beliefs and desires, and these are partly constituted by the set of linguistic concepts available to them. Thus to understand the nature of such actions is dependent upon an understanding of the agents' language. Third, the understanding of linguistic utterances is a necessary means to knowledge of the systems of belief, values and attitudes that are important objects of sociological enquiry.

This last point was indicated in our account of Weber's interpretation of Franklin's writings. Let us now return to this, and consider what else is involved, in addition to linguistic understanding. The ethical views which Weber ascribes to Franklin are not simply a summary of Franklin's explicit comments. Rather, the latter are used as 'evidence' for the former, and the correctness of Weber's interpretation depends upon the plausibility of the argument that these explicit comments in some way rest upon, or derive their sense from, the ethical views. One feature of such an argument would be the claim that the ethical views are logically presupposed by these comments: that the former provide the assumptions from which the latter derive their rationale. Clearly, this feature of the interpretation bears a strong resemblance to certain forms of *philosophical* analysis, in which one attempts to discover the assumptions behind particular beliefs or doctrines, in order to make a critical evaluation of them. But, in interpretative understanding in the social sciences, there are greater restrictions on the assumptions and presuppositions that can reasonably be postulated: we must be partly guided, in this, by our knowledge of the kinds of beliefs and concepts that were present in the society concerned.

Linguistic understanding, and the kind of philosophical-logical analysis just outlined, are not the only elements involved in interpretive understanding. We cannot give a full account of these other elements, but we suggest that the most illuminating source for these is to be found in the types of analysis used in *literary* interpretation and criticism. Consider, for example, some of the questions often posed about Shakespeare's *Hamlet*: is it 'a study in the passion of grief, ... a dramatization of the conflict between optimism and pessimism as these doctrines were understood in the Elizabethan age, ... a symbolization of the theme of life versus death' (Weitz, 1965, p. 210)? An account of the nature of questions like these, particularly of their epistemological status, is important for social theory for at least two reasons. First, in many studies of social reality, the social scientist has to use evidence such as *Hamlet* to characterize the beliefs, attitudes and values that are present in a specific society or social group. Second, by examining the problems faced by literary theorists in assessing the truth or falsity of literary interpretations, we can gain some insight into the epistemological issues raised by interpretative understanding in general. We will now discuss one of these problems, commonly termed the 'hermeneutic circle'.

Consider the second of the three questions about *Hamlet* noted above. It assumes, amongst other things, that we already know there was a 'conflict between optimism and pessimism' in the Elizabethan age, and how these doctrines were at that time understood. Yet, in discovering these facts, we might well use literary products such as *Hamlet* as part of the evidence. In other words, it seems necessary to understand the social context in which this play was written in order to interpret it, whilst at the same time we have to interpret *Hamlet* in order to understand that context. Similar points could be made about Weber's interpretation of Franklin's writings. The same difficulty arises in the interpretation of a single text: to understand each part we require a prior grasp of the meaning of the whole, yet to understand the whole we need an understanding of each of its parts. Indeed, it is in terms of this problematic relation between whole and part that the general concept of the hermeneutic circle is often formulated.[21]

This concept is relevant to many types of enquiry. We will briefly note two of these, in anthropology, and in ethnomethodological investigation of conversational practice (see chapter 6, section 4). Consider the following problem posed by Martin Hollis (1967, p. 221 – our italics):

> Certain primitive Yoruba carry about with them boxes covered with cowrie shells, which they treat with special regard. When asked what they are doing, they apparently reply that the boxes are their heads or souls and that they are protecting them against witchcraft. *Is that an interesting fact or a bad translation?*

Why is this an interesting and difficult question? To know what the Yoruba believe, we must be able to translate their language. But one of our tests for correct translations is that the translated statement in some way 'makes sense'. To make this assessment, we have to examine the logical relations between the statement concerned and others. But to do this, we must already understand these other statements – a necessary condition of which is the intelligibility, or sense, of their translations. We are thus involved in the hermeneutic circle.

By contrast, although interpretive difficulties often arise, it seems that our understanding of each other in everyday conversation is normally unproblematic. One thing that makes everyday understanding possible, in practice, is the existence of a large variety of shared background assumptions and conventions between the communicants. It is the relative absence of these that makes the hermeneutic circle a particularly difficult practical problem for the anthropologist. Nonetheless, the more abstract or philosophical problem of how conversational understanding is possible is of considerable importance. Thus, we can suggest that one way of regarding ethnomethodological studies of conversational practice is as attempts to formulate the contextual requirements and interpretive procedures involved in the practical solution of the hermeneutic circle in everyday life. If this is correct, we should be wary of criticizing ethnomethodology on the grounds that its subject-matter is essentially mundane or insignificant.[22]

Finally, let us consider the relevance of what we have said about interpretive understanding to the question of the methodological unity of social and natural science. An important issue here is the relation between the criteria of validity for interpretive understanding, and those for explanatory understanding. It is sometimes held that the claims of, for example, literary interpretation to the title of 'knowledge' or 'science' are dubious, because there are no objective criteria for correct interpretations. But this view is mistaken, and with it, the implied contrast between the objectivity of the natural sciences, whose aim is explanatory understanding, and the subjectivity of those studies of social reality that involve interpretive understanding. There are three main reasons why this is mistaken. First, it assumes that explanatory understanding is the only legitimate form of knowledge, and that anything else must be judged by the criteria of validity appropriate to it. It thus ignores the possibility that different forms of understanding may have their own criteria of validity, which should not be seen as non-existent, or non-objective, merely because they differ from those of explanatory understanding. Second, this view is based upon an over-simple characterization of the criteria of validity for causal explanations in the natural sciences. In chapter 2 we noted various difficulties in stating such criteria. One of these, concerning the theory-loaded nature of observational-statements, has clear analogies with the problem of the hermeneutic circle. In both cases, we could say that every interpretation (or theory) is judged by reference to facts that are themselves loaded with theories (or interpretations). Third, as we will now conclude by arguing, any adequate account of the natural sciences, and of the way in which explanatory understanding is achieved in them, must include an analysis of interpretative understanding, and thus of its criteria of validity.

This argument rests upon the essentially social nature of any knowledge-seeking enterprise, whether this aims at knowledge of physical or social reality. As Kuhn and others have emphasized, to analyse this enterprise we must examine the nature of the scientific community. One fundamental feature of such communities is the presence of linguistic communication between its members. Without this, scientific activity would be impossible. But what is involved in this communicative interaction is the interpretive understanding of each scientist by others. Thus, to account for the possibility of explanatory understanding, we must provide a philosophical analysis of the nature and status of the interpretive processes, the shared linguistic and contextual meanings, upon which this is based. Nonetheless, we must also recognize an important asymmetry between the place of interpretive understanding in our conceptions of the natural and social sciences. In the latter, it is one of the forms of understanding that the practitioners of social sciences are aiming to achieve. In the natural sciences, interpretive understanding is presupposed by the attempt of its practitioners to gain explanatory understanding. But this asymmetry does not justify a straightforward defence of anti-naturalism. For the social nature of all human knowledge requires an analysis of interpretive understanding in both social and natural sciences. Finally, although interpretive understanding is peculiar to our knowledge of social reality, it does not replace or eliminate explanatory understanding in the social sciences.[23]

8 Reification and realism

1 The Marxist concept of ideology

The term ideology has a complex history and is presently used in a large variety of different ways.[1] If we try to identify what is common to these uses, we may say that the term is applied to sets of beliefs, or concepts, or theories, and is normally derogatory or pejorative. In particular, in the social sciences, to refer to a theory as ideological involves the claim that that theory is in some way distorted. It fails to meet appropriate criteria of knowledge or validity, and is to that extent objectionable or mistaken.

However, the kinds of distortion regarded as ideological are highly varied; let us distinguish two. First, within what we may term 'orthodox' or 'mainstream' social science, the form of distortion most frequently referred to is that resulting from the intrusion of 'values', which include political, moral and religious beliefs, the subjective and affective preferences and tastes of the individual scientist, and so on. Such values are seen as causing the social scientist either directly to misperceive what actually exists, or more indirectly to misapply techniques of theory-construction, operationalization, measurement or testing. The contrast here is between value-free and value-contaminated social science, the latter being seen as non-objective and ideological because of the intrusion of subjective elements. Much controversy has been generated as to whether, in this sense, all social science is ideological, whether it is in fact possible to exclude values, and indeed whether this is desirable. One response to this controversy has been to maintain that, if all social science is necessarily value-impregnated and ideological, the appropriate procedure is self-consciously to adopt one's preferred value-standpoint and to construct one's sociology directly in relationship to this.[2]

The 'Marxist' conception of ideology is quite different. One reason for this is that it is held, not that values contaminate our acquisition of factual knowledge of the world, but that the very distinction between facts and values cannot be maintained. There is a rejection of the logical heterogeneity of fact and value. We will not, however, elucidate in detail what Marx means by ideology. Rather we will consider certain methodological criticisms made by Marx and Marxists of other writers and theories. These raise central issues concerning the status and validity of the social sciences.

Essentially, for Marx, the manner in which knowledge is produced in a society, and its content, are directly related to the social relations of material production. For Marx, the class which is the ruling material force in a society also has control over the means of mental production. The ruling ideas are those ideas held by the ruling class. Such ideas represent in an ideal form the social relations of production. There are two central and connected elements in Marx's concept of ideology. First, a specification of particular forms of distortion. Second, a claim that these forms of distortion are dependent upon the relations of material production. In particular, it is held that the acceptance of ideologically distorted beliefs serve the *interests* of specific social classes. It is not that the ruling class intentionally and conspiratorially aims to dominate ideologically; rather that the structure of social relationships systematically generates ideological distortions which serve the class-interests of the dominant class. We will now consider further these two elements in Marx's conception of ideology, beginning with the first.

The term 'ideology' refers to a loosely connected set of errors and distortions. We are not interested here in the specific content of those ideas which serve to legitimate the dominance of a particular ruling class. Rather we shall consider one set of general types of ideological distortion associated with the notions of commodity fetishism and reification. There are important continuities between what Marx regards as the correct methodological approach in his later economic writings and the kinds of criticism he makes of other writers in works written earlier. Thus in *The German Ideology* (Marx and Engels, 1965) he criticizes social theories and philosophies of history which ignore the historical specificity of the 'laws' of social relationships. He considers as ideological distortion the seeing of the social relations of production specific to the capitalist mode, as natural and eternal. Further, he rejects those theories which take the psychological characteristics displayed by the members of such societies as part of human nature itself, as an unchanging given set of attitudes, motives and beliefs, which both explain and justify the continued existence of capitalist social relations.

Marx also objects to the ascription of an independent existence to the social products of human activity, and to regarding them as determinative of human behaviour. He argues that in the use of the notions of 'society', 'history', 'the invisible hand', and what we now call 'roles', there is a failure to recognize how it is that it is people themselves that constitute societies and make history.[3] Any adequate social analysis must begin from the basic premisses of the actions and material conditions of life of given, real individuals. To fail to see that it is they that make up society and make history is to commit an ideological error.

We can develop the second element of Marx's conception of ideology by noting how the distinction between appearance and reality functions in his later writings. Marx, as we saw in section 1 of chapter 5, criticizes the 'vulgar' economists for their failure to get beyond the 'appearances' of capitalist society. Part of what he means by this is that their theories are constructed in terms of the concepts, categories and everyday distinctions used by the members of that society in coping with and understanding its mode of operation. For Marx, this 'self-understanding' of a society by its members is itself distorted and ideological. Ideology, then, is not only a possible feature of explicitly theoretical attempts to understand the nature of any society, but it also infects in a systematic and patterned way the beliefs and concepts widely accepted and used by the members of that society.

Marx holds that these systems of ideological belief serve to maintain the established position of the dominant class or classes within a given social formation. Such ideologies, which contain theories, concepts, moral, social and political beliefs, and everyday assumptions and rules, are taken by Marx as serving the interests of that class or classes. It is not that the dominant class consciously promulgates an ideology which is in its interests; for example, the fetishism of commodities is seen by Marx as an unintended but pervasive aspect of the ideological superstructure in the capitalist mode. These distortions are produced by the systematic conditions which ensure the continued reproduction of capitalist relations of production, in which there is exploitation of labour by capital. For Marx the dominant ideology is that of the capitalist class. This is so in the sense that its content can be explained partly in terms of the interests of that class, given its structural location; and in the sense that the dominance of this ideology is due to the domination of this class. Marx's own theory is seen as being in the interests of the class of wage-labourers; both in that it exposes the ideological nature of the dominant systems of belief, and in that it supports the political interests of the dominated class. But Marx also believes that his own theory is not itself ideological, although it is of course class-related and class-interested. Thus for Marx, the explanation of given beliefs in terms of their class-relatedness, does not mean that those beliefs are necessarily distorted. Let us now consider why he thinks that his own class-based theory is scientific and non-ideological.

A non-ideological theory is one which, at the minimum, does not involve distortions, some of which have been mentioned above. Marx sometimes characterizes distorted theories as those that mistakenly take the appearances of capitalist society for its reality or essence. But this distinction between appearance and reality or essence is problematic. We did not employ it in our account of Marx in chapter 5; let us consider it here.

The term 'essence' is unhelpful since it may imply, contrary to Marx's belief, that all the constituent elements of a society are the phenomenal forms or appearances of a single underlying kernel or essence.[4] The term 'reality' is problematic since it may suggest that the appearances of a society are, by contrast, unreal. Yet Marx clearly emphasizes that what people experience within capitalism, and how they conceptualize it, is not illusory. It is rather that capitalist society appears to its members in a systematically misleading form. In failing to understand the underlying structural mechanisms of that society people do not merely make a mistake which arises out of stupidity, ignorance or prejudice. Thus, in his use of the terms 'essence' or 'reality', Marx is in fact referring to the central structural relationships within the CMP; these he analyses in a realist manner as both genuinely existent and causally determining. It is his theory of these relationships which explains that what appears to people, how they perceive and interpret their experiences within capitalist society, is misleading or false.

To show further that this distinction is unhelpful to our comprehension of Marx's method, let us also consider the term 'appearance'. One possible interpretation of this term is that of a theory-free observation. But we saw in chapters 1 and 3 that this notion is problematic. Consider the example of an appearance that Marx gives from the natural sciences, that is, of air as undifferentiated. When Marx says that the essence of air is different from its appearance, what he must mean is that the original observation is incorrect, because it assumes the truth of a false theory. For Marx then appearances are not empirically incorrect yet theoretically-free observations; rather they are our everyday observations and conceptions of phenomena, which rest on erroneous theories. We can also see how this is the case in the social sciences. What is wrong with the 'observation' that capital is naturally productive is that it is underlain by a false theory, not simply that the observation is itself incorrect. Capitalist society, for Marx, is not observed a-theoretically yet incorrectly; it is rather that the mechanisms of that society produce false theories embedded within the descriptions, perceptions, and experiences of people that live in that society.

Thus, Marx's professed aim to get to the reality behind the appearances can be seen in two different ways. First, that we explain, in a realist manner, observable features of capitalist society in terms of unobservable structures and mechanisms. Second, that we criticize members' everyday concepts and understandings because they are based on false theories. However, what is problematic is the characterization of both of these in terms of the single distinction between appearance and reality. However, in either case for Marx, it is necessary to go beyond such appearances. But there is one problem in this. For Marx the correct scientific theory enables one to reject the ways in which social phenomena are normally conceptualized and described. But if we are able to redescribe what takes place in a society in terms of a new scientific theory, then how can that theory itself be defended against those who reject the view that the existing descriptions are themselves distorted? What is it about one theory-dependent description which makes it preferable to another? What sort of reasons could we give for why Marx's description of the exploitative transactions between capitalist and wage-labourers is preferable to the descriptions provided by non-Marxist economists which do not involve the notion of exploitation? In discussing the relation between theories and perception in chapter 3 we suggested in the natural sciences that it is normally possible to find another description that could be agreed upon to judge between the competing theories. In the social sciences it may be that agreement on such descriptions is more problematic.

Let us now analyse in more detail certain categories of ideological falsity or distortion based on the concept of reification. We will consider the contributions of Georg Lukács and Peter Berger and Stanley Pullberg. Also we will consider whether Marx's own theory is reified on account of its predication upon a realist conception of science.

2 Lukács' analysis of reification

For Lukács the essential feature of capitalism is commodity fetishism; and the main product of such fetishism is reification.[5] In capitalism the relations between people acquire a 'phantom objectivity'. They take on the appearance of autonomous, all-embracing and rational relations between things. Society and history appear not as the products of social activity but as alien and impersonal forces, as laws of nature determining people's behaviour. Even men's own abilities and faculties are seen as properties to be owned and disposed of like things in the natural world.

It is only in capitalism that the production of commodities dominates the whole of society. This is linked with the growth of the market and exchange, and the consequent development of the division of labour and of the interdependent character of production. Labour becomes increasingly rationalized; there is a progressive elimination of the qualitative, human and individual attributes of the worker. The process of work is split up into abstract, rational and specialized operations which have to be completed within calculated and imposed periods of time. This calculability itself leads to an enhanced need for specialization and a heightened division of labour. Each individual worker becomes merely a mechanical element incorporated into a mechanical system, which is experienced as pre-existing and self-sufficient. His idiosyncrasies are seen only as sources of error. The principles of rationalization and calculability are extended from the place of work to every aspect of social life, to credit, finance, law, bureaucracies, the state, ideology, and ultimately to the 'very depths of man's physical and psychic nature' (Lukács, 1971, p. 101).

Such reification extends to science, or at least to bourgeois science, which is the ultimate expression of capitalist reification. This is because bourgeois science reflects the two features of reified capitalist society in which commodity exchange is dominant. First, there is the splitting up or fragmentation of all aspects of social life; there are the different commodities, work-tasks, roles, institutions, and so on. Second, within each sphere of life there are laws which govern the relationships between each commodity, or between each work-task, and so on. The individual finds these laws of economic life, of organizational structures, and so on, as pre-existent, unchanging, uncontrollable, and determinative of human action.

A reified science for Lukács follows these features of a reified society. It takes the appearances of that society and fails to penetrate to their essence or reality. In capitalism these appearances consist of isolated facts and complexes of facts produced by the reification of human relations. The structure of capitalism produces discrete thing-like classes of facts. They appear to be the obvious and given object for scientific study. Each such complex of facts gives rise to separate disciplines, of economics, political science, sociology, and so on. Further, in each of these disciplines reified science seeks to discover the general laws which relate together the normally measurable individual facts. Such general laws are seen as natural and eternal. Thus certain of the features of what we have identified as the positivist tradition in the philosophy of science are seen by Lukács as aspects of a reified science, of bourgeois or non-proletarian science.

Let us now consider how Lukács links the nature of science with specific classes and class-interests. For him in any society the major social formations are social classes; different societies are dominated by one or other class; history is the product of the conflict between classes; and within capitalism the bourgeoisie and the proletariat are the two significant social classes. Each class gives rise to a particular form of consciousness, bourgeois and proletarian consciousness. For Lukács there is no thought or knowledge or ways of thinking which are not class based. However, he further holds that the class consciousness of the proletariat is in fact true, whilst other forms are false; in particular, they are reified. He is not arguing that *actual* proletarian class consciousness is true; rather he regards that which logically the proletariat could develop, and which over time they will be forced to develop, as true. It is only from the vantage point of the proletariat that true theory can emerge. Let us now consider why, for Lukács, although the *ascribed* or *imputed* class consciousness of the proletariat is true, bourgeois consciousness must remain false.

First, it is inherent within the class position of the bourgeoisie that they will not analyse the possibility of a post-capitalist society. History is seen as ending with the system of capitalist production; and the laws of capitalist economics are taken to be natural and eternal. Second, the capitalist must minimize the importance of class conflict, and generally of the contradictory character of capitalism, at the time when such conflicts and tensions are becoming increasingly important. If the bourgeoisie did understand the contradictory character of capitalism and the means of its resolution, then they would see that this could not be achieved except by the abolition of the system itself. Third, capitalists necessarily view society from the standpoint of their own enterprise and they are therefore oblivious to the *social* implications of their *individual* activities. They will tend to believe that history is made, either by great men, analogous to the capitalists' running of their enterprises, or by a system of natural and eternal laws, analogous to those which confront their individual enterprises. Bourgeois consciousness thus reproduces the confrontation between the individual and the laws which naturally and eternally impel social phenomena. Bourgeois thought, however class-conscious, always remains partly falsely conscious because it cannot discover the solutions to the central problems of capitalist society.

Why, by contrast, is the class-position of the proletariat one in which true theory can be realized? First, we should note that class consciousness is an historically specific phenomenon. In particular, it is only with the development of capitalism that economic class interest emerges explicitly as a basis for consciousness. Further, in capitalism there are two classes, both of which are able to organize society in terms of their overall general interests. But it is the proletariat, whose interests are for Lukács genuinely universal, which, corresponding to Hegel's category of the Absolute Spirit, is both the producer and the product of history. The proletariat moves in a self-created world which imposes itself upon the proletariat, within which it acts, and with which the proletariat will be finally reunited.

The duality of subject and object, like other dualities such as freedom and necessity, can only be resolved when the proletariat acts as the first identical subject-object in history. It is only the proletariat, placed at the centre of capitalist society, that can perceive the total workings of that society. Further, Lukács argues, more sociologically, that since it is the most alienated class in that society, it must abolish itself in order to liberate itself. And the proletariat's liberation of itself involves the liberation of the whole. But the proletariat cannot assert itself without exact knowledge of the whole; and that knowledge will be based, for Lukács, on the notion of totality.

What exactly Lukács means by the concept of totality is problematic. We may note the following. First, Lukács criticizes the 'blinkered empiricist' who fails to see that there are no theory-free facts, facts which have not been interpreted by some theoretical system. There are no brute facts. Further, he argues, it is crucial to acknowledge the historical character of these facts; they are not timeless and unchanging but merely the facts peculiar to some given historical period. All individual facts and complexes of facts can only be understood in terms of the whole social and historical process from which they have become detached. We should not view each set of facts on their own but as linked to the social whole. Moreover, adequate comprehension of these facts involves their identification as distorted or mistaken appearances. The analysis of the totality involves identifying how capitalist society functions; it enables us to grasp the essence of that society.

However, when we inspect the content of Lukács's analysis of capitalism it seems less convincing than that of Marx. In particular Lukács fails to produce a theory of the *structure* of the CMP; there is no systematic analysis of labour, of the links between the social relations of production (that is, labour: capital) and reified exchange relations, or of the connections between the relations of production and the proletariat as a revolutionary class. Rather he adopts reification as the master-principle which characterizes capitalist societies. All parts of the totality are taken to embody this particular principle. Furthermore, Lukács appears to claim that the way to eliminate capitalism is to eliminate reification. If the proletariat came to realize full class-consciousness then this would be itself tantamount to the overthrow of capitalist society.[6] Also Lukács, unlike Marx, fails to distinguish between the processes of reification and objectification. The latter is the inevitable process by which people objectify themselves in material objects and related patterns of social organization. The failure to make this distinction implies for Lukács that de-reification will mean that there are no objects, either material or social, which are external to each individual. Although the distinction between reification and objectification is problematic, it is necessary to make some such distinction. Only in certain forms of society is there reification of external objects and reified social theory.

3 Berger and Pullberg's analysis of reification

Let us now consider Berger and Pullberg's analysis of reification which is based on the distinction between objectifying and reifying processes. They make the following four-fold distinction.[7] *Objectivation* refers to man's production of material and social objects; and *objectification* to the process by which such objects are named, classified, and thereby partly detached from their producers. These processes are seen by Berger and Pullberg as anthropologically necessary. We both objectivate ourselves in objects and objectify them in a language. *Alienation* refers to that situation in which the objectivated product stands as an alien facticity or power set over and against its producer. It refers to the situation in which men forget that the world in which they live has been produced by themselves. *Reification* is that moment in the process of alienation in which objective reality is seen as comprised only of material things. There is a failure to acknowledge that the world has been man-made.

Let us note the following general points about their analysis. First, they argue that reification results from certain 'terrors' of human existence, in particular that of uncertainty and chaos which is only transcended by the firm order of a reified consciousness. Their analysis is thus couched in terms of the relations between 'man' and his 'world', and the more general category of alienation is taken to follow from the fact that man 'forgets' that he has made the world in which he lives. Unlike a Marxist explanation in terms of the overall structure of the society, alienation and reification for Berger and Pullberg is accounted for by whether or not people remember that social phenomena are human products. Second, de-reification (and de-alienation) is not achieved, according to Berger and Pullberg, once and for all with the ending of capitalism. Rather, it is dependent upon people being in situations of social disintegration, cultural shock or social marginality. These situations make explicit the social rather than the thing-like nature of reality. This is more likely to occur in modern rather than pre-modern societies; in the past, there was no Golden Age of a non-reified society. Further, interestingly, they fail to point out that de-reification can only result, not from the actions of single individuals, but from the coordinated and organized activity of specific social groups. Third, in the bulk of their article the term 'alienation' is dropped, and Berger and Pullberg concentrate upon reified consciousness, and seem to think that a reified society is one in which there is reified consciousness. However, when we consider this analysis at the level of consciousness, we find that they conflate a number of different elements. This can be seen in terms both of the examples of reified consciousness to which they refer, and of their more abstract characterizations.

Let us begin by considering their main examples of reification, social roles and social institutions. When we explain someone's actions by describing the role that that person is playing, this is a reification since we are taking the role rather than the person as the basic reality. Roles thus are reified since they are detached from human purpose and expressivity. Further, people themselves may come to believe that roles are the basic reality and that since they are the incumbent of a particular role, they could not have acted differently. Reified thinking on the theoretical level may thus become part of each person's taken-for-granted everyday world and language. Social institutions similarly are reified by mystifying their true nature as human objectivations. They are seen instead as supra-human facticities in which what takes place is founded upon the will of the gods, upon natural law, or upon human nature. This reification of social institutions, such as the family, the state, or the nation, occurs both at the theoretical level and at the level of participants within each institution. Thus while in fact 'men produce society as, at the same time, society produces men, what is now conceived of and actually experienced is only a situation in which society produces men' (Berger and Pullberg, 1966, p. 68).

Let us now consider this account of reification more critically. It contains a number of different elements, not all of which are consistent with each other, or entail each other, or, for that matter, are obviously erroneous. The first is the claim that there is nothing that is real which does not have the character of a *thing*; given then that social phenomena are real, they are taken to be things (Berger and Pullberg, 1966, p. 61). Second, the products of human activity are seen as having an *independent existence* separate from the activity that produces them (pp. 62–3). Third, reification involves the ascription of *ontological* status to social roles and institutions, whereas we should only ascribe such status to persons (pp. 67–8). Fourth, such roles and institutions are taken to determine *causally* how human beings behave; society is seen as producing men and not vice versa (pp. 67–8). Fifth, reification involves the claim that humans are *powerless* to change their social and historical circumstances (p. 68).

Initially we may note that the fifth claim, that human beings are powerless to change their historical circumstances, does not follow from the first three claims. In other words, the fact that we regard a set of institutions as a set of things with independent, ontological status, does not mean that they cannot be brought under our control and changed. To regard something as a thing, that is, as part of nature, is not *necessarily* to regard it as immutable, since many of our activities are directed precisely to the control of nature. Nevertheless, although powerlessness does not follow logically from the first three claims, one reason why people often feel powerless is that they do ascribe independent, thing-like, ontological status to social roles and institutions.

However, the view that products of human activity have an 'independent existence' is itself problematic. If we take this to mean that we fail to see that such products originate in human activity, then clearly this view is erroneous. But, if it means that such products are able to persist without continuing human activity, this is not a mistake in the case of one category of human products, namely material objects (tables, machinery, books, etc.). However, for other categories there would be a mistake involved; social institutions, roles and symbols could not persist without individuals engaging in constitutive patterns of human action. The other claims are also problematic. Berger and Pullberg hardly refer to the first element, that reification involves seeing social phenomena as material things. It seems to be articulated mainly to link their discussion with the Marxist tradition, and especially to Lukács. Anyway, it appears that the third element, that social phenomena are accorded an ontological status only properly attributable to people, is not dependent upon this first claim. In other words, we may well hold that social phenomena are real, that they have an ontological status as the effects of human activity, while denying that this status is that of a thing. Also it is not clear that the claim that social phenomena have ontological status is incorrect, although it would be wrong to ascribe to such phenomena the ontological status of a person.

The main argument then of Berger and Pullberg is that the second and third claims ('independent existence' and 'ontological status') entail the fourth, that such entities causally determine human actions. For them the prime example of reification is the viewing of social roles and institutions as having an independent existence, an ontological status, and a consequential causal efficacy in determining human action. Further, they seem to consider that these claims in turn entail powerlessness, the fifth element of reification. This is problematic however; the fifth element follows psychologically rather than logically. Thus, if people see social roles and institutions as causally determining their behaviour, then they will tend to feel powerless to change such external social forces. Also, interestingly, Berger and Pullberg sometimes appear to argue that any explanation of human action in terms of the causal operation of social factors constitutes a reification. We believe however that one can in fact distinguish between reified and non-reified causal explanations of human action. In the final section of this chapter we shall try to show why a realist causal analysis does not necessarily involve reification.

Before that, though, we shall consider how reification has been perhaps over-extended in its use as an undifferentiated term of ideological condemnation in contemporary social science.

4 Reification and the critique of sociological orthodoxy

The article by Berger and Pullberg is one of a number of works which, in the last ten years or so, have criticized, explicitly or implicitly, certain reified features of contemporary sociology.[8] In particular there has been criticism of such sociology because it is based upon taking 'society', 'structural' or 'social' factors as directing and determining each individual's patterns of behaviour. One type of criticism made is that it is erroneous to view society as a person directing and controlling human beings to fit into preordained and neatly organized social roles. Dahrendorf points out: 'Society is patently not a person, and any personification of it obscures its nature and weakens what is said about it' (Dahrendorf, 1968, p. 44). This personification or reification of 'society' is sometimes thought to be supported by, or to follow from, Durkheim's analysis of social facts. In chapter 4 we saw that such social facts are regarded by Durkheim as external to the individual, general, and coercive in their consequences. One such fact can only be explained in terms of another preceding social fact. These social facts constitute an irreducible social level of reality.

Let us consider Durkheim's analysis further. We may note that he uses the term 'society' to refer to a mere organized collection of individuals; to the basic reality responsible for transmitting and inculcating beliefs and practices; to a 'great moral power'; and to an actual concrete society (see Lukes, 1973a, p. 21). There are also a variety of referents of the contrast term, 'individual': the biologically given unit; the abstract individual with certain invariant properties (economic man, for example); the pre- or extra-social individual; and an actual concrete person (p. 22). Lukes argues that Durkheim employs different sorts of distinction between the generally social and the generally individual, but he mistakenly conflates them: 'he reified them into the abstractions of "society" and "the individual" ' (Lukes, 1973a, p. 21). Lukes suggests that by adopting this single and sharp dichotomy between society and the individual, Durkheim is led to the view that explanations must be either exclusively holist or exclusively individualist in their form. And in his concern to establish the specific subject matter and method of the science of sociology, Durkheim chooses the holist alternative, to explain social facts only in terms of other social facts. Different writers have chosen the individualist alternative; sometimes because they regard the holist position as one which involves reification. In particular they oppose the

187

ascription of ontological status to social phenomena. We will not enter into the debates between methodological holists and individualists except to note the fact that this conceptually mistaken controversy may well have arisen precisely because of Durkheim's over-rigid single distinction between society and the individual, resulting from the conflation of different distinctions.[9] Durkheim is wrong in thinking that we have to choose between holism and individualism. He need only have claimed that social facts cannot be fully explained in terms of facts about individuals, and there is thus a place for social or sociological explanations. But does Durkheim's position involve reification?

First, it might be argued that his injunction to treat social facts as things involves the first element of reification, identified in the previous section. However, it is unclear what Durkheim means by this. Initially, we may note that it is odd to suggest that facts of any sort are things. Thus we may restate his claim as: social phenomena are to be treated as things. But even so Durkheim is not saying that social phenomena *are* material things: 'We assert not that social facts are material things but that they are things by the same right as material things, although they differ from them in type' (Durkheim, 1938, p. xliii). Thus, not only does Durkheim think that social facts are not *material* things; also his injunction is merely that we should *treat* social phenomena as (non-material) things. That is, sociologists should adopt a certain attitude to them: they must abandon all the preconceptions they may hold about them; they must realize that they are ignorant of their nature, that their properties cannot be discovered by introspection, and that their analysis must proceed from external observation and experimentation. Thus Durkheim does not claim that social phenomena are things, only that they must be analysed in a similarly 'scientific' way.

Let us now turn to the second, third and fourth elements ('independent existence', 'ontological status' and 'causal efficacy') in Berger and Pullberg's account. For Durkheim social phenomena, like natural phenomena, are real. He says that his fundamental principle is the 'objective reality' of social facts, that 'social phenomena, although immaterial, are nevertheless real things, the proper objects of scientific study' (Durkheim, 1938, p. lvii). Clearly for Durkheim they have a distinctive ontological status and causal efficacy. But it is questionable whether he considers that they have an existence independent of their generative human activity. Consider the following ambiguous characterization of a social fact (Durkheim, 1938, p. lvi – our italics):

collective ways of acting or thinking have a reality outside the *individuals* who, at every moment of time, conform to it. These ways of thinking and acting exist in their own right. The *individual* finds them completely formed, and he cannot evade or change them.

In this passage social phenomena are at first taken to constitute a reality which is independent of *all* the individuals found within that society. He thus ascribes to such phenomena an existence independent of generative human action. However, later in the passage, these collective phenomena are held to be independent only of the particular individual whose standpoint we may consider. Durkheim here notes how the individual person finds social phenomena given and pre-existent. He also argues that each individual is unable to change collective ways of thinking or acting. But he appears not to see how it is quite possible for groups of individuals to change such established social practices. It seems that this possibility is concealed for him because of his simple differentiation between the individual and society. Finally, we may note that for Durkheim, people may still be powerless even if they do not reify, and this is because of a lack of the complex social theoretical knowledge of exactly how the social world is constructed and at which points it might be changed.

Let us now turn to the concept of social role, noting that for many writers this is the prime example of a Durkheimian social fact. Roles are customarily taken to provide the major link between the social structure and the human personality. People, in that they are social, are seen as role players, and acquire their basic character as social beings by virtue of learning appropriate role behaviour. The organization of the roles played within a society provides the basic matrix of the social structure, as for example in Nadel's *The Theory of Social Structure* discussed in chapter 6.[10] In our discussion of the use of role within the positivist tradition we have already mentioned several relevant criticisms.[11] A person's behaviour within a role is never purely conforming. Individuals bring to any role their previous biographical experiences. These provide them with sets of meanings by which they give their own interpretation to that role. Indeed, behaviour within a role always involves a certain reworking and redefinition of the expectations regarding the ways the incumbent should behave. Role behaviour is partly a construction, since role-expectations never fully specify the nature of a role-player's behaviour. Furthermore such expectations are rarely consistent with each other. There is never complete consensus as to the behaviour expected of the incumbent of a given social position.

Let us state the different ways in which it could be argued that the concept of role is reified; we will follow the five elements identified in section 3. First, roles and the properties of role systems, may be thought of as things or thing-like; they are given, fixed and un-changing. Second, roles may be seen as having an existence indepen-dent of the patterns of human activity which have generated and maintained them in existence. Third, it is social roles rather than individual people that may be seen as having primary ontological status. Fourth, the fundamental causal relationship may be such that social roles are seen as determining individual behaviour. Finally, individuals may feel themselves powerless to attempt to change the complex sets of roles and their interrelationships.

Let us now consider two or three writers who have either employed the role concept or have criticized its reified nature. First of all, in Biddle and Thomas's overview of the role concept, they argue that the dominant perspective 'is a limited, social determinism that ascribes much, but rarely all, of the variance of real-life behaviour to the operation of immediate or past external influences'. But they also point to the importance of 'the individual's own understanding of, and reactions to, these factors' (Biddle and Thomas, 1966, p. 17). To the extent that they reify the notion of role this is in the sense that they ascribe an independent existence to social roles and an unjusti-fied degree of causal efficacy. But they do not appear to reify roles with respect to the other elements of reification that we have dis-cussed.

Dahrendorf, in fact, argues that it is necessary to assume that people do play roles, but it does not follow that any reification is involved. He says: 'The fact that in sociology and social psychology the idea of role helps explain human behaviour implies absolutely nothing about the real existence of men with or without roles' (Dahrendorf, 1968, p. 103). For Dahrendorf the concept of role is instrumentally useful, just as economic man is a useful assumption in economics for the generation of 'powerful explanations and useful predictions' (p. 92). Thus he tries to avoid the accusation of reifica-tion by adopting an instrumentalist view about the logical status of scientific theories. It is clear that the adoption of an instrumentalist position avoids the charge of reification since it means that there are no ontological commitments involved. However, there are two points to note. First, we must consider exactly how the concept concerned is actually used in the analysis of the phenomena in question. Thus some argue, for example, that despite his methodological disclaimers, Dahrendorf does reify the concept of role.[12] Second, we would doubt whether 'powerful explanations' had been provided unless the concepts used in a scientific theory did actually refer to real structures and processes. This point relates more generally to the fact that, although most role analysts adopt a positivist, predictivist interpre-tation of roles, they also claim that this provides a causal explanation of human action in terms of the social roles individuals play. This is of course problematic since we have emphasized how a positivist approach provides us, not with causal explanations, but with law-like predictions about the natural or social world.

Finally, we should note that not all those writers who point to the reification of the role concept maintain that this occurs with respect to all five elements. Some concentrate upon the failure of role theory to analyse how roles are established, maintained, and transformed; that is, to consider the human activity which is generative of social roles. Others point out how roles are often analysed as though they are unchanging, and are hence unproblematically given to each present and future incumbent. Another criticism focuses on the presumption that roles are taken as things or thing-like and are governed by natural laws. It is further pointed out that social roles and their regular relationships should not be seen as eternal; and indeed that such eternalization does not follow from the fact that there may appear to be natural law-like regularities involved. Finally, it is sometimes claimed that if a causal relationship of any sort is thought to hold between a social role and patterns of individual action, then this is itself a reason for believing that reification is involved. This is connected with the view that a social deterministic account of roles may be associated with powerlessness. It is consequently maintained that social theories should not involve causal determination, since this may engender feelings of human powerlessness. In the next section we will consider a specific version of this claim; that is, that a realist social science, in that it focuses upon the causal efficacy of structures and mechanisms, will involve reification.

5 Realism and reified social theory

According to the realist, the question of what exists is of central importance to the scientist. The realist advocates the development of theories which provide causal explanations of regular relations, by reference to the characteristics of actually existing, although not necessarily observable, entities. Thus the realist is centrally concerned with whether a particular theoretical term genuinely refers to something, the ontological class to which such entities belong, and the ways they may be causally related to other such entities. Thus, to the extent that reification involves errors about ontological status and causal efficacy, we would regard realism as generally inimical to errors of this kind.

However, it might be thought that a realist naturalism in the social sciences will lead inevitably to the first element in the concept of reification, the identification of the 'real' with the ontological category of material objects. But this is not so for two reasons. First, if 'material object' is taken to mean macro-sized, observable objects, of the kinds that we perceive and manipulate in everyday life, then realism clearly assigns no privileged status to this type of entity, for reasons outlined in chapter 2. Second, if this phrase is taken to mean *any* kind of 'object', provided it belongs to the general category of the 'physical', there is still no necessary relation between realism and this element of reification. For realism, as a methodological position relating to the nature of scientific theories and explanations, involves no *a priori* commitment to a physicalist ontology. Realism, in the sense we have given to it, is independent of metaphysical disputes between, for example, materialism and dualism.[13]

There are, however, other reasons why realism may be held to generate a reified social science. A clear element in the notion of reification is the feeling of powerlessness in the face of apparently incomprehensible and unchangeable social structures. Thus a realist social science, in its focus upon causal mechanisms and structures, may be thought to lead to a mechanistic view of social life, where human action is governed by apparently natural and eternal laws, and which people are powerless to change. We will try to assess these problems by examining the kinds of relationships between social formations and individual action that are involved in our earlier realist interpretation of Marx.

Let us approach this by noting a particular reason why it may be held that Marxist realism must be reified. Since realist theories are intended to depict reality, then if that reality is characterized by reified social relations, then the social theory representing it will also embody reified elements (see Markovic, 1972). This is a specific application of the general thesis that the form of a social theory should mirror the social reality which it is meant to depict. Thus it is held that, if social reality were to change, then the concepts which denote that reality should also change (see Ollman, 1971). If this general thesis was correct with regard to the necessity for social theory to mirror the reified social world, then the only ideological element in the analysis would be in taking the relationship so identified as being eternally true.

We think, however, that this view is incorrect both as an account of Marx's own method and as a general characterization of an appropriate methodological position. For Marx, two elements of an adequate theory are: first, to represent the beliefs which are held by the members of a given society; second, to show how some of these are false, and why they develop and are sustained. Thus in his discussion of commodity fetishism, Marx talks of 'the fetishism peculiar to bourgeois Political Economy, the fetishism which metamorphoses the social, economic character impressed on things in the process of social production into a natural character stemming from the material nature of those things' (Marx, 1961, p. 225). For Marx, commodity fetishism consists in seeing the relations between commodities, particularly their exchange-values, as due to their natural properties as objects, when in fact they are the result of the historically specific social relations of the CMP. For Marx, in such a form of society, people are dominated by the structure of social relations which lie behind the exchange-values. This structure has two effects. First, certain properties of objects which are really social appear as natural. Second, the social relations themselves appear as things, governed by natural and eternal laws. A non-reified social theory is thus crucial in elucidating how it is that people came erroneously to believe that certain properties of commodities are natural and that social relations are things.

Let us now consider the minimal constituent claims of a non-reified theory. People are, it is clear, dominated in important ways by the structure of social relations. However, such relations do not have an existence in a society apart from the human activity that produced and continues to produce them. Social phenomena are thus irreducibly made by humans. But for any single person such relations have an existence apart from his or her activity. Individually, people correctly perceive the powerless nature of their situations. The form that social relations take is unintended by any single individual, but results from the interdependent activities of the past and present members of that and related societies. These social relations are not material things but they are real. They have ontological status, but not that of a person. Such social relations are causally effective but they do not fully determine the course of individual behaviour. Also crucial are the subjective meanings through which individuals assess, interpret, and actively construct their patterns of action within the given structures. Such meanings are not simply individual. Their content is logically dependent upon the shared meanings, rules, and conventions and their structured interrelationships, within the language at the societal level.

All human action is therefore caused or determined by the patterns of both social relations and individual meanings. However, we must distinguish between this kind of general determinism, and the specific forms of determination found within particular types of society. In other words, we hold that, although human action is everywhere determined, there is variation in the nature of such determination. That in turn, however, involves us in the analysis of the structures characterizing different forms of society. Let us briefly state why we consider that Marx's analysis of such structures, and particularly that of the CMP, does not involve reification. We will conclude with some comments on the nature of socialist society and especially upon probable forms of social science within that society.

Roughly speaking, we do not think that Marx's analysis involves

193

reification because its basic premises are those which we have just identified as the minimal constituent claims of a non-reified theory. Althusser, however, maintains that there is a radical break between the early and the late Marx. While the subject of history in the former is 'man' or 'men', in the latter it is classes or even the social relations of production. We will not concern ourselves with whether Althusser is strictly correct. Rather, let us summarize Marx's view in his later writings of the relationships between 'men', 'classes' and the 'relations of production'.[14]

Within the social relations of material production men act as the bearers of determinate and specified functions. As such, as agents, they carry out particular functions which are necessary to the continued reproduction of those productive relations. Men and the structures of social relations are internally related. It is not men who are the subjects of history, but rather it is those social classes, which are not reducible to, but which are generated within, the structures of social relations. In other words, the link between classes and human action is provided by those social relations of material production in which the systemic objective requirements become subjectively internalized. In acting as agents men develop needs, aspirations and objectives which are shared with others, and potentially involve conflict. Capitalism therefore, for Marx, involves specific determinations resulting from the fact that each person acts as a bearer of highly specific functions within the overall structure.

We have emphasized that for Marx social classes and class conflict are systematically generated within the social relations of material production; and the needs, purposes and objectives of individuals are likewise developed through the objective functions that they perform. Thus, to this extent, Althusser is correct in maintaining that, in Marx, humans are analysed primarily as 'bearers' of these functions (see Althusser, 1969, 1970). But one problem with this formulation is that it is unclear what would happen in a socialist society. Does it mean that there are bearers of specific functions analogous to the bearers of capitalism? We think that, although there will still be a sense in which people will bear functions or parts, the relationship between human action and the structural configuration of such functions will be different. We can consider this by returning to the issue of reification. A socialist society will be characterized by the following. First, certain elements of reification will disappear. The social world will not be seen to consist of things or to be thing-like in constitution; it will be clearly the result of human activity; and people will correctly feel that collectively they both have changed and can change it. But social relations will still have ontological status and causal power, although people will not ascribe erroneous status to such relations (such as that of a person).

There will clearly be social phenomena external to each individual and partly determinative of individual action. Such 'social facts' will include the social organization of production, language, norms of appropriate socialist behaviour, and so on.

Finally, as a result of these changes the place and function of social science will be altered. It might be thought that, because in a socialist society there will no longer be any gap between appearances and reality, we can expect an eventual 'withering away of social science' (the ideological analogue to the withering away of the state: see Cohen, 1972). But this seems partly mistaken. First, there will be social scientific analyses of a 'technical' nature of different social phenomena, such as those just mentioned. Indeed the study of language, if based on Chomskyan or similar principles, will involve the positing of different structural levels and the explanation of the possible 'appearances' of language (grammatical sentences) by its 'essence' or 'reality' (innate linguistic principles). Thus the argument that social science will wither away is a claim that general, systematic social theories, and especially that of historical materialism, will progressively disappear. Let us suggest the following. Because socialist society will not be dependent for its continued existence upon systematically generated false theories embodied in the perceptions and experiences of everyday life, there will be no need for a theoretical understanding which will emancipate people from these erroneous conceptions. A socialist society will be so structured that its everyday understandings will not be distorted, that is, by false theories. This does not mean that there will not be erroneous conceptions held by many people. It is rather that, first, the continued existence of that structure is not dependent upon systematically generated distortions; and second, the sources of error do not lie in the structural features that characterize that society. But this does not mean, as the members of that society progressively come to understand that society correctly, that all systematic social theory will disappear. It would seem that, since in capitalism social science has served both cognitive-emancipatory and ideological functions, so in socialism there will still be a need for theory to serve the former function. A socialist society, as Lukács seemed not to realize, will be highly organized, industrialized and rationalized (see Stedman-Jones, 1971). Systematic theory will be necessary, for example, to indicate exactly how its members can intervene in its workings so as to control and transform its constitutive relationships.

9 Values, theory and reality

1 Weber and value-freedom

Weber's conception of the place of values in social science involves several different claims, which are partly independent of one another. This is often concealed by discussions which ascribe to him a single, general position called 'value-freedom'. So we begin by outlining the six main elements which together constitute Weber's view of the relation between values and social science. First, *value-judgments*, which he defines as 'practical evaluations of the unsatisfactory or satisfactory character of phenomena subject to our influence', cannot be logically derived from factual statements (Weber, 1949, p. 1). Thus the social sciences, which are concerned with factual descriptions and explanations, cannot establish the truth or falsity of any value-judgment. Second, social scientists should not make value-judgments, in either their teaching or their writing. Weber emphasizes that this is itself a value-judgment. Third, social scientists are necessarily committed to the scientific values of truth, objectivity, and so on. Fourth, it is important to study other people's values, since these may often be significant causal determinants of their actions; and it is possible to do this without the social scientist's own values distorting such studies. Fifth, we need some way of selecting objects of investigation from the infinitely complex concrete reality that confronts us. This we do by reference to the relationship that parts of this reality have to one or more different values. But to select objects in this way, by their *value-relevance*, does not mean that we make favourable value-judgments about either the objects selected, or the values to which they are related. Sixth, once this selection is made, neither value-relevance nor value-judgments have any further function in the investigation. The process of causal explanation must, and can, be guided solely by the objective canons of scientific argument and evidence.

Two central concepts in this multi-faceted position are those of value-judgments and value relevance.[1] We will examine these in turn, together with those elements of Weber's position to which they relate. Weber's claim that value-judgments cannot be derived from the results of social science is based on a particular philosophical view of the logical status of such judgments. In adopting this view, he was strongly influenced by both Kant and Nietzsche. Weber holds that there is no way of rationally and objectively deciding between competing, substantive ethical doctrines. In particular, specific value-judgments about concrete phenomena cannot be justified by reference to factual enquiries. From such enquiries, all that can be discovered are the likely consequences of different courses of action, and thus the most effective means of achieving various ends. But the results of social scientific investigations do not enable one to make favourable or unfavourable judgments of the ends themselves. Nor does the fact that a particular course of action is the most efficient means to a favourably judged end mean that it should be performed; for one may also make a value-judgment about the means, that runs counter to the judgment of the end.

When Weber claims that the social scientist should not make value-judgments, he is well aware that this is itself a value-judgment, and that it cannot be supported solely by his philosophical view about such judgments. Thus Weber does not argue against making value-judgments on the grounds that this policy is, for social scientists, required by the logical status of their enquiry. Instead, Weber's grounds for this judgment are related both to his own political and ethical values, and to his views about the probable consequences of adopting or rejecting the policy. We will not discuss his values here. But we should note that, in assessing the likely consequences, Weber distinguishes between the effects of social scientists making value judgments in their writing, and in their teaching in universities. It is with the second of these that he is mainly concerned. And one of his main arguments is that political pressures on universities at the time were such that many legitimate and significant political and moral positions would be prevented from being expressed.[2]

Let us now turn to the concept of value-relevance, and the relationship between selecting objects of study and causally explaining them. The need for such selection is justified by Weber (1949, p. 72) in the following way: reality presents itself to us as

an infinite multiplicity of successively and coexistently emerging and disappearing events. . . . All the analysis of infinite reality which the finite human mind can conduct rests on the tacit assumption that only a finite portion of this reality constitutes the object of scientific investigation, and that only it is 'important' in the sense of being 'worthy of being known'. But what are the criteria by which this segment is selected?

197

Weber argues that the answer to this question lies in the relations of various features of reality to cultural values. Through such relations, these features gain 'cultural significance'. Thus (1949, p. 76):

> Empirical reality becomes 'culture' to us because and insofar as we relate it to value ideas. It includes those segments and only those segments of reality which have become significant to us because of this value-relevance. . . . We cannot discover . . . what is meaningful to us by a 'presuppositionless' investigation of empirical data. Rather, perception of what is meaningful to us is the presupposition of its becoming an *object* of investigation.

To illustrate his doctrine of value-relevance, let us consider what, for Weber, makes the emergence of European capitalism a significant object of investigation. It is, primarily, that capitalism embodies a particular form of 'rationalization', a systematic attempt to organize human activities in an efficient, calculable and impersonal manner. The growth of rationalization, manifested especially in the increasing dominance of bureaucracy, poses the central value-problem of contemporary society. For it leads to the progressive 'disenchantment' of humans with the world, to a state of 'mechanized petrifaction', from which only some kind of 'spiritual renewal' can rescue them. For Weber, this value-relevance of capitalism leads him not only to select it as an object of investigation, but also to select those of its features that are especially significant. Weber regards the 'internal rationality' of capitalism as its most essential feature, not in any absolute or metaphysical sense, but in relation to his particular value-conditioned interest. Thus Weber's characterization of capitalism is *'ideal-typical'*. For Weber, an ideal-type involves the deliberately one-sided accentuation of specific features that an object, or class of objects, may have. No concrete phenomenon precisely corresponds to an ideal-type, for three main reasons. First, any such phenomenon will have many features that are not included in the ideal-type. Second, those features that are included are represented in an idealized or 'purified' form. Third, not all the features of the ideal-type are present in each concrete exemplification of it.

For Weber, then, all knowledge of social reality is ideal-typical. And one cannot criticize one ideal-type, say of capitalism, as less objectively 'correct' than another. Relative to different values, one might wish to emphasize other features, such as its class structure, which are not so central to Weber's particular concerns in, for example, *The Protestant Ethic* (Weber, 1930). But Weber insists that, once an object of a study has been selected and defined in relation to values, these have no further part in the investigation: neither they, nor any value-judgments, should affect the objectivity of causal explanations. Everything else that is studied gains its significance not from values, but either from the fact that it is a causal determinant of the object of investigation, or because it provides evidence of such causal relations. Weber's position on these issues is explicitly and strongly expressed in the following passage (1949, p. 159):[3]

> This imputation of causes is made with the goal of being, in principle, 'objectively' valid as empirical truth absolutely in the same sense as any proposition at all of empirical knowledge. Only the adequacy of the data decides the question, which is wholly factual, and not a matter of principle, as to whether the causal analysis attains this goal to the degree which explanations do in the field of natural events. It is not the determination of the historical 'causes' for a given 'object' to be explained which is 'subjective' in a certain sense . . . – rather is it the delimitation of the historical 'object', of the 'individual' itself, for in this the relevant values are decisive.

Having identified the different elements in Weber's conception of value-free social science, and examined the two central notions involved in it, we will now consider a number of objections that have been made against his position. In doing so, we will show that attacks on some of these elements, even if successful, do not entail the rejection of others. In particular, Weber's views about value-relevance can be defended independently of his views about value-judgments. It is the former, which support his claim that values are relevant only to the selection of objects of study, and not to their explanation, which are the most significant for the philosophy of social science.

We begin by briefly examining some claims made by Charles Taylor (Taylor, 1967). His attack on 'neutrality in political science' is primarily directed against the first element in Weber's position, the claim that social scientific investigations do not support or justify specific value-judgments. Taylor's opposition to this derives from two main arguments. First, he rejects Weber's philosophical view of the logical status of value-judgments. For Taylor, such judgments are rationally defensible. To show that some state of affairs leads to the satisfaction of human wants, needs or interests is to show that it is morally desirable. It is unintelligible, though not strictly self-contradictory, to deny that such a state of affairs is desirable, unless it can also be shown that it contains elements leading to non-satisfactions. Second, Taylor argues that political science, once it goes beyond the mere collection of data, must develop theories embodying 'explanatory frameworks'. Such frameworks involve a set of assumptions about the relative importance of different causal variables, such as economic or political relations. The theories based upon them demonstrate that only a limited number of social and political arrangements are possible. We are thus posed with a choice between these options. And Taylor argues that, typically, this choice is straightforward, since it will be obvious which of the options is morally preferable.

We will not criticize Taylor's position here, though we believe that both of the main arguments for it are partly defective. Instead, we will note that, even if correct, it would not affect Weber's claims about value-relevance. What it would show is that value-judgments are 'objective', in the sense that they can be supported by social theories. But it would not show that those theories are themselves influenced or distorted by values. The acceptance or rejection of value-judgments would be dependent upon social theories, but the truth or falsity of the latter would not be affected by the former.[4]

If Taylor's view of the logical status of value-judgments were correct, it would remove one of the grounds for the second element in Weber's position, the prohibition on value-judgments by social scientists. But this policy was, as we saw, advocated by Weber on other grounds as well. We will now examine how Alvin Gouldner challenges this prohibition on value-judgments. In 'Anti-Minotaur: The Myth of a Value-Free Sociology' (Gouldner, 1964), he tries to explain why this policy has proved so popular amongst orthodox sociologists, especially since few of them show any understanding of the complex issues involved in Weber's defence of it. Gouldner disclaims any interest in the logical arguments relevant to value-freedom. Instead he analyses the function of the dogma 'Thou shalt not commit a value judgment': for individual sociologists, for the development of sociology as an institutionalized profession, and for the apparent autonomy of the modern university from the political arena. He claims, for example, that this dogma enables sociologists to resolve the personal problem generated by fearing the consequences of taking a critical attitude to their own society, yet not wishing to be seen as 'unmanly or lacking in integrity' (Gouldner, 1964, pp. 204–7). They resolve the dilemma by arguing that it is not legitimate for them, in their role as social scientists, to make value-judgments.

Gouldner's explanation is thus partly functionalist. But he does not regard these functional consequences of the dogma as justifying its adoption in contemporary sociology. On the contrary, he claims that it diminishes and impoverishes the content of political debate, and prevents the taking of an openly critical stance towards society. It therefore supports the *status quo*. And it is harmful to the process of education, since students are subject to the unwitting influence of the values that are normally implicit in what they are taught. Thus Gouldner rejects Weber's value-judgment about social scientists making such judgments in their teaching. Why do they disagree about this? Partly, because of their different political values, and partly because of their different assessments of the actual consequences of this policy. Further, we should note that the latter disagreement is itself affected by differences in the conditions of political life, and in the relation of universities to society, that existed at the times Weber and Gouldner were writing.

We can give additional support to Gouldner's position, with which we basically agree, by briefly elaborating on one of his points. Many academics who defend value-neutrality in their work as teachers and writers do so on a doubly erroneous basis. First, they present their stand as following from the fact that value-judgments cannot be logically derived from the results of social science. They thus disguise a value-judgment as a purely methodological claim. Second, they equate their responsibilities as people working in universities with what they mistakenly regard as the methodological requirements of their role as professional academics. By thus identifying themselves with their professional roles, they further justify their commitment to neutrality. But both manoeuvres are wrong, the first logically, and the second morally.

We turn now to a later attack by Gouldner on the doctrine of value-freedom. In 'The Sociologist as Partisan' (Gouldner, 1968), he is not concerned with the prohibition on value-judgments. Instead, he criticizes the deficiences of a contemporary approach in sociology, advocated especially by Howard Becker (Becker, 1963, 1964). This approach involves sociologists adopting the standpoint of those whom they study: in particular, in studies of the 'underdog', the sociologist in some way 'takes sides' with people such as drug addicts, jazz musicians, prostitutes, or street gangs. Gouldner (1968, p. 106) claims that Becker's interest in the underdog derives in part from

> a titillated attraction to the underdog's exotic difference, and easily takes the form of 'essays on quaintness'. . . . It expresses the satisfaction of the Great White Hunter who has bravely risked the perils of the urban jungle to bring back an exotic specimen.

Gouldner maintains that the nature of this orientation to the study of the underdog results in two failings in Becker's work. First, there is no analysis of the way in which social deviance is generated by the 'master institutions' of society. Second, the deviant is seen as a passive 'victim', and there is no conception of the deviant's life as an attempt to oppose those institutions. The overall effect is a failure to identify the possibilities for radical social and political change, which would, indeed, destroy this connoisseur's collection of specimens. Thus, for Gouldner, Becker's approach lends further

201

support to the *status quo*. For this way of identifying with the underdog ultimately involves adopting the values and standpoint of the
highly placed bureaucratic officialdom, of the American administra-
tive class. Its critical edge is directed only at middle-level bureaucrats,
an attack that is perfectly acceptable to the powerful liberal establishment in universities and political life.

Gouldner himself presents the following reasons for studying the
life of the underdog. First, it is a part of social reality generally
ignored or misrepresented by other members of society. Second, it is
a life of human suffering, and this alone should make a compelling
demand upon the sociologist. Third, much of this suffering is
avoidable, though this fact is concealed by the way in which the
underdog's life is often regarded. Gouldner believes that these
reasons imply the adoption of specific value-commitments, but he
argues that these, rather than being inimical to sociological objectivity, are instead required by it. What is objectionable about
Becker's value orientation is not merely the values themselves, but
that they lead to an erroneous and inadequate explanatory analysis.
For Gouldner, the sociologist's commitment to the elimination of
human suffering will lead to a less distorted analysis. In particular,
it will point our attention to the master institutions of society, and to
the potentialities for changing society in a morally preferable
direction.

How do Gouldner's claims affect Weber's conception of a value-
free social science? We suggest that they do not involve the direct
rejection of any of its various elements. Rather they should be seen as
mainly concerned with a different, though significant set of issues,
about the kinds of motivation and values that are most likely to
generate an adequate, and objectively correct analysis of society.
Thus the fifth and sixth elements of Weber's position, which deny
the logical relevance of values to the truth or falsity of causal explanations, is not undermined by Gouldner's arguments.[5] So let us now
consider a writer whose wide-ranging attack on Weber would, if
successful, seriously challenge his view of value-relevance.

Leo Strauss (1953), not only rejects Weber's theory of the logical
status of value-judgments, but also argues that it is neither possible
nor desirable to expel such judgments from our descriptions and
explanations of social phenomena. Strauss notes that, although
Weber characterized the alternatives for contemporary society as
'mechanical petrifaction' or 'spiritual renewal', he claimed that this
did not belong to a 'purely historical presentation', since it involved
'judgments of value and faith'. Strauss (1953, pp. 49–50) responds:

But is this not absurd? Is it not the plain duty of the social
scientist truthfully and faithfully to present social phenomena?

How can we give a causal explanation of a social phenomenon if we do not first see it as it is? Do we not know petrifaction or spiritual emptiness when we see it? And if someone is incapable of seeing phenomena of this kind, is he not disqualified from this very fact from being a social scientist, just as much as a blind man is disqualified from being an analyst of paintings?

Thus for Strauss, to describe a social phenomenon is necessarily also to evaluate it. Value-judgments cannot be avoided, since they are an essential part of knowing what something is. He considers, as examples, the problems facing a sociologist of art or religion. In both cases, the sociologist must be able to make value-judgments, to distinguish between art and trash, or between genuine and spurious religion. Without such evaluations, we would have the absurd situation of a sociologist who 'claimed to have written a sociology of art but who had actually written a sociology of trash' (Strauss, 1953, p. 50). So, whereas on Weber's view, values function only in the *selection* of objects for study, Strauss maintains that values are partly *constitutive* of these objects, and also of those to which we refer in causal explanations. It is not that there is a pre-existing, value-free social reality from which, because of its infinite complexity, we must select and define objects for investigation by reference to values. Rather, the value of those objects is part of their real nature, so that any adequate description of them must involve their correct evaluation.

We can best examine Strauss's claims by considering what precisely would be wrong with a sociology of art that was actually about trash. In particular, would it follow from the fact that systematic errors had been made in the identification of 'works of art', that the explanations of the items wrongly identified as art were thereby mistaken? In other words, does the fact that a sociology of art is 'really' an explanation of trash mean that it is an erroneous explanation of trash? We think not. What matters is whether the objects picked out by means of the concept of art that is being used have been correctly explained. Their status as art or trash is not relevant to this issue. Thus, although the dispute about their artistic status may involve value-judgments, the truth or falsity of their explanation is not dependent upon the acceptance or rejection of these value-judgments.

Our response to Strauss's position can be further developed by considering the place of specifically political value concepts, such as *justice*, in the description and explanation of social phenomena. On this issue, MacIntyre (1971, p. 278) claims that:

> to insist that political science be value-free is to insist that we never use in our explanations such clauses as 'because it was unjust' or 'because it was illegitimate' when we explain the collapse of a policy or a regime. ... I take it to be no objection

to the methodology which I propose that it is clearly not able to purge its explanations of evaluative elements.

MacIntyre notes how political scientists tend to redefine concepts such as justice in terms of people's beliefs. For example, that something is just may be defined as meaning that it is believed or perceived to be just by the agents concerned. He objects that such definitions rule out the possibility of explaining, say, the collapse of a regime by reference to its actual injustice, as distinct from people's perceptions of this.

What would the kind of explanation that MacIntyre wishes to allow be like? Consider the fairly common definition of justice in terms of equal distribution of goods and resources between all the members of a society. Using this definition, we might explain the collapse of a regime by referring to its injustice, that is, to its unequal pattern of distribution. There are, however, many competing conceptions of justice, disagreements about the relative value of justice and other political ideals, and differences about what, if anything, makes justice a desirable ideal. To resolve such disagreements is, at least partly, to make value-judgments. Nonetheless, we believe that, just as explanations of art can be assessed independently of the judgment 'art or trash', the truth or falsity of explanations in terms of 'injustice' can be assessed independently of questions such as whether the concept of justice involved is the correct one. What matters is that, whatever definition of justice is used, the justice or injustice of a society can be identified independently of value-judgments.[6]

It is unclear which specific elements in the concept of value-freedom MacIntyre sees himself as attacking. But our response to his, and other arguments we have examined, has so far involved a defence of Weber's views about value-relevance, and a separation of these from his claims about value-judgments. A successful challenge to the former would require a rejection of the ontological assumptions that enable Weber to regard values as performing a purely selective function upon an independently existent reality. We will consider the problematic nature of these assumptions later in the chapter. But first, we turn to a different set of issues, raised by one element in Marx's concept of ideology: the class-relatedness of systems of beliefs, and thus their social determination.

2 Rationality and the explanation of beliefs

It is often held that giving a causal explanation for the beliefs of some person or group undermines the truth, rationality or objectivity of those beliefs. Conversely, it is held that causal explanations are only required, or legitimate, for beliefs that are in some way defective.

Thus, at the most general level, it has been argued that the thesis of determinism – that every phenomenon is causally determined – is incompatible with the ascription of truth or rationality to beliefs. More specifically, it has been claimed that any sociology of knowledge committed to the view that all systems of belief are socially determined, must inevitably lead to some form of relativism, to the denial of universal, objective standards of truth or reason.[7]

We disagree with these claims. We can develop an alternative position by returning to one of the main themes in our discussion of reasons and causes in section 2 of chapter 7. We argued there that reason-explanations are open to two, mutually compatible, modes of assessment: causal and evaluative. One can assess whether the reasons proffered by agents are the causes of their actions; and also whether these constitute 'good' or 'bad' reasons for the kinds of actions concerned. A negative evaluative assessment does not entail that these bad reasons were not causally explanatory; nor does the claim that these reasons were 'rationalizations' (that is, not causally operative) entail a negative evaluation of them. Let us apply these points to the explanation of beliefs. The reasons that people give for their beliefs can be both evaluatively and causally assessed. If such reasons provide inadequate justification, this does not show that these are not why people accept those beliefs. Equally, our judgment that these reasons are not why the beliefs are accepted is consistent with our assessment of them as either good or bad reasons for those beliefs.

Thus, to give a causal explanation of beliefs does not entail that the beliefs are defective. First, because the causal explanation may often make reference to reasons that constitute justifications for them. Second, because even if this is not so, there may well be justifications, despite the justifying reasons not being part of the causal explanation for the beliefs' acceptance. We can elaborate these claims by examining briefly the so-called 'genetic fallacy', which involves a distinction between the causal 'origins' of a belief, and its 'validity'. What is usually seen as fallacious by those who attack the genetic fallacy is to regard the origins of a belief as in any way relevant to its validity. But what precisely is the nature of the 'relevance' that is denied? We accept that it is mistaken to argue from the fact that a belief has causal origins to its justification or dismissal as valid or invalid. To make this mistake is basically to deny the compatibility of causal and evaluative assessment. But it does not follow that the origins of a belief are, in every sense, 'irrelevant' to its validity. For it may be possible to establish empirical relationships between the specific ways in which beliefs have been generated, and the defective or non-defective nature of their content. We can illustrate this last point with a very simple example. Suppose someone makes predictions about which horse will win a race, by sticking a pin in a list of runners. One can demonstrate that this is a poor method of prediction, and perhaps also explain why this is so. Thus, if we know that a particular prediction has been made by this method, our causal knowledge about the origins of the belief gives good grounds for doubting the truth of that belief. For pin-sticking tends to generate defective beliefs. To argue in this way would not be to commit the genetic fallacy, since all that is involved is an analysis of the way in which the specific origins of the belief affect the likelihood of its validity.

What is the relationship between the position we have so far defended, and the conception of ideology in Marx's writings, and its later development by Lukács? As we noted in section 1 of the previous chapter, Marx regarded the ideological nature of systems of belief as explicable in terms of features of the class structure of a given society. But he did not see these causal explanations as, by themselves, constituting a rebuttal of those beliefs. Rather, he paid considerable attention to the analysis of their defects, and to the specification of the kinds of methodological errors involved in them. Thus there is no reason to think that Marx was guilty of the genetic fallacy. Further, we can reasonably ascribe to Marx, both a general commitment to the social determination of beliefs, and a defence of the possibility of arriving at correct, undistorted theoretical accounts of different social formations. We have argued that this is a consistent position to maintain. So, also, is Lukács's view of historical materialism as the theoretical articulation of the class-consciousness of the proletariat, combined with his view that historical materialism is a methodologically correct and undistorted theoretical standpoint. For there is no essential error in positively evaluating a system of beliefs whose content is held to be related to the structural location and interests of a specific social class. Likewise, Lukács's attempts to identify the methodological defects of bourgeois consciousness, the inadequacy of its fundamental categories and dichotomies, and to explain these by reference to certain features of the position and interests of the bourgeoisie in capitalism, are in principle defensible, whatever doubts we may have about the actual substance of his analyses. And if Lukács's claims were correct, there would be good reason to doubt the adequacy of particular bourgeois theories whose generation and acceptance could be explained in this way.[8]

Thus we are opposed to any general rejection of the legitimacy or necessity of causally explaining non-defective beliefs. Let us now consider some arguments which are partly designed to challenge this position. MacIntyre argues that there are important differences between the types of explanation that are logically appropriate for non-rational, and rational, beliefs (MacIntyre, 1971, pp. 244–59). He says that, because of this difference, the social scientist must assess the rationality of the beliefs that are being explained, since otherwise an inappropriate type of explanation may be given. MacIntyre illustrates the contrast between non-rational and rational beliefs, and their respective explanations, by two examples. First, he outlines the explanation given by H. R. Trevor-Roper for the European witch-craze in the sixteenth and seventeenth centuries (Trevor-Roper, 1967, chap. 3). According to this, the social tensions resulting from religious conflicts generated fears and anxieties for which the widespread belief in witches, and their active persecution, provided a convenient rationale and outlet. Such an explanation, for MacIntyre, is perfectly appropriate for these non-rational beliefs. But it would be thoroughly inappropriate in his second example, the acceptance by most astronomers, by 1630, of the existence of Jupiter's satellites. To explain this rational belief, one must refer to the use by scientists of various canons of argument and observation; and to the way in which the results of Galileo's telescopic investigations were regarded, in terms of these canons, as constituting good reasons for the belief.

Contrary to some earlier claims (MacIntyre, 1962), MacIntyre holds that an agent's viewing something as a reason for doing or believing something can be a cause of the action or belief (see MacIntyre, 1967, pp. 214–17). Nonetheless, he maintains (1971, p. 247 – our italics) that:

> the explanation of rational belief *terminates with an account of the appropriate intellectual norms and procedures*; the explanation of irrational belief must be in terms of causal generalizations which connect antecedent conditions specified in terms of social structures or psychological states – or both – with the genesis of beliefs.

Furthermore, MacIntyre denies the possibility of finding causally sufficient conditions for the emergence and institutionalization of the norms and procedures involved in the explanation of rational beliefs. Such conditions have never been discovered, and to insist that they can be discovered is only to express the conviction that every event or state of affairs must be fully determined causally.

MacIntyre's arguments would, if correct, have important consequences for the sociology of knowledge, and especially the sociology of science. We will consider some features of the latter further on. But first we will introduce a distinction between two senses in which a belief can be said to be 'rational', which will enable us to criticize MacIntyre's position. In the first sense, 'rational (1)', a rational belief is one for which there are good reasons, whether or not those who accept the belief do so because of these reasons. In the second sense, 'rational (2)', a person's belief can only be called rational if, not only are there good reasons for it, but also it is because of these that the person accepts it. In other words, someone's belief is rational (2) if and only if it is rational (1), and the reasons that make it rational (1) also causally explain its acceptance. Which of these two senses is involved in MacIntyre's argument? If MacIntyre means rational (2) beliefs, then his claim that the social scientist must assess the rationality of a belief, in order to explain it appropriately, is peculiar. For, to identify a belief as rational (2), we must already know what at least some of its causal determinants were, that is, the reasons which justify it as rational (1). If, on the other hand, he means rational (1) beliefs, he is wrong in thinking that there is any necessary relation between the rationality of a belief and the nature of its causal determinants. Thus, in his astronomy example, it is perfectly consistent to maintain that the belief is rational (1), since there are good reasons for it, whilst also claiming that these were not the reasons why it was accepted, and that these latter reasons do not constitute an adequate justification for it.

Such a situation is quite common in the history of science. Rational (1) beliefs are often discovered to have been accepted for reasons which we regard as insufficient, misguided, irrelevant, and so on. One obvious type of example concerns the part of religious beliefs in governing scientific activity. Thus, it has been argued that one of the main reasons for Newton's belief in absolute space and time, was his theological conviction about the omnipresence and everlasting existence of God. Whatever the merits of this explanation, it would be wrong to regard it as 'appropriate' only if the belief in absolute space and time can be shown to be non-rational (1). In other words, even though, on at least some criteria of rationality, this belief is rational (1), there is nothing essentially misguided in explaining Newton's acceptance of it by reference to reasons which do not in fact justify it.

The distinction we have drawn between rational (1) and (2) beliefs is however highly simplified. An adequate formulation of it would require a specification of what are to count as justifying reasons; a differentiation between, for example, reasons, good reasons, and sufficient reasons; and an examination of the relations between justifying reasons in different types of discourse, such as science and religion.[9] The complexity of these issues is partly indicated by the kinds of reasons which are normally operative for the members of a scientific community when they accept or reject the results and theories of other scientists. A plausible account of this aspect of scientific activity is given by Barry Barnes (1972b, p. 279):

Of the work he utilizes, no scientist personally checks more than a small fraction, even of that he is fully competent to evaluate, nor, in general, is any responsibility laid upon him to do so. Instead more limited norms of scepticism exist: critical attention is directed to work anomalous with respect to a paradigm, results produced by a recently developed technique, and experiments either charged with technical inadequacy or unavoidably unreliable due to external constraints or dependence on measurements near a technical threshold. Results produced by practitioners reputed to be technically unreliable are given a similarly guarded reception whereas other work is likely to be accepted routinely, especially if it emanates from a highly reputable source. On logistic grounds alone such channelling probably makes good sense; without it work would proceed very much more slowly, and the consequent gain in reliability would be minimal.

This passage raises two interesting points. First, should we charac-
terize these scientific practices as rational or non-rational? This will depend partly on what criteria of rational (1) beliefs are adopted. But there will clearly be some such criteria according to which the acceptance by scientists of many of their beliefs must be seen as *not* rational (2); since, although there may be good reasons for these beliefs, these are not why they are generally held. Instead, something more akin to an 'appeal to authority' is involved, which, on stringent criteria of rationality (1), would be non-rational. Second, the last sentence of Barnes's account suggests that the practices he describes are beneficial to the development and progress of science. However, to make this kind of claim requires a prior, philosophical specification of the nature and objectives of scientific enquiry. Only by doing this can we assess the merits of specific types of practice in promoting or retarding the development of scientific knowledge.

A similar point is relevant to the following statements made by Kuhn: 'Whatever scientific progress may be, we must account for it by examining the nature of the scientific group, discovering what it values, what it tolerates, and what it disdains. That position is intrinsically sociological' (Kuhn, 1970c, p. 238). For, although it is partly correct to describe this kind of account as 'intrinsically sociological', it is important to emphasize that it must also be 'intrinsically philo-
sophical'. If the object of Kuhn's enquiry is 'scientific progress', we must first know what sorts of belief and enquiry are to count as *science*: and this is a philosophical issue, that cannot be avoided or eliminated by any amount of sociological, psychological, or historical investigation. Furthermore, we have reservations about the substantive content of Kuhn's sociological enterprise: in particular, his failure to analyse the relations between the institutional features of the scientific community, and other elements of the societies in which

these institutions exist. Connected with this, there is a tendency in Kuhn's work to assume that, once established, institutional arrangements do not historically change in response to, amongst other things, changes in these other elements in society. Perhaps because of this, Kuhn does not consider the important question of whether the institutional organization of science that, at one time, is responsible for its 'progress', may become subject to external influences that weaken or destroy the tendency of that organization to generate true or rational beliefs.

The remarks we have made about the essential place of philosophical issues in the sociology of science are related to those made in our discussion of Strauss's objections to a value-free social science, in the previous section. We argued there that a sociological explanation of 'art' might be a correct account of the objects which this term is taken to denote, whether or not their evaluation as 'art' is itself correct. Nonetheless, for such investigations to be properly described as a sociology of *art*, it must also be true that the objects explained are genuine instances of this concept. And this will depend upon the philosophical issues involved in the question 'what is art?'. It is precisely this point that we have just made about the sociology of science. This parallel between the two cases suggests a further point about attempts to account, sociologically, for 'scientific progress'. For if the conception of science which these assume is philosophically unsound, what may result is a correct explanation of social phenomena that are not 'science', but something else – perhaps a more general type of phenomenon, of which science is only one species.[10]

Let us return now to MacIntyre's argument that the explanations appropriate for rational beliefs differ from those for non-rational beliefs. He concludes from this that, since it is therefore necessary for the sociologist to assess the rationality of the beliefs that are to be explained, 'the positivist account of sociology in terms of a logical dichotomy between facts and values must break down. For to characterize actions and institutionalized practices as rational or irrational is to evaluate them' (MacIntyre, 1971, p. 258). One significant feature of this conclusion is that MacIntyre broadens the way in which the concepts of value, and evaluation, have normally been interpreted in disputes about the value-free nature of social science. Typically, these concepts have been limited to moral and political values. But MacIntyre also includes rationality-assessments as evaluative. Our own suggestions, in the previous paragraph, about the parallels between Strauss's claims and the problems involved in the sociology of science, give support to this broader concept of evaluation. We will consider this issue again in section 4. But we believe that MacIntyre is wrong to locate the importance of such evaluations in the way that he does, as prerequisites to appropriate forms of explanation. Instead, we should see philosophical evaluation as relevant to the correct specification of objects of sociological investigation as 'science', 'art', and so on. Yet the kinds of explanation given for such phenomena are not logically dependent, as MacIntyre claims, upon the correctness of these evaluations. For there is no *a priori* relation between, for example, the rationality (1) of a belief, and the nature of its causal determinants.

Nonetheless, as we noted in our earlier discussion of the genetic fallacy, there may well be important *empirical* relations between the rationality (1) of beliefs, and their causal determinants. In particular, it would be strange if we discovered that rational (1) beliefs could typically be explained with no reference to the reasons which justify those beliefs as rational. In other words, it is unlikely that the reasons why people accept beliefs that are rational (1) bear no close relation to the justifying reasons. Thus we should expect the cases where people's beliefs are rational (1) but not rational (2), to be relatively rare. But this is an empirical question, that cannot be settled purely by philosophical argument.

However, if this suggestion about the relation between rational (1) beliefs and their causal determinants is correct, it has an important implication for the sociology of knowledge, and especially for the study of science: it is essential to begin such investigations by examining the reasons which people give for their beliefs. Indeed, much of the opposition to the sociology of knowledge can be seen as deriving from the way in which many sociological theories systematically dismiss, as causal determinants of beliefs, the agent's reasons for these. In the case of science, such an approach may lead to an exclusive interest in social determinants that cannot possibly explain the specific content of scientific beliefs and theories. We argued against such rejections of agents' reasons in section 3 of chapter 7. For us, sociological accounts of science must neither exclude this level of explanation, nor be limited to it. The question, for example, of what it was that led to the emergence of a particular conception and practice of science in seventeenth-century Europe is a legitimate one, for which, in principle, sociological answers may be discovered. But such answers will not be found without an examination of how those who were involved in this historical episode both perceived, and explained, what they were doing. With beliefs, as with actions, the agent's viewpoint can be neither ignored nor left unexplained.

We conclude this section by briefly considering the consequences of our position for some arguments often used against determinism and relativism. One such argument is this. If the causal determination of beliefs entails that they are defective, then the statement of the general thesis of determinism must be self-refuting. For the determinist is claiming that this thesis is correct: but if it were correct, then all beliefs, including the belief in determinism, would be defective. Thus the determinist cannot, without self-contradiction, defend the truth of determinism. Further, it is sometimes argued that this counter to determinism also provides a strong reason for rejecting relativism, the view that there are no universal and objective standards of truth and rationality, but only standards that are accepted by particular social groups or societies. For, if relativism is defended by reference to determinism, as it often is, then the self-refuting nature of determinism entirely undermines its support for relativism.

For us, however, these arguments against determinism and relativism are mistaken. They rest upon the assumption that the causal explanation of beliefs is incompatible with a positive evaluation of their truth or rationality. We have argued against this assumption. And we should note that these kinds of objection to determinism often rely upon the view that people's reasons for beliefs and actions cannot be interpreted as causes. On this view, the causal explanation of beliefs cannot be given in terms of the reasons which justify those beliefs. But we reject this view, and with it, these arguments against determinism and relativism. Nonetheless, we must distinguish the argument against relativism which rests upon the self-refuting nature of determinism, and an apparently similar objection to relativism which is in fact independent of the issue of determinism. According to this, the statement of the general thesis of relativism is self-refuting, since it claims that relativism is true, whilst at the same time denying the existence of universal standards of truth. We regard this objection as a significant one. We should note, however, that our position does not entail any form of relativism to which such an objection could reasonably be made.[11]

3 Concepts and reality: the problem of Zande witchcraft

In 'Understanding a Primitive Society' (Winch, 1964), Winch argues against certain elements in Evans-Pritchard's account of Zande witchcraft. According to Evans-Pritchard, the Azande explain particular types of misfortune that befall them in everyday life by reference to the activities of witches. Witches are people with a specific physical condition, the presence of *mangu* in their intestines, which gives them the power of witchcraft. The witch's soul goes out at night and harms those towards whom the witch has a hostile attitude. When a Zande believes that his misfortunes are due to witchcraft, he may resort to a complex procedure of oracular divination, to discover the identity of the witch. One part of this procedure involves feeding a fowl with *benge*, a reddish powder (probably containing strychnine), while asking if a named individual is the witch concerned. It has been decided in advance whether the fowl's dying, or living, will count as an affirmative or negative answer to this question. The procedure is then reversed, by feeding *benge* to a second fowl, and asking if the first answer was correct. If the two answers are inconsistent, a variety of explanations may be given: that bad *benge* was used, or that the procedures had been carried out incorrectly, or that the oracle was itself influenced by witchcraft.[12]

The main disagreement between Evans-Pritchard and Winch is whether to interpret these beliefs and practices as 'poor science'; or as not science at all, but some other form of activity which should be understood in terms of the specific context in which it occurs, and its relation to certain central features of human existence, namely birth, death, and sexual relationships. According to Winch, Evans-Pritchard adopts the former view, whilst the latter is in fact the correct one. Why does Evans-Pritchard evaluate Zande witchcraft, as science, unfavourably? He has three main reasons. First, since witches do not exist, its claims are 'not in accordance with objective reality'. Second, it makes use of 'mystical notions', which he defines as 'patterns of thought that attribute to phenomena supra-sensible qualities which, or part of which, are not derived from observation or cannot be logically inferred from it, and which they do not possess'. Third, the Azande do not abandon their beliefs despite internal inconsistencies, and contradiction by experience. Nonetheless, Evans-Pritchard does not regard the acceptance of such beliefs as indicating the inferior intelligence, or irrationality, of those who adopt them. For the members of modern Western societies accept their scientific beliefs for much the same reasons that groups like the Azande accept witchcraft beliefs: in both cases, people adopt the patterns of thought provided for them by the societies they live in.

We can begin our analysis of this dispute by noting how Evans-Pritchard's evaluation of witchcraft rests upon a conception of science that we have challenged, in several respects, in part 1. Thus, his third criticism assumes an over-simplified view of the procedures involved in the testing of scientific theories, and of the point at which it becomes reasonable to abandon them (see chapter 3, section 1). His second criticism involves a definition of 'mystical notions' which would rule out, as unscientific, many theoretical concepts which have been central to the development of science, especially when this is viewed from a realist standpoint (see chapter 2, *passim*). Finally, although, as we will argue later, it is legitimate to criticize belief in the existence of witches as false, it is wrong to identify good science with true beliefs, and poor science with false ones. To do so would be to write off a large proportion of the major achievements in the history of science, since many of these have later been abandoned as incorrect. It is the general adequacy and rationality of methods and

213

theoretical frameworks that are important in evaluating scientific activity, not the truth or falsity of particular results.[13]

We do not wish to exaggerate the similarities between witchcraft and science. But it is important to notice how philosophical issues about scientific knowledge affect the way in which a social phenomenon such as Zande witchcraft is characterized and evaluated. Let us turn now to Winch's reasons for objecting to Evans-Pritchard's account. For us, this account implies an unduly negative evaluation of the merits of witchcraft as science. For Winch, however, Evans-Pritchard's account is more radically mistaken: it interprets as science a social practice that does not belong to this category. Indeed, it is partly because Winch accepts that to interpret witchcraft as science would entail a strong rejection of its merits, that he objects to that interpretation. Winch, it seems, is committed to some form of the following principle: if, as a consequence of interpreting a system of beliefs and practices in a particular way, we are forced to regard it as fundamentally erroneous and irrational, we can be sure that we have misinterpreted it. Thus, to characterize Zande witchcraft as even an attempt at scientific explanation and prediction must be mistaken, since if we do so, we must evaluate it as systematically erroneous and irrational.

For Winch, this principle of interpretation (which, we should emphasize, is not explicitly advocated by him), is supported by some radical claims about the concepts of reality and rationality. Thus he objects to the view that Zande witchcraft does not accord with 'objective reality', on the grounds that there is no intelligible concept of reality that can be used to evaluate the truth or falsity of the belief-systems involved in every form of life or social practice. In a much-quoted passage, Winch (1964, p. 82) claims that:

> Reality is not what gives language sense. What is real and what is unreal shows itself *in* the sense that language has. Further, both the distinction between the real and the unreal and the concept of agreement with reality themselves belong to our language.

In particular, there is not only a *scientific* concept of reality, that is internal to the language of science, but also a *religious* concept of reality, internal to its language, and so on. The same is true of logic and rationality. In an earlier work, Winch (1958, pp. 100–1) claimed that criteria of logic

> arise out of, and are only intelligible in the context of, ways of living or modes of social life. It follows that one cannot apply criteria of logic to modes of social life as such. For instance,

science is one such mode and religion another; and each has criteria of intelligibility peculiar to itself. So within science or religion actions can be logical or illogical. . . . But we cannot sensibly say that either the practice of science itself or that of religion is either illogical or logical; both are non-logical.

How do these philosophical claims support Winch's principle of interpretation? Since each form of life has its own criteria of reality and rationality, to interpret any such form in a way that leads us to reject it as systematically failing to accord with reality, or as irrational and inconsistent, must result from a basic misidentification of it. A correct identification will show each form of life to be, in its own terms, coherent and accordant with reality. Winch accepts that it is legitimate to criticize particular beliefs within one form of life as false, or inconsistent with others. But we should do so only by reference to the concepts of reality and rationality specific to that form. We cannot employ universal standards to evaluate the form as a whole: for there are no such standards available. It follows that we must not use the criteria of Western science to evaluate the form of life involved in Zande witchcraft.

But Winch's position generates serious difficulties. Two of these have been identified and criticized by Ernest Gellner (Gellner, 1962 and 1968). First, the operation of the principle of interpretation implicitly adopted by Winch inevitably conceals a significant aspect of most societies: the existence of systematic divergences between beliefs and reality, and inconsistencies between beliefs, which are functional to the continuation of those societies in their present form. Gellner's claim can be illustrated by noting that Winch's principle excludes the applicability to any belief-system of the concept of ideology, a central feature of which is the specification of various kinds of distortion. Amongst these is the misrepresentation of the nature of, and the possibilities of change within, a particular society. Second, Gellner argues that Winch's claims about the concepts of reality and reason make it impossible to give a logically coherent account of a certain type of historical change that often takes place. Such changes result partly from the rejection, by members of some social group, of the truth or rationality of that group's basic beliefs and practices. Consider, for example, the European Reformation. Gellner claims that this involved the rejection of the pre-Reformation form of religious life, 'X', as incoherent and irrational. This view of X was an essential part of the Reformers' religious life, 'Y'. How is Winch to deal with the view, held in Y, that X is irrational? He is committed to challenging neither X nor Y. But not to challenge Y is to accept Y's rejection of X. So, as Gellner puts it, 'either the pre-Reformation Church was wrong, or the Reformers were, in supposing

215

it to be wrong. . . . One way or another, *someone* must be wrong' (Gellner, 1968, p. 61). For Gellner, it is clearly Winch who is wrong.[14]

One interesting feature of the example Gellner uses here is that it assumes the possibility of different forms of life within the general category of 'the religious form of life'. If Gellner's argument about this example is correct it indicates another difficulty for Winch's position: how is one to distinguish between different forms of life; or, what is to count as a single form? Without criteria for these discriminations, there is a considerable danger that Winch's arguments about the relations between forms of life, and concepts of reality and rationality, will become circular. For, whenever it seems that the members of two different forms of life are engaged in mutually intelligible, systematic criticisms of each other's beliefs and practices, we would be faced with the claim that, by definition, the two forms must in fact be one. We can elaborate upon these difficulties in Winch's position by comparing it with Kuhn's views about the incommensurability of scientific paradigms, and the nature of scientific revolutions, which were outlined in sections 3 and 4 of chapter 3. In the first edition of *The Structure of Scientific Revolutions* (Kuhn, 1970a), Kuhn suggested that those who operate within different paradigms live in 'different worlds'. If this suggestion is taken seriously, it becomes unintelligible to evaluate the merits of competing paradigms with respect to the truth or falsity of their claims about what exists, or what the characteristics of these items are. Yet an important fact about scientific revolutions is that many scientists live through them. And at least some of them are able to give reasons for preferring the later paradigm to the earlier one. Thus we have another example of the type of historical change that Gellner points to, in his criticism of Winch. If different paradigms have their own standards of reality and rationality, then it is difficult to make sense of the objections made by supporters of the later paradigm to the views they accepted as supporters of the earlier one. Once again, someone must be wrong. It is perhaps to avoid this problem that Kuhn often likens the scientist's change of allegiance to a 'conversion experience'. But even if this correctly describes the psychological experience that at some point normally occurs, it does not remove the necessity of providing a consistent account of the criticisms of one paradigm made by advocates of another.

Kuhn, though, recognizes the philosophically problematic consequences of his claims about incommensurability, especially as they make it difficult to construct a concept of scientific 'progress' which, as we noted in the previous section, is important for the specification of his sociological approach to science. But for Winch, a strong sense of incommensurability is required, to rule out the possible evaluation of Western science as superior in its account of reality to that given by Zande witchcraft. As we can now see, however, the view that he adopts of the relationship between language and reality is such that it tends to generate the paradoxical consequences of Kuhn's views about scientific paradigms. For Winch does not provide a means of distinguishing different forms of life that would prevent one from talking of different forms *within* both science and religion, and not merely of the differences between them.[15]

We conclude this section by making some remarks about the relations between language and reality. Whatever the defects of Winch's and Kuhn's positions, they are correct in emphasizing the centrality of these relations to any philosophical account of our knowledge of physical and social reality. First, let us make two general claims that it is reasonable to accept, and which function as 'outer limits' for more precise articulations of these relations. On the one hand, many of the beliefs that might possibly be proposed, especially in scientific theories, can properly be judged defective because they ignore, deny, or mis-describe features of a world that exists independently of those beliefs. On the other hand, there can be no beliefs about such features which are not couched within a particular set of concepts; and there is a considerable diversity in the conceptual frameworks that have seemed to their users both convenient and successful in their dealings with physical and social reality.

Second, the phrase 'concept of reality' is open to misinterpretations that lead to unnecessarily relativistic consequences. For example, it might be said that, whilst witches are 'real for the Azande', they are not 'real for the Western scientist'; that this shows that the two groups have different 'concepts of reality'; and that, since one cannot talk about what is real independently of any concepts, one cannot intelligibly claim that one of these concepts of reality is correct and the other incorrect. But this kind of argument is misleading. Instead, we should say that the Azande believe that witches exist, whilst Western scientists do not: the two groups do not have different 'concepts of reality', except in the sense that they disagree about what exists. But it does not follow from the fact that people disagree whether a certain type of item exists, that it is in principle mistaken to regard one group as right and the other wrong. Thus there is no inconsistency in maintaining both that 'witches are real for the Azande', and that 'witches do not exist'. In particular, there is no need to add, to the second statement, *'for us'*. We may nonetheless be wrong about the existence of witches, and the Azande right: what matters is that this situation, too, can be intelligibly described.

Third, we must distinguish between concepts, and statements or propositions. It is an important feature of any language that it is always possible to express the negation of any statement made within it. Thus, from the fact that a group of people, through sharing a language, share the concepts embodied in that language, it does not follow that they must also share the same set of beliefs. To have common concepts is not thereby to have common beliefs, since, for any statement made within a particular set of concepts, it is always possible to deny the truth of that statement. It is therefore misleading to talk of a set of beliefs as constituting a 'conceptual framework', since it may seem to follow, either that it is impossible to reject those beliefs without also rejecting the 'conceptual framework', or that people whose beliefs differ must therefore be operating within different 'conceptual frameworks'. There is thus an important sense in which concepts do not *determine* beliefs.

But finally, although no one set of concepts determines a single set of beliefs, it is equally true that not all beliefs can be expressed in a given set of concepts. As a simple example: we can believe either that a table is red, or that it is not red, while using the same concepts; but we cannot believe that it is square without an additional concept. Concepts therefore limit beliefs, so there is a genuine problem about what makes one set of concepts preferable to another. More specifically, we have to consider whether one such set can be preferred because it enables us to make more, or all, true statements about a reality that exists independently of those concepts, and thus independently of the beliefs expressed by means of them. Such problems themselves depend, for their solution, upon an adequate analysis of the relations between the knower and the known, between the subject and object of knowledge. We turn now to an examination of a group of writers for whom this analysis, together with closely connected issues, is of central importance. In doing so, we will be returning to the problems of value-free social science left partly unresolved at the end of section 1.

4 Critical theory

The expression 'critical theory' has been applied to a wide range of different theoretical standpoints. In its narrowest sense, it refers to the views advocated by members of the Frankfurt School, especially in the early writings of Max Horkheimer and Herbert Marcuse. We will begin by outlining some of their basic claims. Later we will examine, in greater detail, a more recent writer connected with the School, Jürgen Habermas.[16]

A central concept in the early attempts to articulate a critical social theory is that of *reason*. Its meaning derives from the primarily Hegelian tradition within which these attempts were made. Marcuse (1937, pp. 135–6) characterizes the concept of reason in the following way:

Reason is the fundamental category of philosophical thought, the only one by means of which it has bound itself to human destiny. Philosophy wanted to discover the ultimate and most general grounds of Being. Under the name of reason it conceived the idea of an authentic Being in which all significant antitheses (of subject and object, essence and appearance, thought and being) were reconciled. Connected with this idea was the conviction that what exists is not immediately and already rational but must rather be brought to reason. Reason represents the highest potentiality of man and existence; the two belong together. . . . Reason was established as a critical tribunal . . . [and] the concept of reason contains the concept of freedom as well. For such examination and judgment would be meaningless if man were not free to act in accordance with his insight and to bring what confronts him into accordance with reason.

Thus, for Marcuse, reason can be used to criticize and challenge the nature of existing societies. Reason is a 'critical tribunal'; and its judgments are based upon the values of both freedom and pleasure. Marcuse, like Horkheimer, opposed the way in which personal gratification and hedonic pleasure are rejected in bourgeois culture. They also defended the ideal of humans as free, autonomous agents, able to create and control their own lives in a society where there is an absence of the forms of alienation and reification characteristic of capitalism. Further, unlike many political and moral philosophers, they did not regard the ideals of pleasure and freedom as ultimately conflicting with each other. But existing types of pleasure are to be evaluated in the light of freedom. For Marcuse especially, the satisfactions available in capitalist society reflected the presence of 'false' wants and needs: only in a free society could true wants and needs be generated. Thus capitalism leads not only to the non-satisfaction of existing wants, but also to the satisfaction of false ones. The elimination of this irrational state of affairs requires the transformation of society into one where the means of production are controlled by the community, who actively participate in directing the productive processes towards the needs and wants of the whole society (Marcuse, 1968, p. 193).

For Marcuse and others, a transformation of this kind must take place through political practice guided by a critical theory of society. We can note four important features of such a theory. First, it starts from an evaluation of existing reality as fundamentally irrational. Second, it attempts to identify the possibilities for change in that reality, the relations and developments that are already operating to undermine the continuation of its present form. Third, critical theory challenges the ideological, reified consciousness which is generated by existing social reality, and which systematically conceals these potentialities for radical transformation. Finally, it is opposed to positivism, and to the positivistic assumptions of most types of social science. Let us consider this last point in more detail. For the early critical theorists, 'positivism' refers not only to the specific view of science which we outlined in chapter 1, but also to the divorce of facts from values, to the denial of any distinction between essence and appearance, and to the claim that empirical science is the only legitimate form of human knowledge. The restriction of human knowledge to science is seen by these writers as leading to the elimination of philosophy itself. For philosopical knowledge is not empirical science, and the positivist's conception of knowledge means that most of the traditional concerns of philosophy are condemned as meaningless metaphysics. In particular, positivism is regarded by critical theorists as denying the intelligibility of the concept of reason. As a consequence, positivism performs the function of supporting the *status quo*, since it rules out the possibility of a theory of society based upon the critical, philosophical concept of reason.[17]

We will now consider how far this conception of critical theory departs from Weber's claims about the place of values in social science. First, critical theorists reject Weber's view of the status of value-judgments. We can see the differences between their positions by contrasting their concepts of rationality. For Weber, judgments of rationality are limited to an assessment of the relations between means and ends, and of the internal consistency of a given set of ends. But there is no possibility of evaluating the ends themselves as rational or irrational. It follows that the only sense that can be given to the idea of a rational society is that of a society organized in such a way that the most effective means of achieving the values accepted in it are systematically employed. For critical theorists, however, a rational society is one that embodies the values supported by reason. A society that is rational, in Weber's sense, can thus be criticized for the irrationality of the ends pursued in it. Second, though, we must examine how this disagreement about the status of value-judgments affects Weber's view of value-relevance, his claim that values can be limited to a selective function and are not relevant to the truth or falsity of social theories which investigate the objects selected in this way. A Weberian might argue that one should regard the 'values dictated by reason' as directing the social scientist's interest towards specific features of an infinitely complex reality. These value-relevant features would be the elements in a given society that are potential causes of its transformation into a form which realized the values of human freedom and pleasure. But there could be no guarantee that a social theory oriented in this way would in fact discover such potential sources of change, or be able to show the present likelihood of the hoped-for transformation. To think otherwise would be to permit interest-directing values to distort the objectivity of social science.

Could critical theorists accept this Weberian characterization of the place of values in their theory of society? Certainly, they did not regard the values of reason as guaranteeing the 'right' results for sociological enquiries. Indeed, the early members of the Frankfurt School were generally pessimistic about the chances of a radical transformation of capitalism. This pessimism was partly due to their belief that the proletariat was no longer the potential agent of revolution, and partly also to the growth of Fascism at the time they were writing. Nonetheless, critical theorists entirely rejected a basic assumption of Weber's position, the logical heterogeneity of facts and values. They regarded this assumption as itself deriving from a more fundamental philosophical error, a denial of the essentially *active* part of the human subject in the process of cognition. They therefore rejected the view of perception and knowledge as passive processes of sensory reception by which humans can achieve a correct representation of a world that exists independently of them. Thus Weber's position is seen as resting upon mistaken epistemological and ontological doctrines.[18]

Before going on to examine Habermas's work, which has several themes in common with the early critical theorists, we will explore some of the epistemological and ontological issues raised in the previous paragraph. We will do so by outlining the position developed by Leszek Kolakowski (1969), who, it should be emphasized, is regarded neither by himself nor by the Frankfurt School as a critical theorist. But his attempt to rescue, reconstruct and defend the epistemological views in Marx's early writings is of considerable relevance to the discussion of critical theory.

Marx, especially in the 'Theses on Feuerbach' (Bottomore and Rubel, 1963, pp. 82–4), accepts the view of philosophical idealists that human perception and cognition are active, rather than passive, processes; yet he insists, against idealism, that the activity involved is not that of a detached consciousness, but the conscious activity of human agents engaged in a dialectical interaction with nature. In that interaction, humans attempt to satisfy their existing needs, and as a result, both the natural world, and human agents, are repeatedly transformed. Kolakowski (1969, p. 66) states the implications of Marx's views for the relations between concepts and reality thus:

Human consciousness, the practical mind, although it does not produce existence, produces existence as composed of individuals divided into species and genera. From the moment man in his onto- and phylogenesis begins to dominate the world of things intellectually – from the moment he invents instruments that can organize it and then express this organization in words – he finds that world already constructed and differentiated, not according to some alleged natural classification but according to a classification imposed by the practical need for orientation in one's environment. The categories into which this world has been divided are not the result of a convention or a conscious social agreement; instead they are created by a spontaneous endeavour to conquer the opposition of things. It is this effort to subdue the chaos of reality that defines not only the history of mankind, but also the history of nature as an object of human needs – and we are capable of comprehending it only in this form.

The position outlined here contains elements of what is normally termed 'pragmatism'. But it differs from several forms of pragmatism. For it accepts the idea of a world of things that exists independently both of our practice upon it, and of our theories about it. And it locates the philosophical significance of human practice primarily in the constitution of categories and concepts, rather than in the assessment of the truth or falsity of the beliefs and theories that are expressed within those concepts. It thus rejects two views often associated with pragmatism. First, the view that the main importance of practice is in the testing of beliefs and theories. Second, the view that truth or falsity is to be identified with successful or unsuccessful practice. Further, we should note that, if human needs change historically in the way that Marx suggests, one should expect consequent changes in the concepts and categories through which our beliefs and theories about nature can most appropriately be expressed.[19]

A central feature of Marx's epistemology is the attempt to relate the foundations of knowledge to fundamental characteristics of the human species. In *Knowledge and Human Interests* (Habermas, 1971), Habermas accepts this general approach but argues that Marx was mistaken in his exclusive concern with one of these characteristics, namely work or labour. For Habermas, there are three distinctive forms of knowledge, of which only one, involved in the *empirical-analytic* sciences, can properly be understood by reference to this characteristic of the human species. The other two forms are those involved in the *historical-hermeneutic* sciences, and in *self-reflection*. Habermas says that each form of knowledge is constituted as such by a separate 'knowledge-constitutive interest'. The three interests are, respectively, the *technical*, the *practical* and the *emancipatory*. It

222

is important to notice that Habermas does not use the term 'practical' in the way we have used it in our discussion of Marx and Kolakowski. Instead, the latter sense of 'practical' is closest, in Habermas's definitions, to what he calls 'technical'. We will see this in examining Habermas's account of the relation between empirical-analytic science and its technical, knowledge-constitutive interest.

Habermas claims that the empirical-analytic sciences, which include both the natural sciences, and economics, sociology, and political science, are aimed at the discovery of nomological know-ledge about natural and social relations. Their particular status as knowledge is constituted by their interest in technical control, in increasing the possible extent of human domination over natural and social reality. These sciences provide us with the information that is required for rational, feedback-controlled instrumental activity. Let us consider two questions raised by these claims. First, what does Habermas mean by 'technical interest'? Second, in what sense is this interest 'constitutive' of knowledge? Concerning the first question, Habermas does not mean that scientists typically engage in their enquiries intending to discover laws that can be used for instru-mental control. The technical interest is not a particular type of motivation on the part of scientists. Rather, it is related to an essential characteristic of the manner in which the human species historically transforms itself: to labour, productive activity upon nature, by which the human species reproduces itself biologically and culturally. This productive activity both requires and generates a specific 'interest' in technical control. Thus Habermas maintains that his concept of interest is neither purely empirical nor purely transcendental: it does not refer to actual intentions, yet it remains rooted in the general characteristics of human existence, and not in an abstract realm of philosophical categories.

As for the second question, about 'constitution', Habermas argues that the technical interest constitutes knowledge at two related levels. First, it provides a criterion for what is to count as 'real', that is, for what counts as an 'object', about which the propositions of empirical-analytic science give us knowledge. What is real, in relation to the technical interest, is what can be detected, measured and manipulated in the situation of controlled experiments, in which information is received through our perceptual mechanisms. Second, the technical interest determines the general character of the standards employed in assessing the truth or falsity of statements made about these objects. An example of such a standard is that of falsification, which requires us to reject those statements whose predictive consequences are unsuccessful. For Habermas, it is only by reference to the technical interest that we can understand, and justify, the limitations that are imposed in the empirical-analytic sciences upon what is real, and upon what is an acceptable statement or system of statements about such real objects.[20]

But Habermas maintains that the empirical-analytic sciences cannot be seen as definitive of human knowledge: they involve only one form of knowledge, whose criteria of reality and standards of validity are relative to the interest in technical control. This interest derives from one essential characteristic of the human species. But, just because there are other such characteristics, that give rise to non-technical interests, there are also other, distinctive forms of knowledge, with their own criteria of reality and validity. One of these forms is involved in the historical-hermeneutic sciences, and is constituted by the practical interest. The objects of these sciences (that is, what is defined as real), are inter-subjectively established meanings. Their criteria of validity, or standards of assessment, are those of *interpretation*, the paradigmatic example of which is the interpretive understanding of linguistic communication in everyday discourse. For Habermas, communicative interaction is an irreducible category of the mode of existence and self-transformation of the human species. In particular, it cannot be reduced to the category of work. Thus the hermeneutic-historical sciences involve a distinctive form of knowledge that is constituted by the practical interest. It follows that these sciences cannot intelligibly be criticized for failure to define their objects, and criteria of validity, in the manner of the empirical-analytic sciences.

The third form of knowledge that Habermas distinguishes is that constituted by the emancipatory interest, an interest in human autonomy and responsibility (*Mündigkeit*). It is a form of knowledge that involves *self-reflection*, and which is itself involved in critical theory. To understand what Habermas means by these claims, we must consider his general opposition to 'positivism', a term which has, for him, a similarly broad sense to that given it by the earlier critical theorists. His central criticism of positivist philosophy is that it is unable to account for the epistemological status of its own claims. We can best see the point of this criticism by an example that is not used by Habermas himself. Consider the principle proposed by many logical positivists in the twentieth century, that all statements are either empirical (synthetic), *a priori* (analytic), or meaningless. A frequent objection to this has been that this principle conforms to neither of the two 'meaningful' types of statement allowed by it. It thus has the paradoxical character of being meaningless if true. Habermas, we believe, would regard it as a philosophical claim, for which various grounds could be advanced: but such grounds could not justify it in either of the ways that logical positivists allow as legitimate types of knowledge.

For Habermas, philosophical knowledge involves self-reflection,

224

by which we reflect upon particular features of human existence, and especially upon the nature and status of human knowledge itself. Thus Habermas regards the examination of the relations between technical and practical interests, and their respective forms of knowledge, as itself a case of self-reflection, which positivism, through its implicit abolition of philosophical knowledge, cannot comprehend. Further, philosophical knowledge, in its concern with issues such as the criteria of validity appropriate to different types of science, is thereby concerned with questions about values and standards. These questions are to be answered by means of critical argument, which is concerned with the defence or challenging of any kind of evaluative standard. Critical argument is one of the three general uses of language. Thus Habermas (1974, p. 216 – our italics and insertion) states:

> A critical discussion, regardless of whether it concerns the acceptance of proposals or propositions, includes a threefold use of language: the descriptive, in order to describe a state of affairs; the postulatory, in order to establish rules of procedure; and *the critical, in order to justify such decisions*. Logically these forms of speech mutually presuppose each other. The descriptive usage is in no way limited to a certain class of 'facts'. [e.g. the facts about the 'objects' of empirical-analytic science]. The postulatory usage covers *the establishment of norms, standards, criteria and definitions of all kinds, no matter whether practical, logical or methodological rules* are involved. The *critical* usage employs *arguments for considering, evaluating, judging and justifying the choice of standards*; it includes therefore language transcendent approaches and attitudes in its discussion.

What, then, is the relationship between self-reflection (embodying critical argument), the emancipatory interest, and the nature of a critical theory of society? To answer this absurdly complex question, we must note how Habermas treats Freud's theory of psycho-analysis. He regards this theory as especially important as the only tangible example of a science incorporating methodical self-reflection. Habermas claims that psycho-analysis involves a kind of 'depth-hermeneutics', in which the 'distorted texts' of the patient's behaviour become intelligible to the patient through the analyst's interpretations, and the patient's self-reflection. As a result of successful psycho-analysis, the previously concealed and causally determinative motives are revealed to the patient, and at the same time lose their power as unconscious determinants of the patient's actions. For Habermas, psycho-analytic theory involves both empirical-analytic and historical-hermeneutic forms of knowledge: the former in, for example, the discovery of the past episodes that lead to repressions; and the

225

latter in, for example, the interpretation of dreams. Further, Habermas (1971, p. 226) claims that psycho-analysis presupposes a specific norm or ideal standard of human relations:

> In the methodically rigorous sense, 'wrong' behaviour means *every deviation from the model of the language-game of communicative action*, in which motives of action and linguistically expressed intentions coincide. . . . This model, however, could be generally applicable only under the conditions of a non-repressive society. Therefore deviations from it are the normal case under all known social conditions.

In two more recent articles (Habermas, 1970a, 1970b), Habermas extends his account of the norms involved in communicative action, by outlining a 'general theory of communicative competence'. A central feature of this is the specification of an 'ideal speech situation', which is presupposed by the actual communicative competence that all language-users display. This ideal situation involves, in addition to the norm of motive-and-expressed-intention coincidence, others which Habermas suggests are related to the traditional ideals of truth, freedom and justice. And he puts forward two hypotheses. First, that the degree to which *actual* speech-situations deviate from the ideal one is dependent upon the degree of repression that characterizes the institutional system within a given society. Second, that the degree of repression depends on the developmental stage of the productive forces and the system of political and economic power (Habermas, 1970b, p. 374).

We conclude by stating the implications of Habermas's position for the nature of a critical theory of society, and our own critical response to these. For Habermas, a critical theory of society is not itself a distinctive form of knowledge. Thus the relationship between such a theory and the emancipatory interest, is not symmetrical with the relationships between empirical-analytic and historical-hermeneutic sciences, and their knowledge-constitutive interests. Rather, a critical theory of society is one which involves both of these other forms of knowledge; which is methodologically self-conscious of the distinctive nature of these forms; and which is oriented towards the emancipatory values embodied in the activity of that philosophical self-reflection which makes methodological self-consciousness possible. More specifically, such a theory would include the following types of enquiry. First, the interpretive understanding, by the methods of historical-hermeneutic science, of the systems of belief and modes of communication present in a given society. Second, their critical evaluation by reference to the norms of an ideal speech-situation. Third, the investigation, by the methods of empirical-analytic science, of the causal determinants of those modes of communication and belief, and of their departure from the norms that can be justified by self-reflection and critical argument. Finally, a specification of the kind of non-repressive society in which these values can be realized.

We believe that a critical theory of society of this kind has many desirable features. But it also has at least two serious defects. First, Habermas's account of the nature of the empirical-analytic-sciences is essentially positivistic. This is revealed partly by the way he characterizes the objects of these sciences, in terms of what is open to detection and manipulation in controlled experiments; partly by the way he describes their aim as the discovery of nomological knowledge; and partly by his inclusion of what he calls the 'systematic sciences of social action', namely economics, sociology and political science, as examples of empirical-analytic science (Habermas, 1971, p. 310). We suggested, in part 2, that most social theories have been based upon positivist conceptions of science. Further, we noted that a major exception to this, Marx's structural theory, involves the adoption of a non-positivist, realist conception of science. And we argued in part 1 that realism, at least in the natural sciences, is preferable to both positivism and conventionalism. Thus we regard Habermas's analysis of the empirical-analytic sciences as failing to challenge the positivist understanding of scientific knowledge, its view of theories and explanations, and its ontological and epistemological restrictions. Second, though Habermas is correct to distinguish the forms of knowledge involved in interpretive understanding and causal explanation, there is a danger that critical social theory will be split into two irreconcilable components: the investigation of causal relations that do not involve the subjective states of human agents; and the interpretive understanding of human actions and beliefs. Against this, we maintain the necessity of a social theory which, whilst involving both interpretive and explanatory understanding, unifies these in the analysis of structural relations, and of the way in which these affect, and are affected by, the subjective meanings of human agents. For example, we need interpretive understanding to identify the intentions of individual agents, and the contents of the systems of belief and value that are present in a given society. But this must be combined with an analysis of how an agent's acceptance of such beliefs and values is causally operative in his or her actions; and of how systems of belief are causally related to the structural relations and mechanisms present in specific social formations.[21]

Postscript

In this book we have tried to establish the overall character of an objective science of social life and social formations. We have done this at two distinct, though related, levels. First, we argued in general for a realist conception of science, in opposition to both positivist and conventionalist alternatives. Second, we argued for several methodological features specific to the social sciences, especially those involved in the Marxist concept of ideology, and in the interpretive understanding of social phenomena.

One consequence of our approach is that the way in which the issue of objectivity in social science is normally analysed can be seen to be defective. Typically the issue is examined as if the question of what it is to be scientific is unproblematic, and the discussion is focused upon various sources of distortion, and on the possibility of their elimination. We argued, however, that there is a more basic problem about objectivity, that is, the precise nature of an objective science. It is this which is problematic, and only when it is satisfactorily resolved can we identify the nature of ideological distortion.

We are aware, nonetheless, of several difficulties and further questions that arise from our own position. These concern both the epistemological and ontological foundations of an adequate science of society, and also the development of substantive theories based upon these foundations. Amongst the former issues are, first, the nature and criteria of validity of interpretive understanding; and second, the complex relationship between the knower and the known. We gave only a brief and minimal account of the first: much remains to be done in distinguishing the different types of interpretation, and in specifying the criteria of validity for these. As for the second, we have attempted little more than establishing the general limits within which a more precise and sophisticated analysis must proceed. In particular, there is the question of how scientific concepts are related to human needs and activity. Further, since conceptions of human needs are themselves related to general characterizations of human nature, we need some way of evaluating the many competing views of human nature that have been espoused, if an adequate epistemology is to be articulated.

At the level of substantive social theory, the primary problem is how to develop theories that satisfactorily synthesize the structural analysis of different social formations, and the explanation of human action in terms of subjective states and meanings. We argued that both of these must be seen as causal accounts, and thus we have defended a framework within which the necessary synthesis can intelligibly be made. But we have given no clear indications of how this can be done in practice. One important area in which our position would be fruitfully applied, is in the analysis of ideologies, that is, in a theory of the generation, dissemination, and abandonment of systems of true and false beliefs. This would necessarily involve the interpretive understanding of beliefs; an account of the structural features of particular social formations in which these beliefs are generated and disseminated; and an examination of the ways in which people perceive, and act in, the situations located within these structures. No adequate theory of this kind at present exists; and only by basing it upon an appropriate conception of scientific knowledge can it be constructed.

Notes

Introduction to part 1

1 Losee (1972) is a useful account of the major historical figures and ideas in the philosophy of science. On the realist tradition, see Wallace (1972); on conventionalism in astronomy, Duhem (1969); on Berkeley's positivism, Popper (1969c); on late nineteenth-century writers, Alexander (1964). In this century, philosophy of science has been much influenced by developments in relativity theory and quantum mechanics, but we will not discuss these: Capek (1961) presents most of the issues. Bohm (1957) defends a realist approach to quantum mechanics, in contrast to the positivist interpretation by Heisenberg (1959); Smart (1968), ch. 5, contains a useful discussion from a realist standpoint.

2 For a general history of positivist philosophy, see Kolakowski (1972). On logical positivism, and the analytical movement, see Passmore (1968), chs 16 and 18. Examples of scientific realism are Sellars (1963), Smart (1963), and Mandelbaum (1964), though this movement is somewhat heterogeneous.

3 Cf. Ayer (1946), whose logical positivism involves a rejection of metaphysics, theology and ethics as spurious, cognitively meaningless forms of 'knowledge'; with Popper (1969a), who argues, against the logical positivists, that what is important is to distinguish between science and non-science, and not between the meaningful and the meaningless. Duhem combines a part-positivist, part-conventionalist view of science with defence of a neo-Aristotelian metaphysics compatible with his Catholicism. He rejects the idea that scientific theories should attempt to *explain* phenomena, on the grounds that explanation means the discovery of unobservable realities beneath the appearances. Explanatory science would therefore be unnecessarily subject to *metaphysical* disputes (see especially (1954), chs 1, 2, and the appendix).

4 The term 'realism' is applied to several philosophical doctrines, such as Platonic Realism, that have little connection with our own use of it. In contemporary philosophy of science, the term is sometimes restricted to a particular view about theoretical entities. Our wider use is justifi-

able, though unlike chapter 1, where we analyse positions that have frequently been maintained by philosophers of science, chapter 2 contains some developments of realist views that have not been advanced in the same form before. Our threefold classification is not intended as complete: see n. 11 to chapter 6, on the *rationalist* conception of science.

1 Positivist philosophy of science

1 Thus positivists have analysed scientific theories as 'interpreted formal calculi'. We will not discuss this concept in what follows. For a simple account of its main features, see Introduction to Shapere (1965). A critical assessment by one of its former exponents is in Hempel (1970). For general characterizations and evaluations of twentieth-century positivism, see the papers in Achinstein and Barker (1969). We have tried to avoid the use of symbolic formalizations; but where these occur, they are always preceded by 'translations' in non-symbolic language.

2 Hempel's views were first stated in Hempel (1942); then in Hempel and Oppenheim (1948); and more fully, with detailed consideration of objections, in Hempel (1965b). Similar views were proposed in Popper (1959), itself a translation of the 1934 German edition. Important critical discussions include: Scriven (1962), Scheffler, I. (1964), Donagan (1966), and Suchting (1967).

3 In the third model, the 'Deductive-Statistical', it is statistical laws that are explained, by deducing them from premises containing at least one other such law: see Hempel (1965b), pp. 380–1. An example of this, in sociology, will be given in chapter 4, section 4. This contrasts with the I-S model, where it is particular phenomena that are explained.

4 We have omitted reference to another popular criterion, that laws 'support counter-factual conditionals', since we believe this has proved fruitless; see Walters (1967) for a useful account. For general discussions of the criteria for scientific laws, see Popper (1959), ch. 3; Nagel (1961) ch. 4; Ayer (1963); Jobe (1967). On the issue of necessity, see n. 19 to chapter 2.

5 On the logical problem of induction, see Black (1967). Barker (1957) is a useful analysis of different views about the relations between theories and observations. For discussion of various types of confirmation theory, see Swinburne (1973). Popper's rejection of inductive argument, and defence of hypothetico-deductivism, are in Popper (1959) and (1969a): Medawar (1969) gives very readable support. Chapters 6 and 7 of Achinstein (1971) contain an interesting discussion of several forms of argument from observation to theory, illustrated with case-histories.

6 Ashby (1967) is a useful survey of the problems of formulating the positivist criterion; see also Scheffler (1964), pp. 127–62, and the Introduction to Ayer (1946). We have excluded reference to analytic statements, which most positivists regard as non-empirical but meaningful, and important in science. On the difference between criteria of scientificity and meaningfulness, see n. 3 to the Introduction to part 1.

231

7 Strictly speaking, the observation-language contains not only observational terms, but 'logical' terms, such as 'and', 'all', 'if', 'not', etc.: see the Introduction to Shapere (1965) on this. For discussion of strategies not using correspondence rules, such as the use of Craig's Theorem, or Ramsey Sentences, see Hempel (1958); Scheffler (1964), pp. 162–203; and Smart (1968), ch. 5.

8 See Spector (1967) for a fuller account of these different attempts to characterize observational terms.

9 See the Introduction to Shapere (1965) for an outline of the more technical aspects of these two types of correspondence rule. Our account here, and the examples, are drawn from Shapere. For a critical discussion of the use of operational definitions in psychology, see Taylor, C. (1964), ch. 4: we discuss this in chapter 7, section 3. In Spector (1967), a different but equally common sense is given to 'partial interpretation'.

10 For discussion of the many different distinctions that can be drawn, see Spector (1967), and Achinstein (1968), chs 5 and 6. On the problem of distinguishing sets of terms, as against uses of terms, see Suppe (1972).

11 See Shapere (1966) pp. 41–4 on these aspects of 'the logic of science', and n. 1 to this chapter on the analysis of theories as interpreted calculi.

12 The distinction between logic and psychology is closely related to that between the 'contexts of justification and discovery': on this latter distinction, see Achinstein (1971), pp. 137–41. For support of the logic versus psychology distinction, see Popper (1959), ch. 1; and on his dispute with Kuhn on this issue, see Kuhn (1970b) and Popper (1970). For an extreme dismissal of models and analogies as psychologistic, see Duhem (1954), part I, ch. IV. A fuller discussion of models and analogies occurs in chapter 2, section 2, below.

13 See Agassi (1963) for a spirited attack on inductivist historians of science, from a hypothetico-deductivist standpoint. The whole question of the relations between history and philosophy of science is one of the main themes of the papers in Lakatos and Musgrave (1970).

14 On the phlogiston and oxygen theories of combustion, see McKie (1952), chs 10–14; Toulmin (1957); Hall (1962), ch. 11; and Freund (1968), ch. 1. Another episode favoured by positivists is the elimination of 'vitalism' from nineteenth-century biology: for a stimulating account of positivist misrepresentation of this, see Benton (1974).

15 See Hempel (1969), pp. 185–94, on the several different aspects of the 'unity of science' ideal. On the reduction of scientific theories, see Oppenheim and Putnam (1958), Nagel (1961), and Sklar (1968).

2 Realist philosophy of science

1 The contrast here is similar to that drawn by Scheffler, I. (1964) between the 'substantiation' and the 'explanation' of an event's occurrence: see pp. 19–57. It is also closely related to the medieval distinction between 'ratio cognoscendi' and 'ratio essendi': roughly, between a reason for knowing or believing, and a reason for being or existing.

2 This account of Hume is a deliberately 'modernized' one, using the concepts of modern empiricism. For a critical discussion of Hume, including this problem of modernization, see Bennett (1971), chs 9–12. Hume's own position is most easily approached in section 7 of 'An Enquiry Concerning Human Understanding', in Hume (1902). The precise relationship between individual causal judgments and regularities is problematic: see ch. 3 of White, M. (1965), and Davidson (1967).

3 It is no solution to restrict the concept of causal relations to cases where one kind of event is not only always followed by another, but also always precedes it. For this runs into the problem of causal 'plurality', i.e. of there being more than one possible cause of the same effect. For useful discussions of this generally neglected issue, see Pap (1963), ch. 14 and Gruner (1967a).

4 For somewhat different approaches, see Madden (1969), and Maxwell N. (1968). In the latter, it is argued that there is no unintelligibility in causal relations being *logically* necessary.

5 See Harré (1964b), and (1970) ch. 4, for this argument about meaning and evidence. Our view of the natural sciences is heavily indebted to Rom Harré's systematic development of the realist position.

6 The restriction of science to how questions and descriptions, is sometimes used to protect religion from the claims of science: cf. n. 3 to the Introduction to part 1, and the accompanying text. For a brief discussion of some of these issues, see Edwards (1967).

7 For Mill's account of causation, see Mill (1898), book 3. Several refinements have been added in more recent work, such as the requirement of non-redundancy of causal conditions, and the concept of a causal field. On these, and for a seminal discussion of the relation between particular causal conditions and the complete set, see Mackie (1965). M. White's treatment of explanation and causation in history shows the close relation between the D-N model and the Millian view of causes as sufficient conditions: see M. White (1965), especially chs 3–4.

8 On the use of models and analogies in science, see Hesse (1963), Spector (1965), Achinstein (1968), chs 7–8, and Harré (1970), ch. 2. Discussion of this issue is beset by terminological differences between writers. Our distinctions between source, subject and model follow those of Harré; on 'representational' models as physical objects, see Achinstein (1968) pp. 209–11.

9 On idealizations in science, see Nagel (1961) pp. 129–45, and Shapere (1969). Hempel (1952) compares their use in natural and social science. In chapter 5, section 5, below, Marx's use of abstraction and idealization is examined and compared with Weber's.

10 For a lively account of this use of models as hypothetical mechanisms, see Harré (1961). The form of argument involved is often termed 'retroductive inference': on this, see Hanson (1958), ch. 4, and Achinstein (1971), ch. 6.

11 The inadequacy of inductive arguments for arriving at hypotheses about unobservables is discussed in Barker (1957), ch. 5 and Mandelbaum (1964), ch. 2. On the nature and status of analogical argument,

see Hesse (1963), and Achinstein (1971) ch. 6. It should be noted that some existential hypotheses have the characteristic of being verifiable, but not falsifiable: unlike general laws, the discovery of positive instances may be conclusive. On this asymmetry, see Watkins (1958). This undermines the rationale for any general commitment to falsification: cf. section 2 of the previous chapter. On the importance of existential hypotheses, see Harré (1961).

12 We have omitted any discussion of the sense of 'model' in mathematics, often used by positivists in their accounts of scientific theories, when viewing them as interpreted calculi. On this, see Achinstein (1968) ch. 8.

13 In fact, the restrictive criterion of scientificity that we have ascribed to positivists was abandoned fairly soon in this century, and less restrictive formulations substituted for it. It is arguable that these do not generate the positivist 'problem of theoretical terms': but discussions of theoretical terms long continued as if this problem did exist. Why this is so is an interesting historical question.

14 On this realist interpretation of correspondence rules, see Schaffner (1969), and Harré (1970), ch. 1. For general defences of the realist view of theoretical terms as making ontological commitments, see Maxwell, G. (1962), and Smart (1968), ch. 5. We have used the example of 'magnetic' as a theoretical term for the sake of simplicity. Since, though, it is a *dispositional* term, not directly referring to an entity such as an atom, it might be thought appropriate to give its meaning via hypothetical statements about observations. But even with dispositional terms, we believe a realist analysis is preferable. For defence of realism about dispositions, see Armstrong (1968), ch. 6.

15 For an interesting general discussion of the nature of definitions in science, see Achinstein (1968), chs 1-2. In a recent article which marks a considerable departure from positivist views, Hempel (1970) argues that the demand for precise definitions of theoretical terms is unfounded. On the verificationist theory of meaning, see Passmore (1968), chs 16 and 18.

16 Harré (1964a), pp. 8-20, distinguishes 'reticular' and 'explanatory' theories, denying explanatory power to the former. The distinction is similar to that between 'abstractive' and 'hypothetical' theories; see Nagel (1961), pp. 125-8. Hempel (1965b), pp. 247-54, regards the explanatory power of non-causal laws such as those of pendular motion as good grounds for not restricting the D-N model's laws to *causal* laws: cf. section 1 of the previous chapter, p. 12.

17 It is doubtful, however, whether positivist views of explanation and theory adequately represent even reticular laws and theories.

18 Cf. the comments on descriptive and prescriptive approaches to science in section 4 of the previous chapter. One difficulty with basing philosophical theories on scientific practice is that this practice is itself guided by (often implicit) philosophical views. A good example is quantum mechanics: see n. 1 to the Introduction to part 1.

19 Kneale (1961) contains an influential argument for the need of the concept of necessity to characterize scientific laws. The argument is convincingly re-stated by Molnar (1969).

20 Some realists might be willing to accept this attenuated version of positivism whilst emphasizing that, in practice, the realist position generates a significantly different type of theoretical activity in science than the less-attenuated type of positivism leads to. Others might argue that the ultimate level of explanation need not be in terms of brute regularities; Harré, for example, argues for a universe made up of point-powers, in (1970), chs 10–11. On the finitude of nature, and its relevance for the philosophy of science, see Kneale (1968).

21 For Popper's rejection of essentialism, see his (1969b), pp. 103–7. More will be said about the reality-appearance distinction in parts 2 and 3, especially in section 1 of chapter 8.

22 Another form of essentialism will be discussed in chapter 4, section 3. For an interesting defence of the Aristotelian view of scientific explanation, involving a concept of essence, see Brody (1972): he argues that this avoids the problems of the D-N model. In chapter 9, we return briefly to the issue of natural kinds, in discussing the relations between language and reality.

23 On the early development of the gene-concept, see Goodfield (1969). On phlogiston and oxygen theories, see n. 14 to chapter 1.

3 Forms of conventionalism

1 Cf. the discussion of verification, confirmation and falsification in chapter 1, section 2, and chapter 2, section 2. On the verification of existential hypotheses, see n. 11 to chapter 2.

2 See Hempel (1966), pp. 3–6. Chapters 2 and 3 of this book contain a useful account of the logic of theory-testing, with several scientific examples.

3 Duhem's and Quine's positions are sometimes mistakenly conflated in what is called 'the Duhem-Quine Thesis'. For criticism of this conflation, and exegesis of Duhem's position, see Laudan (1965). Grünbaum (1966) argues against both positions, claiming that Quine's view is only true if trivial. Assumptions introduced solely to 'save' a theory are often termed *ad hoc*.

4 For examples demonstrating this historical point, see Swinburne (1964). The phrase 'naive methodological falsification' is Lakatos's: see his (1970), where the issue of Popper's changing views is also discussed, pp. 180–4. Notice that 'abandoning' a theory is ambiguous between (a) no longer regarding it as *true*, and (b) no longer *using* it.

5 Feyerabend's reasons for this last claim will emerge at the end of the next section. For his defence of proliferation, see his (1963a): his criticisms of Lakatos are in his (1970). It should be noted that Lakatos's main concern is slightly different from the way we have presented his views: he wishes to distinguish 'progressive and degenerating problem shifts'. Also, his Popperian concept of 'corroboration' is not strictly equivalent to that of 'confirmation'.

6 For similar accounts to Hanson's, see Toulmin (1961), chs 3–6; Feyerabend (1962), (1963a); Kuhn (1970a), especially ch. 10. Many of their arguments are inspired by the later writings of Wittgenstein, especially (1963), part 2, sec. xi. The theory-dependence of meanings is

also maintained by these writers, particularly Feyerabend, and the arguments here display an interesting isomorphism to those about perception. For criticism of these views about meaning, see Putnam (1965), Shapere (1966), and Achinstein (1968), pp. 91–105. For criticisms of both forms of attack on theory-neutrality, see Scheffler, I. (1967), and Kordig (1971).

7 Our account of Hanson's position is based upon his (1958): he defends a similar view in (1969). Unlike, for example, Kuhn, he is not *explicitly* concerned to challenge the function of observation as an objective control for theory-comparisons. In what follows, the terms 'theory' and 'theoretical belief' are used in a deliberately imprecise and general sense. Cf., with the present section, the arguments against a single theoretical-observational dichotomy, in chapter 1, section 3.

8 This argument depends upon his claim that seeing involves seeing *that* something is the case: ' "Seeing that" threads knowledge into our seeing' (1958, p. 22).

9 This is why, at the end of chapter 1, section 3, we claimed that the issues of theory-neutrality, and epistemological certainty, must be clearly separated. The position we have defended here is partly based on that of Hooker (1973). See also Dretske (1969), for defence of a concept of 'non-epistemic seeing', i.e. seeing without presuppositions of knowledge or belief.

10 For Feyerabend on proliferation, see his (1963a). The necessity for challenging the theoretical assumptions of observational descriptions is emphasized by Mepham (1973a), who talks of 'the theoretical critique of the facts'. A related problem is whether, for the purposes of such 'theoretical critiques', we should regard *ordinary language* as itself a theory, which is open to revision by scientific discoveries. On this, in the context of the mind-body problem, see Feyerabend (1963b), and Rorty (1965).

11 But note that the first edition of *The Structure of Scientific Revolutions* appeared in 1962, before Lakatos's position was fully developed. Our account of Kuhn is mainly based on this edition: in the second, a *Postscript* is added, containing several refinements and partial retractions, for example on the concepts of paradigms and of seeing: further 'second thoughts' are in his (1970c). Exegesis of Kuhn is made difficult by his frequent use of weakening qualifications: on this feature, see the important review-article by Shapere (1964). We have kept to the stronger versions of his claims. Useful critical discussions are in Scheffler, I. (1967), Lakatos and Musgrave (eds) (1970), and Kordig (1971). We discuss further aspects of Kuhn's position in sections 2 and 3 of chapter 9.

12 For Kuhn, paradigms are also incommensurable because of meaning-changes in the theoretical and observational vocabularies, and because, in some sense, scientists operating within different paradigms inhabit 'different worlds'. On the latter, see Section 4 below: on the former, see n. 6 above. It seems doubtful whether Kuhn can consistently maintain, as he often does, that paradigms are both incommensurable *and* incompatible: see, e.g. Kordig (1971), pp. 52–9.

13 On seventeenth-century theories of light, and their methodological assumptions, see Sabra (1967): especially chs 6, 8 and 11, on Huygens's wave theory, and Newton's (implicitly) corpuscular position. It should also be noted that there were many distinctive standpoints within a generally corpuscularian framework, which strongly affected disputes about what counted as a *substantively* adequate 'ultimate explanation': but much 'normal science' was carried on despite these differences. See also Dijksterhuis (1961), part IV, and Mandelbaum (1964), chs 1–2.

14 The conflict between their views on 'normal science' is apparent if one compares the title of Kuhn (1963), 'The Function of Dogma in Scientific Research', with Feyerabend's defence of an 'anarchistic epistemology' in his (1970). But Feyerabend, like Kuhn, is a strong advocate of meaning-variance: see n. 6 above. For a recent attempt to develop an *evolutionary* view of the growth and development of science and human knowledge, see Toulmin (1972).

15 See Feyerabend (1970), p. 72. For this feature of Popper's position, see Magee (1973), chs 6 and 7. Thus, underlying the methodological disagreements between Popper, Kuhn, and Feyerabend are important *political* implications: the three have been taken as providing defences for, respectively, liberal-democracy, totalitarianism, and anarchism – though Feyerabend now prefers the label 'dadaism': see footnote 33 to his (1970).

16 For a similar point, see Hooker (1972), a sympathetic review of Feyerabend's work. The contrast we have drawn between 'rational standards' and 'practical guides' is too simple as it stands: for example, Lakatos's 'sophisticated methodological falsificationism' (section 1 above), and the attempts to formulate a 'logic of confirmation' (see n. 5 to chapter 1), fall somewhere between the two.

17 Kolakowski's definition is mainly related to nineteenth-century writers, in a chapter significantly entitled 'Conventionalism: Destruction of the Concept of Fact' (1972, ch. 6). Our elaborations on it reflect the changing concerns and assumptions of more recent philosophers of science. Many earlier conventionalists were interested in the extent to which scientific laws involved definitional, rather than empirical, truths: on these writers, see Alexander (1964). There was also concern with the relations between language and reality: see chs 10–11 of Poincaré (1958). 'Conventionalism' is sometimes applied to the view that logical principles are based on conventions: see, e.g., Ayer (1946), ch. 4.

18 For a partial withdrawal of his 'different worlds' claim, see Postscript to Kuhn (1970a), pp. 192–3: and in his (1970c), pp. 259–66, he emphasizes how individual scientists may apply their shared standards differently. The relation between aesthetic or moral values, and the objectivity or rationality of science, is more complex than we have presented it. For example, one frequently advocated criterion for theory-choice is simplicity: should this be seen as a subjective, or objective standard? This partly depends on which of the numerous criteria of simplicity is used, and for what reason: on these issues, see the symposium in *Philosophy of Science*, 28, pp. 109–71, especially

Rudner (1961). We return to the issues of values, objectivity, and the theory-dependence of reality, in chapter 9.

19 On positivists and the history of science, see section 4 of chapter 1. Historical studies by the writers examined include: Duhem (1917) and (1969), Hanson (1958), (1963), and Kuhn (1959).

20 The argument outlined here is far from conclusive, and positivists might claim that radical changes in theoretical vocabularies could be accounted for by the discovery of unsuspected general laws.

21 Using the distinction made between two senses of 'abandonment' in n. 4 above, the realist sees this use of models as indicating abandonment (a), but not (b). Another argument against realism by instrumentalists concerns the function of idealizations: for the realist view on this, see chapter 2, section 2. On the general contrast between realism and instrumentalism, see Popper (1969b), and Nagel (1961), ch. 6, who argues that the difference between them concerns only 'preferred modes of speech'. This claim is strongly rejected in G. Maxwell (1962).

22 Thus Kolakowski (1972) correctly treats conventionalism as a 'chapter' in the history of positivism; and the tradition of viewing astronomical theories as 'saving the phenomena' can be seen as part-instrumentalist, part-conventionalist: see the Introduction to part 1. But most instrumentalists would be opposed to a denial of the theory-neutrality of the observational facts predicted by theories. The variety of definitions given by philosophers of science to such terms as 'positivism', 'realism', 'instrumentalism' and 'conventionalism' is somewhat confusing, and our own differ from several others: but what matters is the specific content of the positions these terms are used to denote.

Introduction to part 2

1 Positivist interpretations of Marx were common at the end of the last century and at the beginning of this; best known are Bukharin, Kautsky and Plekhanov. A set of papers which criticizes this interpretation and support an alternative humanistic one is Fromm (1967).

2 A good example of a social scientist who explicitly adopts a single distinctive position in the philosophy of science is Homans. See his (1964) where he adopts a Hempelian positivism which he then uses to criticize sociological orthodoxy.

3 The account that would be given by a hypothetico-deductivist of the history of social science would of course be different again; see our discussion of these writers in section 4, of chapter 1. There are no histories of social thought which are based on the types of methodological distinction that we make. On the Scottish Enlightenment see Swingewood (1970).

4 Sociology and positivism

1 On the general history of Comtean positivism see Simon (1963). For Comte's own writings the most convenient source is *Positive Philosophy* vols 1 and 2 (Comte, 1853). Two useful and interesting nineteenth-

century discussions, both relevant to the next section, are Mill (1965) and Spencer (1968). Three modern methodological discussions are in Aron (1968), Kolakowski (1972), and Laudan (1971). On the role of sociology in the Comtean system, see Swingewood (1970). The fact that the following account is only of Comte should not be read as historically minimizing the role and importance of Saint-Simon. We will not enter into the debate as to whether the Comtean system is merely the systematization and elaboration of basically Saint-Simonian arguments. Furthermore, our account is mainly of Comte's theses as set out in the *Cours de Philosophie Positive*, written between 1830 and 1842.

2 We will discuss aspects of methodological individualism in chapter 8.

3 In general, see Mill (1898), book VI, 'On the Logic of the Moral Sciences', as well as Mill (1965). The best methodological discussion is in Ryan (1970a), especially chapter 1 on deduction, chapter 3 on induction, and chapter 4 on whether or not he is suitably classified as an empiricist, epistemologically. Also see Chapter 2, section 1 above, for a discussion of the Millian approach to causation.

4 Spencer's own views can best be seen in Spencer (1874, 1883, 1893), some of which is included in Andreski (1971). Very useful discussions are in Eisen (1967) and Peel (1971). For other aspects of his work see Barker (1915) and Burrow (1966).

5 This reorientation of social thought is interestingly and helpfully discussed in Hughes (1959), although his use of the term 'positivism' is much broader than ours set out in chapter 1. We discuss positivism and behaviourism in chapter 7, section 3.

6 For Durkheim's own writings see especially *The Rules of Sociological Method* (Durkheim, 1938); also Durkheim (1915, 1933, 1952). We are now fortunate in having available Steven Lukes's work on Durkheim (Lukes, 1973a). The other most useful methodological discussions are in Alpert (1961) and Douglas (1967). On Durkheim's possibly changing views on the character of social facts, see Parsons (1968, vol. 1). Useful general discussions are in Giddens (1971, 1972).

7 We will discuss aspects of this issue in chapter 8. There is anyway much controversy. Some writers, such as Alpert (1961) argue that we can only grasp Durkheim's thesis if we distinguish carefully between the different notions of the 'individual' that he uses. Other writers, Giddens (1971) for example, do not think this so important. In general on this topic see Alpert (1961, p. 149f.) and Lukes (1973a, pp. 11–15).

8 We should note that *Elementary Forms* is a rather different work from the other two, partly at least because it is based upon a functionalist mode of explanation.

9 Durkheim's method of rejecting alternative explanations apart from his own suffers from two defects. First, he may very well not reject *all* the possible explanations so it does not follow that his own, the sociological, is left as the only alternative. Second, Durkheim's method of presentation excludes the possibility that the alternative explanations are interdependently plausible and only implausible when given as separate and mutually incompatible. We examine his rejection of

individualistic explanations of suicide in chapter 7, section 3. Durkheim's same effect–same cause principle involves denial of causal plurality. On this see n. 3 in chapter 2.

10 It should be noted that one consequence of Durkheim's classification of suicide in terms of causes is that it has tended to prevent consideration of whether there is in fact a preferable typology of suicide, or whether there are in fact alternative causes operative. See chapter 9 in Lukes (1973a) for an excellent discussion of *Suicide*.

11 Our account of this is indebted to Douglas (1967). For an example of a highly formal algebraic interpretation of *Suicide*, see Willer (1967). Also see the useful article by Hinkle (1964).

12 See chapter 1, section 1, especially n. 3. This is an example of the deductive-statistical model.

13 Our presentation of Durkheim's argument is of course over-simplified; specifically it neglects the fact that the rate of suicide is U-functionally related to the degree of social integration.

14 Douglas (1967) even suggests that Durkheim's central proposition, the inverse relationship between the suicide rate and social integration, may represent no more than the fact that where there is high social integration a death is less likely to be labelled as suicidal, not that suicides are less likely to occur.

15 See Taylor, Walton and Young (1973) on positivism in criminology and the response of various anti-positivists. We might note their emphasis upon the inductivist aspects of positivism.

16 We ought to note the positivist movement in some areas, such as criminology, has been more explicitly and clearly framed with regard to immediate practical action.

17 See chapter 1 on the different styles of positivist natural science, e.g. inductivist versus hypothetico-deductivist.

18 For a much lengthier and partly similar critique of the related concept of the reference group, see Urry (1973a).

19 It might be noted here that functionalism is not going to be considered in this book. We do however make certain references to functionalist aspects of Marx's theory in the following chapter.

20 We will discuss other aspects of roles, in chapters 6 and 8 below. Also in chapter 7 we will analyse the realist approach to meanings and causes.

21 For further discussion of American positivism, see Brown and Gilmartin (1969), Friedrichs (1970), and Gouldner (1971).

5 Marx and realism

1 On Marx there are two useful collections of his more sociological writings, Bottomore and Rubel (1963) and Jordan (1971). Many of his early writings are collected together in Easton and Guddat (1967). Recent works which advocate versions of the one-Marx thesis are Nicolaus (1968), Avineri (1969), and Walton and Gamble (1973). This thesis is strongly criticized by Althusser (1969); also see the journal *Theoretical Practice*. The best sources for contemporary methodological

debates on Marx's writings are in the *Bulletin of the Conference of Socialist Economists, Economy and Society, New Left Review,* and *Radical Philosophy.* We have greatly benefited from reading unpublished chapters of a forthcoming book on Marx's political economy by Mike Howard and John King. As with Durkheim a new full length biography has recently appeared; see McLellan (1973). On Marx's political economy, see the collections in Horowitz (1968) and Hunt and Schwartz (1972), as well as Mandel (1968), Mattick (1969), Meek (1967, 1973), and Sweezy (1968).

2 Marx objects to Comtean positivism because of its predication upon a speculative philosophy of history, because of its artificial separation of the social from the political and the economic, and because of its positivist methodological foundation. He thought Comte much inferior to Hegel. For a very brief account, see Bottomore and Rubel (1963, pp. 28–30).

3 The 'vulgar' economists are mainly discussed in part 3 of *Theories of Surplus-Value* (Marx, 1972b), Adam Smith in part 1 (Marx, 1969a) and Ricardo in part 2 (Marx, 1969b).

4 This relational aspect of Marx is sometimes interpreted to mean both that all the elements within a given structure are internally related with each other, and that any single element contains the rest of that structure viewed from the particular angle of that element. Ollman (1971) presents the most systematic formulation of the 'philosophy of internal relations' approach to Marx.

5 However, we should note that some philosophers of science have tried to apply the positivist model of explanation to history by using 'laws' which are limited in their scope to specific historical periods or societies: see, e.g., Joynt, C. and Rescher, N. (1961).

6 We will discuss this distinction further in chapter 8, particularly section 1. It is interestingly discussed in Cohen, G. (1972), Geras (1971), and Mepham (1972); and given a rather different meaning in Althusser (1970). This is briefly discussed in the following chapter, section 3.

7 This distinction, and the relationship between value and price, is discussed in section 2 below.

8 We should note that Marx is not *always* consistent in his usage here; occasionally, the base refers to both the forces *and* the relations of production. We shall discuss below the functional and causal interdependencies between the base and superstructure; we should note here the problem of their possible conceptual interdependence. Specifically, is it possible to define the base without referring to elements in the superstructure, such as the system of legal rules? If not, how can base determine superstructure when the former is partly defined in terms of the latter? This point is forcibly made by Plamenatz (1954, pp. 21–8), but criticized by Cohen, G. (1970), and Miller (1972). For Ollman (1971), on the contrary, this is a necessary and desirable aspect of Marx's 'internal relations' approach.

9 These remarks of Engels are especially interesting in view of one common interpretation of his work. In this it is held that the more positivistic and deterministic elements in the works of Marx and Engels

are to be found in the latter. See for two accounts of this interpretation, Avineri (1969) and Coulter (1971).

10 In the following we present an analysis of this passage which is not found elsewhere. The passage provides a conception of the base in terms apparently different from an analysis in terms of the forces and the relations of production.

11 The units in terms of which labour is measured are those of 'abstract labour', or labour in general abstracting from the concrete forms which it takes. 'Abstract labour' is what is common to all productive activity. Further this reduction of labour to a common denominator, so that units of labour can be compared, added and subtracted, is an abstraction particularly appropriate to the capitalist mode of production.

12 'Constant' capital refers to the value of the materials and machinery used up in production which does not increase value. 'Variable' capital refers to the value of the labour power (expressed in units of abstract labour) which is responsible for producing a surplus. In general, the 'transformation problem' in Marx, the transforming of values into prices (of production) is highly complex. The classic critique and defence of Marx's solution were produced by Böhm-Bawerk and Bortkiewicz respectively. See the discussions in Sweezy (1966) and Meek (1973), especially the Introduction to the Second Edition and the Appendix.

13 This raises a whole series of issues too complex to be considered here. For a survey of articles on capital theory in modern economics, see Harcourt (1969), especially on the differences between the neoclassical, Ricardian and Marxist approaches.

14 For an up-to-date and interesting general discussion of Marx's approach to social classes, see Giddens (1973). For an approach influenced by the work of Louis Althusser see Poulantzas (1973). For an older, although still provocative discussion, see Ossowski (1963). Our account here is a development from Urry (1973b).

15 This criticism has been most famously developed by Popper (1960, 1962). It is critically discussed in Suchting (1972). It is an interpretation most applicable to Marx and Engels's *Manifesto of the Communist Party* (1888).

16 For a general discussion of Marx's analysis of pre-capitalist societies, see Hobsbawm (Marx, 1964). In this Marx's differing formulations are brought out clearly. It should be noted that in the text we will not mention the Slavonic form of society. Also, see Dobb (1946) and Ashcraft (1972) on feudalism, Terray (1972) on primitive societies, and Balibar (1970) generally on an approach to Marx's analysis of different modes of production. Also see Marx's ethnological notebooks (Marx, 1972a).

17 Engels, for example, says that: 'The less the development of labour ... the more preponderatingly does the social order appear to be dominated by ties of sex' (Marx and Engels, 1962b, p. 171). The possible dominance of kinship and the distinction between determination and dominance has been much discussed in French Marxist writing. See Godelier (1967), Balibar (1970), and Terray (1972). For a set of papers

which discuss this issue in depth, see *International Journal of Sociology*, 1972.

18 An implication of this is that we should not confuse the logical-historical method with the argument that there are highly determinate laws of development propelling societies from one mode of production to another. See n. 15 above.

19 It should be noted that Marx intended to introduce further logical-historical stages: the state, the international organization of production, and the world market. This work was not completed.

20 Giddens's account of Marx's theory of capitalism (as in Giddens, 1971) rests on an ideal typical interpretation. Such an interpretation is criticized in Althusser (1970). We might in passing note Marx's criticism of the Physiocrats that they conflated feudalism and capitalism. On the realist view of models and idealizations, see chapter 2, section 2.

21 We shall consider this passage only briefly since, as Nicolaus points out (Marx, 1973, pp. 36–9), Marx soon rejects this formulation.

22 Our brief discussion here is indebted to Althusser's *For Marx* (Althusser, 1969) and his concept of a structure-in-dominance.

23 Many of the most useful papers on functionalist explanation are collected together in Demerath and Peterson (1967). There is a helpful discussion in Lessnoff (1974). Two of the best known functionalists in sociology, Merton and Parsons, are discussed in Mulkay (1971). Cohen, G. (1970) suggests that Marx's functionalist interpretation can be seen in terms of the following analogy. Consider four struts which are driven into the ground each protruding an equal distance above it. If a roof is attached it is both supported by these struts but at the same time makes them more stable. Cohen suggests that the struts correspond with the base, the roof with the superstructure; the latter being in some sense functionally necessary for the former.

24 On the concept of the dialectic there is some helpful discussion in the articles in the *International Journal of Sociology* (1972); also see Nicolaus's Foreword to Marx (1973). We are not going to discuss the dialectic in Hegel nor its relationship to that in Marx.

25 A very interesting and clear example of this positivist interpretation is Banks (1970), see especially chapter 1. Other examples include Popper (1960, 1962) and the bulk of the literature on value in modern economics.

6 Structure and structuralism

1 Some writers, Piaget (1971) for example, argue that the structuralist method is also employed by certain schools of mathematical, physical and biological science. We will not consider this here.

2 This view is most forcibly maintained by Boudon (1971). A similar sort of position is argued for by Runciman (1969).

3 There is a useful discussion of these issues in Martinet (1970).

4 These two conceptions of structure correspond with the distinction often drawn between realism, on one hand, and instrumentalism, on the other. In section 4 of chapter 3 we discussed this distinction and rejected it as over-simple.

5 See, for example, Evans-Pritchard (1951), Firth (1961), Malinowski (1944), Nadel (1957), Radcliffe-Brown (1952), as well as standard textbook definitions of social structure. For a more unorthodox conception, see Leach (1954). For a general discussion and critique, see Goddard (1972), and Glucksmann, M. (1974). Also see section 3 of chapter 9 for discussion of Evans-Pritchard's positivist conception of science.

6 See the 'Introduction to part 1', n. 3, where we point out a similar feature of Duhem's position. Duhem rejects an explanatory function for scientific theories, although, as a matter of fact, the kinds of theories he does advocate would provide 'explanation' as defined by the positivist.

7 For general methodological discussions of 'structuralism' see the various articles in Ehrmann (1970), Lane (1970) and Robey (1973). Note our use of 'scarequotes' when referring to writers or positions associated with this movement.

8 This is most clearly found in the work of Lévi-Strauss; see (1968), part I. Also this is helpfully discussed in Leach (1970, chs 2 and 6), and Ardener (1971). There is good critical discussion in Scheffler, H. (1970, especially pp. 62–5).

9 For a general introduction to Chomsky, see Lyons (1970). For his methodological views, see Chomsky (1965, 1969 plus following articles, and 1972). Also see the exchange, Chomsky (1967) and Putnam (1967).

10 It should be noted that linguistic competence refers, for Chomsky, to grammatical ability. This ignores other systems of linguistic competence: semantic competence and conversational competence. On both of these, see Coulter (1973); on the latter Hymes (1971).

For an argument that the latter can be studied in a 'structuralist' manner, see Cicourel (1973).

11 The rationalist conception of science was an important element in, for example, Galileo and Descartes: see Koyré (1968), and Burtt (1932), chs 3 and 4. Sabra (1967), however, ch. 1, emphasizes the empiricist element in Descartes's actual scientific work. Rationalism in science derives partly from the Platonic view that 'the world is written in numbers': on this, see Wartofsky (1968), ch. 4, and Losee (1972). See Chomsky (1966), on the Cartesian tradition in linguistics.

12 See for a general account of Lévi-Strauss, Leach (1970). Also see many of the papers in Ehrmann (1970), especially Scheffler, H. (1970), and in Lane (1970). Also see Ardener (1971). Many of Lévi-Strauss's methodological views are to be found expressed in the convenient collection, Lévi-Strauss (1968).

13 See Douglas, M. (1970) for an attempt to construct a total system of classification which would account for the prohibitions and exclusions practised by any given society.

14 We are mainly going to consider Althusser's arguments as set out in Althusser (1969 and 1970). We will not refer to his later mainly untranslated work, except for Althusser (1971). Two interesting critical articles are Geras (1972) and Glucksmann (1972). A more obviously 'structuralist' Marxist writer is Godelier (1967) who more directly equates Marx's method with that of Lévi-Strauss.

15 See our discussions of phlogiston and oxygen theories in the last sections of chapters 1, 2 and 3.

16 This discussion of Althusser's analysis of classes and the social relations of production is partly based on Mepham's very interesting article on who, for Marx and Althusser, 'makes history' (see Mepham, 1973b).

17 This is of course a much discussed issue, especially in the history of Marxism. For a convenient and interesting summary, see Marek (1969). For an attempt to repair a structural theory of revolution with the analysis of subjective meanings, see Urry (1973a).

18 For a collection of 'structuralist' and related writings which point to the socially constructed character of social reality, see Douglas (1973). An influential book which emphasizes the dialectical interaction between man and society is Berger and Luckmann (1967). In chapter 8 we will discuss Berger and Pullberg's formulation of the notion of reification.

19 The term 'ethnomethodology' was coined by Harold Garfinkel. See his essays (Garfinkel, 1967) and the important article (Garfinkel and Sacks, 1967). There is a useful introduction to his work, Filmer (1972). There are three helpful collections of ethnomethodological writings, Douglas (1971), Sudnow (1972) and Turner (1974). For a writer influenced by both ethnomethodological and Chomskyan linguistic perspectives, see Cicourel (1973). We will briefly return to certain issues connected with ethnomethodology in the last section of chapter 7.

Introduction to part 3

1 On the problem of uniqueness in history, cf. Dray (1957) with Joynt and Rescher (1961). Popper (1960) is a classic attack on the possibility of long-term predictions in the social sciences: Gibson (1968) is a useful critical review of the main issues about prediction. Nagel (1961), pp. 447–59, discusses some of the problems about experiments and their relevance to social science.

2 Roughly, these two questions separate the main interests of Anglo-American, and Continental philosophers, in their discussions of the nature of human action. For an interesting account of the relations between the two philosophical traditions, and their increasingly complementary positions *vis-à-vis* the social sciences, see Apel (1967).

3 For a brief account of the intellectual context of Weber's methodological writings, and his attempt to mediate between several extreme dichotomies, see Runciman (1972), sec. 1.

7 The explanation and understanding of social action

1 For Weber's views about understanding and explanation, see Weber (1947), pp. 88–115. Useful critical accounts include: Parsons (1968), chs 13 and 16; Giddens (1971) ch. 10; Runciman (1972), sections 3, 5, and 6; Schutz (1972), ch. 1.

2 Weber's ideas about the nature and testing of causal explanation, especially in history, are developed in 'The Logic of the Cultural

Sciences', in Weber (1949). This essay is also important for his views about interpretive understanding. His ideas about causation are similar to J. S. Mill's, but are developed in a different intellectual context, Continental jurisprudence, which is outlined in Hart and Honoré (1959), chs 16 and 17.

3 Weber also argues that, by working out the deviations of any actual course of action from those that would occur if it were 'rational', we can assess the causal significance of non-rational factors determining the action: see Weber (1947), pp. 92–3. On the gap between rational and explanatory understanding, cf. our criticisms of the D-N model in chapter 2, section 1: the deductive argument gives us only rational understanding, and not necessarily causal explanation.

4 Cf. Parsons (1968), ch. 15, with Giddens (1971), ch. 12, for different views of the methodological significance of Weber's comparative studies. Weber's account of the emergence of European capitalism is in Weber (1930): Green (ed.) (1959) contains a useful collection of critical discussions of 'The Weber Thesis': see also Sprinzak (1972). Giddens (1970) is an interesting discussion of Weber's opposition to materialist accounts of capitalism, including Marx's.

5 The literature on reasons, causes, and the status of action-explanations is enormous. A useful summary of the issues, with bibliographical references, is in Bernstein (1972), pp. 260–80. On the nature of rational explanation in history, cf. Hempel (1965b), pp. 463–87, with Dray (1963). Our own position owes much to White, M. (1965), ch. 5; MacIntyre (1967); and Toulmin (1970).

6 Thus we disagree with MacIntyre (1962), pp. 54–6, who argues both that the connection was a rational-logical one, and that Weber was wrong to think that empirical testing was relevant. Cf., also, our remarks about the relations between formal-logical, and causal, relations in Lévi-Strauss and Chomsky, in chapter 6, section 2.

7 For an interesting discussion of what is involved in *following* a rule, with reference to Chomsky's theories, see Fisher (1971). We do not attempt to discuss the many difficult issues about the concept of a rule, which is central to, for example, Winch (1958); see Ryan (1970b), chs 6 and 7, for a useful account of Winch's position; and Schwayder (1965), part 3, for a classification of different types of rules and rule-following behaviour.

8 Our account of the relations between the concepts of reason, purpose, intention, motive, and so on, is highly schematic. For a useful discussion of some of the differences between these concepts, see White, A. (1967), ch. 6. On motives, see especially Kenny (1963), ch. 4. Notice that this concept, in ordinary English usage, is a more limited one than Weber's technical definition of 'motive', given in section 1 above.

9 For the purposes of the discussion that follows, we assume a Humean view of causation, especially that causal relations are not logically necessary. Cf. our discussion of Hume in chapter 2, sections 1 and 4.

10 On the problems of specifying preventing conditions, see Block (1971). This issue is central to the philosophical problem of 'weakness of will': a useful collection on this is Mortimore (ed.) (1971). The claim that

actions follow logically from beliefs and desires is defended in MacIntyre (1962), and, in a different form, by von Wright (1971), ch. 3. A further argument against desires and beliefs as causes, that no relevant generalizations relating them to actions can be found, is supported in Lessnoff (1974), ch. 4. For a general defence of the causal status of such explanations, see Fodor (1968), chs 1 and 2.

11 Cf. Schutz (1972), pp. 25–31, who notes that Weber's examples of direct understanding can also be seen to involve motivational understanding. He also argues that Weber's definition of 'motive' is seriously ambiguous, between what seems an adequate ground to the *agent*, or to the *observer*.

12 See Schutz (1954), as an example of those who assume that naturalism involves a social science based on purely behavioural action descriptions. Our views about the causal assumptions of descriptions are based on our position about theory-neutral observations, developed in chapter 3, section 2. We make further use of this in chapter 8, section 1 in discussing Marx's distinction between 'appearance' and 'reality'.

13 The classical attempt to define purposeful action using cybernetic concepts is Rosenblueth *et al.* (1943): Taylor, R. (1950) is an equally classical criticism. A good general discussion of such attempts is Scheffler, I. (1964), section 9. On behaviourism in psychology, see the interesting collection in Wann (ed.) (1964). On the use of operational definitions, an important symposium is in the *Psychological Review*, vol. 52, 1945. For a critical discussion of B. F. Skinner's form of 'radical behaviourism', see Keat (1972). In the rest of this section, we will use the phrase 'subjective states' to refer to items such as beliefs, desires, emotions, and so on.

14 See Fodor (1968), chs 2 and 3, and Bloor (1970), for similar contrasts between realism and positivism in relation to behaviourism, though their main concern is with specifically philosophical behaviourism. Fodor, unlike Bloor, regards realism as entailing some form of materialism, in which mental states are identified with physical ones. But his argument for this, on pp. 97–9, is, we believe, mistaken. Harré and Secord (1972), use a realist view of science to attack behaviourist psychology, but they seem to regard reason-explanations as non-causal.

15 MacIntyre (1967) argues that Durkheim's definition of suicide rules out, in principle, reference to the agent's intentions in explaining acts of suicide. Douglas, by contrast, argues that Durkheim does in fact make reference to the social meanings of suicide, but in an unsystematic and arbitrary way: see Douglas, J. (1967). On Durkheim's anti-individualism, see chapter 4, section 3, and for more detailed discussion, chapter 8, section 4. On 'ultimate explanations', see chapter 2, section 4.

16 For Schutz's views on the relation between scientific and everyday concepts, see especially Schutz (1953). On the way in which concepts change from 'technical' to 'everyday' status, cf. chapter 1, section 3. The problem of describing people's subjective states, using concepts unavailable to them, is particularly important in Freud's theories. We should also note, though, that many everyday explanations do not

involve reference to purposes and beliefs, but to 'external' determinants, such as physiological, social, or more 'theoretical' items.

17 MacIntyre (1967) argues that Winch's position excludes the possibility of using the concepts of ideology and false-consciousness: we believe this argument rests partly on the conception of ideology we reject here. But Winch certainly rejects the legitimacy of any systematic challenging of the agent's professed reasons – see, e.g. Winch (1958), p. 46. Both Durkheim and Pareto rely partly, in their rejection of agent's reasons, on the denial of the possible plurality of causes, i.e. of alternative reasons or causes for the same action. See n. 3 to chapter 2 on this issue.

18 For a useful classification of different senses of 'meaning' and 'understanding' see Brodbeck (1963). On the general relation between explanation and understanding, see Gruner (1967b) and (1969). We are not trying, in this section, to give a complete catalogue of different senses of 'understanding': cf. our discussion of Weber's concept of 'rational understanding', in section 1 of this chapter. In the present section, we use 'explanatory understanding' in a wider sense than Weber gives it: see section 1 above.

19 An influential statement of the positivist view of *verstehen* is Abel (1948): see also Nagel (1961), pp. 480–5. It is clear from Weber's discussion of imaginitive re-enactment that he did not regard this as central to *verstehen*: see section 1 above. Another positivist response to *verstehen* is to claim that it involves a 'reproductive fallacy': for an appropriately sceptical discussion of this claim, see Gruner (1969). Recently, *verstehen* has been interpreted as a special type of judgment made by the professional expert: on this, see Cohen, H. (1973). Positivist views of *verstehen* are similar to their views of models and analogies in the natural sciences: see chapter 1, section 4, and chapter 2, section 2.

20 The example we use here is discussed in Skinner, Q. (1972), though in a somewhat different context. For a similar rejection of intentionalist accounts of meaning, see Margolis (1973). A useful survey of such accounts is Facione (1973). Our comments on linguistic meaning are very brief and selective – for example, there are several behaviourist theories of meaning. An introduction to many of the issues is Alston (1964), chs 1 and 2.

21 On hermeneutics see Habermas (1971), chs 7–11; Taylor, C. (1971); and Radnitzky (1972), vol. 2, chs 3–5. Hirsch (1967) is a stimulating discussion of literary interpretation, especially of the place of authors' intentions in analysing the meaning of their works. On the relations between context and intention in the methodology of the history of ideas, see Skinner, Q. (1969).

22 On problems of interpretation in anthropology, see Gellner (1962), and Hollis (1967a), (1967b). Schutz (1954) emphasizes the idea that *verstehen* is what goes on in our everyday interpretive understanding of each other, though he includes a number of very different types of knowledge in this. Cf. also our discussion of Lévi-Strauss, in chapter 6, section 2: in his work, further types of interpretation are apparently used.

23 Our position on the place of interpretive understanding in the natural sciences owes much to Apel (1972); the idea of different criteria of

validity for interpretive and explanatory understanding is explored
further in our discussion of Habermas, in chapter 9, section 4.

8 Reification and realism

1 For an interesting discussion of the historical development of the
concept of ideology, see Lichtheim (1967). For a rather different general
discussion, see Plamenatz (1970); also see Harris (1968). Marx's own
views are stated most systematically in *The German Ideology* (Marx and
Engels, 1965); but also see Mepham (1972) on the concept of ideology
in the later writings. The non-Marxist formulations are famously found
in Daniel Bell's *The End of Ideology* (1962). These are contrasted with
Marxist formulations in Miller (1972).
2 We will discuss aspects of Weber's analysis of values in sections 1, 2
and 4 of chapter 9. See Parsons (1951) for an example of this mainstream interpretation of the notion of ideology.
3 Marx gives as examples of 'roles', those of 'hunter' or 'fisher', and
characterizes them as 'fixations of human activity . . . consolidations of
our own products into an objective power above us, growing out of our
control, thwarting our expectations, and nullifying our calculations'
(Easton and Guddat, 1967, p. 425). Also see the last two papers in
Berger (1969).
4 This is discussed by Althusser, who argues that Hegel's thought is
dominated by the notion of 'expressive causality'; that is: 'that the
whole in question be reducible to an *inner essence*, of which the elements
of the whole are then no more than the phenomenal forms of expression, the inner principle of the essence being present at each point in the
whole . . . *a 'spiritual' whole in which each element was expressive of the
entire totality*' (1970, pp. 186–7).
5 We will only consider Lukács's *History and Class Consciousness* (1971).
Note the Preface in which he presents many criticisms of the work.
There are useful collections of relevant papers in Parkinson (1970) and
Mészáros (1971). Other useful discussions are Revai (1971), Stedman-
Jones (1971), and in Hamilton (1974: chapter 3).
6 Lukács says, for example, that the knowledge that produces dereifica-
tion: 'brings about an objective structural change in the object of
knowledge' (Lukács, 1971, p. 169).
7 See Berger and Pullberg (1966); also see the related more general
phenomenological sociology of knowledge, Berger and Luckmann
(1967). On the former see Brewster (1966) and Walton and Gamble
(1973). Note the distinction between objectifying and objectivating
processes and how the latter corresponds to our term 'objectifying' at
the end of the previous section.
8 See, for explicit examples, Berger (1966), Dahrendorf (1968), Coulson
and Riddell (1970), Urry (1970) and Coulson (1972). The claim is
implicit in Wrong (1964) and Atkinson (1971).
9 The debates between methodological individualists and holists have
given rise to an enormous literature. A very clear discussion of the
main issues is in Dray (1967); and see Lukes (1968) who also argues

that the debates involves conceptual confusion. Many relevant articles are collected together in O'Neill (1973), see especially Watkins. There is also a helpful discussion in Danto (1965) on the relationship between this debate and the issue of reductionism in the philosophy of natural science.

10 Three very different writers who adopt roles as the conceptual basis for their analysis of social organization, are Parsons (1951), Gerth and Mills (1954), and Berger (1966).

11 See the last section of chapter 4. Some of the relevant critical works, are: Gross *et al.* (1958), Naegele (1960), Goffman (1961), Preiss and Ehrlich (1966), Dahrendorf (1968), Urry (1970), Coulson (1972).

12 We should note that Dahrendorf's original article on role theory ('Homo Sociologicus') in which his argument is developed, gave rise to enormous controversy in German sociology. In Dahrendorf (1968, pp. 88–106) there is a discussion of some of this critical literature.

13 See section 3, chapter 7, especially n. 14.

14 We introduced this topic in section 3 of chapter 6. We noted then the helpful article by Mepham (1973b); although there are possible inadequacies in his characterization of the relations between 'men' and 'material circumstances' in the early Marx.

9 Values, theory and reality

1 We will not discuss a third concept that Weber employs, 'value-interpretation' – see especially 'The Logic of the Cultural Sciences', and pp. 22 and 33, in Weber (1949). This concept has been ignored by most commentators, but is important in relating his views about values and understanding: on the latter, see section 1 of chapter 7. Our account here is drawn mainly from the first two essays in Weber (1949). Useful discussions of Weber and value-freedom are Runciman (1972), sections 3 and 4; and Lessnoff (1974), ch. 6.

2 On Weber's political values, see Giddens (1971), pp. 190–5. On the intellectual context of the dispute about value-judgments in teaching, see Dahrendorf (1968), ch. 1. See Strauss (1953), for an attack on Weber's philosophical theory of value-judgments, as leading to 'moral nihilism'.

3 Our account of Weber's position about the relation of values to causal explanation departs from that of most commentators, e.g. Ashcraft (1972). For examples of how values have, in fact, distorted social scientific work, see Myrdal (1958). On Weber's concepts of rationalization and disenchantment, see Giddens (1971), pp. 214–16, and 178–84. On idealization and abstraction, see n. 9 to chapter 2, and section 5 of chapter 5. For a stimulating discussion of the Kantian influence on Weber's position, see Goddard (1973).

4 Taylor also argues (1967) that the rejection of the value-judgments supported by a social theory entails the rejection of the theory's explanatory framework. But this argument depends, we believe, on mistakenly assuming that a variable that is significant for value-judgments is necessarily causally significant also. Taylor's moral theory

seems to ignore issues about the distribution of satisfactions – see Lessnoff (1974), pp. 139–40. For an interesting discussion of the way values may be involved in setting appropriate levels of 'statistical significance' in theory-testing, see Leach (1968).

5 For Gouldner's later development of the idea of 'reflexive sociology', which contain many of the elements in the two papers we have discussed, see Gouldner (1971), ch. 13. For a critical review of this book, see Urry (1972).

6 Cf. our remarks about Strauss and MacIntyre, with Nagel's distinction between 'characterizing' and 'appraising' value-judgments. We should note that several definitions of 'justice' make use of the concept of human *needs*: the precise status of this concept, and thus its use in explaining social phenomena, is problematic.

7 On the denial of universal standards for assessing competing theories in the natural sciences, see chapter 3, sections 3 and 4. For a useful discussion of the relations between determinism and the free-will problem, see Honderich (1971), ch. 5. Lukes (1973b) examines many arguments about truth and social determination. The idea that only 'odd' or 'abnormal' phenomena require causal explanation is common in many ordinary language philosophers: for a decisive rebuttal of one such view, see Mandelbaum (1958). We return to arguments against determinism and relativism at the end of this section.

8 On Lukács's position, see section 2 of chapter 8. See Cohen, G. (1968), for an interesting defence of the claim that the proletariat, unlike the bourgeoisie, can develop true theories. Plamenatz (1970), ch. 5, criticizes the way 'class-interest' is typically used in making such claims. Note that causal explanations of beliefs must concern not only their *origins*, but also their *continued acceptance*.

9 For discussion of different criteria of rationality, see Schutz (1943), and Lukes (1967). On the difference between reasons, good reasons, and sufficient reasons, see Alexander (1962). MacIntyre emphasizes the importance of distinguishing truth from rationality: (1971), p. 248. On Newton's theology, and his beliefs about space and time, see Burtt (1932), ch. 7. On sixteenth- and early seventeenth-century astronomy, see Kuhn (1959). For support of the legitimacy of causally explaining non-defective beliefs, see Peel (1969), and Barnes (1972b).

10 Cf. Popper (1970), who claims that Kuhn concentrates too much on what is, for Popper, 'bad' science (i.e. 'normal' science). For an assessment of Kuhn as a sociologist of knowledge, see Urry (1973c). A useful collection of papers on the sociology of science is Barnes (1972a). Ravetz (1971) contains a stimulating discussion of the problem of 'quality-control' in science, and the deleterious effects of various external influences on the scientific community.

11 See Trigg (1973), ch. 7, for a typical defence of the claim that determinism supports relativism, and is self-refuting: in ch. 1 he also argues that relativism is self-refuting. It seems that Mannheim (1960) was led to support a version of relativism by his belief in social determination: but this is unclear, as is the precise nature of his relativism. Some form of conceptual relativism is probably implied by the relations between

concepts and reality derivable from Marx's early writings – see section 4 below.

12 For Evans-Pritchard's account of the Azande, see Evans-Pritchard (1937): a useful summary is in Gluckman (1944), who emphasizes that witchcraft explanations are typically invoked in cases of *coincidence*, and where the Azande's technical knowledge (important to an adequate analysis of their witchcraft beliefs) provides no explanation. We will not examine the many other interpretations of witchcraft by anthropologists: see Skorupski (1973), for a helpful discussion of these, and their philosophical relevance. Marwick (1970) contains a number of important papers on witchcraft and magic.

13 See Polanyi (1958), pp. 286–94, on witchcraft, science and falsification; and Horton (1967), for a seminal discussion of witchcraft and magic on the basis of a generally realist view of science. Note that our account of Evans-Pritchard's evaluation of Zande witchcraft is constructed from his comments in several different publications. Our quotations are taken from those used by Winch (1964): the bibliographical data are in that paper.

14 Cf. this argument of Gellner's against Winch, with the 'self-refuting' argument against relativism outlined at the end of section 2. On the concept of ideology, see chapter 8, *passim*. Note that the identification of inconsistencies between beliefs is made difficult by the problem of the hermeneutic circle: see chapter 7, section 4, and n. 21. (I sometimes wonder what the Azande would make of their misfortune if they read all this – R.N.K.)

15 See Sherry (1972), and Mounce (1973), for criticisms of the way Winch interprets Wittgenstein's (1963) views on language-games and forms of life. On the relations between Kuhn, Winch and Wittgenstein, see Trigg (1973). Kuhn discusses the question of what, on his views, counts as 'scientific progress', in the Postscript to (1970a), and in (1970c).

16 Our account of early critical theorists owes much to Jay (1973), ch. 2. He notes their rejection of certain features of Hegel's philosophy, especially the subject-object identity – cf. our discussion of Lukács, in section 2 of chapter 8. We have ignored the differences between, e.g. Horkheimer and Marcuse. Many of Marcuse's early papers are translated in Marcuse (1968): Horkheimer's, in Horkheimer (1972).

17 On the broader sense of 'positivism', see the Introduction to part 1, and the discussion of Habermas later in this chapter. For Horkheimer's attacks on positivism, see 'Traditional and Critical Theory', 'The New Attack on Metaphysics', and 'The Social Function of Philosophy', in Horkheimer (1972). For Marcuse's, see his (1937), and 'The Concept of Essence', in Marcuse (1968). For Marcuse's defence of hedonism, see 'On Hedonism', in (1968); the attack on capitalism's generation of false wants is continued in his later (1964). See also our discussion of Marx's essence-appearance distinction in chapter 8, section 1.

18 The pessimism of critical theorists is related to the later studies of the 'authoritarian personality', by Adorno and others. These are discussed by Jay (1973), who also notes the ambivalence of Horkheimer on the relations between true theories, reason, and social change: see pp. 63–4.

19 For discussions of American pragmatists, see Habermas (1971), chs 5–6, and Bernstein (1972), part III. On the idea of language producing 'different dissections of nature', see Whorf (1956): Hoijer (ed.) (1954) contains several important discussions of his ideas, especially in the papers by Hoijer and Hockett. Lawton (1968), ch. 4, gives a useful summary of work on the relations between language, thought and perception. On Marx's early epistemology, see Rotenstreich (1965).

20 On Habermas's conception of interests, see especially ch. 9 of (1971); his (1974), p. 203, is helpful on what he means by 'constitutive'. Both these, and other features of his position have generated considerable discussion. A useful summary of the main criticisms is Dallmayr (1972): for Habermas's replies, see his (1973). Our own account is based mainly on Habermas (1971) and (1974), which is part of an important exchange with Albert (1974).

21 We should note that Habermas, in the writings we consider, is not explicitly concerned with the nature of a critical *social* theory: our view of the implications of his position for this are based on his general standpoint, and occasional specific remarks – e.g. the analogy he suggests between Freudian 'rationalizations' and the concept of ideology. We believe his analysis of Freud, in chs 10–11 of (1971), indicates that he regards only *unconscious* motives and intentions as causal determinants, and that he thus rejects the causal interpretation of reasons we defended in chapter 7, sections 2 and 3. See McCarthy (1973), on Habermas's theory of communicative competence.

Bibliography

ABEL, T. F. (1948). 'The Operation Called Verstehen', *American Journal of Sociology*, 54, 211–18.

ACHINSTEIN, P. (1968). *Concepts of Science*, Baltimore: Johns Hopkins Press.

ACHINSTEIN, P. (1971). *Law and Explanation*, Oxford University Press.

ACHINSTEIN, P. and BARKER, S. F. (eds) (1969). *The Legacy of Logical Positivism*, Baltimore: Johns Hopkins Press.

AGASSI, J. (1963). *Towards an Historiography of Science, History and Theory*, Middletown: Wesleyan University Press.

ALBERT, H. (1974). 'The Myth of Total Reason', trans. G. Adey and D. Frisby, in Giddens (ed.) (1974).

ALEXANDER, P. (1962). 'Rational Behaviour and Psychoanalytic Explanation', *Mind*, 71, 326–41.

ALEXANDER, P. (1964). 'The Philosophy of Science, 1850–1910', in *A Critical History of Western Philosophy* (ed. D. J. O'Connor), New York: Free Press.

ALPERT, H. (1961). *Emile Durkheim and his Sociology*, New York: Russell & Russell.

ALSTON, W. P. (1964). *Philosophy of Language*, Englewood Cliffs: Prentice-Hall.

ALTHUSSER, L. (1969). *For Marx*, Harmondsworth: Penguin.

ALTHUSSER, L. (1970). 'From *Capital* to Marx's Philosophy' and 'The Object of *Capital*' in Althusser and Balibar (1970), 11–198.

ALTHUSSER, L. (1971). *Lenin and Philosophy and other Essays*, trans. B. Brewster, London: New Left Books.

ALTHUSSER, L. and BALIBAR, E. (1970). *Reading Capital*, London: New Left Books.

ANDRESKI, S. (1971). *Herbert Spencer: Structure Function and Evolution*, London: Michael Joseph.

APEL, K. O. (1967). *Analytical Philosophy of Language and the Geisteswissenschaften*, trans. H. Holstelilie, Dordrecht: D. Reidel.

APEL, K. O. (1972). 'Communication and the Foundations of the Humanities', *Acta Sociologica*, 15, 7–27.

ARDENER, E. (1971). 'Introductory Essay', in E. Ardener (ed.), *Social Anthropology and Language*, London: Tavistock, ix–cii.

ARMSTRONG, D. M. (1968). *A Materialist Theory of the Mind*, London: Routledge & Kegan Paul.

ARON, R. (1968). *Main Currents in Sociological Thought*, vol. 1, Harmondsworth: Penguin.

ASHBY, R. W. (1967). 'Verifiability Principle', in P. Edwards (ed.), *The Encyclopedia of Philosophy*, vol. 8, New York: Free Press.

ASHCRAFT, R. (1972). 'Marx and Weber on Liberalism as Bourgeois Ideology', *Comparative Studies in Society and History*, 14, 130–68.

ATKINSON, D. (1971). *Orthodox Consensus and Radical Alternative*, London: Heinemann.

AVINERI, S. (1969). *The Social and Political Thought of Karl Marx*, Cambridge University Press.

AYER, A. J. (1946). *Language, Truth and Logic*, 2nd edn, London: Gollancz.

AYER, A. J. (1963). 'What is a Law of Nature?', in *Concept of a Person*, London: Macmillan.

BALIBAR, E. (1970). 'The Basic Concepts of Historical Materialism', in Althusser and Balibar (1970), 199–308.

BANKS, J. A. (1970). *Marxist Sociology in Action, A Sociological Critique of the Marxist Approach to Industrial Relations*, London: Faber & Faber.

BARKER, E. (1915). *Political Thought from 1848 to 1914*, London: Butterworth.

BARKER, S. (1957). *Induction and Hypothesis*, Ithaca, New York: Cornell University Press.

BARNES, B. (ed.) (1972a). *Sociology of Science*, Harmondsworth: Penguin.

BARNES, B. (1972b). 'On the Reception of Scientific Beliefs', in Barnes (ed.) (1972a).

BARTHES, R. (1967). *Element of Semiology*, London: Jonathan Cape.

BECKER, H. and BARNES, H. E. (1938). *Social Thought from Lore to Science*, vol. 2, New York: D. C. Heath.

BECKER, H. S. (1963). *Outsiders*, New York: Free Press.

BECKER, H. S. (1964). *The Other Side*, New York: Free Press.

BELL, D. (1962). *The End of Ideology*, London: Collier-Macmillan.

BENNETT, J. (1971). *Locke, Berkeley, Hume*, Oxford University Press.

BENTON, E. (1974). 'Vitalism in Nineteenth Century Scientific Thought – a Typology and Reassessment', *Studies in History and Philosophy of Science*, 5, 17–49.

BERGER, P. (1966). *Invitation to Sociology*, Harmondsworth: Penguin.

BERGER, P. (ed.) (1969). *Marxism and Sociology, Views from Eastern Europe*, New York: Appleton-Century-Crofts.

BERGER, P. and LUCKMANN, T. (1967). *The Social Construction of Reality*, London: Allen Lane.

BERGER, P. and PULLBERG, S. (1966). 'Reification and the Sociological Critique of Consciousness', *New Left Review*, 35, 56–71.

BERNSTEIN, R. (1972). *Praxis and Action*, London: Duckworth.

BIDDLE, B. J. and THOMAS, E. J. (eds) (1966). *Role Theory Concepts and Research*, New York and London: John Wiley.

BLACK, M. (1967). 'Induction', in P. Edwards (ed.), *The Encyclopedia of Philosophy*, vol. 4, New York: Macmillan and Free Press.

BLOCK, N. (1971). 'Are Mechanistic and Teleological Explanations of Behaviour Incompatible?', *Philosophical Quarterly*, 21, 109–17.

BLOOMFIELD, L. (1935). *Language*, London: Allen & Unwin.

BLOOR, D. (1970). 'Is the Official Theory of Mind Absurd?', *British Journal for the Philosophy of Science*, 21, 167–83.

BOHM, D. (1957). *Causality and Chance in Modern Physics*, London: Routledge & Kegan Paul.

BOTTOMORE, T. and RUBEL, M. (eds) (1963). *Karl Marx: Selected Writings in Sociology and Social Philosophy*, Harmondsworth: Penguin.

BOUDON, R. (1971). *The Uses of Structuralism*, London: Heinemann.

BRADBURY, M., HEADING, B. and HOLLIS, M. (1972). 'The Man and the Mask: A Discussion of Role Theory' in J. A. Jackson (ed.), *Role, Sociological Studies 4*, Cambridge University Press, 41–64.

BREWSTER, B. (1966). 'Comment on Berger and Pullberg's "Reification and the Sociological Critique of Consciousness" ', *New Left Review*, 35, 72–5.

BRODBECK, M. (1963). 'Meaning and Action', *Philosophy of Science*, 30, 309–24.

BRODY, B. A. (1972). 'Towards an Aristotelian Theory of Scientific Explanation', *Philosophy of Science*, 39, 20–31.

BROWN, J. S. and GILMARTIN, B. G. (1969). 'Sociology Today: Lacunae, Emphases and Surfeits', *Amer. Sociologist*, 4, 283–91.

BURROW, J. (1966). *Evolution and Society: A Study in Victorian Social Theory*, Cambridge University Press.

BURTT, E. (1932). *The Metaphysical Foundations of Modern Science*, London: Routledge & Kegan Paul.

CAPEK, M. (1961). *The Philosophical Impact of Contemporary Physics*, New York: Van Nostrand.

CHOMSKY, N. (1959). 'Verbal Behaviour by B. F. Skinner', *Language*, 35, 26–58.

CHOMSKY, N. (1965). *Aspects of the Theory of Syntax*, Cambridge, Mass.: M.I.T. Press.

CHOMSKY, N. (1966). *Cartesian Linguistics*, New York: Harper & Row.

CHOMSKY, N. (1967). 'Recent Contributions to the Theory of Innate Ideas', *Boston Studies in the Philosophy of Science*, vol. 3, Proceedings of the Boston Colloquium for the Philosophy of Science, 1964/1966, 81–90.

CHOMSKY, N. (1969). 'Linguistics and Philosophy', in S. Hook (ed.), *Language and Philosophy*, University of London Press, 51–94.

CHOMSKY, N. (1972). *Language and Mind*, New York: Harcourt Brace Jovanovich.

CICOUREL, A. V. (1973). *Cognitive Sociology*, Harmondsworth: Penguin.

COHEN, G. A. (1968). 'The Workers and the Word: Why Marx had the Right to think he was Right', *Praxis*, 4, 376–90.

COHEN, G. A. (1970). 'On Some Criticisms of Historical Materialism', *Supplementary Proceedings of the Aristotelian Society*, 44, 121–41.

COHEN, G. A. (1972). 'Karl Marx and the Withering Away of Social Science', *Philosophy and Public Affairs*, 1, 182–203.

COHEN, H. (1973). '*Das Verstehen* and Historical Knowledge', *American Philosophical Quarterly*, 10, 299–307.

COMTE, A. (1844). *Discours sur l'esprit positif*, Paris.

COMTE, A. (1853). *The Positive Philosophy of Auguste Comte* (translated and condensed by Harriet Martineau), London: Chapman.

COULSON, M. A. (1972). 'Role: A Redundant Concept in Sociology? Some Educational Considerations', in J. A. Jackson (ed.), *Role, Sociological Studies 4*, Cambridge University Press, 107–28.

COULSON, M. A. and RIDDELL, D. S. (1970). *Approaching Sociology, A Critical Introduction*, London: Routledge & Kegan Paul.

COULTER. J. (1971). 'Marxism and the Engels Paradox', in R. Miliband and J. Saville (eds), *Socialist Register*, London: Merlin, 129–56.

COULTER, J. (1973). 'Language and the Conceptualization of Meaning', *Sociology*, 7, 173–90.

DAHRENDORF, R. (1968). *Essays in the Theory of Society*, London: Routledge & Kegan Paul.

DALLMAYR, F. R. (1972). 'Critical Theory Criticized', *Philosophy of the Social Sciences*, 2, 211–29.

DANTO, A. C. (1965). *Analytical Philosophy of History*, Cambridge University Press.

DAVIDSON, D. (1963). 'Actions, Reasons and Causes', *Journal of Philosophy*, 60, 685–700. Reprinted in B. Berofsky (ed.), *Free Will and Determinism*, New York: Harper & Row, 1966. Page references are to this.

DAVIDSON, D. (1967). 'Causal Relations', *Journal of Philosophy*, 64, 691–703.

DEMERATH, N. J. III and PETERSON, R. A. (eds) (1967). *System, Change, and Conflict*, New York: Free Press.

DIJKSTERHUIS, E. J. (1961). *The Mechanization of the World Picture* (trans. C. Dikshoorn), Oxford University Press.

DOBB, M. (1946). *Studies in the Development of Capitalism*, London: Routledge.

DONAGAN, A. (1966). 'The Popper-Hempel Model Reconsidered', in W. H. Dray (ed.), *Philosophical Analysis and History*, New York: Harper & Row.

DOUGLAS, J. D. (1967). *The Social Meanings of Suicide*, Princeton University Press.

DOUGLAS, J. D. (ed.) (1971). *Understanding Everyday Life. Toward the Reconstruction of Sociological Knowledge*, London: Routledge & Kegan Paul.

DOUGLAS, M. (1970). *Purity and Danger: an Analysis of Concepts of Pollution and Taboo*, Harmondsworth: Penguin.

DOUGLAS, M. (ed.) (1973). *Rules and Meanings, The Anthropology of Everyday Knowledge*, Harmondsworth: Penguin.

DRAY, W. H. (1957). *Laws and Explanation in History*, Oxford University Press.

DRAY, W. H. (1963). 'The Historical Explanation of Actions Reconsidered', in S. Hook (ed.), *Philosophy and History*, New York University Press.

DRAY, W. H. (1967). 'Holism and Individualism in History and Social Science', in P. Edwards (ed.), *Encyclopaedia of Philosophy*, vol. 4, New York: Macmillan and Free Press.

257

DRETSKE, F. (1969). *Seeing and Knowing*, London: Routledge & Kegan Paul.

DUHEM, P. (1917). *Le Système du monde*, 5 vols, 1913–17, Paris: Hermann.

DUHEM, P. (1954). *The Aim and Structure of Physical Theory* (trans. P. Wiener), Princeton University Press.

DUHEM, P. (1969). *To Save the Phenomena* (trans. E. Dolan and C. Maschler), University of Chicago Press.

DURKHEIM, E. (1897). Review of A. Labriola: 'Essais sur la conception matérialiste de l'histoire', in *Revue Philosophique*, 44, 645–51.

DURKHEIM, E. (1915). *The Elementary Forms of the Religious Life*, London: Allen & Unwin.

DURKHEIM, E. (1933). *The Division of Labour in Society*, New York: Macmillan.

DURKHEIM, E. (1938). *The Rules of Sociological Method*, Chicago: Free Press.

DURKHEIM, E. (1952). *Suicide: A Study in Sociology*, London: Routledge & Kegan Paul.

EASTON, L. D. and GUDDAT, K. H. (eds) (1967). *Writings of the Young Marx on Philosophy and Society*, New York: Anchor.

EDWARDS, P. (1967). 'Why', in P. Edwards (ed.), *The Encyclopedia of Philosophy*, vol. 8, New York: Macmillan and Free Press.

EHRMANN, J. (ed.) (1970). *Structuralism*, New York: Anchor.

EISEN, S. (1967). 'Herbert Spencer and the Spectre of Comte', *Jnl of Brit. Studies*, 7, 48–67.

EVANS-PRITCHARD, E. E. (1937). *Witchcraft, Oracles and Magic amongst the Azande*, Oxford University Press.

EVANS-PRITCHARD, E. E. (1951). *Social Anthropology*, London: Routledge & Kegan Paul.

FACIONE, P. A. (1973). 'Meaning and Intending', *American Philosophical Quarterly*, 10, 277–89.

FEYERABEND, P. K. (1962). 'Explanation, Reduction, and Empiricism', in H. Feigl and G. Maxwell (eds), *Minnesota Studies in the Philosophy of Science*, vol. 3, University of Minnesota Press.

FEYERABEND, P. K. (1963a). 'How to be a Good Empiricist – A Plea for Tolerance in Matters Epistemological', in B. Baumrin (ed.), *Philosophy of Science, The Delaware Seminar*, vol. 2, New York: Interscience Publishers. Reprinted in P. Nidditch (ed.), *The Philosophy of Science*, Oxford University Press.

FEYERABEND, P. K. (1963b). 'Materialism and the Mind-Body Problem', *Review of Metaphysics*, 17, 49–66.

FEYERABEND, P. K. (1970). 'Against Method: Outline of an Anarchistic Theory of Knowledge', in M. Radner and S. Winokur (eds), *Minnesota Studies in the Philosophy of Science*, vol. 4, University of Minnesota Press.

FILMER, P. (1972). 'On Harold Garfinkel's Ethnomethodology', in Filmer, P. *et al.*, *New Directions in Sociological Theory*, London: Collier-Macmillan.

FIRTH, R. (1961). *Elements of Social Organisation*, 3rd edn, London: Watts.

FISHER, J. (1971). *On Being Guided by a Rule*, University of Minnesota

Ph.D. Thesis, microfilm by University Microfilms, Ann Arbor, Michigan.

FODOR, J. A. (1968). *Psychological Explanation*, New York: Random House.

FREUND, I. (1968). *The Study of Chemical Composition*, New York: Dover.

FRIEDRICHS, A. W. (1970). *A Sociology of Sociology*, New York: Free Press.

FROMM, E. (ed.) (1967). *Socialist Humanism*, London: Allen Lane.

GARFINKEL, H. (1967). *Studies in Ethnomethodology*, Englewood Cliffs, N.J.: Prentice-Hall.

GARFINKEL, H. and SACKS, H. (1970). 'On Formal Structures of Practical Actions', in J. C. McKinney and E. A. Tiryakian (eds), *Theoretical Sociology: perspectives and developments*, New York: Appleton, 337–66.

GELLNER, E. (1962). 'Concepts and Society', *Transactions of the Fifth World Congress of Sociology*, 1, 153–83. Reprinted in Wilson (ed.) (1970).

GELLNER, E. (1968). 'The New Idealism – Cause and Meaning in the Social Sciences', in I. Lakatos and A. Musgrave (eds), *Problems in the Philosophy of Science*, Amsterdam: North-Holland. Reprinted in E. Gellner, *Cause and Meaning in the Social Sciences*, London: Routledge & Kegan Paul, 1973: page references are to this.

GERAS, N. (1971). 'Essence and Appearance: Aspects of Fetishism in Marx's *Capital*', *New Left Review*, 65, 69–85.

GERAS, N. (1972). 'Althusser's Marxism: An Account and Assessment', *New Left Review*, 71, 57–86.

GERTH, H. and WRIGHT MILLS, C. (1954). *Character and Social Structure*. London: Routledge & Kegan Paul.

GIBSON, Q. (1968). 'The Limits of Social Prediction', *Monist*, 52, 359–73.

GIDDENS, A. (1970). 'Marx, Weber, and the Development of Capitalism', *Sociology*, 4, 289–310.

GIDDENS, A. (1971). *Capitalism and Modern Social Theory*, Cambridge University Press.

GIDDENS, A. (1972). *Emile Durkheim: Selected Writings*, Cambridge University Press.

GIDDENS, A. (1973). *The Class Structure of the Advanced Societies*, London: Hutchinson.

GIDDENS, A. (ed.) (1974). *Positivism and Sociology*, London: Heinemann.

GLUCKMAN, M. (1944). 'The Logic of African Science and Witchcraft', *Human Problems in British Central Africa*, 1, 61–71. Partly reprinted in Marwick (ed.) (1970).

GLUCKSMANN, A. (1972). 'A Ventriloquist Structuralism', *New Left Review*, 72, 68–92.

GLUCKSMANN, M. (1974). *Structuralist Analysis in Contemporary Social Thought. A Comparison of the Theories of Claude Lévi-Strauss and Louis Althusser*, London: Routledge & Kegan Paul.

GODDARD, D. (1972). 'Anthropology: The Limits of Functionalism', *New Left Review*, 58, 79–89.

GODDARD, D. (1973). 'Max Weber and the Objectivity of Social Science', *History and Theory*, 12, 1–22.

GODELIER, M. (1967). 'System, Structure and Contradiction in "Capital" ', *Socialist Register*, 91–119.

GOFFMAN, E. (1961). *Encounters. Two Studies in the Sociology of Interaction*, Indianapolis and New York: Bobbs-Merrill.

GOODFIELD, J. (1969). 'Theories and Hypotheses in Biology', in R. Cohen and M. Wartofsky (eds), *Boston Studies in the Philosophy of Science*, vol. IV, Dordrecht: D. Reidel.

GOULDNER, A. W. (1964). 'Anti-Minotaur: The Myth of a Value-Free Sociology', in I. L. Horowitz (ed.), *The New Sociology*, New York: Oxford University Press.

GOULDNER, A. W. (1968). 'The Sociologist as Partisan: Sociology and the Welfare State', *American Sociologist*, 3, 103–16.

GOULDNER, A. W. (1971). *The Coming Crisis of Western Sociology*, London: Heinemann.

GREEN, R. W. (ed.) (1959). *Protestantism and Capitalism*, Boston: D. C Heath.

GROSS, N., MASON, W. and MCEACHERN, A. (1958). *Explorations in Role Analysis*, New York: John Wiley.

GRÜNBAUM, A. (1966). 'The Falsifiability of a Component of a Theoretical System', in P. K. Feyerabend and G. Maxwell (eds), *Mind, Matter, and Method*, University of Minnesota Press.

GRUNER, R. (1967a). 'Plurality of Causes', *Philosophy*, 42, 367–74.

GRUNER, R. (1967b). 'Understanding in the Social Sciences and History', *Inquiry*, 10, 151–63.

GRUNER, R. (1969). 'The Notion of Understanding: Replies to Cunningham and Van Evra', *Inquiry*, 12, 349–56.

HABERMAS, J. (1970a). 'On Systematically Distorted Communication', *Inquiry*, 13, 205–18.

HABERMAS, J. (1970b). 'Towards a Theory of Communicative Competence', *Inquiry*, 13, 360–75.

HABERMAS, J. (1971). *Knowledge and Human Interests*, trans. J. J. Shapiro, Boston: Beacon Press (published in German in 1968).

HABERMAS, J. (1973). 'A Postscript to *Knowledge and Human Interests*', *Philosophy of the Social Sciences*, 3, 157–89.

HABERMAS, J. (1974). 'Rationalism Divided in Two', trans. G. Adey and D. Frisby, in Giddens (ed.) (1974).

HALL, A. R. (1962). *The Scientific Revolution 1500–1800*, London: Longmans.

HAMILTON, P. (1974). *Knowledge and Social Structure*, London: Routledge & Kegan Paul.

HANSON, N. R. (1958). *Patterns of Discovery*, Cambridge University Press.

HANSON, N. R. (1963). *The Concept of the Positron*, Cambridge University Press.

HANSON, N. R. (1969). *Perception and Discovery, an Introduction to Scientific Inquiry* (ed. W. C. Humphreys), San Francisco: Freeman, Cooper.

HARCOURT, G. C. (1969). 'Some Cambridge Controversies in the Theory of Capital', *Jnl Econ. Literature*, 7, 369–405.

HARRÉ, R. (1961). *Theories and Things*, London and New York: Sheed & Ward.

HARRÉ, R. (1964a). *Matter and Method*, London: Macmillan.

HARRÉ, R. (1964b). 'Concepts and Criteria', *Mind*, 73, 353–63.

HARRÉ, R. (1970). *The Principles of Scientific Thinking*, London: Macmillan.

HARRÉ, R. and SECORD, P. F. (1972). *The Explanation of Social Behaviour*, Oxford: Basil Blackwell.

HARRIS, N. (1968). *Beliefs in Society, The Problem of Ideology*, London: Watts.

HART, H. L. A. and HONORÉ, A. M. (1959). *Causation in the Law*, Oxford University Press.

HEISENBERG, W. (1959). *Physics and Philosophy: The Revolution in Modern Science*, London: Allen & Unwin.

HEMPEL, C. G. (1942). 'The Function of General Laws in History', *The Journal of Philosophy*, 39, 35–48. Reprinted in Hempel (1965a): page references are to this.

HEMPEL, C. G. (1952). 'Typological Methods in the Natural and Social Sciences', in *Science, Language and Human Rights*, American Philosophical Association, Eastern Division, Symposia, vol. 1, Philadelphia: University of Pennsylvania Press. Reprinted in Hempel (1965a).

HEMPEL, C. G. (1958). 'The Theoretician's Dilemma: a Study in the Logic of Theory Construction', in H. Feigl, M. Scriven and G. Maxwell (eds), *Minnesota Studies in the Philosophy of Science*, vol. 2, University of Minnesota Press. Reprinted in Hempel (1965a): page references to this.

HEMPEL, C. G. (1965a). *Aspects of Scientific Explanation*, New York: Free Press.

HEMPEL, C. G. (1965b). 'Aspects of Scientific Explanation', in Hempel (1965a).

HEMPEL, C. G. (1966). *Philosophy of Natural Science*, Englewood Cliffs, N.J.: Prentice-Hall.

HEMPEL, C. G. (1969). 'Logical Positivism and the Social Sciences', in Achinstein and Barker (1969).

HEMPEL, C. G. (1970). 'On the "Standard Conception" of Scientific Theories', in M. Radner and S. Winokur (eds): *Minnesota Studies in the Philosophy of Science*, vol. 4, University of Minnesota Press.

HEMPEL, C. G. and OPPENHEIM, P. (1948). 'Studies in the Logic of Explanation', *Philosophy of Science*, 15, 135–75. Reprinted in Hempel (1965a): page references are to this.

HESSE, M. (1963). *Models and Analogies in Science*, London and New York: Sheed & Ward.

HINDESS, B. (1973). *The Use of Official Statistics in Sociology*, London: Macmillan.

HINKLE, R. C., JR (1964). 'Durkheim in American Sociology', in Durkheim, E. *et al.*, *Essays on Sociology and Philosophy*, ed. K. Wolff, New York: Harper & Row, 267–95.

HIRSCH, D. (1967). *Validity in Interpretation*. New Haven: Yale University Press.

HOIJER, H. (ed.) (1954). *Language in Culture*, University of Chicago Press.

HOLLIS, M. (1967a). 'Reason and Ritual', *Philosophy*, 43, 231–47. Reprinted in Wilson (ed.) (1970): page references are to this.

HOLLIS, M. (1967b). 'The Limits of Irrationality', *Archives Européennes de Sociologie*, 7, 265–71. Reprinted in Wilson (ed.) (1970).

HOMANS, G. C. (1964). 'Bringing Men Back In', *American Sociological Rev.*, 29, 809–18.

261

HONDERICH, T. (1971). *Punishment: The Supposed Justifications*, Harmondsworth: Penguin.

HOOKER, C. A. (1972). 'Critical Notice of Paul K. Feyerabend's "Against Method" ', *Canadian Journal of Philosophy*, 1, 489–509.

HOOKER, C. A. (1973). 'Empiricism, Perception and Conceptual Change', *Canadian Journal of Philosophy*, 3, 59–75.

HORKHEIMER, M. (1972). *Critical Theory*, trans. by Mathew J. O'Connell *et al.*, New York: Seabury.

HOROWITZ, D. (ed.) (1968). *Marx and Modern Economics*, London: MacGibbon & Kee.

HORTON, R. (1967). 'African traditional thought and Western Science', *Africa*, 37, 50–71 and 155–87. Reprinted in Wilson (ed.) (1970), and, in part, in Marwick (ed.) (1970).

HUGHES, H. STUART (1959). *Consciousness and Society*, London: MacGibbon & Kee.

HUME, D. (1902). *Enquiries concerning the Human Understanding and the Principles of Morals*, ed. D. A. Selby-Biggs, Oxford University Press.

HUNT, E. K. and SCHWARTZ, J. G. (eds) (1972). *A Critique of Economic Theory*, Harmondsworth: Penguin.

HYMES, D. (1971). 'Sociolinguistics and the Ethnography of Speaking', in E. Ardener (ed.), *Social Anthropology and Language*, London: Tavistock.

ISRAEL, J. (1972). 'Is a Non-Normative Social Science Possible?', *Acta Sociologica*, 15, 69–89.

JAY, M. (1973). *The Dialectical Imagination*, Boston: Little, Brown & Co.

JOBE, E. K. (1967). 'Discussion: Some Recent Work on the Problem of Law', *Philosophy of Science*, 34, 363–81.

JORDAN, Z. A. (1971). *Karl Marx: Economy, Class and Social Revolution*, London: Nelson.

JOYNT, C. and RESCHER, N. (1961). 'The Problem of Uniqueness in History', *History and Theory*, 1, 150–61.

KEAT, R. N. (1971). 'Positivism, Naturalism and Anti-Naturalism in the Social Sciences', *Journal for the Theory of Social Behaviour*, 1, 3–17.

KEAT, R. N. (1972). 'A Critical Examination of B. F. Skinner's Objections to Mentalism', *Behaviorism*, 1, 53–70.

KENNY, A. (1963). *Action, Emotion and Will*, London: Routledge & Kegan Paul.

KNEALE, W. (1961). 'Universality and Necessity', *British Journal for the Philosophy of Science*, 12, 89–102.

KNEALE, W. (1968). 'Scientific Revolution for Ever?', *British Journal for the Philosophy of Science*, 19, 27–42.

KOLAKOWSKI, L. (1969). 'Karl Marx and the Classical Definition of Truth', in *Marxism and Beyond* (trans. J. Z. Peel), London: Pall Mall Press.

KOLAKOWSKI, L. (1972). *Positivist Philosophy*, Harmondsworth: Penguin.

KORDIG, C. R. (1971). *The Justification of Scientific Change*, Dordrecht: D. Reidel.

KOYRÉ, A. (1968). *Metaphysics and Measurement*, London: Chapman & Hall.

KUHN, T. S. (1959). *The Copernican Revolution*, New York: Vintage Books.

KUHN, T. S. (1963). 'The Function of Dogma in Scientific Research', in A. C. Crombie (ed.), *Scientific Change*, London: Heinemann.

KUHN, T. S. (1970a). *The Structure of Scientific Revolutions* (2nd edn: includes 1st edn and a postscript), University of Chicago Press.

KUHN, T. S. (1970b). 'Logic of Discovery or Psychology of Research?', in Lakatos and Musgrave (eds) (1970).

KUHN, T. S. (1970c). 'Reflections on my Critics', in Lakatos and Musgrave (eds) (1970).

LAKATOS, I. (1970). 'Falsification and the Methodology of Scientific Research Programmes', in Lakatos and Musgrave (eds) (1970).

LAKATOS, I. and MUSGRAVE, A. (eds) (1970). *Criticism and the Growth of Scientific Knowledge*, Cambridge University Press.

LANE, M. (ed.) (1970). *Structuralism: A Reader*, London: Jonathan Cape.

LAUDAN, L. (1965). 'Grünbaum on "the Duhemian Argument" ', *Philosophy of Science*, 32, 295–9.

LAUDAN, L. (1971). 'Towards a Reassessment of Comte's "Méthode Positive" ', *Phil. of Science*, 38, 35–53.

LAWTON, D. (1968). *Social Class, Language, and Education*, London: Routledge & Kegan Paul.

LEACH, E. (1954). *Political Systems of Highland Burma: a study of Kachin social structure*, London: Bell.

LEACH, E. (1970). *Lévi-Strauss*, London: Fontana.

LEACH, J. (1968). 'Explanation and Value-Neutrality', *British Journal for the Philosophy of Science*, 19, 93–109.

LESSNOFF, M. (1974). *The Structure of Social Science*, London: Allen & Unwin.

LÉVI-STRAUSS, C. (1968). *Structural Anthropology*, London: Allen Lane.

LICHTHEIM, G. (1967). *The Concept of Ideology and Other Essays*, New York: Vintage Books.

LOSEE, J. (1972). *A Historical Introduction to the Philosophy of Science*, Oxford University Press.

LUKÁCS, G. (1971). *History and Class Consciousness, Studies in Marxist Dialectics*, London: Merlin.

LUKES, S. (1967). 'Some Problems about Rationality', *Archives Européennes de Sociologie*, 8, 247–64. Reprinted in Wilson (ed.) (1970).

LUKES, S. (1968). 'Methodological Individualism Reconsidered', *British Jnl of Sociology*, 19, 119–30.

LUKES, S. (1973a). *Emile Durkheim: His Life and Work*, London: Allen Lane.

LUKES, S. (1973b). 'On the Social Determination of Truth', in R. Finnegan and R. Horton (eds), *Modes of Thought*, London: Faber & Faber.

LUNDBERG, G. A. (1964). *Foundations of Sociology*, New York: David McKay.

LYONS, J. (1970). *Chomsky*, London: Fontana.

MCCARTHY, T. A. (1973). 'A Theory of Communicative Competence', *Philosophy of the Social Sciences*, 3, 135–56.

MACINTYRE, A. (1962). 'A Mistake about Causality in the Social Sciences', in P. Laslett and W. G. Runciman (eds), *Philosophy, Politics, and Society*, second series, Oxford: Basil Blackwell.

MACINTYRE, A. (1967). 'The Idea of a Social Science', in *Supplementary Proceedings of the Aristotelian Society*, 1967, 95–114. Reprinted in MacIntyre (1971): page references are to this.

MACINTYRE, A. (1971). *Against the Self-Images of the Age*, London: Duckworth.

MCKIE, D. (1952). *Antoine Lavoisier*, London: Constable.

MACKIE, J. L. (1965). 'Causes and Conditions', *American Philosophical Quarterly*, 2, 245–64.

MCLELLAN, D. (1973). *Karl Marx*, London: Macmillan.

MADDEN, E. H. (1969). 'A Third View of Causality', *Review of Metaphysics*, 23, 67–84.

MAGEE, B. (1973). *Popper*, London: Fontana/Collins.

MALINOWSKI, B. (1944). *A Scientific Theory of Culture and Other Essays*, Oxford University Press.

MANDEL, E. (1968). *Marxist Economic Theory*, 2 vols, London: Merlin.

MANDELBAUM, M. (1958). 'Professor Ryle and Psychology', *Philosophical Review*, 68, 522–30.

MANDELBAUM, M. (1964). *Philosophy, Science and Sense Perception*, Baltimore: Johns Hopkins Press.

MANNHEIM, K. (1960). *Ideology and Utopia*, London: Routledge & Kegan Paul.

MARCUSE, H. (1937). 'Philosophy and Critical Theory', originally published in *Zeitschrift für Sozialforschung*, 6. Trans. J. J. Shapiro, in Marcuse (1968): page references to this.

MARCUSE, H. (1964). *One-Dimensional Man*, London: Routledge & Kegan Paul.

MARCUSE, H. (1968). *Negations*, London: Allen Lane.

MAREK, F. (1969). *Philosophy of World Revolution*, London: Lawrence & Wishart.

MARGOLIS, J. (1973). 'Meaning, Speakers' Intentions, and Speech-Acts', *Review of Metaphysics*, 26, 681–95.

MARKOVIC, M. (1972). 'The Problem of Reification and the *Verstehen-Erklären* Controversy', *Acta Sociologica*, 15, 27–38.

MARTINET, A. (1970). 'Structure and Language', in J. Ehrmann (ed.), *Structuralism*, New York: Anchor.

MARWICK, M. (ed.) (1970). *Witchcraft and Sorcery*, Harmondsworth: Penguin.

MARX, K. (1933). *Wage-Labour and Capital*, London: Lawrence & Wishart.

MARX, K. (1960). *The Class Struggles in France*, 1848–50, Moscow: Progress.

MARX, K. (1961). *Capital*, vol. 2, London: Lawrence & Wishart.

MARX, K. (1962). *Capital*, vol. 3, London: Lawrence & Wishart.

MARX, K. (1963). *The Eighteenth Brumaire of Louis Bonaparte*, New York: International Publishers.

MARX, K. (1964). *Pre-Capitalist Economic Formations* (trans. J. Cohen, ed. E. Hobsbawm), London: Lawrence & Wishart.

MARX, K. (1965). *Capital*, vol. 1, London: Lawrence & Wishart.

MARX, K. (1969a). *Theories of Surplus-Value*, part 1, London: Lawrence & Wishart.

MARX, K. (1969b). *Theories of Surplus-Value*, part 2, London: Lawrence & Wishart.

MARX, K. (1972a). *The Ethnological Notebooks of Karl Marx* (ed. L. Krader), Assen: Van Gorcum & Co.

MARX, K. (1972b). *Theories of Surplus-Value*, Part Three, London: Lawrence & Wishart.

MARX, K. (1973). *Grundrisse, Foundations of the Critique of Political Economy* (trans. with Foreword by M. Nicolaus), Harmondsworth: Penguin.

MARX, K. and ENGELS, F. (1888). *Manifesto of the Communist Party*, Moscow: Foreign Languages.

MARX, K. and ENGELS, F. (1962a). *Selected Works*, vol. 1, Moscow: Foreign Languages.

MARX, K. and ENGELS, F. (1962b). *Selected Works*, vol. 2, Moscow: Foreign Languages.

MARX, K. and ENGELS, F. (1965). *The German Ideology*, Moscow: Progress.

MATTICK, P. (1969). *Marx and Keynes: The Limits of a Mixed Economy*, Boston: Porter Sargent.

MAXWELL, G. (1962). 'The Ontological Status of Theoretical Entities', in H. Feigl and G. Maxwell (eds), *Minnesota Studies in the Philosophy of Science*, vol. 3, University of Minnesota Press.

MAXWELL, N. (1968). 'Can there be Necessary Connections between Successive Events?', *British Journal for the Philosophy of Science*, 19, 1–25.

MEAD, G. H. (1934). *Mind, Self and Society*, University of Chicago Press.

MEDAWAR, P. B. (1969). *Induction and Intuition in Scientific Thought*, London: Methuen.

MEEK, R. L. (1967). *Economics and Ideology and Other Essays*, London: Chapman & Hall.

MEEK, R. L. (1973). *Studies in the Labour Theory of Value*, London: Lawrence & Wishart.

MEPHAM, J. (1972). 'The Theory of Ideology in Capital', *Radical Philosophy*, 2, 12–19.

MEPHAM, J. (1973a). 'The Structuralist Sciences and Philosophy', in Robey (ed.) (1973).

MEPHAM, J. (1973b). 'Who Makes History?', *Radical Philosophy*, 6, 23–9.

MERTON, R. K. (1957). *Social Theory and Social Structure*, Chicago: Free Press.

MÉSZÁROS, I. (ed.) (1971). *Aspects of History and Class Consciousness*, London: Routledge & Kegan Paul.

MILL, J. S. (1965). *Auguste Comte and Positivism*, Ann Arbor: University of Michigan Press.

MILL, J. S. (1898). *A System of Logic*, London: Longmans.

MILLER, D. (1972). 'Ideology and the Problem of False Consciousness', *Political Studies*, 20, 432–47.

MOLNAR, G. (1969). 'Kneale's Argument Revisited', *Philosophical Review*, 78, 79–89.

MORTIMORE, G. W. (ed.) (1971). *Weakness of Will*, London: Macmillan.

MOUNCE, D. (1973). 'Understanding a Primitive Society', *Philosophy*, 48, 347–62.

MULKAY, M. J. (1971). *Functionalism, Exchange and Theoretical Strategy*, London: Routledge & Kegan Paul.

MYRDAL, G. (1958). *Value in Social Theory*, London: Routledge & Kegan Paul.

NADEL, S. F. (1957). *The Theory of Social Structure*, London: Cohen & West.

NAGEL, E. (1961). *The Structure of Science*, London: Routledge & Kegan Paul.

NATANSON, M. (ed.) (1963). *Philosophy of the Social Sciences*. New York: Random House.

NICOLAUS, M. (1968). 'The Unknown Marx', *New Left Review*, 48, 41–61.

OLLMAN, B. (1971). *Alienation, Marx's Conception of Man in Capitalist Society*, Cambridge University Press.

O'NEILL, J. (ed.) (1973). *Modes of Individualism and Collectivism*, London: Heinemann.

OPPENHEIM, P. and PUTNAM, H. (1958). 'Unity of Science as a Working Hypothesis', in H. Feigl, G. Maxwell, and M. Scriven (eds), *Minnesota Studies in the Philosophy of Science*, vol. 2, University of Minnesota Press.

OSSOWSKI, S. (1963). *Class Structure in the Social Consciousness*, Routledge & Kegan Paul.

PAP, A. (1963). *An Introduction to the Philosophy of Science*, London: Eyre & Spottiswoode.

PARKINSON, G. H. R. (ed.) (1970). *Georg Lukács. The man, his work and his ideas*, London: Weidenfeld & Nicolson.

PARSONS, T. (1951). *The Social System*, Chicago: Free Press.

PARSONS, T. (1968). *The Structure of Social Action*, New York: Free Press.

PARSONS, T., BALES, R. F. and SHILS, E. (1953). *Working Papers in the Theory of Action*, Chicago: Free Press.

PASSMORE, J. (1968). *A Hundred Years of Philosophy*, Harmondsworth: Penguin.

PEEL, J. D. Y. (1969). 'Understanding Alien Belief-Systems', *British Journal of Sociology*, 20, 69–84.

PEEL, J. D. Y. (1971). *Herbert Spencer: the Evolution of a Sociologist*, London: Heinemann.

PIAGET, J. (1971). *Structuralism* (trans. and ed. C. Maschler), London: Routledge & Kegan Paul.

PLAMENATZ, J. (1954). *German Marxism and Russian Communism*, London: Longman.

PLAMENATZ, J. (1970). *Ideology*, London: Pall Mall.

POINCARÉ, H. (1958). *The Value of Science*, New York: Dover.

POLANYI, M. (1958). *Personal Knowledge*, University of Chicago Press.

POPPER, K. R. (1959). *The Logic of Scientific Discovery*, London: Hutchinson.

POPPER, K. R. (1960). *The Poverty of Historicism*, London: Routledge & Kegan Paul.

POPPER, K. R. (1962). *The Open Society and its Enemies*, vol. 2, 4th edn, London: Routledge & Kegan Paul.

POPPER, K. R. (1969a). 'Science: Conjectures and Refutations', in *Conjectures and Refutations*, London: Routledge & Kegan Paul.

POPPER, K. R. (1969b). 'Three Views Concerning Human Knowledge', in *Conjectures and Refutations*, London: Routledge & Kegan Paul.

POPPER, K. R. (1969c). 'A Note on Berkeley as Precursor of Mach and Einstein', in *Conjectures and Refutations*, London: Routledge & Kegan Paul.

POPPER, K. R. (1970). 'Normal Science and its Dangers', in Lakatos and Musgrave (1970).

POULANTZAS, N. (1973). *Political Power and Social Classes*, London: New Left Books and Sheed & Ward.

PREISS, J. J. and EHRLICH, H. J. (1966). *An Examination of Role Theory. The Case of the State Police*, Lincoln: University of Nebraska Press.

PUTNAM, H. (1965). 'How Not to Talk about Theories', in R. Cohen and M. Wartofsky (eds), *Boston Studies in the Philosophy of Science*, vol. 2, New York: Humanities Press.

PUTNAM, H. (1967). 'The "Innateness Hypothesis" and Explanatory Models in Linguistics', *Boston Studies in the Philosophy of Science*, vol. 3, Proceedings of the Boston Colloquium for the Philosophy of Science, 1964/1966, 91–101.

QUINE, W. V. (1961). 'Two Dogmas of Empiricism', in *From a Logical Point of View*, Cambridge, Mass.: Harvard University Press.

RADCLIFFE-BROWN, A. R. (1952). *Structure and Function in Primitive Society*, London: Cohen & West.

RADNITZKY, G. (1972). *Contemporary Schools of Metascience*, Göteborg: Akademiförlaget.

RAVETZ, J. R. (1971). *Scientific Knowledge and its Social Problems*, Oxford University Press.

REVAI, J. (1971). 'A Review of Georg Lukács' "History and Class Consciousness" ', *Theoretical Practice*, 1, 22–30.

ROBEY, D. (ed.) (1973). *Structuralism: an Introduction*, Oxford: Clarendon Press.

RORTY, R. (1965). 'Mind-Body Identity, Privacy, and Categories', *Review of Metaphysics*, 19, 24–54.

ROSENBLUETH, A., WIENER, N. and BIGELOW, J. (1943). 'Behavior, Purpose and Feedback', *Philosophy of Science*, 10, 18–24.

ROTENSTREICH, N. (1965). *Basic Problems of Marx's Philosophy*, New York: Bobbs-Merrill.

RUDNER, R. S. (1961). 'An Introduction to Simplicity', *Philosophy of Science*, 28, 109–19.

RUNCIMAN, W. G. (1969). 'What is Structuralism?', *Brit. Jnl of Sociology*, 20, 253–65.

RUNCIMAN, W. G. (1972). *A Critique of Max Weber's Philosophy of Social Science*, Cambridge University Press.

RYAN, A. (1970a). *John Stuart Mill*, New York: Pantheon.

RYAN, A. (1970b). *The Philosophy of the Social Sciences*, London: Macmillan.

SABRA, A. I. (1967). *Theories of Light: from Descartes to Newton*, London: Oldbourne.

SAUSSURE, F. DE (1960). *Course in General Linguistics*, London: Owen.

SCHAFFNER, K. F. (1969). 'Correspondence Rules', *Philosophy of Science*, 36, 280–90.

SCHEFFLER, H. W. (1970). 'Structuralism in Anthropology', in Ehrmann (1970), 56–79.

SCHEFFLER, I. (1964). *The Anatomy of Inquiry*, London: Routledge & Kegan Paul.

SCHEFFLER, I. (1967). *Science and Subjectivity*, Indianapolis: Bobbs-Merrill.

SCHUTZ, A. (1943). 'The Problem of Rationality in the Social World', *Economica*, 10, 130–49. Reprinted in D. Emmet and A. MacIntyre (eds), *Sociological Theory and Philosophical Analysis*, London: Macmillan.

SCHUTZ, A. (1953). 'Common-Sense and Scientific Interpretation of Human Action', *Philosophy and Phenomenological Research*, 14, 1–37. Reprinted in Natanson (ed.) (1963).

SCHUTZ, A. (1954). 'Concept and Theory Formation in the Social Sciences', *Journal of Philosophy*, 51, 257–73. Reprinted in Natanson (ed.) (1963): page references are to this.

SCHUTZ, A. (1972). *The Phenomenology of the Social World*, trans. G. Walsh and F. Lehnert, London: Heinemann.

SCHWAYDER, D. (1965). *The Stratification of Behaviour*, London: Routledge & Kegan Paul.

SCRIVEN, M. (1962). 'Explanation, Prediction and Laws', in H. Feigl and G. Maxwell (eds), *Minnesota Studies in the Philosophy of Science*, vol. 3, University of Minnesota Press.

SEEMAN, M. (1959). 'On the Meaning of Alienation', *Am. Sociol. Rev.*, 24, 783–91.

SELLARS, W. (1963). *Science, Perception and Reality*, London: Routledge & Kegan Paul.

SHAPERE, D. (1964). 'The Structure of Scientific Revolutions', *Philosophical Review*, 73, 383–94.

SHAPERE, D. (ed.) (1965). *Philosophical Problems of Natural Science*, New York: Macmillan.

SHAPERE, D. (1966). 'Meaning and Scientific Change', in R. G. Colodny (ed.), *Mind and Cosmos*, University of Pittsburgh Press.

SHAPERE, D. (1969). 'Notes towards a Post-Positivistic Interpretation of Science', in Achinstein and Barker (1969).

SHERRY, P. (1972). 'Truth and the "Religious Language-Game" ', *Philosophy*, 47, 18–37.

SIMON, W. M. (1963). *European Positivism in the Nineteenth Century*, Ithaca, New York: Cornell University Press.

SKINNER, B. F. (1957). *Verbal Behaviour*, New York: Appleton-Century-Crofts.

SKINNER, Q. (1969). 'Meaning and Understanding in the History of Ideas', *History and Theory*, 8, 3–53.

SKINNER, Q. (1972). ' "Social Meaning" and the Explanation of Social Action', in P. Laslett, W. G. Runciman, and Q. Skinner (eds), *Philosophy, Politics and Society*, fourth series, Oxford: Basil Blackwell.

SKLAR, L. (1968). 'Types of Inter-Theoretic Reduction', *British Journal for the Philosophy of Science*, 18, 109–24.

SKORUPSKI, J. (1973). 'Science and Traditional Religious Thought', parts I and II, *Philosophy of the Social Sciences*, 3, 97–115. (Parts III and IV forthcoming, same journal.)

SMART, J. J. C. (1963). *Philosophy and Scientific Realism*, London: Routledge & Kegan Paul.

SMART, J. J. C. (1968). *Between Science and Philosophy*, New York: Random House.

SPECTOR, M. (1965). 'Models and Theories', *British Journal for the Philosophy of Science*, 16, 121–42.

SPECTOR, M. (1967). 'Theory and Observation', *British Journal for the Philosophy of Science*, 17, 1–20 and 89–104.

SPENCER, H. (1874). *The Study of Sociology*, London: Appleton.

SPENCER, H. (1883). *Essays: Scientific, Political, and Speculative*, London: Williams & Norgate.

SPENCER, H. (1893). *The Principles of Sociology*, vol. 1, London: Williams & Norgate.

SPENCER, H. (1968). *Reasons for Dissenting from the Philosophy of M. Comte and Other Essays*, Berkeley: Glendessary Press.

SPRINZAK, E. (1972). 'Weber's Thesis as an Historical Explanation', *History and Theory*, 11, 294–320.

STEDMAN-JONES, G. (1971). 'The Marxism of the Early Lukács: an Evaluation', *New Left Review*, 70, 27–64.

STRAUSS, L. (1953). *Natural Right and History*, University of Chicago Press.

SUCHTING, W. A. (1967). 'Deductive Explanation and Prediction Revisited', *Philosophy of Science*, 34, 41–52.

SUCHTING, W. A. (1972). 'Marx, Popper, and "Historicism" ', *Inquiry*, 15, 235–66.

SUDNOW, D. (ed.) (1972). *Studies in Social Interaction*, New York: Free Press.

SUPPE, F. (1972). 'What's Wrong with the Received View on the Structure of Scientific Theories?', *Philosophy of Science*, 39, 1–19.

SWEEZY, P. M. (ed.) (1966). *Karl Marx and the Close of the System*, New York: Kelley.

SWEEZY, P. M. (1968). *The Theory of Capitalist Development*, New York: Modern Reader Paperbacks.

SWINBURNE, R. G. (1964). 'Falsifiability of Scientific Theories', *Mind*, 73, 434–6.

SWINBURNE, R. G. (1973). *An Introduction to Confirmation Theory*, London: Methuen.

SWINGEWOOD, A. (1970). 'Comte, Marx and Political Economy', *Sociol Rev.*, 18, 335–50.

TAYLOR, C. (1964). *The Explanation of Behaviour*, London: Routledge & Kegan Paul.

TAYLOR, C. (1967). 'Neutrality in Political Science', in *Philosophy, Politics and Society*, third series (edited by P. Laslett and W. G. Runciman), Oxford: Basil Blackwell.

TAYLOR, C. (1970). 'Explaining Action', *Inquiry*, 13, 54–89.

TAYLOR, C. (1971). 'Interpretation and the Sciences of Man', *Review of Metaphysics*, 25, 3–51.

TAYLOR, I., WALTON, P. and YOUNG, J. (1973). *The New Criminology: for a Social Theory of Deviance*, London: Routledge & Kegan Paul.

TAYLOR, R. (1950). 'Purposeful and Non-purposeful Behaviour: A Rejoinder', *Philosophy of Science*, 17, 327–32.

TERRAY, E. (1972). *Marxism and 'Primitive' Societies, Two Studies*, New York: Modern Reader.

269

TIMASHEFF, N. F. (1950). 'Sociological Theory Today', *Am. Catholic Sociol Rev.*, 11.

TOULMIN, S. (1957). 'Crucial Experiments: Priestley and Lavoisier', *Journal of the History of Ideas*, 18, 205–20.

TOULMIN, S. (1961). *Foresight and Understanding*, London: Hutchinson.

TOULMIN, S. (1970). 'Reasons and Causes', in R. Borger and F. Cioffi (eds), *Explanation in the Behavioural Sciences*, Cambridge University Press.

TOULMIN, S. (1972). *Human Understanding*, vol. I, Oxford University Press.

TREVOR-ROPER, H. R. (1967). *Religion, Reformation and Social Change*, London: Macmillan. Chapter 3, 'The European Witch-Craze of the Sixteenth and Seventeenth Centuries', partly printed in Marwick (ed.) (1970).

TRIGG, R. (1973). *Reason and Commitment*, Cambridge University Press.

TURNER, R. (ed.) (1974). *Ethnomethodology*, Harmondsworth: Penguin.

URRY, J. R. (1970). 'Role Analysis and the Sociological Enterprise', *Sociological Review*, 18, 351–63.

URRY, J. R. (1972). 'More Notes on Sociology's Coming Crisis', *British Journal of Sociology*, 23, 246–8.

URRY, J. R. (1973a). *Reference Groups and the Theory of Revolution*, London: Routledge & Kegan Paul.

URRY, J. R. (1973b). 'Towards a Structural Theory of the Middle Class', *Acta Sociologica*, 16, 175–87.

URRY, J. R. (1973c). 'Thomas S. Kuhn as sociologist of knowledge', *British Journal of Sociology*, 24, 462–73.

WALLACE, W. A. (1972). *Causality and Scientific Explanation*, vol. 1, Ann Arbor: University of Michigan Press.

WALTERS, R. S. (1967). 'Contrary-to-Fact Conditional', in *The Encyclopedia of Philosophy* (ed. P. Edwards), vol. 2, New York: Macmillan and Free Press.

WALTON, P. and GAMBLE, A. (1973). *From Alienation to Surplus Value*, London: Sheed & Ward.

WANN, T. (ed.) (1964). *Behaviourism and Phenomenology*, University of Chicago Press.

WARTOFSKY, M. (1968). *Conceptual Foundations of Scientific Thought*, New York: Macmillan.

WATKINS, J. (1958). 'Confirmable and Influential Metaphysics', *Mind*, 67, 344–65.

WEBER, M. (1930). *The Protestant Ethic and the Spirit of Capitalism*, trans. T. Parsons, London: Allen & Unwin.

WEBER, M. (1947). *The Theory of Social and Economic Organization*, trans. A. Henderson and T. Parsons, Chicago: Free Press.

WEBER, M. (1949). *The Methodology of the Social Sciences*, trans. E. Shils and H. Finch. Chicago: Free Press.

WEITZ, M. (1965). *Hamlet and the Philosophy of Literary Criticism*, London: Faber & Faber.

WHITE, A. (1967). *The Philosophy of Mind*, New York: Random House.

WHITE, M. (1965). *The Foundations of Historical Knowledge*, New York: Harper & Row.

WHORF, B. L. (1956). *Language, Thought, and Reality* (ed. J. B. Carroll), Cambridge, Mass.: M.I.T. Press.

WILLER, D. (1967). *Scientific Sociology*, Englewood Cliffs: Prentice-Hall.

WILSON, B. (ed.) (1970). *Rationality*, Oxford: Basil Blackwell.

WINCH, P. (1958). *The Idea of a Social Science and its Relation to Philosophy*, London: Routledge & Kegan Paul.

WINCH, P. (1964). 'Understanding a Primitive Society', *American Philosophical Quarterly*, 1, 307–24. Reprinted in Wilson (ed.) (1970): page references are to this.

WITTGENSTEIN, L. (1963). *Philosophical Investigations*, trans. G. E. M. Anscombe, Oxford: Basil Blackwell.

VON WRIGHT, G. H. (1971). *Explanation and understanding*, Ithaca, New York: Cornell University Press.

WRONG, D. (1964). 'The Oversocialized Conception of Man in Modern Sociology', in L. A. Coser and B. Rosenberg (eds), *Sociological Theory*, London: Collier-Macmillan, 112–22.

Index

Routledge Social Science Series

Routledge & Kegan Paul   London and Boston

68–74 Carter Lane   London EC4V 5EL
9 Park Street   Boston   Mass 02108

Contents

*Authors wishing to submit manuscripts for any series in
this catalogue should send them to the Social Science Editor,
Routledge & Kegan Paul Ltd, 68–74 Carter Lane,
London EC4V 5EL*

●*Books so marked are available in paperback*
All books are in Metric Demy 8vo format (216 × 138mm approx.)

International Library of Sociology

General Editor   John Rex

GENERAL SOCIOLOGY

Barnsley, J. H. The Social Reality of Ethics. *464 pp.*
Belshaw, Cyril. The Conditions of Social Performance. *An Exploratory Theory. 144 pp.*
Brown, Robert. Explanation in Social Science. *208 pp.*
● Rules and Laws in Sociology. *192 pp.*
Bruford, W. H. Chekhov and His Russia. *A Sociological Study. 244 pp.*
Cain, Maureen E. Society and the Policeman's Role. *326 pp.*
Gibson, Quentin. The Logic of Social Enquiry. *240 pp.*
Glucksmann, M. Structuralist Analysis in Contemporary Social Thought. *212 pp.*
Gurvitch, Georges. Sociology of Law. *Preface by Roscoe Pound. 264 pp.*
Hodge, H. A. Wilhelm Dilthey. *An Introduction. 184 pp.*
Homans, George C. Sentiments and Activities. *336 pp.*
Johnson, Harry M. Sociology: *a Systematic Introduction. Foreword by Robert K. Merton. 710 pp.*
Mannheim, Karl. Essays on Sociology and Social Psychology. *Edited by Paul Keckskemeti. With Editorial Note by Adolph Lowe. 344 pp.*
   Systematic Sociology: *An Introduction to the Study of Society. Edited by J. S. Erös and Professor W. A. C. Stewart. 220 pp.*
Martindale, Don. The Nature and Types of Sociological Theory. *292 pp.*
●**Maus, Heinz.** A Short History of Sociology. *234 pp.*
Mey, Harald. Field-Theory. *A Study of its Application in the Social Sciences. 352 pp.*
Myrdal, Gunnar. Value in Social Theory: *A Collection of Essays on Methodology. Edited by Paul Streeten. 332 pp.*
Ogburn, William F., and **Nimkoff, Meyer F.** A Handbook of Sociology. *Preface by Karl Mannheim. 656 pp. 46 figures. 35 tables.*
Parsons, Talcott, and **Smelser, Neil J.** Economy and Society: *A Study in the Integration of Economic and Social Theory. 362 pp.*
●**Rex, John.** Key Problems of Sociological Theory. *220 pp.*
   Discovering Sociology. *278 pp.*
   Sociology and the Demystification of the Modern World. *282 pp.*
●**Rex, John** (Ed.) Approaches to Sociology. *Contributions by Peter Abell, Frank Bechhofer, Basil Bernstein, Ronald Fletcher, David Frisby, Miriam Glucksmann, Peter Lassman, Herminio Martins, John Rex, Roland Robertson, John Westergaard and Jock Young. 302 pp.*
Rigby, A. Alternative Realities. *352 pp.*
Roche, M. Phenomenology, Language and the Social Sciences. *374 pp.*
Sahay, A. Sociological Analysis. *220 pp.*
Urry, John. Reference Groups and the Theory of Revolution. *244 pp.*
Weinberg, E. Development of Sociology in the Soviet Union. *173 pp.*

FOREIGN CLASSICS OF SOCIOLOGY

●**Durkheim, Emile.** Suicide. *A Study in Sociology. Edited and with an Introduction by George Simpson. 404 pp.*
Professional Ethics and Civic Morals. *Translated by Cornelia Brookfield. 288 pp.*
●**Gerth, H. H.,** and **Mills, C. Wright.** From Max Weber: *Essays in Sociology. 502 pp.*
●**Tönnies, Ferdinand.** Community and Association. *(Gemeinschaft und Gesellschaft.) Translated and Supplemented by Charles P. Loomis. Foreword by Pitirim A. Sorokin. 334 pp.*

SOCIAL STRUCTURE

Andreski, Stanislav. Military Organization and Society. *Foreword by Professor A. R. Radcliffe-Brown. 226 pp. 1 folder.*
Coontz, Sydney H. Population Theories and the Economic Interpretation. *202 pp.*
Coser, Lewis. The Functions of Social Conflict. *204 pp.*
Dickie-Clark, H. F. Marginal Situation: *A Sociological Study of a Coloured Group. 240 pp. 11 tables.*
Glaser, Barney, and **Strauss, Anselm L.** Status Passage. *A Formal Theory. 208 pp.*
Glass, D. V. (Ed.) Social Mobility in Britain. *Contributions by J. Berent, T. Bottomore, R. C. Chambers, J. Floud, D. V. Glass, J. R. Hall, H. T. Himmelweit, R. K. Kelsall, F. M. Martin, C. A. Moser, R. Mukherjee, and W. Ziegel. 420 pp.*
Jones, Garth N. Planned Organizational Change: *An Exploratory Study Using an Empirical Approach. 268 pp.*
Kelsall, R. K. Higher Civil Servants in Britain: *From 1870 to the Present Day. 268 pp. 31 tables.*
König, René. The Community. *232 pp. Illustrated.*
●**Lawton, Denis.** Social Class, Language and Education. *192 pp.*
McLeish, John. The Theory of Social Change: *Four Views Considered. 128 pp.*
Marsh, David C. The Changing Social Structure of England and Wales, 1871-1961. *288 pp.*
Mouzelis, Nicos. Organization and Bureaucracy. *An Analysis of Modern Theories. 240 pp.*
Mulkay, M. J. Functionalism, Exchange and Theoretical Strategy. *272 pp.*
Ossowski, Stanislaw. Class Structure in the Social Consciousness. *210 pp.*
Podgórecki, Adam. Law and Society. *About 300 pp.*

SOCIOLOGY AND POLITICS

Acton, T. A. Gypsy Politics and Social Change. *316 pp.*
Hechter, Michael. Internal Colonialism. *The Celtic Fringe in British National Development, 1536–1966. About 350 pp.*
Hertz, Frederick. Nationality in History and Politics: *A Psychology and Sociology of National Sentiment and Nationalism. 432 pp.*

Kornhauser, William. The Politics of Mass Society. *272 pp. 20 tables.*

Laidler, Harry W. History of Socialism. *Social-Economic Movements: An Historical and Comparative Survey of Socialism, Communism, Co-operation, Utopianism; and other Systems of Reform and Reconstruction. 992 pp.*

Lasswell, H. D. Analysis of Political Behaviour. *324 pp.*

Mannheim, Karl. Freedom, Power and Democratic Planning. *Edited by Hans Gerth and Ernest K. Bramstedt. 424 pp.*

Mansur, Fatma. Process of Independence. *Foreword by A. H. Hanson. 208 pp.*

Martin, David A. Pacifism: *an Historical and Sociological Study. 262 pp.*

Myrdal, Gunnar. The Political Element in the Development of Economic Theory. *Translated from the German by Paul Streeten. 282 pp.*

Wootton, Graham. Workers, Unions and the State. *188 pp.*

FOREIGN AFFAIRS: THEIR SOCIAL, POLITICAL AND ECONOMIC FOUNDATIONS

Mayer, J. P. Political Thought in France from the Revolution to the Fifth Republic. *164 pp.*

CRIMINOLOGY

Ancel, Marc. Social Defence: *A Modern Approach to Criminal Problems. Foreword by Leon Radzinowicz. 240 pp.*

Cain, Maureen E. Society and the Policeman's Role. *326 pp.*

Cloward, Richard A., and **Ohlin, Lloyd E.** Delinquency and Opportunity: *A Theory of Delinquent Gangs. 248 pp.*

Downes, David M. The Delinquent Solution. *A Study in Subcultural Theory. 296 pp.*

Dunlop, A. B., and **McCabe, S.** Young Men in Detention Centres. *192 pp.*

Friedlander, Kate. The Psycho-Analytical Approach to Juvenile Delinquency: *Theory, Case Studies, Treatment. 320 pp.*

Glueck, Sheldon, and **Eleanor.** Family Environment and Delinquency. *With the statistical assistance of Rose W. Kneznek. 340 pp.*

Lopez-Rey, Manuel. Crime. *An Analytical Appraisal. 288 pp.*

Mannheim, Hermann. Comparative Criminology: *a Text Book. Two volumes. 442 pp. and 380 pp.*

Morris, Terence. The Criminal Area: *A Study in Social Ecology. Foreword by Hermann Mannheim. 232 pp. 25 tables. 4 maps.*

Rock, Paul. Making People Pay. *338 pp.*

●**Taylor, Ian, Walton, Paul,** and **Young, Jock.** The New Criminology. *For a Social Theory of Deviance. 325 pp.*

SOCIAL PSYCHOLOGY

Bagley, Christopher. The Social Psychology of the Epileptic Child. *320 pp.*

Barbu, Zevedei. Problems of Historical Psychology. *248 pp.*

Blackburn, Julian. Psychology and the Social Pattern. *184 pp.*

● **Brittan, Arthur.** Meanings and Situations. *224 pp.*

Carroll, J. Break-Out from the Crystal Palace. *200 pp.*

● **Fleming, C. M.** Adolescence: Its Social Psychology. *With an Introduction to recent findings from the fields of Anthropology, Physiology, Medicine, Psychometrics and Sociometry. 288 pp.*

● The Social Psychology of Education: *An Introduction and Guide to Its Study. 136 pp.*

Homans, George C. The Human Group. *Foreword by Bernard DeVoto. Introduction by Robert K. Merton. 526 pp.*

● Social Behaviour: *its Elementary Forms. 416 pp.*

● **Klein, Josephine.** The Study of Groups. *226 pp. 31 figures. 5 tables.*

Linton, Ralph. The Cultural Background of Personality. *132 pp.*

● **Mayo, Elton.** The Social Problems of an Industrial Civilization. *With an appendix on the Political Problem. 180 pp.*

Ottaway, A. K. C. Learning Through Group Experience. *176 pp.*

Ridder, J. C. de. The Personality of the Urban African in South Africa. *A Thematic Apperception Test Study. 196 pp. 12 plates.*

● **Rose, Arnold M.** (Ed.) Human Behaviour and Social Processes: *an Interactionist Approach. Contributions by Arnold M. Rose, Ralph H. Turner, Anselm Strauss, Everett C. Hughes, E. Franklin Frazier, Howard S. Becker, et al. 696 pp.*

Smelser, Neil J. Theory of Collective Behaviour. *448 pp.*

Stephenson, Geoffrey M. The Development of Conscience. *128 pp.*

Young, Kimball. Handbook of Social Psychology. *658 pp. 16 figures. 10 tables.*

SOCIOLOGY OF THE FAMILY

Banks, J. A. Prosperity and Parenthood: *A Study of Family Planning among The Victorian Middle Classes. 262 pp.*

Bell, Colin R. Middle Class Families: *Social and Geographical Mobility. 224 pp.*

Burton, Lindy. Vulnerable Children. *272 pp.*

Gavron, Hannah. The Captive Wife: *Conflicts of Household Mothers. 190 pp.*

George, Victor, and **Wilding, Paul.** Motherless Families. *220 pp.*

Klein, Josephine. Samples from English Cultures.
 1. Three Preliminary Studies and Aspects of Adult Life in England. *447 pp.*
 2. Child-Rearing Practices and Index. *247 pp.*

Klein, Viola. Britain's Married Women Workers. *180 pp.*

 The Feminine Character. *History of an Ideology. 244 pp.*

McWhinnie, Alexina M. Adopted Children. *How They Grow Up. 304 pp.*

● **Myrdal, Alva,** and **Klein, Viola.** Women's Two Roles: *Home and Work. 238 pp. 27 tables.*

Parsons, Talcott, and **Bales, Robert F.** Family: Socialization and Inter- action Process. *In collaboration with James Olds, Morris Zelditch and Philip E. Slater. 456 pp. 50 figures and tables.*

SOCIAL SERVICES

Bastide, Roger. The Sociology of Mental Disorder. *Translated from the French by Jean McNeil. 260 pp.*

Carlebach, Julius. Caring For Children in Trouble. *266 pp.*

Forder, R. A. (Ed.) Penelope Hall's Social Services of England and Wales. *352 pp.*

George, Victor. Foster Care. *Theory and Practice. 234 pp.*
Social Security: *Beveridge and After. 258 pp.*

George, V., and **Wilding, P.** Motherless Families. *248 pp.*

● **Goetschius, George W.** Working with Community Groups. *256 pp.*

Goetschius, George W., and **Tash, Joan.** Working with Unattached Youth. *416 pp.*

Hall, M. P., and **Howes, I. V.** The Church in Social Work. *A Study of Moral Welfare Work undertaken by the Church of England. 320 pp.*

Heywood, Jean S. Children in Care: *the Development of the Service for the Deprived Child. 264 pp.*

Hoenig, J., and **Hamilton, Marian W.** The De-Segregation of the Mentally Ill. *284 pp.*

Jones, Kathleen. Mental Health and Social Policy, 1845-1959. *264 pp.*

King, Roy D., Raynes, Norma V., and **Tizard, Jack.** Patterns of Residential Care. *356 pp.*

Leigh, John. Young People and Leisure. *256 pp.*

Morris, Mary. Voluntary Work and the Welfare State. *300 pp.*

Morris, Pauline. Put Away: *A Sociological Study of Institutions for the Mentally Retarded. 364 pp.*

Nokes, P. L. The Professional Task in Welfare Practice. *152 pp.*

Timms, Noel. Psychiatric Social Work in Great Britain (1939-1962). *280 pp.*

● Social Casework: *Principles and Practice. 256 pp.*

Young, A. F. Social Services in British Industry. *272 pp.*

Young, A. F., and **Ashton, E. T.** British Social Work in the Nineteenth Century. *288 pp.*

SOCIOLOGY OF EDUCATION

Banks, Olive. Parity and Prestige in English Secondary Education: a Study in Educational Sociology. *272 pp.*

Bentwich, Joseph. Education in Israel. *224 pp. 8 pp. plates.*

● **Blyth, W. A. L.** English Primary Education. *A Sociological Description.*
1. Schools. *232 pp.*
2. Background. *168 pp.*

Collier, K. G. The Social Purposes of Education: *Personal and Social Values in Education. 268 pp.*

7

Dale, R. R., and **Griffith, S.** Down Stream: *Failure in the Grammar School.* *108 pp.*

Dore, R. P. Education in Tokugawa Japan. *356 pp. 9 pp. plates.*

Evans, K. M. Sociometry and Education. *158 pp.*

●**Ford, Julienne.** Social Class and the Comprehensive School. *192 pp.*

Foster, P. J. Education and Social Change in Ghana. *336 pp. 3 maps.*

Fraser, W. R. Education and Society in Modern France. *150 pp.*

Grace, Gerald R. Role Conflict and the Teacher. *About 200 pp.*

Hans, Nicholas. New Trends in Education in the Eighteenth Century. *278 pp. 19 tables.*

● Comparative Education: *A Study of Educational Factors and Traditions.* *360 pp.*

Hargreaves, David. Interpersonal Relations and Education. *432 pp.*

● Social Relations in a Secondary School. *240 pp.*

Holmes, Brian. Problems in Education. *A Comparative Approach. 336 pp.*

King, Ronald. Values and Involvement in a Grammar School. *164 pp.*

School Organization and Pupil Involvement. *A Study of Secondary Schools.*

●**Mannheim, Karl,** and **Stewart, W. A. C.** An Introduction to the Sociology of Education. *206 pp.*

Morris, Raymond N. The Sixth Form and College Entrance. *231 pp.*

●**Musgrove, F.** Youth and the Social Order. *176 pp.*

●**Ottaway, A. K. C.** Education and Society: An Introduction to the Sociology of Education. *With an Introduction by W. O. Lester Smith. 212 pp.*

Peers, Robert. Adult Education: *A Comparative Study. 398 pp.*

Pritchard, D. G. Education and the Handicapped: *1760 to 1960. 258 pp.*

Richardson, Helen. Adolescent Girls in Approved Schools. *308 pp.*

Stratta, Erica. The Education of Borstal Boys. *A Study of their Educational Experiences prior to, and during, Borstal Training. 256 pp.*

Taylor, P. H., Reid, W. A., and **Holley, B. J.** The English Sixth Form. *A Case Study in Curriculum Research. 200 pp.*

SOCIOLOGY OF CULTURE

Eppel, E. M., and **M.** Adolescents and Morality: *A Study of some Moral Values and Dilemmas of Working Adolescents in the Context of a changing Climate of Opinion. Foreword by W. J. H. Sprott. 268 pp. 39 tables.*

●**Fromm, Erich.** The Fear of Freedom. *286 pp.*

● The Sane Society. *400 pp.*

Mannheim, Karl. Essays on the Sociology of Culture. *Edited by Ernst Mannheim in co-operation with Paul Kecskemeti. Editorial Note by Adolph Lowe. 280 pp.*

Weber, Alfred. Farewell to European History: *or The Conquest of Nihilism. Translated from the German by R. F. C. Hull. 224 pp.*

SOCIOLOGY OF RELIGION

Argyle, Michael and **Beit-Hallahmi, Benjamin.** The Social Psychology of Religion. *About 256 pp.*

Nelson, G. K. Spiritualism and Society. *313 pp.*

Stark, Werner. The Sociology of Religion. *A Study of Christendom.*
Volume I. *Established Religion. 248 pp.*
Volume II. *Sectarian Religion. 368 pp.*
Volume III. *The Universal Church. 464 pp.*
Volume IV. *Types of Religious Man. 352 pp.*
Volume V. *Types of Religious Culture. 464 pp.*

Turner, B. S. Weber and Islam. *216 pp.*

Watt, W. Montgomery. Islam and the Integration of Society. *320 pp.*

SOCIOLOGY OF ART AND LITERATURE

Jarvie, Ian C. Towards a Sociology of the Cinema. *A Comparative Essay on the Structure and Functioning of a Major Entertainment Industry. 405 pp.*

Rust, Frances S. Dance in Society. *An Analysis of the Relationships between the Social Dance and Society in England from the Middle Ages to the Present Day. 256 pp. 8 pp. of plates.*

Schücking, L. L. The Sociology of Literary Taste. *112 pp.*

Wolff, Janet. Hermeneutic Philosophy and the Sociology of Art. *About 200 pp.*

SOCIOLOGY OF KNOWLEDGE

Diesing, P. Patterns of Discovery in the Social Sciences. *262 pp.*

● **Douglas, J. D.** (Ed.) Understanding Everyday Life. *370 pp.*

● **Hamilton, P.** Knowledge and Social Structure. *174 pp.*

Jarvie, I. C. Concepts and Society. *232 pp.*

Mannheim, Karl. Essays on the Sociology of Knowledge. *Edited by Paul Kecskemeti. Editorial Note by Adolph Lowe. 353 pp.*

Remmling, Gunter W. (Ed.) Towards the Sociology of Knowledge. *Origin and Development of a Sociological Thought Style. 463 pp.*

Stark, Werner. The Sociology of Knowledge: *An Essay in Aid of a Deeper Understanding of the History of Ideas. 384 pp.*

URBAN SOCIOLOGY

Ashworth, William. The Genesis of Modern British Town Planning: *A Study in Economic and Social History of the Nineteenth and Twentieth Centuries. 288 pp.*

Cullingworth, J. B. Housing Needs and Planning Policy: *A Restatement of the Problems of Housing Need and 'Overspill' in England and Wales. 232 pp. 44 tables. 8 maps.*

Dickinson, Robert E. City and Region: *A Geographical Interpretation* *608 pp. 125 figures.*

The West European City: *A Geographical Interpretation. 600 pp. 129 maps. 29 plates.*

● The City Region in Western Europe. *320 pp. Maps.*

Humphreys, Alexander J. New Dubliners: *Urbanization and the Irish Family. Foreword by George C. Homans. 304 pp.*

Jackson, Brian. Working Class Community: *Some General Notions raised by a Series of Studies in Northern England. 192 pp.*

Jennings, Hilda. Societies in the Making: *a Study of Development and Redevelopment within a County Borough. Foreword by D. A. Clark. 286 pp.*

●**Mann, P. H.** An Approach to Urban Sociology. *240 pp.*

Morris, R. N., and **Mogey, J.** The Sociology of Housing. *Studies at Berinsfield. 232 pp. 4 pp. plates.*

Rosser, C., and **Harris, C.** The Family and Social Change. *A Study of Family and Kinship in a South Wales Town. 352 pp. 8 maps.*

RURAL SOCIOLOGY

Chambers, R. J. H. Settlement Schemes in Tropical Africa: *A Selective Study. 268 pp.*

Haswell, M. R. The Economics of Development in Village India. *120 pp.*

Littlejohn, James. Westrigg: *the Sociology of a Cheviot Parish. 172 pp. 5 figures.*

Mayer, Adrian C. Peasants in the Pacific. *A Study of Fiji Indian Rural Society. 248 pp. 20 plates.*

Williams, W. M. The Sociology of an English Village: *Gosforth. 272 pp. 12 figures. 13 tables.*

SOCIOLOGY OF INDUSTRY AND DISTRIBUTION

Anderson, Nels. Work and Leisure. *280 pp.*

●**Blau, Peter M.,** and **Scott, W. Richard.** Formal Organizations: *a Comparative approach. Introduction and Additional Bibliography by J. H. Smith. 326 pp.*

Eldridge, J. E. T. Industrial Disputes. *Essays in the Sociology of Industrial Relations. 288 pp.*

Hetzler, Stanley. Applied Measures for Promoting Technological Growth. *352 pp.*

Technological Growth and Social Change. *Achieving Modernization. 269 pp.*

Hollowell, Peter G. The Lorry Driver. *272 pp.*

Jefferys, Margot, *with the assistance of Winifred Moss.* Mobility in the Labour Market: *Employment Changes in Battersea and Dagenham. Preface by Barbara Wootton. 186 pp. 51 tables.*

Millerson, Geoffrey. The Qualifying Associations: *a Study in Professionalization. 320 pp.*

Smelser, Neil J. Social Change in the Industrial Revolution: *An Application of Theory to the Lancashire Cotton Industry, 1770-1840. 468 pp. 12 figures. 14 tables.*

Williams, Gertrude. Recruitment to Skilled Trades. *240 pp.*

Young, A. F. Industrial Injuries Insurance: *an Examination of British Policy. 192 pp.*

DOCUMENTARY

Schlesinger, Rudolf (Ed.) Changing Attitudes in Soviet Russia.
2. The Nationalities Problem and Soviet Administration. *Selected Readings on the Development of Soviet Nationalities Policies. Introduced by the editor. Translated by W. W. Gottlieb. 324 pp.*

ANTHROPOLOGY

Ammar, Hamed. Growing up in an Egyptian Village: *Silwa, Province of Aswan. 336 pp.*

Brandel-Syrier, Mia. Reeftown Elite. *A Study of Social Mobility in a Modern African Community on the Reef. 376 pp.*

Crook, David, and **Isabel.** Revolution in a Chinese Village: *Ten Mile Inn. 230 pp. 8 plates. 1 map.*

Dickie-Clark, H. F. The Marginal Situation. *A Sociological Study of a Coloured Group. 236 pp.*

Dube, S. C. Indian Village. *Foreword by Morris Edward Opler. 276 pp. 4 plates.*
India's Changing Villages: *Human Factors in Community Development. 260 pp. 8 plates. 1 map.*

Firth, Raymond. Malay Fishermen. *Their Peasant Economy. 420 pp. 17 pp. plates.*

Firth, R., Hubert, J., and **Forge, A.** Families and their Relatives. *Kinship in a Middle-Class Sector of London: An Anthropological Study. 456 pp.*

Gulliver, P. H. Social Control in an African Society: a Study of the Arusha, Agricultural Masai of Northern Tanganyika. *320 pp. 8 plates. 10 figures.*
Family Herds. *288 pp.*

Ishwaran, K. Shivapur. *A South Indian Village. 216 pp.*
Tradition and Economy in Village India: *An Interactionist Approach. Foreword by Conrad Arensburg. 176 pp.*

Jarvie, Ian C. The Revolution in Anthropology. *268 pp.*

Jarvie, Ian C., and **Agassi, Joseph.** Hong Kong. *A Society in Transition. 396 pp. Illustrated with plates and maps.*

Little, Kenneth L. Mende of Sierra Leone. *308 pp. and folder.*
Negroes in Britain. *With a New Introduction and Contemporary Study by Leonard Bloom. 320 pp.*

11

Lowie, Robert H. Social Organization. *494 pp.*

Mayer, Adrian C. Caste and Kinship in Central India: *A Village and its Region. 328 pp. 16 plates. 15 figures. 16 tables.*
    Peasants in the Pacific. *A Study of Fiji Indian Rural Society. 248 pp.*

Smith, Raymond T. The Negro Family in British Guiana: *Family Structure and Social Status in the Villages. With a Foreword by Meyer Fortes. 314 pp. 8 plates. 1 figure. 4 maps.*

SOCIOLOGY AND PHILOSOPHY

Barnsley, John H. The Social Reality of Ethics. *A Comparative Analysis of Moral Codes. 448 pp.*

Diesing, Paul. Patterns of Discovery in the Social Sciences. *362 pp.*

●**Douglas, Jack D.** (Ed.) Understanding Everyday Life. *Toward the Reconstruction of Sociological Knowledge. Contributions by Alan F. Blum. Aaron W. Cicourel, Norman K. Denzin, Jack D. Douglas, John Heeren, Peter McHugh, Peter K. Manning, Melvin Power, Matthew Speier, Roy Turner, D. Lawrence Wieder, Thomas P. Wilson and Don H. Zimmerman. 370 pp.*

Jarvie, Ian C. Concepts and Society. *216 pp.*

Pelz, Werner. The Scope of Understanding in Sociology. *Towards a more radical reorientation in the social humanistic sciences. 283 pp.*

Roche, Maurice. Phenomenology, Language and the Social Sciences. *371 pp.*

Sahay, Arun. Sociological Analysis. *212 pp.*

Sklair, Leslie. The Sociology of Progress. *320 pp.*

International Library of Anthropology

General Editor   Adam Kuper

Brown, Paula. The Chimbu. *A Study of Change in the New Guinea Highlands. 151 pp.*

Lloyd, P. C. Power and Independence. *Urban Africans' Perception of Social Inequality. 264 pp.*

Pettigrew, Joyce. Robber Noblemen. *A Study of the Political System of the Sikh Jats. 284 pp.*

Van Den Berghe, Pierre L. Power and Privilege at an African University. *278 pp.*

International Library of Social Policy

General Editor   Kathleen Jones

Bayley, M. Mental Handicap and Community Care. *426 pp.*

Butler, J. R. Family Doctors and Public Policy. *208 pp.*

Holman, Robert. Trading in Children. *A Study of Private Fostering. 355 pp.*

12

Jones, Kathleen. History of the Mental Health Service. *428 pp.*
Thomas, J. E. The English Prison Officer since 1850: *A Study in Conflict.* *258 pp.*
Woodward, J. To Do the Sick No Harm. *A Study of the British Voluntary Hospital System to 1875. About 220 pp.*

International Library of Welfare and Philosophy

General Editors Noel Timms and David Watson

● **Plant, Raymond.** Community and Ideology. *104 pp.*

Primary Socialization, Language and Education

General Editor Basil Bernstein

Bernstein, Basil. Class, Codes and Control. *2 volumes.*
　1. *Theoretical Studies Towards a Sociology of Language. 254 pp.*
　2. *Applied Studies Towards a Sociology of Language. About 400 pp.*
Brandis, W., and **Bernstein, B.** Selection and Control. *176 pp.*
Brandis, Walter, and **Henderson, Dorothy.** Social Class, Language and Communication. *288 pp.*
Cook-Gumperz, Jenny. Social Control and Socialization. *A Study of Class Differences in the Language of Maternal Control. 290 pp.*
● **Gahagan, D. M.,** and **G. A.** Talk Reform. *Exploration in Language for Infant School Children. 160 pp.*
Robinson, W. P., and **Rackstraw, Susan D. A.** A Question of Answers. *2 volumes. 192 pp. and 180 pp.*
Turner, Geoffrey J., and **Mohan, Bernard A.** A Linguistic Description and Computer Programme for Children's Speech. *208 pp.*

Reports of the Institute of Community Studies

Cartwright, Ann. Human Relations and Hospital Care. *272 pp.*
●　Parents and Family Planning Services. *306 pp.*
　Patients and their Doctors. *A Study of General Practice. 304 pp.*
● **Jackson, Brian.** Streaming: *an Education System in Miniature. 168 pp.*
Jackson, Brian, and **Marsden, Dennis.** Education and the Working Class: *Some General Themes raised by a Study of 88 Working-class Children in a Northern Industrial City. 268 pp. 2 folders.*
Marris, Peter. The Experience of Higher Education. *232 pp. 27 tables.*
　Loss and Change. *192 pp.*

Marris, Peter, and **Rein, Martin.** Dilemmas of Social Reform. *Poverty and Community Action in the United States. 256 pp.*

Marris, Peter, and **Somerset, Anthony.** African Businessmen. *A Study of Entrepreneurship and Development in Kenya. 256 pp.*

Mills, Richard. Young Outsiders: *a Study in Alternative Communities. 216 pp.*

Runciman, W. G. Relative Deprivation and Social Justice. *A Study of Attitudes to Social Inequality in Twentieth-Century England. 352 pp.*

Willmott, Peter. Adolescent Boys in East London. *230 pp.*

Willmott, Peter, and **Young, Michael.** Family and Class in a London Suburb. *202 pp. 47 tables.*

Young, Michael. Innovation and Research in Education. *192 pp.*

● **Young, Michael,** and **McGeeney, Patrick.** Learning Begins at Home. *A Study of a Junior School and its Parents. 128 pp.*

Young, Michael, and **Willmott, Peter.** Family and Kinship in East London. *Foreword by Richard M. Titmuss. 252 pp. 39 tables.*
The Symmetrical Family. *410 pp.*

Reports of the Institute for Social Studies in Medical Care

Cartwright, Ann, Hockey, Lisbeth, and **Anderson, John L.** Life Before Death. *310 pp.*

Dunnell, Karen, and **Cartwright, Ann.** Medicine Takers, Prescribers and Hoarders. *190 pp.*

Medicine, Illness and Society

General Editor   W. M. Williams

Robinson, David. The Process of Becoming Ill. *142 pp.*

Stacey, Margaret, *et al.* Hospitals, Children and Their Families. *The Report of a Pilot Study. 202 pp.*

Monographs in Social Theory

General Editor   Arthur Brittan

● **Barnes, B.** Scientific Knowledge and Sociological Theory. *About 200 pp.*

Bauman, Zygmunt. Culture as Praxis. *204 pp.*

● **Dixon, Keith.** Sociological Theory. *Pretence and Possibility. 142 pp.*

● **Smith, Anthony D.** The Concept of Social Change. *A Critique of the Functionalist Theory of Social Change. 208 pp.*

Routledge Social Science Journals

The British Journal of Sociology. *Edited by Terence P. Morris. Vol. 1, No. 1, March 1950 and Quarterly. Roy. 8vo. Back numbers available. An international journal with articles on all aspects of sociology.*
Economy and Society. *Vol. 1, No. 1. February 1972 and Quarterly. Metric Roy. 8vo. A journal for all social scientists covering sociology, philosophy, anthropology, economics and history. Back numbers available.*
Year Book of Social Policy in Britain, The. *Edited by Kathleen Jones. 1971. Published annually.*

Printed in Great Britain by Unwin Brothers Limited
The Gresham Press Old Woking Surrey
A member of the Staples Printing Group